A Guide to Formulation in Coaching

Lane, Corrie and Kovács present a foundational text for coaches wishing to improve their coaching practice through use of formulation.

A Guide to Formulation in Coaching examines the nature and purpose of formulation and how to develop effective formulations that can inform and improve practice. It combines theoretical perspectives with case studies illustrating its use in different coaching contexts to provide a comprehensive and accessible account of the purpose, perspectives and processes used in formulation. In addition to providing practice-based examples and drawing on the literature, the book provides a series of exercises to enable readers to refine their individual approaches.

Practical and accessibly written, this book will be a valuable resource for coaches and coaching psychologists, coaching supervisors and trainers, and academics interested in understanding the role of formulation and how it applies in a coaching context.

David A. Lane is a psychologist and coach who has researched and taught formulation for several decades. He has contributed to the development of the field of coaching, supervision as well as to counselling psychology. Previous books include *The Case for Coaching, Supervision in the Psychological Professions* and *A Critical Introduction to Coaching and Mentoring*.

Sarah Corrie is a psychologist and coach and has developed methods for teaching formulation in both coaching and professional psychology. She has published widely, including books on decision-making, supervision and formulation in applied psychology. Sarah is also a Professor of Cognitive Behaviour Therapy and Counselling at the University of Suffolk.

Louise C. Kovács is a practitioner–researcher, executive coach and coaching supervisor. In completing her doctoral-level research she developed a framework for applying the concept of formulation in an executive coaching context. She has co-authored a number of articles on the topic of formulation and in her work as a supervisor continues to advance the case for formulation as an essential skill for coaches.

The Professional Coaching Series

This series brings together leading exponents and researchers in the coaching field to provide a definitive set of core texts important to the development of the profession. It aims to meet two needs - a professional series that provides the core texts that are theoretically and experimentally grounded, and a practice series covering forms of coaching based in evidence. Together they provide a complementary framework to introduce, promote and enhance the development of the coaching profession.

Titles in the series:

The Art of Inspired Living: Coach Yourself with Positive Psychology
By Sarah Corrie

Supporting the Family Business: A Coaching Practitioner's Handbook
By Manfusa Shams

Developing and Sustaining a Successful Family Business: A Solution-Focused Guide
By Louis Cauffman

The Evidence-Based Practitioner Coach: Understanding the Integrated Experiential Learning Process
By Lloyd Chapman

An Integral Approach to Transformative Leadership: Dancing Through the Storm
By Dorrian Aiken

A Guide to Formulation in Coaching
By David A. Lane, Sarah Corrie and Louise C. Kovács

For further information about this series please visit https://www.routledge.com/The-Professional-Coaching-Series/book-series/KARNPROFC

"Formulation in coaching is an art that has long been underrepresented in the literature, yet it is essential to understanding and guiding clients effectively. This book shines a light on the often-overlooked process of formulation, offering practical guidance for coaches to systematically make sense of their clients' experience and organise their approach accordingly. With clear examples and thoughtful analysis, it empowers coaches to integrate this powerful tool into their work. A must-read for coaches seeking to deepen their practice and enhance their effectiveness and a marvellous contribution to the field!"

Dr Marc Kahn, *chief strategy and sustainability officer at Investec Plc, senior associate at Cambridge Institute of Sustainability Leadership and visiting professor at Middlesex University*

"This book is an important resource, providing experienced and beginning coaches a powerful way of thinking about their work. Disciplined case formulation provides a roadmap for coaches to understand and make sense of the complex dynamics with their clients. It also helps clients to navigate the world of development which is often new, scary and uncharted for them. Lane, Corrie and Kovács are master coaches who move seamlessly between theory and practice. It is a delight to watch them dance."

Joshua Ehrlich, *Global Leadership Council*

"This book makes a great contribution to coaching! For a coach to widen their repertoire in order to offer most help to their coachee, they need an approach to deciding which approach under which circumstances. The concept of case formulation offers just that! Another great set of insights from Lane, Corrie and Kovács!"

Bob Garvey, *managing partner with The Lio Partnership, consultant with Coachmentoring Ltd*

"Case formulation, while widely used in many aspects of psychology, is an underdeveloped concept in coaching. The authors, having pioneered the development of the concept in coaching, have produced a book which I hope will become part of the canon of work in coaching. Through case formulation the coach can better both understand themself, their client and the work they engage with. The result is improved client outcomes and a deeper insight about ourselves as an active agent in the coaching process. Detailed, definitive and developmental, this is a book to add to your coaching library."

Jonathan Passmore, *professor Henley Business School and EZRA Coaching LHH*

"This is a colossus of a book, fascinating, challenging and rewarding, well researched and with a breadth that makes it stand out. I was absorbed and engaged from the beginning – with its narrative and different style of introduction from the authors – to the end, and grateful that such an important topic was being presented to aid the development of coaching practice. *A Guide to Formulation in Coaching* brings together much disparate thinking in the field and draws it into a coherent framework. It has a range of case studies to make it come alive and it is rich in resources including excellent questions, and themes such as understanding the role of power and different worldviews. The 4Ps framework (Positionality, Purpose, Perspective and Process), a development of the original 3Ps I have drawn from for many years, is an excellent addition to practitioners and trainers alike."

Eve Turner, *author, researcher, accredited master executive coach and master supervisor, co-founder of the Climate Coaching Alliance, founder of the Global Supervisors' Network, former Chair, APECS (Association for Professional Coaching and Supervision); 2023 EMCC Global Special President's Award for contributions to supervision and society*

"As coaches, we must relentlessly sharpen and elevate our craft given the increased competition and the rise of AI coaching bots. Mastering formulation offers us another powerful tool in our kit to better understand clients, design impactful interventions, and drive meaningful change. This book provides cutting-edge insights and practical applications of formulation that will enhance your effectiveness and refine your coaching approach. If you're serious about staying ahead, this book is a necessity."

Brian O. Underhill, Ph.D., PCC, *founder and CEO CoachSource LLC. Author of* Executive Coaching for Results: The Definitive Guide to Developing Organizational Leaders

"By introducing a fourth P – Positionality, this revision is a most welcome addition for enhancing the universally applied 3P approach of Purpose, Perspective and Process. Through encouraging reflection and examination of practice the 4P framework stimulates us to determine how we and our clients influence our work together when attempting to function in the complex world in which we operate. I've appreciated the advantages gained in developing my practice by applying the 3P framework and encouraged coaches in training to adopt the same approach. *Formulation* with the creation of Positionality acts as a productive conduit for seeking the rewards realised by the deep reflection on practice offered with this approach. What I find particularly helpful in emphasising ways of applying *Formulation* to practice are the case studies. These offer scenarios that guide and inform how the revised framework challenges us to identify a unique way of explaining our offering as coaches and to reassure clients of the benefits of working with us. The construction of the text offering a compilation of methodologies from a range of contributors brings variety and versality and succeeds in encouraging the adoption of *Formulation*. A fully recommended addition to coaching literature."

Dr Lise Lewis, *executive and relational leadership coach, coach supervisor*

"*A Guide to Formulation in Coaching* is a misleading title. While it deals fully and excellently with the process of formulation or case conceptualisation in coaching, this book is so much more. It is both an eminently scholarly and genuinely practical account of a wide range of coaching approaches that will benefit practising coaches and the users of coaching alike. For practising coaches, it provides a wealth of information enabling the coach to reflect on and implement their chosen theories and approaches to coaching. For those who purchase and manage coaching engagement, this book provides an excellent source of information to help identify coaching approaches that might be useful for their needs, and a guide that might help them evaluate the progress of coaching in a more sophisticated and ultimately effective way. I heartily endorse this book and will be setting it as a key text in our Master of Coaching Psychology course at the University of Sydney."

Michael Cavanagh, *coaching psychology unit, University of Sydney*

"For any coach striving to anchor their practice on theoretical grounded, evidence-based scientist-practitioner models and research, this book will prove to be a valuable resource. At no point do the authors prescribe a model or a way of coaching. Instead, they offer the coach a formulation framework that will enable the coach to make explicit the foundational assumptions and worldviews to which the coach and client subscribe, to explore and adopt the perspectives most relevant to the situation and to define the purpose of the coaching intervention. In so doing, they enable the coach to become a scientist-practitioner. I highly recommend this book. The formulation approach has been the foundation of my work and the two books I authored."

Lloyd Chapman, D.Prof, *MBA executive coach; author of*
The Evidence-Based Practitioner Coach: Understanding the
Integrated Learning Process *and* Integrated Experiential
Coaching: Becoming an Executive Coach

A Guide to Formulation in Coaching

David A. Lane, Sarah Corrie
and Louise C. Kovács

Routledge
Taylor & Francis Group

LONDON AND NEW YORK

Designed cover image: Getty Images

First published 2025
by Routledge
4 Park Square, Milton Park, Abingdon, Oxon OX14 4RN

and by Routledge
605 Third Avenue, New York, NY 10158

Routledge is an imprint of the Taylor & Francis Group, an informa business

British Library Cataloguing-in-Publication Data
A catalogue record for this book is available from the British Library

Library of Congress Cataloging-in-Publication Data
Names: Lane, David A., 1947- author | Corrie, Sarah author | Kovács,
Louise C. author
Title: A guide to formulation in coaching / David A. Lane, Sarah Corrie,
and Louise C. Kovács.
Description: Abingdon, Oxon ; New York, NY : Routledge, 2025. | Series: The
professional coaching series | Includes bibliographical references and
index. |
Identifiers: LCCN 2024059330 (print) | LCCN 2024059331 (ebook) |
ISBN 9781032005300 hardback | ISBN 9781032005287 paperback |
ISBN 9781003174585 ebook
Subjects: LCSH: Personal coaching | Executive coaching
Classification: LCC BF637.P36 L34 2025 (print) | LCC BF637.P36 (ebook) |
DDC 158.3--dc23/eng/20250507
LC record available at https://lccn.loc.gov/2024059330
LC ebook record available at https://lccn.loc.gov/2024059331

ISBN: 978-1-032-00530-0 (hbk)
ISBN: 978-1-032-00528-7 (pbk)
ISBN: 978-1-003-17458-5 (ebk)

DOI: 10.4324/9781003174585

Typeset in Times New Roman
by KnowledgeWorks Global Ltd.

Contents

Who Are We – A Note From the Authors

It is common for the authors of a book to introduce themselves with brief bios setting out achievements and prior publications; that is, the outcomes of their journeys. However, we make much in this book about the importance of positionality. We argue that it is important for the coach to spend time considering their own history, their position as persons and practitioners and the themes and experiences that have influenced their approach to their practice. This can then enable similar conversations with their clients. So, we have decided that rather than set out our outcomes we would explore some of the themes that have led each of us to see ourselves and the world in particular ways. Given limited space this can only cover a few of those influences so is a partial picture, but we hope nonetheless that it will be useful to our readers.

David A. Lane

My early memories are much taken up with stories. We pleaded for stories about the olden times. Rather than fairy tales, we, as children, were introduced to life in the 1930s, the poverty, the grind to find food for the family, the constant search for work and the politics of the time. George Lansbury was the family hero, and the Labour movement was deeply ingrained in our sense of the world. Later, I realized that my grandfather, contributing quietly, was also a hero to many. Those stories were about community and how people helped each other even if they had little to share. Subsequent stories were about the years 1939–1945, life serving in the Navy and life at home under constant threat. Again, there was a thread around comradeship and the power of communities to work together to overcome adversity. Growing up on a council estate in East London there was still much poverty alongside wealth, but also joy and community and new stories. On the estate and via the local church people gave their time to run clubs including a film club, dancing, games and trips to the seaside. There was also the annual trip to pick hops. However, we were also very aware of the gangs, criminality and of the racism in 1950s England which was manifest everywhere.

I was fortunate at the age of 3 to attend the local nursery. There at Wentworth were new stories, light, music, painting and learning about others. Thank you, Wentworth, and thank you to librarians everywhere and the mobile library that visited the estate for the opening into the world of books. Books gave me a picture of the world that I could not have imagined. At primary school I discovered song and for the first time had a sense of the joy that brings and my own sense of achievement. In my teenage years the family bought our first house, a small suburban semi, and we became middle class. I still attended school in East London, travelling in each day, and as a commuter had much time to read, and the bookstand I passed each day became a new source of books. At secondary school I was led to discover drama and poetry. With two friends I discovered the power of research to elucidate difficult issues. The importance of stories, community and research have informed my work ever since.

The other theme was place. I was fortunate enough to live opposite Vicky Park (Victoria) and spent countless hours in the park and wandering around London's canals. It gave me a sense of the value of exploration of places, people and experiences. Later, working across the globe meeting people doing amazing things with very little, I greatly expanded this sense.

I became eventually, via various missteps, a teacher, psychologist and coach who had the privilege of working with people and organizations globally and wrote as well as read books. Continually, from the age of 16, I have been involved in voluntary work, and this has been a blessing as I have gained so much from others. While teaching, I became involved in work in the field of drug education and prevention and was fortunate to be asked to join The Kings Fund Drug Dependency Discussion Group. This brought together those working in the field, across professions and settings to share ideas. This taught me the power of sharing learning.

On establishing the Islington Educational Guidance Centre, we ran weekly skill sharing groups to which anyone could contribute and adopted the position that ideas are to be freely given away. We shared ideas, supported each other in research all in a spirt of a community of learning. Operating in a multi-cultural area I had to recognize that being from a white working-class family (even in one that knew the area and had always challenged prejudice) we saw the world differently from many of our clients. They taught us the importance of listening to their stories, being vigilant in self-monitoring and the impact of the service we provided. We had to constantly reach out to see the world from their point of view, and recognize that we could impact their life positively and negatively so had to be aware of our own power.

Qualifying as a psychologist and later developing the field of coaching, it was within a community that impacts were made. To quote Ellen Kuzwayo, with whom I had the pleasure of working and whose life was so different from my own, the key is "learning from each other". The work in Islington formed the basis for the creation of the Professional Development Foundation, which has occupied 50 years of my professional life but also promotes stories, community and research. Its motto is, "Sharing our passion for learning". These themes are present throughout this book.

Sarah Corrie

My first career was in the performing arts. At the age of 11, I left my home in the suburbs of London to begin my professional training with one of the world's premier ballet schools. Between the ages of 11 and 17, I completed a rigorous and demanding training that prepared me for a career as a classical dancer.

My experiences of the ballet world had a profound and enduring impact on me both in terms of my identity and values, and how I came to understand the meaning of having a career. My training was steeped in a set of values that included self-discipline, dedication and respect for hierarchy. Indeed, the relationship between teacher and pupil was a distinct form of the "expert–apprentice" model of training that I was later to discover embedded in several models of supervision in psychotherapy and applied psychology.

Having passed my annual assessments, I worked with a ballet company that toured the UK and took me to New Zealand, Singapore, South Korea and India. However, my career was to be short-lived. Injury led to treatment which, when unsuccessful, resulted in surgery. After a year of rehabilitation, I realized that my career as a dancer was over. I had just turned 19.

Guided by the recommendations of my former teachers, I completed a dance teaching qualification. At the same time as studying for my qualification, I made the transition from dancer to actor – a long-standing interest that I now had an opportunity to pursue in a committed fashion. I was fortunate to be trained by a number of highly respected actors and directors who taught me the art of character interpretation for the purposes of performance. It was during this time that I learned about working with narrative and the ways in which playwrights might approach constructing stories for optimum effect. Through an introduction to the work of Stanislavski I had my first exposure to the task of formulation which, as in my later work as a clinical psychologist and therapist, was deemed to be the backbone of understanding the characters whom we were portraying on stage.

Following a year of study, I auditioned successfully for a theatre company and had my first experience of working as a professional actor. Touring schools and community centres was very different from the opera house audiences with which I was familiar. I was introduced to deprived areas within London and to young people whose prospects seemed confined by fiscal and social realities that I had not previously encountered. These experiences opened up an interest in how performance generally and storytelling in particular could represent a force for empowerment and social change.

At this time in my life, I realized that the questions and possibilities I was interested in exploring would benefit from the scaffolding of some formal, disciplinary knowledge. I decided to go to university where I studied for a degree in psychology and counselling psychology. My degree provided a structure for knowledge acquisition through which I could structure my learning and which brought together the themes of interest and commitment that were materializing. A vocation in psychology and in mental health was taking form and a new life was beckoning. This became the gateway for a subsequent training in clinical psychology and then a post-doctoral qualification in cognitive behaviour therapy where learning how to work skilfully with individuals' stories featured heavily.

My career as a psychologist has opened up many opportunities to learn and develop my knowledge and practice. A particularly significant one, in the context of this book, was the opportunity to start working with individuals and organizations who were seeking ways of flourishing. A contrast to working with distress and psychopathology that had been the main focus of my clinical psychology career, this new type of work stretched my knowledge and skills in new ways, providing opportunities to reflect, refine and develop innovative approaches to practice. The inauguration of the British Psychological Society's Special Group in Coaching Psychology (later to become the Division of Coaching Psychology) of which I was a founder member, provided a much-needed home for developing my knowledge and practice with a community of like-minded and inspirational colleagues and clients. Becoming a chartered coaching psychologist and undertaking additional studies to become a certified professional executive coach led me to a point where my interests could intersect.

At the heart of all of my careers – ballet dancer, actor, clinical psychologist and coach – has been a fascination with how stories and the act of storytelling can be enabled by disciplinary knowledge, and how disciplinary knowledge can in turn be enriched by stories and the act of storytelling. For me, writing this book has represented a journey into some of the many ways in which we can all use stories to enrich our lives and engage many different audiences in the task of designing interventions for healing, growth and success.

Louise C. Kovács

I grew up in the south of England in a white middle-class family. I attended the local schools and benefited from the government's policies (in the 1980s) to fully fund university study, enabling me to complete a BEd (Hons). On leaving university I chose to enter the business world rather than teach, and secured a graduate position in the sales team of a technology company. I was the first woman hired in a sales role by the organization and this experience helped me gain the skills needed to navigate a corporate environment and develop strategies to deal with the bias that I encountered. I learned to set goals and strive to achieve them, but I also felt that I needed to outperform my male peers in order to be taken seriously. It would be easy to emphasize the minoritized aspect of my identify in this context. However, other aspects of my social identity afforded me the opportunity to pursue this career.

Having spent 15 years in the technology industry in Europe and Australia I had achieved some success and had gained valuable commercial experience. Additionally, through working for several start-up companies, I developed my entrepreneurial skills. However, I was also suffering the effects of burnout. Seeking a change in direction, I completed the Master of Organizational Coaching at the University of Sydney. The evidence-based approach taught in this programme initially informed the primary perspectives that I brought to my executive coaching practice. These theoretical models are largely based on Western approaches to psychology and are underpinned by cultural values, such as individualism and personal striving, which resonated with my background. While these approaches are appropriate for many clients, I also recognize the potential for these to marginalize other perspectives.

This challenge was highlighted during the seven years in which I lived and worked as a coach in Singapore, where I had the opportunity to coach leaders across Southeast Asia as well as China and India.

Since beginning my practice in 2004, my personal and professional experiences have continued to shape and reshape how I think about coaching. I have pursued further study, completing a Professional Doctorate and courses in neuroscience, adult developmental theory and coaching supervision. It was during my doctoral study, through the Professional Development Foundation, that I discovered the concept of formulation. I apply formulation in my practice as a means to ensure that I am creating space for the client's perspective, to hear their story, and to assist me in broadening my thinking beyond the individual to consider, with the client, the systemic factors that may be involved in each coaching engagement. I now consider myself an eclectic coach who interweaves my knowledge and experience with the client's story, and the wider context, to facilitate positive change.

As a formative working experience, my career in the technology industry influences how I frame the purpose of my work as an executive coach. Many of my coaching engagements focus on working with people from minoritized groups who have chosen to pursue their careers in large, Western organizations. In working with executives in these organizations I aim to challenge the norms of leadership to develop more inclusive, systemic approaches to leading. Having been a coach for 20 years, I have had the privilege to facilitate the learning and growth of many clients and likewise, these experiences have continued to challenge me to constantly evaluate and evolve my practice, as well as stimulating my personal development.

Acknowledgements

This project has benefited from the contribution of a number of people whose support and involvement we would like to acknowledge.

First, we would like to thank Katie Randall and the team at Routledge who have been a source of guidance and support at all stages of the journey. We have greatly appreciated this most recent opportunity to partner with Routledge on this project.

Second, we wish to thank those who have supported the development of the material for the book. In particular we thank those colleagues who participated in the study described in the Introduction to the book and Nicola Hurton who conducted the data analysis. We would also like to thank David Clutterbuck, Catherine Carr, Peter Hawkins, Jacqueline Peters and Sunny Stout-Rostron for permission to reproduce their work. Additional thanks go to Carole Morley for her help with compiling and formatting the references and to Ian Lacey for reviewing the manuscript and for his encouragement, critique and enthusiasm along the way, both for this project and for the work of the authors over many years.

Finally, we owe a debt of gratitude to all of the colleagues and clients who have informed our research and practice. The opportunity to benefit from their experiences and expertise has been an inspiration and a privilege and has formed the foundations for the ideas that feature in the pages that follow.

Confidentiality Statement

The case material included in this book has been inspired by the experiences of and dilemmas encountered in professional practice. However, care has been taken to ensure anonymity and all of the clients and coaches in all of the cases used for illustrative purposes throughout the book are fictitious.

Series Editor's Foreword

Formulation as a Key to Coaching in a Complex World

The Professional Coaching Series has been developed to provide key texts to inform practice in coaching. Colleagues from across the world have generously contributed their expertise to inform and challenge practice in multiple areas that coaches face in the increasingly complex context in which they operate.

As series editor, one area I have been asked to include is the role of formulation to address complexity in coaching. Formulation is a core element of practice in many areas of psychology but has been marginal for many coaches who have preferred to apply given frameworks to their work with clients. Yet, formulation is increasingly appearing in the work of leading practitioners faced with clients who are trying to address multiple, complex issues. As series editor I have tried to avoid featuring my own work. However, formulation is an area that has fascinated me throughout my career in coaching, education and therapy. Together with my colleague Sarah Corrie in applied practice in psychology and with Louise Kovács, formulation has formed a central part of our work as coaches. Hence this current volume.

We have set out in the first section of the book to make the case for why formulation adds value to the work of coaches, explain what formulation looks like within practice and provide a revised framework for its application.

The 4P Framework proposed in the second section of the book is a development from the previous Purpose, Perspective and Process approach that has formed the basis for our work over many years. It continues to provide a structure for consideration of the nature of professions and to guide practitioner research within defined areas of practice. Adding the fourth P – Positionality – makes explicit elements that were previously included in the way we defined the Purpose of our work and the Perspectives we adopted. By considering Positionality as a discrete element, we have given more weight to the role of the way we and our clients see ourselves and the world as a feature of practice. This section of the book explores the framework in some detail. We provide brief case vignettes and questions to ponder.

The third section of the book looks at some examples of areas of practice. Coaching has become so comprehensive that we cannot cover more than a fraction of the areas of practice encompassed within our field. We have chosen to illustrate formulation within areas where we feel there are specific challenges that help to illustrate the depth of the thinking that formulation encourages. The case studies we use in this section are more detailed to illuminate the ideas that emerge over the course of a coaching journey.

The fourth section of the book provides a way for readers to apply the concepts to their own work. A detailed case study, a generic framework and a personalized approach are explored which will, we believe, enable readers to fully appreciate why and how applying formulation within their coaching can benefit clients and wider stakeholders as well as their own practice. The section also explores formulation within a diverse world and the challenges this brings. We offer a brief conclusion to the book to encourage further exploration of the role of formulation in enhancing coaching practice.

I trust this will be a welcome addition to the series.

Professor David A. Lane
Professional Development Foundation

Introduction

Coaching is now well established as an effective intervention for addressing a wide range of issues facing individuals, teams and organizations. Its theoretical influences are expanding, and although still somewhat dependent on ideas from other psychology disciplines, one central feature of much psychology practice has been largely missing, namely, formulation. The concept of formulation is central to practice in many areas of psychology and beyond. This process for working with the client to understand the issues faced and the factors that influence them enables innovative interventions to emerge but also generates practice beyond the simple to encompass complex contexts. The application of formulation as an approach to coaching does, in our view, need to be more widely applied. Our aim in this book is to make the case for its use and enable understanding and application of the concept to practice.

We hope that this book will become the primary resource for coaches wishing to improve their practice through the use of formulation. While it has yet to be fully embraced within coaching, formulation is increasingly identified as a necessary skill for coaches to acquire. In our discussions with experienced coaches, for example, it is clear that they typically use formulation as a core process to aid their understanding of their clients' circumstances and needs, and as a basis for selecting interventions to bring about desired change. Additionally, formulation has become a topic of scholarship and offerings in the literature are starting to appear (e.g., Chapman, 2023; Corrie, Kovács & Lane, 2021; Drake, 2010; Kahn, 2014; Kovács & Corrie, 2021; Lane & Corrie, 2006; Lane et al., 2024; Stout-Rostron, 2009, 2014). Scholars advocating the importance of formulation have pioneered formulation in coaching and have passionately (yet carefully) promoted this to coaches at workshops across the globe. Thus, while it is not always a priority on training programmes, formulation is attracting increased interest and is becoming a significant growth area for the field of coaching as a whole.

This book examines the essence, purpose and function of formulation and explores how to create effective formulations that can enhance practice. Across the chapters, formulation is explored through theoretical perspectives and debates, brief case vignettes and longer case studies illustrating its use, and questions and tasks with which the reader can engage to develop their own formulation skills.

DOI: 10.4324/9781003174585-1

Why Formulation Is Important for Coaches

As noted above, recent years have witnessed an emerging literature examining the role of formulation in coaching. This interest appears reflected in our conversations with experienced coaches. Many of these colleagues use formulation as a core process to aid understanding of their clients' circumstances and needs, and as a basis for selecting interventions to bring about desired change. For example, prior to writing this book, and as a basis for developing the themes and content, we wanted to learn more about why and how experienced coaches used formulation in their work. Generously, a number of colleagues provided detailed information which was then independently reviewed and thematically analysed by our long-term collaborator Nicola Hurton. Through her analysis, seven core themes were identified relating to the perceived benefits of formulation, namely that it:

1 Enables coach and client to personalize the use of relevant literature and models
2 Provides a psychologically informed approach
3 Helps to provide a way forward that has implications for change
4 Enables the systematic use of stories/narratives
5 Enables interpretations, making sense of the situation in a shared process
6 Facilitates exploration of the context and different influences at play in a client's circumstances and needs
7 Provides an explanatory framework that can guide and support practice

These benefits were identified as helping coach and client to work to create a framework of co-working that can generate both understanding and future directions and are evident in the quotations from our colleagues below:

"As people tell their stories a considerable amount of information is forthcoming. We need a way to make sense of that and find a coherent and articulate account that enables those working together to recognize their story and be able to re-author unhelpful aspects. So, for me formulation is a process of authoring, and re-authoring our stories as individuals, or as groups of connected people. It is about, first, construction of a coherent account, then the deconstruction of it to understand how different elements impact on us (and others) in order to reconstruct an alternative narrative."

"(Formulation) helps me to keep looking at the emerging story … for elements of coherence and mismatches in the account. It creates ideas that can be subjected to further exploration including testing ideas in real world contexts until eventually, an articulate account is reached. Using this account with the client (person or peoples) we can set up experiments in behaviour to create intervention strategies to generate change. Having the formulation means that we can relate those experiments back to the formulation and see if it still holds up as a viable account. It can then be revisited as necessary. It also provides a basis for evaluation of any work undertaken and as a new story is authored, it provides for a sustainable process of adaptation in the future. As this is a collaborative process the client(s) learns how to use the formulation process for themselves to address future concerns."

"For me it is like holding a bigger container. Part of the reason it informs my work is that formulation provides me with something like a checklist. It also helps me notice what is absent from the picture. If I don't have a formulation then there are times where I just get lost in what the client is saying and do not go beneath that to identify, for example, what are the defensive patterns here. Or what is the emotion underneath this or what is happening with the client late at night and they are on to their second bottle of wine. When I have a sense of my formulation, I am also clear on how I could intervene. For example, should I look at a belief system, or is there an emotion I need to go into? Or is there something around interpersonal skills? Perhaps there is an element of all of the above, but it helps me be clearer about the best way of working with each client."

About This Book

The book features current and historical evidence, knowledge and debates that are central to both coaching and the use of formulation and provides illustrations of formulation in practice.[1] The book is divided into four parts moving from theory to application as follows:

Part 1 introduces the fundamentals of formulation. The chapters in this first section of the book examine the essence, purpose and functions of formulation and how formulation can contribute to effective coaching. Key concepts and terms are introduced, different approaches to formulation are examined and an introduction to the use of formulation in practice is provided. Specifically, Chapter 1 provides a thorough orientation to the concept of formulation, its origins within applied psychology and how it might contribute to effective coaching practice. These ideas are developed in Chapter 2, which examines different approaches to formulation including the approaches that have been dominant in the literature to date. This is followed by Chapter 3, which examines how to use formulation in practice. Chapter 3 introduces the 4P Framework – the approach that has emerged through our own practice, scholarship, collaboration and conversations with colleagues.

Part 2 examines how to build a framework for formulation using the 4P Framework introduced in the previous section. The first of the 4Ps, examined in Chapter 4, is

---

1 All case vignettes and case studies are fictitious. However, we hope that the scenarios presented will resonate with readers as representative of the kinds of clients and settings encountered in different coaching contexts.

concerned with positionality; that is, how we see ourselves, are seen and interact with the world as a function of the cultures and beliefs to which we have been exposed and which shape our personal epistemologies and ontologies in multiple ways. Chapter 5 examines the second of the 4Ps, purpose, and explores how to establish a purpose for the coaching and how formulation can be used to conceptualize the encounter. In Chapters 6, 7 and 8, the book introduces three different versions of the third of the 4Ps, perspectives, that can inform the journey – the individual, the interpersonal and the systemic. Finally, Chapter 9 considers the fourth of the 4Ps, process, and how formulation impacts the design and delivery of the coaching process.

Part 3 provides some illustrations of how formulation can be applied in different coaching contexts. These chapters seek to illuminate some of the creative, diverse and valuable ways in which formulation can be applied to coaching. Although it is not our intention to represent all of the many contexts in which coaching now occurs – there are simply too many contexts for us to be able to include them all – we have sought to identify areas of coaching which we hope will be recognizable to our readers and which will, therefore, provide fertile ground for considering the application of the principles and methods introduced in Parts 1 and 2. Thus, in this section, the chapters focus on the role and benefits of formulation in health and wellness coaching (Chapter 10), executive coaching and leadership development (Chapter 11), teams and systems (Chapter 12) and education (Chapter 13).

Part 4 of the book follows logically from the preceding sections to take the reader through a detailed account of how to construct a formulation. The case example provided in Chapter 14 illustrates in detail the choices and decisions confronting the coach at each stage of the formulation process providing a "step-by-step" account of how the task of formulation might be approached in the context of a specific coaching assignment. This is followed, in Chapter 15, by guidance for readers on how to develop a personalized approach to formulation that takes account of their own positionality, purpose, preferred perspectives and processes. Finally, in Chapter 16, the book considers the challenges to coaching formulation of different worldviews. The chapter examines some of the ways in which specific groups have been marginalized as well as attempts to address some of these issues. Thus, the chapter aims to provide a challenge to much of our collective Western thinking to develop ways of understanding that can foster practices that are genuinely inclusive.

While the overall direction of the book is one of moving from theory to application, embedded within each chapter are specific "anchors" in the form of points to consider to help the reader personalize and use the ideas, either as a basis for personal reflection or for discussion in conversation with peers, training or in supervision. In this way, we invite a continuation of the journey into formulation which the reader can ground within their own coaching practice.

Who This Book Is for

In writing this book our aim is to support the learning and development needs of coaches at all stages of their careers so that regardless of their level of experience and professional context, readers can become increasingly skilled in using formulation in their own practice. We hope, therefore, that this book will be useful for a wide range of audiences including:

- Coaches and coaching psychologists who, having consolidated their core coaching skills, are seeking a flexible but systematic approach to understanding their clients' needs that can be adapted to the unique characteristics of any coaching encounter.
- Experienced coaches and coaching psychologists wishing to extend their approach to a wider range of clients and contexts and who would welcome a useful text to guide them in this endeavour. For experienced practitioners looking to explore ways to extend areas of practice, formulation offers imaginative ways to conceptualize client work.
- All coaches and coaching psychologists who wish to broaden their practice beyond the confines of a single theoretical model.
- Coach supervisors seeking effective ways of helping their supervisees make sense of their clients' needs as the coaching journey unfolds.
- Coach trainers who wish to expand their repertoire of approaches for helping trainees master the art and science of designing effective coaching approaches for their clients. It will also provide a basis for teaching formulation on coach training programmes and we hope encourage others to begin to include this in their curriculum.
- Academics interested in developing an understanding of the role of formulation and how this can contribute to the processes and outcomes of coaching research.

How to Use the Book – A Message to You, the Reader

The intention behind this book is to offer a text that goes beyond the conceptual and theoretical in order to help coaches deliver their best work. Before engaging with the chapters that follow, we recommend, therefore, that you give some thought to what has led you to pick up this book and what you most need from it. This will enable you to personalize your reading and reflections to your own development needs. To engage you in this process we offer you the following questions as orienting prompts:

1 How do you currently seek to understand the client, their issues and the factors that are impacting on them?
2 How do you explore your own personal and professional values while understanding those of your client to arrive at a shared understanding?
3 How do you facilitate coaching relationships that promote an open sharing of your own and your clients' perspectives to leverage the synergies between you?
4 What are your hopes, needs and expectations for reading this book?

Whatever has drawn you to this volume, we hope that through the chapters that follow, you will feel encouraged, challenged and supported to think about your practice in new ways. As you start the journey through the book, we wish you well and look forward to sharing it with you.

Part 1

The Fundamentals of Formulation and an Introduction to the 4P Framework

This first section of the book introduces the concept of formulation and makes the case for formulation as a vital part of coaching practice. In addition to identifying its purpose and functions, the origins of formulation are explored. The characteristics of formulation are introduced with guidance on how to use it in practice. This section also introduces the 4P Framework to assist readers in creating formulations with and for their clients.

DOI: 10.4324/9781003174585-2

Chapter 1

An Introduction and Orientation to Formulation

In coaching, a good part of our time is spent making sense of the concerns, dilemmas, puzzles and requests with which our clients present us. This process of sense-making, whether conducted in the privacy of our personal reflections, carried out discursively in supervision or co-produced through dialogue with our clients, is known as formulation. In comparison with the wide variety of coaching models and techniques that are often the focus of coach training programmes as well as of books and journal articles, formulation is a relatively poorly understood skill. However, and as we hope to demonstrate throughout this book, it is a critical one that is well worth acquiring.

The aim of this first chapter is to provide a broad orientation to formulation as one of the most interesting, complex and sophisticated activities that a coach can undertake. The chapter begins by introducing and describing the nature of formulation and clarifies how it differs from a diagnostic approach and from the working hypotheses that often characterize coaches' thinking. The literature, which suggests a growing interest in formulation as a basis for coaching practice, is introduced and is followed by a discussion of the main functions and benefits of formulation. The chapter then introduces the main capabilities and skills that are needed to construct effective formulations. Finally, consideration is given to whether formulation is essential to all coaching assignments or only some. Through this first chapter the aim is to provide an orientation to what is a multi-layered activity and to raise awareness of current issues, questions and debates surrounding the role of formulation that are elaborated in subsequent chapters.

Finding a Way Through a Client's Story

The act of working with a client presents a coach with multiple choice points. At each stage in the process, the coach is likely to be faced with several options about how to proceed, including which questions to ask, specific avenues of inquiry to explore, which coaching framework might best help make sense of the client's context and needs, or specific techniques that might enable change. Consider, for example, the case scenario in Box 1.1.

DOI: 10.4324/9781003174585-3

Box 1.1 Juliet's decisions about coaching for Mark

Juliet, an experienced executive coach, has been asked to have a chemistry meeting with a senior manager who is an employee of an organization that has recently engaged Juliet's services. Prior to their first meeting, Juliet learns that the prospective client, Mark, brings with him the reputation of "not suffering fools gladly" and "having a short fuse". From her initial contact with the organization, Juliet forms the impression that Mark's behaviour has been tolerated because of the revenue he has brought to the business over a period of years.

At their chemistry meeting, Mark indicates that he would like to work on his leadership style. He reveals that he has had difficulty retaining the staff in his team and is aware that at their exit interviews, several individuals have made complaints about his combative manner. The word "bullying" has also been used. Juliet does not experience his manner as directly combative or bullying, but notes that during their conversation Mark is unusually probing in his questions about her qualifications and experience. At times, he also seems mildly flirtatious, but Juliet wonders whether this could be a misinterpretation on her part.

Mark says that he would like to proceed with coaching and from their initial meeting is optimistic that Juliet "understands him and what he needs". Juliet has mixed feelings about their initial encounter and for reasons she cannot entirely comprehend, feels uneasy in his presence. Nonetheless there is a clear rationale for the coaching to which Mark has indicated he is committed. Juliet also wishes to make a good impression with the organization which is keen that Mark receives coaching to address aspects of his interpersonal style. Juliet and Mark, therefore, agree to work together.

How should Juliet make sense of Mark's presentation and needs as a basis for devising a coaching intervention? On the one hand, at the outset, the information available to Juliet is relatively limited and she will, no doubt, want to gather more data upon which to base the development of a coaching plan. On the other hand, their initial interaction is rich with areas ripe for exploration. For example, there is Mark's own stated aspirations for the coaching: his desire to examine and change his style of leadership, which is a stated objective around which both parties can organize their efforts. There are also the words of warning about his interpersonal style and hints from other stakeholders that Mark is experienced as problematic by his team members in ways that are starting to create difficulties for the business. This suggests the need to consider what might reflect an interpersonal deficit, a broader problem with social cognition or difficulties with regulating his emotional responses, which Juliet might need to consider.

There is also Juliet's own initial impression of and reaction to Mark. Are his prob-ing questions indicative of simply wanting clarification or do they reflect his anxiety about whether Juliet can "manage him"? Is he worried that she, too, might find him interpersonally problematic in the way that others have, or could they be a test to see how Juliet responds to provocations? Additionally, what should Juliet make of Mark's mildly flirtatious style – if, indeed, she detected this correctly? Is this indica-tive of an attempted misuse of power in the context of gender politics? Is he even aware of what he might be communicating? Are his reactions to her, and hers to him, suggestive of character traits that could potentially be interpreted as part of a more enduring personality style? Making sense of the data emerging from the initial interaction with both the organizational sponsor and the client who is to receive the coaching will inevitably give rise to further questions, such as what is relevant infor-mation to include in making sense of Mark's needs and from which sources? What hypotheses might be useful to generate and what type of data should Juliet gather in order to test them? Questions such as these are typical of the decisions that confront coaches as they attempt to make sense of and respond effectively to the many and varied reasons for which clients seek their services. Given that multiple courses of action are potentially available, coaches need to develop a process that enables them to decide upon a plan of action. This is the primary task of formulation.

What Is Formulation?

In broad terms, a formulation can be defined as, "an explanatory account of the issues with which a client is presenting including predisposing, precipitating and maintaining factors that can form the basis of a shared framework of understanding and which has implications for change" (Lane & Corrie, 2009, p. 194). In consid-ering how this type of explanatory account can inform practice, we find it useful to draw on the analogy of having a map to help navigate an unfamiliar terrain. Beginning a coaching assignment may feel akin to finding oneself in a dense forest surrounded by tall trees and thick foliage which block out the rays of the sun. With-out a map, we are likely to feel disoriented and unable to identify how to progress our journey out of the forest. Even if we are not lost, we are more likely to reach our destination safely if we have a sense of the best direction of travel. A map can also protect us from nasty surprises, preventing us from misunderstanding what lies ahead – for example, assuming that the landscape will be flat and shaded only to discover that it leads to a precipice that is exposed to the elements. Equally for coaches, without a map, their interventions are more likely to falter: the success of any method or tool used may be more serendipitous than planned, representing the influence of random factors rather than a coherent understanding of the factors that are truly relevant to consider. In coaching, there are good reasons, then, to underpin the work with a map – that is, a formulation – that can enable us to identify and plan for what lies ahead with greater accuracy and confidence.

The definition above, and the analogy of navigating one's way out of a dense forest, enables us to begin to tease out what formulation is, and what it is not.

First, as Lane and Corrie's (2009) definition implies, a formulation goes beyond a detailed description of the concerns and aspirations of the client in order to arrive at an account which both describes and explains. Second, when developing this explanatory account, the coach will usually need to draw upon multiple sources of information, grounding their conceptual map in the specifics of the client's self-told story, a variety of sources of data and the theories and concepts that inform the coach's professional offering. Thus, in the service of developing this account, some of the questions with which a coach is likely to be concerned include:

- Why is this client presenting with this particular issue (as opposed to any other)?
- Why is this issue arising for them (or others) now?
- Why is coaching being requested at this time as opposed to six months ago or six months from now?
- What is the desired outcome and for whom?
- What are the main factors that are implicated in the client's current circumstances, needs and aspirations?
- What predisposing, precipitating and maintaining factors help explain the client's presentation?
- What strengths and resources (individual, interpersonal and systemic) are available to the client that could be harnessed for the purposes of change?
- What are some of the constraints facing the client (individual, interpersonal and systemic) of which coaching will need to take account?
- Based on the above, what hypotheses might be developed about the client's needs, and what data might be needed to test those emerging hypotheses?

What is immediately evident from the questions above is that coaches can engage with them regardless of the theories or models that inform their preferred approach. This reflects one of the defining functions of formulation, namely, that it provides a vehicle for identifying *where* to look rather than *how* to look. The process of deciding "how to look" comes from the approach to formulation that the coach subsequently adopts. This will be determined by the way the purpose of the work is defined and the perspectives that are adopted, as well as the foundational assumptions (Mahrer, 2000) and worldviews to which the coach and client subscribe.

In their exploration of formulation in applied psychology, Corrie and Lane (2010) identified five principal approaches to formulation that are evident in professional practice, and which have relevance for coaching. These are: (1) the diagnostic perspective – an approach to formulation most evident in health care settings but also used in executive coaching where the coach underpins a formulation with data from psychometric tests; (2) the scientist–practitioner perspective – an approach to formulation that follows the principle of coaches and clients working together to define and test specific hypotheses; (3) the theoretical perspective – where a formulation is derived from the concept and models generated from within a specific theoretical approach such as cognitive, behavioural, psychodynamic or narrative theories; and (4) the strategic perspective – this includes solution-focused approaches which focus on desired future states and how to design ways to achieve them. A fifth perspective that Corrie and Lane (2010) identified is where formulation becomes a vehicle of social control; that is, the ways in which psychological knowledge has been used to complement or challenge prevailing political worldviews and social discourses. Each of these approaches to formulation directs how coaches listen to their clients' stories, provides a basis for gathering certain forms of information over others and directs coaches towards designing particular types of intervention or journey. (These different approaches are considered in Chapter 2.)

In the chapters that follow, different approaches to formulation are considered in detail. In this first chapter it is sufficient to note that the focus of a formulation might range from a specific, pre-identified area of development need for an individual client (e.g. improving a newly appointed team leader's delegation skills) to developing leadership capability for navigating the challenges imposed by a pandemic and global economic crisis. In consequence, developing a formulation may warrant attention to any number of biological, intrapersonal, interpersonal, organizational, systemic, social and cultural factors and will also, as illustrated in the case examples in Part 3, look very different in diverse contexts.

How Formulation Differs From a Diagnosis and a Working Hypothesis

At the same time as introducing what a formulation is, it is also important to note what a formulation is not. A formulation is not a single activity, carried out in isolation at the start of a coaching assignment and imposed upon the work that subsequently takes place. Nor is it a model of coaching, a specific technique or a tool for what Bruch (2015) referred to as "symptom-technique matching" (i.e. a diluted form of professional decision-making where a standardized technique is matched to a symptom, problem or issue in the form of "Problem A = Technique B").

Moreover, a formulation is not a diagnosis. Formulations can be diagnostically informed as described above; a diagnosis is essentially a description that groups together a range of characteristics under a single label. Although potentially useful, diagnosis operates at the descriptive level rather than the deeper, explanatory level that a formulation aims to achieve and fails to accommodate the realities of the professional context with which coaches and their clients will be concerned. The comprehensive approach to data gathering and synthesis that typifies a formulation differs again from the more commonly used working hypothesis, which is often developed in a less systematic way, relying on a potentially limited range of data such as the coach's intuition, professional experience or a preferred way of working. Table 1.1 summarizes some of the main differences between a working hypothesis, diagnosis and formulation to illuminate further what makes formulation distinctive, with illustrations of the application of these principles provided in subsequent chapters.

Table 1.1 The similarities and differences between a working hypothesis, diagnosis and formulation

	Working hypothesis	Diagnosis	Formulation
Type of understanding yielded:	Descriptive or explanatory (depending on the coach's approach)	Descriptive	Descriptive and explanatory
Focus of understanding:	The factors relevant to the individual client	Standardized across groups (i.e. the extent to which the client's profile is consistent with that of a larger, homogeneous group)	The factors relevant to the individual client, supported by relevant concepts from the wider literature
Static vs evolving:	Tends to remain static over time (unless subjected to conscious scrutiny through processes such as critical reflection or supervision)	Remains static over time (the diagnostic criteria themselves remain unchanged even if the client changes)	Evolves as hypotheses are articulated, developed, tested and refined
Range of data used:	May rely on limited information (e.g. the coach's intuition, past experience and preferred model of practice vs a comprehensive approach to data gathering)	Draws on limited information (information is sought to confirm or refute diagnosis, such as a client's responses to a questionnaire)	Requires the use and synthesis of multiple sources of data, drawing on a comprehensive dataset
Nature of data used:	Likely to depend on coach's own preferences and prior experience	Dichotomous (diagnostic criteria are either met or not met)	Continuous and integrated
Source of data:	Subjective (based largely on the coach's own thinking)	Objective (based on normative data)	Combines objective and subjective sources making use of multiple inputs
Development process:	Often developed implicitly, through drawing on prior experience, model preferences and assumptions. May not be easily subjected to external scrutiny	Explicit, based on clear, objective criteria. Accessible to external scrutiny	Can be made explicit. Available to external scrutiny

(Continued)

Table 1.1 (Continued)

	Working hypothesis	Diagnosis	Formulation
Speed of formation:	Can occur swiftly; often based on hunches and the application of sources of data that may be poorly defined (see reference to heuristics in the text below)	Can be applied relatively swiftly once the relevant tool has been selected and applied to determine whether diagnostic criteria are met	Occurs over time as different sources of information are gathered, interpreted and synthesized into a coherent descriptive and explanatory account
Degree of robustness:	Given the factors identified above, may lack robustness	Potentially high	Potentially very high as draws on multiple sources of data, and is capable of articulation so can be subjected to external scrutiny
Ability to predict how the process of coaching unfolds:	Relatively low ability	Low ability	High ability (see the benefits of using formulation below)

© Kovács and Corrie (2021)

In summary, a formulation is the means through which the coach selects certain forms of data and synthesizes those data with relevant theories, models and constructs and the client's self-told story to make sense of the client's needs in a way that that can inform the work that subsequently takes place. This type of account, at its best, has a depth and clarity that the client is unable to achieve unaided and as such adds significant value to the coaching process.

Formulation and Coaching

Formulation has a long and well-established history within applied psychology and therapy, where it has been identified as the foundation of skilled psychological practice (Atter, 2009; British Psychological Society, 2005, 2011; Hallam, 2013; Johnstone & Dallos, 2006; Lane & Corrie, 2006). Indeed, historically some have argued that it is precisely this ability to construct formulations of our clients' needs that differentiates effective and ethically informed professional practice from the types of support offered by lay helpers (see Butler, 1998; Malkin cited in Lane, 1990).

Although it is still a relatively novel application within coaching, formulation is of growing interest to coaches and has begun to attract increased scholarly attention (see Corrie & Kovács, 2019; Drake, 2010, 2018; Kovács & Corrie, 2017b, 2017c; Lane & Corrie, 2009) with the literature providing examples of how formulation can support coaches in working with complexity (Kovács & Corrie, 2021) as well as enabling coaches to make informed decisions about their self-care needs in the context of enabling a psychologically well-resourced workforce (Corrie & Kovács, 2021).

Coaching-specific models of formulation have also been developed. For example, the Purpose, Perspective and Process (PPP) model (Corrie & Lane 2010; Lane & Corrie, 2006, 2009) has been offered as a systematic approach to developing individually tailored explanatory accounts of clients' needs that can enhance a consistency between the process of coaching, the perspectives that are brought to bear on the work and the purpose the coaching is designed to achieve. Drawing on the PPP model, the Purpose–Account–Intervention–Reflect (PAIR) Framework (Kovács, 2016; Corrie & Kovács, 2017; Kovács & Corrie, 2017b, 2017c) provides guidance on how to develop and use formulation within specific coaching assignments, and in particular complex assignments for which linear models of coaching are less likely to be effective (Cavanagh & Lane, 2012).

That formulation is garnering interest and appeal in coaching is perhaps not surprising given the broader national and global context (Lane et al., 2023). Coaches are delivering their services in increasingly complex professional, social, economic and political environments, rendered yet more challenging following the arrival, in 2020, of the COVID-19 pandemic. As noted above, existing models and methods may not prove fit for purpose for optimally meeting the ever-expanding needs of an increasingly diverse range of stakeholders in a rapidly changing world (Cavanagh & Lane, 2012; Smith et al., 2024; Whybrow et al., 2023). Thus, the field needs to remain open to novel, deeper and more sophisticated approaches to making sense of clients' needs and developing novel interventions. It is in this context specifically that formulation might most usefully augment a coach's existing set of methods, models, approaches and techniques. What is it, then, that makes formulation so important? Why might it have been afforded an exalted status within applied psychology and why is it of growing interest to the coaching community? The benefits of underpinning coaching practice with a formulation are considered next.

Why Formulation Matters: The Benefits for Coaches and Their Clients

Given that formulations take time and energy to develop it is not unreasonable to question whether it is worthwhile. Clients want to see results as swiftly as possible, and taking the time to develop a formulation inevitably delays the introduction of specific strategies or techniques. Moreover, as the evidence base for coaching develops, it could be argued that the client's needs are better served by identifying and delivering an empirically supported intervention rather than devising an elaborate individual account. Additionally, a formulation does not necessarily yield immediately obvious or demonstrable benefits; while the effective delivery of a coaching technique might provide a breakthrough moment which is inherently rewarding for coach and client, a formulation is less likely in and of itself to generate transformational change, even though the insights obtained might be experienced as transformational by the client. Nonetheless, formulation is considered to be an important and practice-enhancing activity by many. Across the field of applied psychology (e.g. Butler, 1998; Corrie & Lane, 2010; Corrie et al., 2016; Lane & Corrie, 2006) the benefits of formulation have long been espoused. Commonly cited benefits of formulation are that it:

1 Assists information gathering and supports the identification of appropriate methods of data collection
2 Clarifies core hypotheses and relevant questions
3 Aids the development of a broad, shared understanding of the client's context, circumstances and needs
4 Helps practitioner and client prioritize issues and concerns
5 Places the client's experiences in the context of their circumstances and personal or professional story which can enhance empathy
6 Aids understanding of the connections between past experiences and present behaviours and between present behaviours and environmental factors
7 Identifies patterns in a client's actions and responses that can be examined impartially and collaboratively
8 Aids the identification of any maintenance cycles that appear to be perpetuating the current concerns
9 Supports the process of determining criteria for a successful outcome, including organizing all stakeholders around the same goals
10 Enables predictions of client reactions to specific situations or events

11   Helps predict obstacles to progress
12   Aids the process of thinking systematically and productively about lack of progress, identifies missing information
13   Refines the search for relevant theoretical constructs or processes
14   Can instil hope, especially when positive change is not possible to achieve immediately

The advantages identified above represent the broadly endorsed functions of formulation across applied psychology. For coaching specifically, Corrie and Kovács (2021) have identified the following benefits (see Table 1.2).

Table 1.2 The benefits of using formulation

Type of benefit	Example
Assists information gathering:	Supports information gathering, identifying key stakeholders, gaps in data and appropriate methods of data collection
Helps conceptualize and map complexity:	Provides a framework for systematically capturing the client's needs and background information
	Supports the identification and prioritization of individual and situational factors
	Facilitates understanding of power dynamics and highlights any ethical dilemmas
	Identifies elements of the client's situation that fall outside the coach's expertise or the remit of the coaching assignment
	Provides a structure and process to contain the anxiety that high levels of ambiguity and uncertainty can trigger in both client and coach as well as the organizational sponsor
Fosters collaborative and creative thinking:	Provides a framework for collaborative sense-making and idea generation, which in turn supports the development of the coaching relationship
	Enables the coach and client to broaden their perspective or focus on specific issues, as needed
	Facilitates the coach and client's ability to consider the presenting issues, solutions and process from multiple perspectives
	Supports the identification of likely barriers and enablers of success
Supports transparency and rigor of decision-making:	Brings structure to decision-making
	Encourages collaborative goal setting and alignment
	Promotes transparent communication by providing a vehicle for the coach to share their thinking, allowing for scrutiny and possible challenge
	Provides a means to keep track over time of hypothesis testing, results and progress
	Assists the coach and client in thinking through individual and systemic reactions

(Continued)

Table 1.2 (Continued)

Type of benefit	Example
Encourages reflective practice:	Makes explicit how the coach and client are thinking about the coaching
	Provides an opportunity to evaluate the effectiveness of the coaching and to gather data on factors that might support or hinder effectiveness
	Provides a vehicle for monitoring the quality of the coaching relationship
	Assists the coach in identifying their own learning and development needs

© Kovács and Corrie (2021)

Thus, looking across the literature, the findings suggest that when done effectively, the task of formulation can support both the content of the coaching and the process that unfolds. In terms of content, developing a formulation clarifies key hypotheses and identifies relevant questions and specific hypotheses to be tested; facilitates understanding of the client's needs as a whole; identifies missing information; refines the search for relevant theoretical constructs or processes; determines criteria for a successful outcome; and organizes practitioner and client around the same goals. In terms of the process of coaching, developing a formulation determines which issues are prioritized for exploration, how strategies are selected, planned, introduced and sequenced, helps the coach predict obstacles to progress, aid systematic and productive thinking about lack of progress, identify patterns in a client's actions and responses that can be examined collaboratively and support decisions concerning how the coaching may need to be adjusted in the light of any atypical features. This distinction between content and process is important when it comes to considering how to approach the task of developing effective formulation.

Creating Effective Formulations

Having presented a case for the benefits of formulation, the question arises as to how the task itself is best approached, as well as the types of data that should be included and any method or methods that should be followed. The means by which formulations are constructed, developed and refined are covered in detail in the chapters that follow. However, in broad terms we would see that creating effective formulations relies on the judicious application of skills in three domains: content, capability and process. These elements are introduced briefly below with the implicit invitation to notice how issues relating to content, capability and process are woven into the chapters that follow.

Content

At the level of content, the coach is concerned with identifying the sources of knowledge, data and information that will be used to inform the formulation. This covers the sources of information that the client brings, those available from other stakeholders and the understanding that the coach can offer. The application of content will include constructs, theories, models and evidence that derive from the coaching literature as well as those that relate indirectly to coaching. In his "Research Relevance-to-Coaching" model Grant (2016), for example, highlights how knowledge that informs coaching will often take the form of both coach-specific or coaching-related sources and those deriving from studies conducted in adjacent fields such as social science, psychotherapy, neuroscience, management and leadership. These indirect resources might provide valuable information for the purposes of hypothesis generation even though they do not derive from the field of coaching itself.

The content-related choices that coaches make will reflect what they believe is necessary to help them work with their clients to the best advantage. However, these choices will also reflect what we term the coach's positionality (see Chapter 4), the way the purpose of the work is defined (Chapter 5) and the perspectives adopted (Chapters 6, 7 and 8). In making decisions about content, a coach will also be informed by whether a micro or macro perspective is adopted. Chapter 6, for example, examines how the content of a formulation will be shaped by the extent to which the focus of enquiry is tightly defined (e.g. improving study skills for the purposes of a forthcoming examination) or broadly framed (enabling team functioning in the context of remote working practices necessitated by the onset of a global pandemic) and consider the contribution of Corrie and Kovács' (2019) three levels of formulation: the situation, the pattern and the person as a basis for developing effective formulations. A similar set of reflections applies to the content that the client brings, which encompasses their perspectives on the situation, their sense of self and their wider context.

Capabilities

At the level of capabilities, the coach is concerned with the skills required to help shape the formulation as it emerges. Formulation is perhaps best understood as a meta-skill in that it relies on the application of a range of cognitive abilities such as reflection, hypothesis generation, data gathering, analysis and synthesis, hypothesis testing, decision-making and innovative thinking, among others.

Because the capabilities involved include both accurate and design-based thinking, formulation is typically cognitively demanding, requiring coaches to attend to the factors that enable their thinking as well as impediments to effective decision-making. Such impediments include heuristics (e.g. Tversky & Kahneman, 1973, 1974; Kahneman et al., 1982), cognitive distortions and the impact of schema (e.g. Beck et al., 1979) and other information-processing biases that are well documented in the literature on professional decision-making (see Gambrill, 2005;

Lane & Corrie, 2011). For example, in the clinical field, a considerable body of studies since the 1950s has consistently highlighted a mismatch between professionals' perceptions of their decision-making expertise and the accuracy of those perceptions. In particular, historically it has been noted that there is a poor relationship between training and professional judgement (Carkhuf & Berenson, 1967); that clinicians often fail to draw upon any systematic decision-making process to guide their practice (O'Donohue et al., 1990) and that they over-estimate the influence on outcome of the therapeutic relationship at the expense of empirically tested protocols (Shafran et al., 2009). Additionally, O'Donohue and Henderson (1999) have highlighted a range of biases to which professional practitioners are prone including false descriptive statements, false causal statements, believing that phenomena exist when they do not, false relational claims, false predictions and inaccurate ethical claims (that is, believing certain types of behaviour with clients are acceptable when they are not).

As Lane and Corrie (2011) observe, a quality service relies on a variety of cognitive capabilities and reasoning abilities that include but transcend accuracy. As such, a privileging of accuracy at the expense of a more nuanced understanding of the range of decisions that practitioners make during the course of working with a client provides a potentially misleading picture of the reasoning capabilities of the skilled professional. Nonetheless, the literature on professional decision-making as a whole does not promote a sense of confidence that collectively we are achieving what O'Donohue and Henderson (1999) define as our "ethical and epistemic duties" in ensuring that we remain current in our understanding of relevance and knowledge and are able to make accurate and relevant judgements about that knowledge. Such warnings are likely to be equally relevant to coaches. Thus, when considering the capabilities that coaches will require to develop formulations, it is important to recognize that this activity will entail the skilled use of a variety of reasoning abilities that develop over time, as well as a level of self-awareness that enables coaches to be aware of the types of thinking traps to which they might, individually, be prone. Central to this requires the ability of the coach to be an effective listener in ways that enable the client to tell their story. Unless the client's own agency is at the forefront of the work, a formulation becomes something imposed on the client rather than emerging from their shared concern and decision-making.

Process

At the level of process, coaches need to be attentive to the way in which the formulation is constructed, how the process of its development is approached and managed and how the formulation is refined over time as new information comes to light. Two elements of particular importance here are: (1) the question of ownership of the formulation, and (2) whether a formulation is conceptualized as a product (i.e. having a formula*tion*) or a process (formula*ting*).

Some approaches will foreground formulation and as such produce a formulation ("product") at the outset which is discussed, shared and refined. Other approaches view formulation as an understanding or narrative that emerges over time and thus conceptualize formulation first and foremost as a process. Related to this issue, and a topic of debate in the literature within applied psychology, is the question of who owns the formulation and thus who is entitled to determine its accuracy and where necessary make revisions, or how to manage the process where coach and client have misaligned or even competing formulations. Thus a formulation can be offered to the client by the coach (i.e. a coach-driven formulation that is reviewed by the client for its accuracy and relevance) or collaboratively constructed between coach and client (i.e. developed together with each party contributing specific types of information and expertise to form a co-constructed narrative). Alternatively, it can be developed by the client (which may represent an outcome of the coaching that can guide the client's choices over the longer term).

The question of ownership is more profound than a matter of academic debate. If our starting point is that the coaching encounter is a narrative process in which the perspectives of the client and the coach come together to inform the work, this implies a process that is unproblematically collaborative. Yet, is this always the case? The question of who decides what the formulation is, the types of data that should be included and the hypotheses that are generated and tested are not neutral decisions with benevolent implications for our clients. It is all too easy to confuse offering an understanding to a client with imposing it upon them. Even when coaches are attentive to such issues of power, it is not possible to side-step critiques. The stance adopted in this book is that in a formulation, the client's self-told story will always have precedence in this story-creating process. Nonetheless, the ways in which coaches listen may have what Gergen and Davis (2003) described as the detrimental tendency to "strip the storyteller of the story" (p. 241). This can arise in response to a genuine desire to help clients while inadvertently shaping their stories to our models in a way that reflects our own unthinking adherence.

At the same time, while seeking to honour the client's story and sense of agency, a coach will also use a formulation to help the client see the world differently in ways that might support the pursuit of desired outcomes. The belief systems, knowledge and experience of both parties form part of the emerging narrative that seeks to understand how the client came to this moment and how the journey might unfold. Yet, there may be times when different parties take the lead in shaping the emerging explanation and where the coach plays a more direct role. The challenge is ensuring that, when driven by the coach, the formulation does not become the imposition of the coach's view on the client.

In relation to the points above, this book is organized around the following foundational assumptions:

- Both coach and client bring to the early coaching sessions their own working hypotheses which, when shared, provide a basis for elaboration that can inform the development of a more in-depth, robust explanatory account.
- In most cases, a formulation will be collaboratively developed while recognizing that each party contributes specific forms of knowledge and expertise to the process.

- Formulations are often (but not always) most helpful when they take the form of a co-constructed explanatory account that is developed at the start of coaching and refined as new information comes to light.
- There may be occasions where the coach develops a formulation that "sits behind" the work and is not shared explicitly with the client. This approach may be adopted where a coach finds themselves confronting sensitive issues that could be disadvantageous to the client to share. One example of this might be where a coach wishes to make sense of their own internal negative reactions to a client that they sense are relevant to the wider issues for which the client is seeking help, or where the coach predicts that their own negative reactions might interfere with the coaching process. If unpacked, either through private reflection or in supervision, this privately held formulation may reveal valuable information that can support the coaching.
- Regardless of the approach taken, the client's own agency is central to all formulations which emerge from and synthesize an understanding of a shared process of data gathering and decision-making.
- Coaching entails a willing engagement with the client's story and the stories of other stakeholders and, consequently, at times requires the ability to manage considerable levels of uncertainty and ambiguity.

Is Formulation Always Necessary?

Formulation is widely endorsed and seen by an increasing number of scholars as having a vital role to play in supporting the practice of individual coaches and to progressing the field of coaching more widely (Lane et al., 2023). Yet, it is also contentious. One dilemma for the field is that the connections between formulation and the outcomes obtained are typically difficult to empirically substantiate. This is because aspects of the three broad areas outlined above comprise elements that are themselves challenging to operationalize and measure. For example, it is difficult to discern a direct link between decision-making or reflective practice and coaching outcomes. This would be true of all meta-skills. Thus, as a meta-skill, the direct impact of formulation is difficult to demonstrate objectively.

A second issue is whether formulation is always necessary. In the context of coaching assignments involving a single, clear goal for which there is an established evidence base, a case could be made for omitting a formulation in favour of moving directly towards an empirically supported intervention. For example, there is an increasing use in both therapy (Lane & Corrie, 2009) and coaching of AI led online programmes (Tarry, 2018). Where the issue is simple and there is an evidence base for a specific intervention these approaches can work well. This was demonstrated by Terblanche et al. (2022) in a randomized controlled trail with follow up which found that an AI generated coaching programme did produce effective results in a narrow application of goal attainment but not on measures such as resilience, psychological well-being and perceived stress. An alternative perspective on the research has been presented by Passmore (2024) which raises questions about applicability of the findings. Gray et al. (2016) argue that the future of coaching may take the form of a split between technical skill enhancement type interventions online and more complex adaptive changes which require a coach.

Conclusion

This chapter has provided a broad introduction to formulation – an activity that has a long history within applied psychology but whose contribution to coaching is only starting to be realized. The aim has been to headline some of the opportunities and complexities that arise from adopting a formulation-driven approach to coaching and to raise awareness of some of the dilemmas and debates surrounding the application of formulation.

Formulation is arguably one of the most complex and sophisticated activities that a coach undertakes, comprising skills and capabilities at the level of content and process and utilizing a variety of meta-skills such as decision-making and reflection, which are themselves not necessarily well operationalized or understood. As such, formulation is a multi-layered task that may on initial encounter seem less appealing than acquiring specific techniques with their promise of instant results. Nonetheless, there can be distinct advantages from underpinning coaching with formulation. Although there is no rule book for devising effective formulations, there are certainly good principles, perspectives and approaches to guide us. These principles, perspectives and approaches are the subject of subsequent chapters.

Questions to Consider

Having read this chapter, consider what emerges in relation to your own practice. For the purposes of formulation, you may find it helpful to consider the following questions:

- How would you describe the process by which you come to make sense of a client's needs?
- Reflecting on your practice to date, to what extent is your work informed by formulation as described in this chapter or do you tend to be more frequently informed mainly by a working hypothesis or diagnosis? What factors inform your choice?
- To what extent would you regard it as part of your role to develop a formulation for your client that you present to them for discussion, agreement or modification at the start of coaching? To what extent would you regard the formulation as something that the client ultimately arrives at as the coaching unfolds? In what ways does this perspective influence your practice?

Chapter 2

Approaches to Formulation in Coaching

Formulation can take multiple forms depending on the coach's individual approach and the context in which the coaching is delivered. In the previous chapter we considered what a formulation is and how it adds value to the coaching encounter. While the approaches adopted vary greatly, Corrie and Lane (2010) suggest that they tend to group within five primary forms. Drawing on their work on formulation this chapter introduces and explores five main approaches to formulation:

1 Formulation derived from diagnostic classification
2 The formulation of the scientist–practitioner
3 Formulation as a theoretically driven narrative
4 Strategic formulation
5 Formulation and its role as a means of social control

Examples of what each approach might offer coaching are outlined and readers are encouraged to consider which approaches might be most suited to their practice, background, knowledge and skills. The chapter also outlines the core philosophical dilemma for coaching of the three optional stances of self, other and system. Formulation is primarily concerned with how the knowledge of the coach, client and system come together to create an understanding and stance to the world that is meaningful and worthwhile.

What Informs the Approach to Formulation?

Across psychology and related fields, the five approaches identified above inform how practitioners approach the task of formulation. This chapter starts by considering how these approaches appear within coaching and some of the critiques that apply.

Diagnostic classification – In working with an individual client or an organization it is not uncommon for some form of diagnostic or psychometric instrument to be used. For example, when a coach is asked to work with a client, the sponsoring organization may indicate that detailed information is already available that has given rise to the need for coaching. The need may have been identified in an

DOI: 10.4324/9781003174585-4

annual review, a 360-feedback process or through an assessment centre as part of a promotion exercise. Some form of diagnostic process has been used, leading the organization to suggest that the intended recipient of the coaching needs to work on a particular issue. This is an approach to formulation derived from a diagnostic classification.

With an individual client, the use of psychometrics is also a popular approach (Bourne & Whybrow, 2019). It is similar to an approach in therapy where a client's needs are defined against a set of criteria and the difficulties experienced are assigned to a diagnostic or psychometric category. In individual coaching the coach may encourage the use of questionnaires or tests to help gain a sense of the client. An intervention considered suitable for that category of need is then undertaken. For example, within an organization where a 360-feedback process is used, a diagnostically informed approach might take the form of a request for coaching on delegation skills because the results have suggested that this is an issue for the person referred. The story the coach is being told is externally mandated based on an assumption of a linear relationship between diagnosis (or categorization) and intervention. In an introductory meeting the coach may be presented with a bundle of test results, a personality profile, a 360-feedback process, assessment exercises, competence ratings and peer feedback with a clear assumption on the part of the client that this is what they need to change. It might be suggested that repeat 360-feedback or assessment exercises will be undertaken at the end of coaching to evaluate success. Thus, the purpose of coaching is defined in advance as a process of individual change with a measure of achievement built into the process (Kwiatkowski & Winter, 2006).

In areas of occupational practice, attempts to understand action tendencies, areas of strength, preference and need have often been pursued through personality profiles and other psychometric tools leading to a diagnosis of concerns to be addressed. In working towards a formulation where there is an implication that change within one of those tools will occur, it is still important that the coach hears the client's story. How do they view this information and what implications might it have for change? The individual may complete a questionnaire, or a psychometric test may be used. The danger is when it is assumed that the data determine what the individual must do to change – there is no allowance for possible interpersonal or systemic understanding. Thus, feedback needs to be shared in a way that can be accepted by the client (Bourne & Whybrow, 2019).

Bourne and Whybrow (2019) also refer to the concerns raised by Cripps (2017) regarding the increasing application of big data analytics and algorithms. Consequently, there is a need for more research on when these add value in coaching and how to best communicate findings (McDowall, 2017). Depending on the tools used there will also be an assumed underlying perspective on the nature of behaviour. For example, the Myers Briggs Type Indicator (MBTI) is widely used in coaching. The coach may be presented with a type based on the test. Yet, underpinning this type is a theory based on the work of Jung, then adapted by Myers and Briggs during the 1940s to 1960s (see Quenk, 2009) which divided individuals into

16 personality types. The client is classified into one of these types, with coaching needing to take account of this style as well as meet the predetermined goals for change. Again, if this is the approach taken it matters how the client views these data – do they see themselves as defined by their "type" or do they view their type simply as an interesting factor? Yet, the evidence base that informs the validity and reliability of these various measures for use in coaching is often notably absent according to McDowall's (2017) review of the use of assessments.

Formulation of the scientist practitioner – This approach is predicated on the idea that evidence must determine the approach to formulation adopted (Cavanagh & Grant, 2006; Corrie & Lane, 2006). Evidence in this approach takes two primary forms. The first (widely used in clinical work but rarely in coaching) is based on research that shows that certain interventions work best for defined concerns. For example, the client with social anxiety about presenting to a large group within the organization might be offered a coaching approach that uses a cognitive-behavioural perspective for which there is an evidence base. The second and more common approach in coaching is based on the assumption that a co-constructed enquiry can identify, define and test hypotheses to arrive at an explanation of factors that are influencing the area of concern. The coach using this approach uses data from multiple sources to co-construct the formulation with the client. Coach and client must also between them avoid the temptation to determine in advance what explanatory frame will fit and the goals for coaching that will be most appropriate. There is an emphasis in this approach on working together to conduct an evidence-based enquiry. The enquiry might include individual, interpersonal and systemic data. A key feature of a scientist practitioner focus is the idea that the formulation is always provisional; it is adapted as the work proceeds and as new data become available. The common feature within this process is conducting experiments to test specific hypotheses on potential factors of influence.

A scientist–practitioner approach will honour the available science and diverse forms of knowledge generation activity that inform the underpinnings of a discipline. However, it approaches this engagement differently from the diagnostic approach. Corrie and Lane (2010) suggest that this approach provides the practitioner with an internal "professional compass" that enables a sophisticated grasp of the knowledge of a discipline and how to use this knowledge in the service of a client's particular needs. Thus, rather than using the available science to categorize an individual as a member of a normative group, the individual is understood as "a puzzle to be unlocked through the application of scientific methods" (Corrie & Lane, 2010, p. 85). Attention focuses on how relevant models, methods and modes of knowledge might be drawn upon and used to support a process where both parties – coach and client – seek to make sense of a particular issue of concern and formulate decisions about how to proceed. However, the assumption rarely tested in this approach is the idea that behaviour can be understood in terms of cause-and-effect relationships between events and subsequent behaviours.

Theoretically driven narrative – Many handbooks of coaching include examples of theoretically driven approaches to formulation (e.g. Bachkirova et al., 2017;

Cox et al., 2018; Palmer & Whybrow, 2018; Passmore et al., 2013). The questions asked and the understanding reached is framed by the perspectives embedded in the theory. The enquiry might be individual, interpersonal or systemic depending on the theory used but will be organized around and limited by the parameters of that theory. With rare exceptions, none of the theories used in coaching actually originated in coaching questions or concerns but have been imported from other contexts (Gray et al., 2016). Practitioners approaching formulation from whichever theory they prefer need to identify how those perspectives inform the task. A key challenge is the extent to which the theory determines the locus for change. The form the enquiry takes will be guided by the theory and the importance given to the ideas raised by the client will be judged in terms of that theory.

Formulation from the theoretical perspective shapes both the interpretation of the client's narrative as well as the types of data used to confirm or disconfirm emerging hypotheses. Thus, available to us are, among others, cognitive, behavioural, psychodynamic, narrative and systemic theories, and the models derived from them. Each of these theories provides a conceptual landscape or organizing lens through which the coach hears their client's story, identifies relevant questions and organizes data gathering. Thus, a cognitive approach to formulation will focus on cognitive phenomena such as automatic thoughts, assumptions and beliefs as well as a client's information-processing tendencies (Corrie & Lane, 2021). In contrast, a psychodynamic approach is likely to privilege underlying unconscious patterns and their role in shaping current behaviours (Diamond, 2013). Narrative approaches privilege the types of stories the client occupies and how they portray the different characters and experiences within it (Drake, 2010, 2018).

According to Gray et al. (2016), building a theoretically informed model is the dominant way coaches are trained. Three frameworks seem to be favoured – coaching based on a single theory (e.g. the solution-focused coach or cognitive coach), coaching based on an integrated theory (where related theories are combined) or the coach building their own model of coaching (that is based on their own philosophy). The issue that Gray et al. (2016) raise in considering these frameworks is how the theories underpinning these models may cause practitioners to overlook or notice specific aspects of a client's story in favour of others. Particular models may lead a coach to think about a client in a defined way with any questions asked driven by the perspectives of the model. However, few such coaching models have been subjected to research to substantiate either their underpinning assumptions about the world or their effectiveness beyond a general coaching effect.

Strategic formulation – There are a number of approaches that have adopted a forward-looking view which challenges traditional therapeutically derived models oriented towards problem analysis. Thus, environmental design, systemic and some strengths-based approaches focus on change for the future and seek to design ways to build on the resources that people have available to them to bring about desired outcomes. The emphasis is on how to promote environments in which people can flourish. Some such models build upon our understanding of how we can grow from adversity in order to create 'roads to resilience' (APA, 2024; Joseph, 2012; Tehrani, 2008).

Strategic formulation can be considered at three levels – individual, interpersonal and systemic as discussed in Chapter 3. In formulating understanding, it is important for the coach to think carefully about what is being formulated, and then what level is appropriate. The emphasis on solutions rather than problems is considered a strength of the approach. However, if the focus is too narrowly on the future, it can omit much of the client's account and the potential value generated by the knowledge held by both client and coach.

Formulation and its role as a means of social control – The psychology, sociology and anthropology upon which much coaching literature depends has been critiqued for its role as a means of social control in educational, clinical, forensic and occupational settings. Thus, an offer of coaching might seem innocuous but actually reflect more subtle belief systems and prejudices that penetrate the professions within which we operate. The broader debate in psychology ranges from the marginalization of minorities to the control of those seen as dangerous to the prevailing worldview (this debate is considered further in Chapter 16). Yet, coaches will be asked to help clients ensure that any relevant organizational perspective is respected and that clients are helped to perform in accordance with the dominant narratives of the organization even if those narratives marginalize latent stories (DeFehr, 2017; Kahn, 2014). Thus, it is important to attend to how coaching could represent a form of social control. The offer of coaching might be part of a process by which people are socialized into the norms and expectations of the sponsoring organization.

Behavioural norms within an organization define how people are expected to behave. This includes how corporate culture, competency models and reward systems constitute ways of being within the setting. How the organization requires certain outcomes and who owns the information in coaching forms part of social control (Kahn, 2014; Kwiatkowski & Winter, 2006). However, almost all approaches to coaching were developed by white, largely male Western practitioners (see Chapter 16 for an exploration). The claim that it is possible to simply apply these approaches without reference to cultural and contextual difference cannot be sustained. There is an assumed universality to the perspectives adopted that inevitably marginalizes other voices, which itself can be considered a means of social control. This issue is worthy of further consideration in the coaching literature.

When the approach to formulation adopted is embedded in Western thinking, there is a need to be mindful of the view of the world that it inherits. Even attempts to use Eastern thinking can result in a colonized version, which translates complex understandings into a simplified process. Approaches that try to directly embed Eastern or other thinking in coaching are rare (van Nieuwerburgh & Allaho, 2017; Rowe, 2021). As a number of authors point out, the world does not look the same in different cultures (Lane et al., 2023; Ratele, 2019). Even the concept of research is seen as oppressive by many communities who have been experimented upon, had their philosophies and cosmologies distorted and whose knowledge has been stolen and exploited (Absolon, 2022; DeFehr, 2017).

Critical Issues Arising From the Stance Taken

The relative emphasis given to each of the components considered above will vary as a function of the type of formulation that is used. To return to five of the principal categories of formulation above, a diagnostic approach will make sense of individual needs through reference to normative categories and patterns. A strategic approach to formulation will focus the enquiry on forward-looking approaches that seek to capitalize on clients' strengths and designing solutions. Additionally, many of the theories in psychology, philosophy, adult learning and developmental theory upon which coaches rely to inform their practice adopt what is essentially an individualistic approach to conceptualization and change. However, it is important that allegiance to a preferred way of working is not uncritically adopted. Critics of applied psychology have highlighted how frameworks of psychological understanding collectively assumed to be empowering have in fact contributed to social control (Joseph, 2012, RCPsych, 2008). Where formulation comes to be used as a vehicle of social control, the knowledge base of coaching might be inadvertently used to endorse, enable or challenge current political perspectives.

Formulations have the potential to be used in ways that are not intended. Tobias (1996), for example, highlighted how coaches can be unwittingly drawn into scapegoating clients, especially where organizational stakeholders are resistant to considering how the organizational context might be a contributing factor to the behaviour of the client judged to be unacceptable. Rogers (2014) has referred to the way clients are scapegoated in coaching referrals. In their work examining formulation as a means of navigating complexity in coaching assignments, Kovács and Corrie (2021) also warn of the ways in which power dynamics can draw the coach into a web of complex power dynamics. Hawkins and Smith (2006) discuss the use of power dynamics "as a means of coercing an individual to submit to the will of another – a dynamic which is difficult to resist because it is couched in terms of performance or benefit to the organization" (p. 6). What these warnings alert us to is that our formulations are derived in contexts not entirely of our own choosing and control. Even where we hold the value of formulation as a co-constructed explanatory account, one in which the client is given ownership of the account that unfolds, complex and often subtle processes will arise that need navigating.

A further complicating factor is that we are also governed by perspectives of which we are often only partially aware. Mahrer (2000) argued that psychology itself is change immune, and more recently Eronen and Bringmann (2021) have argued that even if a psychological theory is found to be deficient, psychologists will continue to use it.

When considering which approach to adopt, it is, therefore, necessary to recognize that decisions are not made in a vacuum. The theories and models upon which coaches rely are neither culture- nor value-free, and despite efforts to develop, test and refine ways of working that are grounded in robust methods of investigation and the available evidence base, coaches always work within a set of paradigms and cultural perspectives that determine what they see. Indeed, the notion of evidence-based practice is a cultural phenomenon in its own right and shapes approaches to practice in ways of which we are only partially aware, and which would be difficult to challenge.

Formulation as Storytelling

All the above approaches are forms of storytelling and in the case of formulation, a story told to enable change. Corrie and Lane (2010) propose that clients typically present themselves and their concerns through stories. Often this will be on some part of their lives that they or others believe is not working optimally or where the client has potential they wish to enhance. The practitioner's initial responsibility, they suggest, is to recognize that the client has stories to tell and to be appreciative of those stories. The second duty (implicitly understood by both parties) is that the professional has something to add that can contribute to positive change. While there is a burgeoning literature which looks at the way clients narrate their story, there is far less attention paid to the idea that the professional's account is also a story told to enable change. This they see as placing us at a disadvantage with the potential to strip the storyteller of their story by interpreting it within an existing professional narrative that may not encompass the richness of the client's account or recognize the context that makes it meaningful.

Corrie and Lane (2010) suggest that we can usefully distinguish between tales and stories. A tale is a narrative built around a single perspective that carries with it a given set of values and beliefs – a moral tale. Each of the above approaches to formulation could be considered as tales told from specific perspectives. They prejudge what are and are not considered relevant data. Each will have a place as an approach to formulation in coaching but will also carry inherent limitations based on the values and beliefs they privilege. Mishler (1986) suggested that the felt need of the client to tell their story is often so strong that they will persevere in doing so even when our theoretically driven questions hinder their ability to do so. As Riessman (2012) proposed, when analysing personal narratives participants can resist efforts to fragment their lived experience and the attempt to control meaning through creating codable categories for their own sense of being. The more distant the client's experience from the experience of the coach, the more this tendency will inhibit the coach's understanding.

In contrast, a story, Corrie and Lane (2010) contend, includes a number of players with different tales that need to be woven together around a shared concern to find a common theme, protagonist and plot. To understand that plot requires an attempt to grasp the various tales within the overall story. Each party starts with an existing tale. This includes the coach who comes with a sense of who they are, what they offer as a professional and the purpose, perspectives and process that tend to define their brand of coaching. Even a simple statement like "I am an executive coach" encompasses a number of assumptions that can limit or constrain the offer they make.

Building Relational Narratives Through Dialogue

When the coach attends an initial meeting with a client, several narratives are in play. The client has their own sense of self and a sense of their role in the organization. The sponsor within the organization has a sense of why they made the referral, a sense of their role and a sense of what they believe coaching has to offer. A coach will have a sense of who they are, their role as coach and their role in helping clients look at their current and life-long learning. Each of these influences how the encounter is viewed. The coaching may take the form of a transactional engagement in which capabilities may be enhanced. The purpose is to develop existing skills and attitudes, but fundamentally the view taken by the client is unchanged. They still see the world in the same way. Alternatively, the coach and client develop a relational engagement in which both can change through the encounter (Lane et al., 2023), generating a new sense of self as client or practitioner. (The former is termed horizontal and the latter vertical change by Cavanagh et al., 2016.) Where vertical change occurs it is also the process by which the formation of identity happens in the work context. Thus, in organizations identity is shaped by the engagement with the client in the context of their work. This is similar to the idea that, as Lo (2005) argued, identity arises in sites of action.

For this to happen there has to be an openness to an emergent process. If the coach starts with one of the specific tales introduced above, for example, a theoretically driven position, and seeks to define the client in terms of that understanding, they will privilege certain themes over others. They bring a pre-existing positionality. The stance they take to the world precedes the encounter but also shapes it. This also raises the issue of the role of the knowledge the coach and the client bring and the perspectives embedded in the context in which they operate. How does the coach reconcile these different narratives? This is a core philosophical issue for coaching – what is the knowledge the coach brings that adds value (Hindle Fisher et al., 2023)? This issue is explored below through the concept of dialogic complexity.

Dialogic Complexity Rather Than Cause and Effect

Coaching relationships need to be understood as a process between the coach and client (level 1), the others in the encounter, such as peers, managers, sponsor, etc. (level 2) and the system, such as team, organization or a couple or family (level 3). Thus, there are at least three levels contributing to identity and awareness in the coaching encounter that will shape the process of formulation. The latter is itself embedded in a range of structured interactions and dominant and latent stories about the purpose and values of the system and the place of coaching within it. There are multiple relational narratives in play and in movement. This creates an emerging dialogue and introduces complexity into understanding the relationships between self, other and system. There is no simple linear cause and effect.

Kahn (2014) discusses this in terms of an axis between self and organization expressed through the concept of role. Similarly, there is an axis between coach, client and organization that is also expressed in the role of coach as defined both in an organizational job definition (this is what a coach does) and emergent in specific encounters or sites of action. Thus, the coach becomes a dialogic partner with the client and system (Stelter, 2019).

While a coach might be working with an individual, it should be remembered that they exist as part of a system of relationships. To ignore the possible influence of others could be detrimental to the outcome. All three levels are enacted and voiced in such systems of relationships. There is a constant dynamic interaction between the levels. Awareness of this complexity in the patterns of relationships emerge as an agreed narrative is constructed in the encounters.

The storytelling nature of this process in organizations has been explored in the work of Boje (1991, 2018) and Gabriel (2000). It is defined as a "collective storytelling system in which the performance of stories is a key part of members' sense-making and a means to allow them to supplement individual memories with institutional memory" (Boje, 1991, p. 106). The knowledge the coach brings to this collective storytelling is part of the sense-making process. Storytelling as part of sense-making is seen as a universal process (Bietti et al., 2018). Stories may support or subvert organizational intent (Spear & Roper, 2016) or if used collaboratively can build relationships (Silva & Silva, 2022).

The Influence of the Knowledge the Coach Brings

There is a core philosophical debate in coaching on the place of the coach's knowledge in the process of working (Hindle Fisher et al., 2023). Is the coach just a cypher to assist the client to think through the multiple issues in play to enhance their sense-making? Is it their place to bring their own knowledge and prior experiences in similar contexts as an offer of possibilities for action the client might consider? If their knowledge has no such place, why the emphasis on previous industry experience when appointing an organizational coach? In terms of formulation, what is the place of the coach's knowledge of diagnostics, theory, strategy, control, or experiments in enabling sense-making? As the coach enters an engagement, they are part of the storytelling and need to understand the way their stories about the past, present and future influence any collective acts. Coaching also invites clients to contemplate stories yet to be spoken or realized, and to enter into emergent perspectives that the coach tries to articulate.

Case Vignette

The following case vignette is outlined looking at a coaching within a school and considers the emergence of the agreed purpose for the case.

Box 2.1   Moving beyond initial issue to whole-person response

Irie was 13 when she was first referred for coaching by her school to address management of her anger. She had twice been suspended and was now at risk of permanent exclusion. She felt that she was picked on by certain teachers who she stated disliked her as a loud, energetic, Black girl who did not accept unfairness.

Irie wanted to find other ways to handle her reactions as she saw that she was the one getting into trouble. An agreement was reached between Irie and the school that she would benefit from anger management coaching. The coach also discussed with her the possibility of raising, with the departmental head, her concerns about certain teachers. She responded well to the coaching and for a while matters improved and there were no further referrals. Discussion with the departmental head was inconclusive as he thought she was confusing being strict with unfairness.

Irie was referred again a year later following an outburst in a history class where she challenged the teacher's interpretation of the end of slavery. She had been reading for herself some Black history and was angered that the role of the Black community in resisting slavery was not sufficiently recognized. In discussing this she began to explore a pattern of her strong belief in the importance of justice not just for Black children but for other marginalized groups. This presented an ethical issue for the coach. While it was possible to undertake a programme to teach Irie how to manage her behaviour and adopt a more pro-social approach to dealing with concerns, her sense of injustice was justified and the coach did not want to marginalize her feelings on the matters that engaged her.

The formulation that they developed together raised two shared concerns. Irie recognized that she was at real risk of permanent exclusion and needed to develop a range of different responses to dealing with her feelings. They agreed to establish a series of experiments with behaviours that she could try out to make her points without losing her temper. The second concern was the immediate question of what was being taught in history but more generally how to positively express her stance to the world. It was agreed that she could not do this alone. A meeting with the departmental head was organized initially, and then with two other teachers, where she could explain her concerns. With her coach she roleplayed the meeting in advance to prepare herself for any criticisms and how she would react.

To Irie's surprise, the meeting went very well and it was agreed that she could prepare a presentation for discussion in class on the role of Black resistance to slavery. The history teacher also agreed to include a broader discussion in future lessons. She developed a range of skills for managing conflict. At her own initiative, Irie also started to write rap music lyrics to express her worldviews, including a rap about the coaching.

Some Reflections on the Development of the Purpose of the Coaching

In the case vignette above, the original referral was based on the school's view of the need. Here was an angry girl who needed anger management coaching to deal with her issues. Yet, the student's perspective indicated a more complicated picture in which she felt she had legitimate concerns about how she was treated while agreeing that she needed to do some work to avoid getting into more trouble. The initial coaching went well but the issue with the teachers remained unresolved, leading to a re-referral a year later. This time there was a very specific issue she wanted to raise with the school. Following a dialogic process, the result was a shared concern among student, school and coach. A purpose for the work was agreed, which led to a satisfactory outcome for all.

Some Implications for How to Approach Formulation

At this point, it is useful to reflect on the ways in which a coach might practise and consider the relevance of the ideas raised. This requires a recognition that any approach to formulation is far from neutral, that the explanations coaches develop might favour some individuals while not enabling, or even marginalizing, others. As will be explored in subsequent chapters, the best that can be achieved is to ensure that the coach's own approaches and positionality are made transparent. This includes, as different chapters outline, consideration of particular perspectives (individual, interpersonal, systemic; situation, pattern, person/case and the theory/ theories and principles which are guiding thinking) and ways to articulate them that enable transparency with the client. The client may not, as the case of Irie shows, be an equal partner in the process depending on power relations and how these are constructed in the context in which coaching is taking place. The process of formulation can help make this more visible to the coach and the client.

Conclusion

As described in Chapter 1, it is our belief that in the majority of cases a formulation will need to be collaboratively created and that they are often most helpful when taking the form of a co-constructed explanatory account that is developed at the start of coaching and refined over time. However, in recognizing that each party contributes specific forms of knowledge and expertise to the process, there may be occasions when approaches that have been developed on wider populations also have value. Where research exists on working with similar issues, that knowledge can be used to inform the coaching. Within applied psychology, this is most evident in relation to the diagnostic and theoretically derived perspectives where formulations for specific client concerns have been developed, which are then available to practitioners to adapt to the needs of the individual client. The clearest example here would be of disorder-specific formulations. There are parallels to coaching, such as psychometrics and some coaching models that are very prescriptive. In this sense, there is a choice as to whether the formulation is co-constructed in the coaching encounter or informed by pre-existing knowledge. As long as coach and client are aware of the implications of such positions, appropriate choices can be made, encounter by encounter.

Questions to Consider

Having read this chapter, consider what emerges in relation to your own practice. For the purposes of formulation, you may find it helpful to consider the following questions:

- By framing the conversation through your chosen lens, which areas of a client's experience will you prioritize, and which will remain unexplored?
- What types of coaching journey does your approach facilitate and limit, and who, therefore, is best suited to your coaching offer?
- Our approaches to knowledge, including the models that we prefer, the theories of the world that speak to us as individuals and our approaches to data-gathering and formulation, are not neutral – what implications does this have for your coaching?
- Are your espoused preferences consistent with how you actually work in practice? Are there any discrepancies, and if so, what are the factors that drive these (e.g. coaching context, marketability, lack of training opportunity, needs arising from post-pandemic working patterns)?

Chapter 3

The 4P Framework as a Guide to Formulation in Coaching

From the growing literature in the field of coaching, it is evident that today's coaching practitioners can draw from a diverse range of theories, models, tools and techniques. Given this diversity, there are many ways in which coaches can approach their work with their clients. Similarly, as indicated in the preceding chapters, there is no single model of or correct way to develop a formulation, with each coach approaching the client material differently. While the fundamentals of a coach's training and experience will inevitably be a key influence, other factors will also be evident in influencing the approach to formulation, including the context in which the coaching is taking place and the client themselves. Another major influence, which perhaps is less obvious but of significant importance, is how who we are and how we construct our view of the world impact our approach to our work – a concept that is termed positionality.

Additionally, in developing a formulation with a client, it is likely that there will be significant amounts of information to manage and many decisions to be made. Therefore, it can be useful to have a framework that guides thinking and informs the decision-making that results in how one formulation is prioritised over another. This chapter introduces a comprehensive and flexible framework that is applicable to many coaching approaches and contexts – the 4P Framework. In the following sections we explore each of the four elements in turn: Positionality, Purpose, Perspective, Process. Working through this approach will enable coaches to develop a framework for formulation that is grounded in their positionality, the purpose that their coaching serves, the perspectives they favour and the processes that best fit the purpose and perspectives of their work. While the 4P Framework provides a foundation, it also enables coaches to tailor each formulation to the needs of every individual client.

The Positionality, Purpose, Perspective, Process Framework

There are many decisions that a coach needs to make in preparation to start a formulation. These include:

- What needs to be acknowledged in the coach's worldview that may impact how the client and formulation are approached?

DOI: 10.4324/9781003174585-5

- Is a formulation necessary?
- What themes, events or areas of the client's life or work are going to be the basis of the formulation?
- What outcomes are desired, both with the formulation and for the coaching?
- How do these outcomes fit with the client's purpose for seeking out coaching services?
- What data will be needed and what will inform decisions about what is important to include?
- Whose input and perspectives will be considered in putting together the formulation?
- How will the work be structured to achieve the outcomes?
- Is the coaching process underpinned by the perspectives from which the coach has chosen to base their work?
- How will the coaching process be evaluated against the desired outcomes?

The 4P Framework aids working through some of these decision points and is organized around four elements that are relevant across coaching practices in different contexts.

- Positionality – How does who I am shape what I know about the world and how I approach my work?
- Purpose – Where are we going and why?
- Perspective – What will inform our journey?
- Process – How will we get there?

The 4P Framework has evolved from the original PPP model, which was developed by Lane (2002) and later elaborated (Lane & Corrie, 2006; Corrie & Lane, 2010) and has proven useful in a number of different contexts in the psychological field. The 4P Framework had its origin in an earlier model to create a coherent way to develop formulations in complex settings (Lane, 1975, 1978, 1990) and as Bruch and Bond (1998) and Bruch (2015) identified was influential in the development of the so-called Middlesex and later University College London approach to formulation.

For ease of reading, the 4P Framework is presented in a linear fashion, exploring each element in turn. Developing a formulation following a linear path is one way in which the 4P Framework can be used. However, it can also be considered as a more emergent framework which recognizes that there are complicated and reciprocal relationships between the different elements, with each influencing others in an iterative, emergent process. The evolution of the model to include positionality was driven by the recognition of this complicated relationship between the elements, particularly that between purpose and perspective. The original PPP model (Lane, 2002; Corrie & Lane, 2010) reflected the view that before undertaking any coaching journey it is critical to identify and agree the purpose of the work. As the client and coach explore this, they develop a clear understanding of whether the coach's service offering is a good match for the agreed purpose. The discussion of purpose is also an opportunity to explore the context for the coaching and how this context makes the coaching meaningful to all the stakeholders involved and worthwhile as an engagement.

An alternative view foregrounds perspective or philosophy as the essential underpinning of a coach's approach. This approach argues that any coaching purpose is defined within the constraints of the coach's values and assumptions about life, knowledge and the social world (Bachkirova et al., 2020). Therefore, the service and approach to practice offered by a coach (including how they define the purpose of their work) are wholly dependent on their perspectives. This has led some coach educators to implement the PPP model as philosophy, purpose and process (Bachkirova et al., 2020; Jackson & Bachkirova, 2019). Recognizing the merit of this latter argument, the inclusion of positionality in the 4P Framework proposes that purpose, perspective and process are profoundly influenced by how the coach sees the world. Positionality also encompasses the client's sense of being in the world (Lane, 1990). By drawing on the concept of positionality, the 4P Framework encompasses for the client and the coach not only perspectives on the nature of the self, beliefs about change and the nature of evidence-based practice and ethics, but also how identity and sense of self influence coaching practice. This also retains the original concept that purpose is required before the specific perspectives from which the formulation will be developed can be determined.

Figure 3.1 provides an illustration of the 4P Framework, the relationships between the four elements and how formulation sits at the intersection of those elements.

In the following sections each of the elements of the 4P Framework is explored in turn.

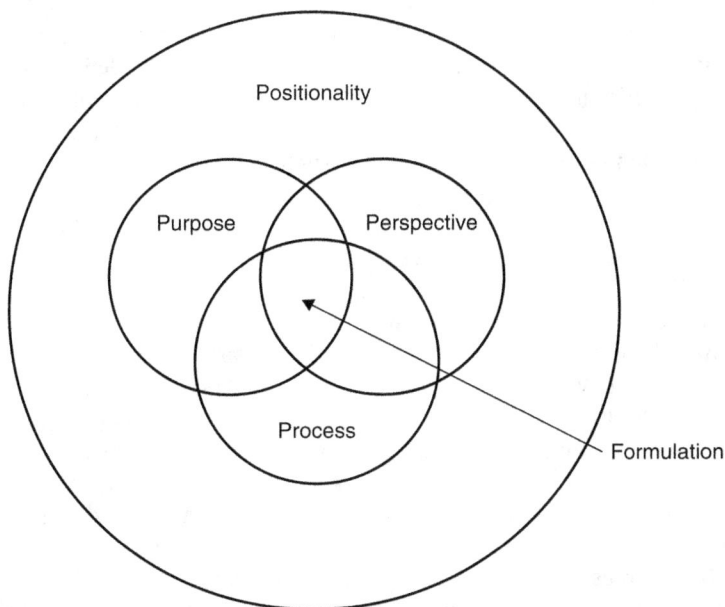

Figure 3.1 The 4P Framework of Formulation

Positionality

Coaches bring to their encounters with clients a reflexive narrative of how they see the world, how they understand themselves in different contexts and how they perceive the role of the coach. This narrative has an impact on all facets of the work, from influencing coaching interests to the approaches that are pursued and the theoretical perspectives that are considered valid. In the shared space of coaching relationships, how the coach and client see the world influences and shapes the coaching interactions and how the task of formulation is approached. Therefore, one of the first tasks in formulation is understanding how the coach's personal narratives could influence the coaching. For example, how does their worldview make them subject to biases that are then brought to the client material and what does this mean for the data that are collected and interpreted? As the encounter continues, the client's reflective narrative also becomes part of the conversation, with coach and client developing together a relational narrative that reflects the shared understandings that emerge (Lane et al., 2018).

In the world of social research, the term used for identifying and reflecting on these influences is positionality, and it is this concept that forms the first element of the 4P Framework. There are many layers of complexity in an individual's positionality, some of which are considered more fluid and more amenable to introspection than others. In Chapter 4 the concept of positionality is described in detail through consideration of three interacting elements: social identity, power relations and context. These elements are introduced below.

A starting point for understanding positionality is each person's multiple intersecting factors of social identity. Social identity has been defined as an individual's recognition that they belong to certain social groups together with an emotional and value significance of being part of this group (Abrams & Hogg, 1990). This includes elements of identify such as gender, ethnicity, nationality, race, age and many others (see Chapter 4 for a fuller account). People can be members of many different groups but only some of these groups will be meaningful in how they define themselves. This self-definition is shared with others who identify as part of that group, such as a female, Australian, or member of the legal profession. However, even if individuals share some characteristics with others in their group, coaches should be wary of assuming that shared elements of identify automatically lead to shared perspectives and experiences. People have multiple elements of identity that are also interwoven with the other facets of positionality such as individual histories, personal attributes and beliefs.

The multiplicity of social identities is connected to the second element of positionality, power relations. Membership of a social group may confer greater access to resources, power, status, and privilege, with those with the most power attempting to maintain the status quo through promulgating their system of values and ideology. This can lead to the marginalization of those who have less access to power and resources (Abrams & Hogg, 1990). The social identities of coach and client are imbued with power relations, making it important that coaches consider how this positions them in relation to their client and what that might mean for the coaching relationship, particularly if the power relations are asymmetrical.

Both social identity and power relations are intertwined with the context in which the coaching takes place. The context also contains influences that have an impact on all aspects of the coaching. The way that individuals make sense of their experiences is influenced by the broader social norms and as all cultures contain a set of encoded social norms, coaches and clients are both subject to influences at multiple levels. For example, major influences on coaching include the commonly accepted views of the profession, attitudes to mental wellbeing, beliefs about personal growth and development as well as the accepted models and approaches to coaching. At a local level, an executive coach and client will be influenced by the beliefs about the use and expected outcomes of coaching within the organization in which they are working.

Coaches can begin to understand positionality through reflection on the three aspects outlined above. While some aspects of positionality cannot be changed, others may alter over time. The aim is to develop an appreciation of the factors that influence how coaching is approached and specifically the impact on the formulations that are subsequently developed.

How Does Positionality Impact Formulation?

How a coach is positioned in relation their practice and each individual client has the potential to influence all aspects of formulation, and hence all other elements of the 4P Framework, including:

- How the purpose of the work is defined
- The data collected for the formulation
- The data considered to be valid
- The processes that are used for data collection
- The stakeholders that are considered important to the work
- The theories on which the formulation is based
- The tools and techniques that are selected as part of the coaching process
- How the success of the coaching is measured and evaluated
- The ethical framework that guides the endeavour

Given the influence of positionality, it is impossible for any approach to formulation to be value-free. Coaches bring not only a level of competence and knowledge, but also all aspects of their positionality which have the potential to directly or indirectly influence the formulation. Therefore, the first step is recognizing that this is the case, and through a self-reflective process to identify, critique and articulate positionality and how this will impact the approach to formulation as well as how a specific formulation is developed. Reflective processes and reflexivity have been conceptualized as existing on a continuum (Shaw, 2010). Reflexivity is considered the active acknowledgement of positionality and its impact before, during and after action, whereas reflection is often completed retrospectively to identify insights gained from a particular encounter or action (Jamieson et al., 2023). Both form an essential part of the formulation process.

Purpose

In understanding any coaching endeavour, it is important to be clear about the fundamental purpose of the work. How the purpose is framed influences not only the direction of the enquiry that follows, but also which perspectives are most useful and the process that will be followed. The purpose of any specific coaching engagement is framed by the context of both the coach's positionality and how they define the purpose of the coaching service they provide. Case by case it is a matter of refining that purpose for each individual client. There are some critical questions that will be addressed at this stage:

- What is the purpose of work with the client (both the coach's and the client's)?
- What are the main questions that will be explored together?
- Who else is/needs to be involved and what are their expectations?
- What is the wider context that will influence the work with this client?

Central to these questions is an understanding of what makes the coaching endeavour worthwhile and why it is meaningful for the coach, the client, team, organization, community and (potentially) society. The topic of purpose is explored in more depth in Chapter 5. However, in the next section we briefly explore each of these questions in turn.

What Is the Purpose of the Work With the Client?

Defining the purpose of the work essentially means agreeing what is important for the coach and client to address in order to make the work worthwhile. Depending on the specific constellation of the factors in each coaching engagement, this may be either a relatively swift and straightforward process or a more protracted procedure involving multiple parties. The way in which the coach has articulated the underpinning purpose for the coaching services they provide will influence how they define the purpose of working with any specific client. For example, a coach who positions the purpose of their service as facilitating the change and development of their clients will define a specific coaching purpose around factors that are amenable to change and largely under the client's control.

Part of the responsibility of coaching practice is to define the type of client that best fits the coaching that is being offered. This means placing some boundaries around the purpose and making referrals for a client to seek support elsewhere if necessary. There will be some clients for whom a specific coach's services will not be appropriate and in agreeing the coaching purpose there is an opportunity to evaluate if they are the best person to facilitate the coaching journey for a particular client at a specific point in time.

What Are the Main Questions That Will Be Explored Together?

The core question/s that the client brings to coaching provides the basis for the direction and form that the coaching will take. The client's dilemma may arise from their desire for a different state, and they may be able to clearly articulate where they see the coaching heading. Alternatively, the client may be less certain of the direction they see for their coaching and instead there may be agreement that the coaching journey will be an exploratory one. One of the key questions to address at this stage is why undertaking the work is important for this client at this time. There may be many reasons for undertaking the coaching, including developing a new understanding of something that has, until now, seemed incomprehensible, seeking improvements to the current circumstances or pursuing a new vision.

Who Else Is/Needs to Be Involved and What Are Their Expectations?

For many engagements, the purpose of the coaching will be decided by the coach and client alone. In other instances, there will be several stakeholders who need to be involved. The context in which the coaching is taking place could dictate that there are different and diverse groups of stakeholders that need to be engaged. For example, in an organizational context, stakeholders might include a manager, human resources sponsors, the board, customers, employees or even the wider community. In a personal coaching example, relatives of the client may be key stakeholders. The aim of engaging with the stakeholders is to establish how each party sees the objectives of any coaching engagement and consider the extent to which these objectives are congruent with what the client is aiming to achieve. In these discussions the coach is exploring why this purpose is meaningful to each of the stakeholders.

What Is the Wider Context That Will Influence the Work With This Client?

The coaching is not taking place in a vacuum, and how the purpose is defined will also be influenced by the wider context. There is a clear link to the coach, client and other stakeholders' positionality contained in this question as many of the factors that influence positionality will flow into how the purpose is defined, e.g. how an organization frames coaching or broader societal beliefs regarding what are acceptable applications of coaching.

Defining Purpose Defines the Direction of the Coaching

The importance of taking the time to gain clarity on the purpose of the coaching rests on the impact that the purpose has on the direction of the coaching that follows. A change in the framing of the purpose of the work alters how the coaching proceeds and a poorly defined purpose will almost certainly be detrimental to the coaching experience and outcomes. The following example illustrates how the different framing of a coaching purpose can influence both the perspective taken and process that follows.

Box 3.1   Defining the purpose of the coaching

Soraya is an experienced health and wellness coach, who was inspired to focus on weight management after her experience of working in a diabetes clinic. She has a new client, Andrea, who stated in their first conversation that her doctor had told her to lose weight as she is at risk of developing diabetes. As with many of Soraya's clients, Andrea attributes her lack of sustained weight loss to her own lack of motivation and laziness and has therefore approached Soraya to help her stay on track. If Soraya defined the coaching purpose purely in these terms, she would likely frame the work through the lens of an individual perspective and design a coaching process aimed at assisting the client in maintaining motivation.

In the process of defining the coaching purpose Soraya and Andrea explored Andrea's health and wellbeing more broadly. This discussion brought to light aspects of her overall wellbeing that were equally important and would also support her original goal. For example, Andrea had recently moved to a new area for her career, was working long hours and was relatively socially isolated. This led to her eating unhealthy takeaway meals at night, and she stated she was reluctant to exercise on her own. By prioritizing her work, where she felt competent, she had neglected her hobbies, which included gardening and cooking.

Taking this information into account, Soraya and Andrea reframed the coaching purpose as improving Andrea's overall wellbeing and reducing her reliance on work as her primary focus and source of confidence. While they would monitor weight, Soraya positioned the coaching as an intervention that conceptualized her overweight condition as a symptom of other factors. This enabled Soraya to consider a formulation at the level of the whole person and take a more systemic view of the coaching. The coaching process that Soraya designed included exploring more broadly the factors affecting Andrea's wellbeing and measures of success that were not exclusively focused on her weight.

Perspectives

With a purpose for the work defined, the next set of decisions concerns those perspectives from which the coach will draw to develop the formulation. As discussed above in relation to positionality, the perspectives held inform many of the decisions made as the coaching proceeds, with or without the coach's awareness. There is a strong relationship between positionality and perspective. In considering positionality the aim is to develop an awareness of the broader influences of social identity, background, experiences, and collective beliefs about how the work should be approached. In considering perspectives the evaluation is more specifically targeting how the beliefs held in relation to the nature of the self and the process of change orient a coach towards the client's story and how the perspectives influence decision-making. This applies to a coach's practice more broadly as well as to the perspective that might be selected with a specific client. The same set of considerations apply to the client, what are they bringing and how will they view the coaching engagement as a result of their experiences. Clients vary in both how they want to tell their story and the role they would prefer the coach to take. Understanding these elements is essential to build towards a shared concern (the relational narrative) that informs the way the work proceeds.

There are myriad theories and frameworks in use in coaching. Some of them have roots in the psychological models that are drawn from three main forces of psychology: behaviourism (latterly cognitive-behaviourism); psychoanalysis; and humanism (Friedman, 1977; Fleuridas & Krafcik, 2019). Coaching also draws on literature from other fields such as adult learning, sports psychology, complexity theory, leadership and management theory. To assist in navigating the complexity of these many different perspectives, it is useful to have an organizing framework to identify how these perspectives view the nature of the self and how change takes place.

The framework proposed in this book organizes approaches based on whether the beliefs are centred on an individual, interpersonal or systemic field of vision. Each of these perspectives enables and constrains the types of explanations that are developed and the methods and interventions that might be considered in designing a coaching process. These three perspectives are described and discussed in detail in the subsequent chapters (see Chapters 6, 7 and 8). This chapter introduces each perspective and the types of approaches that are consistent with that viewpoint.

The Individual Perspective

Coaches working from the individual perspective are concerned with what the person brings to the coaching as a starting point and sees the source of understanding and change as located within the client themselves. The formulation is likely to focus on factors that are directly under the client's control and tend to assume linear cause-and-effect relationships, which leads to coaching that follows a path from goals to actions to results.

Coaching approaches and models that are based in this perspective include:

- Cognitive-behavioural models
- Goal-focused approaches
- Skills coaching, e.g. increasing assertiveness or improving delegation skills
- Performance coaching, i.e. improving individual performance in an agreed domain
- Developmental coaching, e.g. coaching drawing on theories of adult or ego development such as Kegan (1994), Cook-Greuter (1999), Garvey Berger (2012, 2019)

Formulations developed from the individual perspective will be focused on aspects of the client's internal world that can be identified, examined and modified to bring about a positive result. Thus, the formulation will likely include factors such as:

- Thoughts, assumptions and beliefs
- Emotions
- Rules for living and personal values
- Sensations and bodily states
- Stories the client holds about themselves and others
- How a client understands and relates to the influence of factors from their own personal history in the here and now
- External factors that may be barriers or enablers of success

The Interpersonal Perspective

While it is the case that all coaches consider the relationship with the client as part of the process, in the interpersonal perspective this is about the bond formed. This bond is part of building a working alliance to enable the process of coaching. The process of change will still be in relation to the client's worldview and change happens through adjustments in their internal world (thoughts and feelings) leading to new ways to act (behaviours). Those who work within the interpersonal perspective will consider how the client is embedded in a wide variety of one-to-one relationships, including the one between coach and client, and how the client (and coach) is shaped by these encounters. The interpersonal viewpoint holds a foundational assumption that any change or transformation is deeply bound to the relational. Behaviours seen in coaching are considered as potential replications of relationships played out elsewhere. Therefore, the interpersonal perspective emphasizes the importance of what happens in the coaching relationship, seeing this as the key vehicle for any change.

Coaching approaches that prioritize the relational world include:

- Gestalt coaching, which emphasizes what happens between coach and client in their encounter

- Systems psychodynamic perspectives, particularly attachment theory, which emphasizes the way attachments formed early in life play out in later relationships (e.g. how someone behaves towards figures of authority replicates relationships with parents or care givers)
- Eco-systemic approaches which focus on how the individual makes use of the environment they inhabit and the resources for change that emerge
- Social construction approaches that explore the way our sense of self is co-constructed in relation with others often situation by situation
- Role theory which explores how self is expressed in specific job or relationship roles

The formulation and the coaching that follows would consider how any understanding may emerge from interactions between them. The coach is part of that co-construction and may include in their formulation data and observations related to:

- Interactions between the coach and client, and the client and others – they may consider factors operating such as transference or counter-transference as they apply to work roles in particular contexts
- Antecedents and consequences of a particular behaviour and how these patterns serve a function in certain contexts
- Patterns of attachment, drawing on attachment theory and relationships with significant others
- The co-construction of shared narratives of change
- Understanding the axis between the individual and their organization, and how the coaching can be used as a narrative bridge to improve the relationship between the two

Throughout the formulation process, the coach will continue to reflect on the relationship between coach and client and whether there are elements of the relationship that require attention in order for the coaching to be most effective.

The Systemic Perspective

Coaches who work from a systemic perspective view the source of the client's challenges and opportunities not as located with the individual themselves or their relationships, but as a function of the systems in which they are embedded. For example, an executive coach might understand a leader's performance as a product of the interactions and relationships within the organization, team dynamics, or political, economic, and cultural factors. Issues and opportunities are considered to be indicators of wider systemic factors rather than solely a reflection of an individual's limitations or strengths. This will mean that the coaching approach seeks to engage more widely with the organization in order to gain an understanding of this systemic context.

Coaching approaches grounded in a systemic perspective are growing in popularity and draw on theories such as family systems theory (e.g. O'Neill, 2000; Shams & Lane, 2011, 2018; Von Schlippe, 2022; Arnold et al., 2023); or systems thinking or complexity theory (e.g. Cavanagh, 2006; O'Connor, 2020; Hawkins & Turner, 2020; Lawrence, 2021a). From this stance a formulation could include a broad range of factors, couched within wider social, economic and political factors, such as:

- The context in which the specific issue or opportunity is emerging
- The influences of those around the client and their beliefs about the goals of coaching and how they should be pursued
- Patterns of relationships and interactions between the client and others
- Organizational culture and stories within the organization that shape how people behave
- The social, political and economic status of the client and how this might impact the client
- Broader ethical, social, political and economic factors that are likely to influence the coaching

Working from a systemic perspective may be challenging for others in the system to accept, particularly in highly individualistic cultures. This perspective also has the potential to add significant complexity to the coaching engagement. Yet, it also provides the opportunity for the coach and client to view the coaching dilemma from novel perspectives that can open up pathway to change.

Theory-Driven or Data-Driven Formulation

The perspective taken will also influence how the coach tackles the task of developing a formulation. Typically, coaches will start the formulation process from one of two starting points: a top-down, theory-driven approach or a bottom-up, data- or story-driven approach.

Top-Down, Theory-Driven Approach

In this approach the coach holds the view that the key to achieving coaching outcomes comes from the application of a single theory or model of coaching. Coaches who work from this starting point will develop their formulation through the particular lens of their preferred approach. This will lead them to focus on specific aspects of the client's story, rather than the client as a whole. The formulations they develop will likely follow a particular pattern in which certain aspects of the client's story are explored, some forms of data are prioritized over others and a limited, focal set of events or interventions are understood as critical to bringing about change.

As an example of the top-down, theory-driven approach, consider a coach who bases their work on a goal-focused, cognitive-behavioural model. This is the frame through which they view their clients and the pathways to change. If a client recounts a situation in which they noticed they were getting distressed and presents their desired outcome as being able to handle such situations more effectively, the coach will likely develop a formulation that looks at the cycle of situations–emotions–thoughts–behaviour. The assumption underlying this cycle is that central to the client's emotional distress is their interpretation of the event (Corrie et al., 2016). Therefore, it is the client's interpretation of events and their reactions which is the focus of the formulation and the subsequent coaching interventions. It is still the client's story that forms the basis for the formulation, but the coach is suggesting that the client examines their account through the lens of a cognitive-behavioural model. That model is not imposed on the client and offered as a useful way to explore their narrative, but it does direct the attention in specific ways.

Many coaches who are trained in a specific model or framework will favour this approach to formulation and there are a number of advantages to doing so, including:

- The opportunity to gain a high degree of competence in a particular approach
- The ability to clearly define the strengths and limitations of the approach adopted
- Greater ease in creating coherence between the elements of the 4P Framework
- Greater clarity regarding the coaching service offered to clients

There are also some challenges that arise from the use of the top-down approach. In general, it limits the formulation to one model which clearly directs the client and the coaching in particular ways. If the top-down approach is used, the coach will need to manage their intake process to ensure that the clients with whom they work are a good match to the approach which they have adopted. This illustrates the interrelationship between the elements of purpose and perspective as it is in the defining of the purpose that this decision would be made.

Bottom-Up, Data or Story-Driven Approach

In a bottom-up, data or story-driven approach, the coach has a preference for hearing the client's story first and then adopting the perspective or perspectives which are the best fit with the coaching purpose (Corrie & Lane, 2010). The coach may likely consider the data and the client's story through multiple lenses as they work with the client to make sense of the situation. This could involve developing multiple explanations and examining how they might be interconnected, and the data on which the formulation is based may also be derived from multiple sources. As a result, multiple events and interventions may be identified and subsequently woven into an integrated approach to achieving the coaching purpose.

A coach working from a bottom-up approach may well consider a theoretical perspective such as a cognitive-behavioural approach as one avenue to pursue. However, they may also seek to broaden their own and the client's perspective and develop additional accounts based on other approaches. For example, they may consider the broader systemic context in which this situation is unfolding, they may expand the initial cognitive-behavioural formulation to explore the history of the client's patterns of reactions to this or similar situations, or they may draw on the adult or ego developmental theories to identify how the client makes sense of the world. In this approach the client and coach work collaboratively to understand the various factors involved in their situation to create an explanation that has implications for change.

As coaches progress through their careers it is not uncommon for them to add new perspectives and approaches to their practice. Using a bottom-up approach that potentially draws on these multiple perspectives also has advantages and disadvantages. The advantages include:

- Providing an opportunity to develop their practice from a variety of perspectives, broadening the potential client base for their services
- Ensuring that the approach they take is a best fit for the client and the agreed coaching purpose
- Offering the client choices in how the coaching will proceed
- Providing an opportunity for new and diverse approaches to emerge

As with the top-down approach, there are also a number of challenges to approaching formulation in this way. There is the potential for the client and coach to become overwhelmed with the amount of data collected, and this approach relies heavily on the ability of the coach to synthesize and organize information effectively. This story-driven approach can be more difficult to explain to clients who might want more certainty and clarity in how the coaching will unfold. The coach will need to be able to clearly articulate the process of how they work with the client without being able to draw on a specific model or approach. In addition, the use of multiple perspectives requires the coach to develop conceptual and technical competence in a broader range of approaches, which is a potentially more challenging task than becoming competent in one approach. There are also implications for the ability to create a coherent formulation that connects all elements of the 4P Framework. The coach will need to ensure that their approach is grounded in a transtheoretical framework that creates coherence between elements of the formulation.

The key to formulating effectively within either the top-down or bottom-up approach is to maintain a balance between the use of theory and the available evidence with the responsiveness to the client's unique story and context (Denman, 1995). The differences between the two approaches are reflected in the breadth of data and information that is included in a formulation as well as the responsiveness to elements of the client's story that do not fit within a particular theoretical perspective.

The Client's Perspective

While we have focused primarily on the perspectives that the coach brings to the encounter, the client will also hold beliefs regarding the nature of the self and others and beliefs about change. As has already been discussed, certain perspectives will prescribe and proscribe particular avenues of exploration and change, and therefore one key consideration is how coherence between the perspectives of the coach and those of the client is ensured (Corrie & Lane, 2010). It is important to recognize that the formulation that emerges from the encounter is co-created but is owned by the client. It is their story that is being considered.

Process

Having confirmed the purpose and defined the perspectives that will underpin the coaching, it is possible to design a process for the work that follows. Without a link to a defined purpose and perspectives, the process becomes a technical application of coaching tools and techniques uninformed by theoretical perspectives, or an understanding of the client's circumstances which have led them to the coaching. In designing the way forward, there are two intertwined processes that the coach is managing; the process of developing the formulation and the need to synchronize formulating with the overall coaching process. Chapter 9 considers the topic of process in more detail. The following section considers how process is linked to the other elements of the 4P Framework.

Coaches are often trained in a wide range of coaching models, all of which will be based on a particular perspective, and which may prescribe a process and set of tools and techniques. Standard coaching processes that are derived from a particular model of coaching can be effective and may provide substantial benefits to coaches and clients (Tee & Passmore, 2022). However, where a coaching process is implemented regardless of the individual factors and without a deep understanding of the theory that underpins the coaching approach, the coaching is based less on the client's own story and more on the application of one perspective on coaching. This effectively reduces the client's agency. The key question for the coach at this stage of the formulation is, what process (including any methods or tools) is necessary to ensure that the purpose is met within the constraints of the perspectives available to me?

The process reflects what happens as the coach and client work together. It refers to what can be observed by the client or other stakeholders. Designing the process involves making a range of decisions, including:

- How clients are engaged and onboarded into the coaching relationship
- When and how relevant data are gathered
- How the coach and client will share their emerging formulations to create a shared story
- What frameworks will be used to guide the overall coaching journey
- The coaching tools or techniques that will be selected
- The specific timing and pacing of the coaching sessions
- The sequencing of the use of specific coaching interventions

- The point at which other stakeholders are engaged and whether they will have a role in designing the process
- How the coaching will be evaluated

All of these decisions form elements of the coaching process and in this context questions that might need to be considered so as to narrow available choices include:

- What coaching models, frameworks, tools or techniques does the coach favour as a means of ensuring that the coaching purpose is met within the constraints of the positionality and the perspective/s within which the coach chooses to work?
- What is the coach's preferred approach to data gathering in the light of the selected perspective?
- What coaching models, frameworks, tools or techniques are sanctioned or vetoed by those perspectives? How do these influence intervention planning?

To illustrate these points, Table 3.1 compares the decisions regarding process that two coaches might make based on their positionality, purpose and perspectives.

Both coaches would develop a specific formulation for each individual client that would tailor the coaching to the idiosyncratic needs of the client. However, these individual formulations are constrained and enabled by the other elements of the 4P Framework. For example, Coach A would tailor many elements of the coaching process such as the specific psychometrics and coaching techniques used but would be unlikely to design a process based on psychodynamic principles. Similarly, Coach B would tailor the process for each client, but the process remains focused on engaging with the system and the interface between the client and their context.

In terms of designing a process, coaches have available to them a wide range of step-based frameworks which can provide the architecture for the process, or they may design their own. The coaching literature provides many of these frameworks along with a series of questions that the coach can use to take clients through the change process (Corrie & Lane, 2010). Examples of these frameworks include the three-stage framework of Egan's (1975) system of exploration, understanding and action, or the popular four-stage Goal, Reality, Options, Way forward (GROW) model (Whitmore, 2010, first published in 1992) in which many coaches are trained. Stout-Rostron (2014) has identified a series of these frameworks ranging from two to ten steps. The framework a coach may select is dependent on the fit with the purpose and perspectives of the coaching, but regardless of which framework is selected, each stage of the process needs to be consistent with the purpose and create coherence between an individual session and the overall direction of the work (Stout-Rostron, 2014).

Table 3.1 Decision-making about Process based on positionality, purpose and perspective

	Coach A	Coach B
Positionality	Female, mid 30s, clinical psychologist, university-trained, American, based in New York City.	Male, mid 60s, retired senior executive, MBA, coach training in a model based on stakeholder feedback and behavioural change, Australian, based in Singapore.
Purpose	She frames her coaching purpose as helping people fulfil their potential and achieve success in their lives.	He frames his coaching purpose as helping leaders be more effective and create successful businesses.
Perspectives	Individual perspective, theory-driven, drawing on predominantly a cognitive-behavioural (CB) approach.	Systemic perspective, bottom-up, data-driven approach.
Process	Data collection via a range of psychometrics.	Data collected from the client's own story and extensive stakeholder interviews.
	Based on the results of the psychometrics and initial coaching sessions a formulation drawing on CB theory is developed with the client.	May shadow the client to make own observations.
	Given the formulation and the client's reason for commencing coaching, specific goals and outcome measures are agreed.	Synthesizes the data to develop a formulation that identifies key themes in the client's story as a leader and the themes that indicate the culture of the organization that may be enablers or blockers of the leader's success.
	Tools and techniques from CB coaching approaches are introduced.	Agrees areas for development and collaborates with the client to develop an action plan for change.
	Regular coaching at two-week intervals with no fixed endpoint.	"Pulse check" surveys with stakeholders to assess progress.
	Regular review and update of formulation alongside the client.	Re-engages stakeholders towards the end of the coaching to gain feedback on the leader's development and the impact of changes.
	No engagement with other stakeholders.	Six-month programme with regular meetings to suit client's needs.
	Uses goal attainment scales to measure progress.	

Conclusion

This chapter has introduced the 4P Framework, which is an approach that can be adapted to fit any coaching context and can be used to support the development of the ability to formulate. As coaches are offering themselves as facilitators of change, understanding the perspectives and articulating the purpose that underpin their coaching can bring additional rigour and structure to the change process. The 4P Framework is one approach that enables the articulation of the choices that are made and to recognize the advantages and disadvantages of choosing one approach over another. The four aspects of this approach are explored in more detail in the chapters that follow.

Questions to Consider

Having read this introduction to the 4P Framework, it may be helpful to reflect on these questions in relation to your practice:

- What are the key elements of your social identity and how do they position you in relation to your clients?
- How do you define the purpose of the coaching services you provide?
- Considering the perspectives outlined in this chapter, which do you favour in your practice and what would be gained by considering other perspectives?
- What processes, frameworks and tools do you typically use in your practice and what are the links to the perspectives on which you draw?

Part 2

Building a Formulation Using the 4P Framework: Positionality, Purpose, Perspectives and Process

This section of the book examines how to create a framework for formulation using the 4P Framework. Each of the elements of the 4P Framework – Positionality, Purpose, Perspectives and Process – is explored in depth. The chapters in this section illustrate how each of these elements is already present in our coaching practice and also how they can be harnessed to co-create more effective accounts of our clients' needs.

DOI: 10.4324/9781003174585-6

Chapter 4

Formulation and Positionality

In the previous chapter we introduced the concept of positionality as an element of the 4P Framework. This chapter explores positionality in more detail and examines its relationship to and impact on formulation.

Before beginning any formulation process, an examination of a coach's positionality is needed to understand how the knowledge a coach holds about the world is applied in a specific coaching formulation. This is a complex task involving multiple interwoven elements. A reflexive process to articulate positionality may be familiar to scholars in the coaching field, but many practising coaches will be unfamiliar with the term. This exploration is not a one-off activity, but an ongoing and iterative process with each formulation presenting an opportunity to deepen the understanding of the coach's positionality and its effects on the coaching that follows. Examining positionality and the impact it has on a formulation can be challenging as it will likely reveal hidden biases and beliefs which can be an uncomfortable process. However, understanding how their worldview affects every aspect of their coaching can increase coaches' ability to work with clients from different backgrounds and with different perspectives and needs.

The aims of this chapter are to explore the concept of positionality in detail, provide guidance on how to begin exploring it and consider how positionality impacts formulation. The chapter also considers how to work effectively with the client's positionality.

What Is Positionality?

The concept of positionality developed during the late 1980s and 1990s from two distinct but overlapping theoretical perspectives: (1) postmodern feminist theory (e.g. Alcoff, 1988; Harding, 1991), and (2) social psychology (e.g. Davies & Harré, 1990). Both theoretical perspectives propose that the positions from where we make sense of the world, and how we engage with it, are informed by our identities and lived experiences (Acevedo et al., 2015). Specifically, contributors of positionality theory challenged the view of identity as fixed, ongoing and rooted in dominant individual and group characteristics. Instead, individuals are

DOI: 10.4324/9781003174585-7

believed to occupy multiple identities, which may be fluid and evolving, and that are contextually situated (Alcoff, 1988). Differences in perspectives are seen as emerging from unique experiences rather than being something essential about a specific aspect of identity (e.g. gender, race, ethnicity) (Kezar & Lester, 2010). One view of this process from a socio-linguistic perspective examined how culture informs language, which shapes how individuals view the world. We are all socialized into a culture by family and community, which provides a generic sense of the world. We are also influenced by our very particular experiences. Thus, both the general and the particular influence how we see and interact with the world (Lane, 1973). However, as Malik (2023) has argued, humans live neither in the particular nor the universal. We define ourselves through our many immediate identities (generic and particular in Lane's terms) but also in terms of universal aspirations. This more universal sense of being human Malik (2023) argues gives our local rooted identities context and meaning. Thus, individuals seek to make and re-make their worlds, which enables them to reach beyond deterministic categories.

From the perspective of social psychology, positionality theory emerged in an attempt to better account for the complexity of human behaviour in social settings as an alternative to a deterministic view of social participation: "positioning allows for the subjective histories of individuals – identities, personal attributes, experiences as well as preconceived narratives and understandings of our social locations – to play a critical function in the production of interpersonal behaviour" (Acevedo et al., 2015, p. 32).

Post-graduate research students in the social sciences now commonly have to identify and articulate their positionality and its influence on their research. Positionality is seen as influencing all aspects and stages of any study including the interactions researchers have as they undertake their research, the methodology that is selected and the interpretation of outcomes. A researcher's positionality also influences their approach to other scholars' findings, e.g. what findings they accept, how they interpret findings and which theoretical perspectives they favour. Given how positionality can impact on the totality of the research process, reflexive practice is considered essential in reducing potential subjective bias, although it can never be completely eliminated (Holmes, 2020).

A social sciences researcher would typically produce a positionality statement in the initial stages of their project. This statement would include a description of the lenses through which the researcher views the research (e.g. ethical, philosophical, personal, theoretical beliefs), potential influences (e.g. factors of personal identity such as age, social class, religious beliefs, race, gender, ethnicity) and an examination of how, where, when and in what these elements of positionality may or have influenced the research (Savin-Baden & Major, 2013).

In the 4P Framework, a similar process is proposed for coaches. Any formulation process should include an articulation and reflection on the coach's positionality, how it is similar to or different from that of the client, and consider the potential it has to influence the coaching purpose, perspectives and process.

Elements of Positionality

Positionality is recognized as a complex area and one approach to understanding the concept is to consider that it comprises three key interacting strands: intersecting identities, power relations and context (Kezar & Lester, 2010). Using this as a framework for exploring positionality in coaching, the following sections consider these three elements in more detail, how they interact and how they might impact coaching.

Intersecting Identities

Positionality theory assumes people have multiple and fluid overlapping identities that are contextually bound. Being able to name and understand the complexities of social identity is an important step in understanding individual positionality. People make meaning from various aspects of their identity simultaneously, rather than possessing one-dimensional identities associated with essentialist categories (Kezar & Lester, 2010). Therefore, a coach (and client) will bring multiple roles and identities to the coaching, elements of which intertwine to impact the coaching. The complexity of understanding and articulating positionality is increased when we consider that the facets which contribute to social identity are in motion or fluid, shifting over time and place. For example, we are always ageing, educational status changes, class or wealth can shift and other elements of identity are now considered to be more fluid than previously assumed (e.g. gender) depending on the time and place in which someone was raised (Jacobson & Mustafa, 2019).

Adding to the complexity is the consideration that some elements of identity will be more influential than others during specific times and places. This is particularly relevant when considering how social identity interacts with power and context. Facets of social identity may be given more socio-political salience than other factors in different contexts (Jacobson & Mustafa, 2019). All individuals occupy multiple roles in their lives (family, work, informal gatherings) and are multifaceted, adopting different stances as they navigate different social settings and interactions (Acevedo et al., 2015).

Not only does the coach's positionality impact how they make sense of the client and the coaching, but the reverse is also true: how the coach is perceived by the client may be different to how they see themselves. For example, how does the client view the coach from their positionality? What is shared and what is not shared in how the coach and client see the world? It is through conducting this level of reflection that both the shared and differences in aspects of identity can be recognized. While those aspects of identity that are shared may provide useful insights, where there are differences a sense of separation may be created. These aspects may require greater enquiry to understand the client's life experiences and the way in which they have made sense of these. Some of the key elements of identity that are useful to consider are:

- Race
- Ethnicity
- Class
- Abilities

- Neurotypicality and neurodivergence
- Sexuality
- Gender identity
- Nationality
- Religion
- Relationship status
- Age
- Political allegiance
- Cultural factors
- Historical context

Power Relations

From the perspective of positionality theory, power is seen as socially constructed and pervading all contexts, historical situations and interpersonal relationships (Kezar & Lester, 2010). Power is seen as central to the way people make meaning and shape perspectives, and coaches should give consideration of their access to forms of power and how this positions them in relation to the client and the coaching.

Power has been defined as a means of obtaining security and advantage in some way (Smail, 2005). The use of power can involve influencing people, events and outcomes to benefit the interests or needs of individuals as well as organizations or broader social systems. There are multiple closely related forms of power, which operate together, and interact with elements of identity to influence every social interaction, often in complex ways. For example, as noted above, people have multiple intersecting identities. These identities can have conflicting meanings in terms of power, which in turn can cumulatively reinforce or reduce privilege.

Johnstone and Boyle (2018) have categorized the main forms of power, which are summarised in Table 4.1. below.

Table 4.1 Categorizations of power adapted from Johnstone and Boyle (2018)

Type of power	Description
Biological or embodied power	Embodied attributes such as physical appearance, skin shade and colour, physical health or embodied talents.
Coercive power or power by force	Any use of aggression, violence or physical power that is used to intimidate or ensure compliance.
Legal power	A wide range of rules and sanctions exist which regulate and control many aspects of people's lives. These legal powers can support or limit other aspects of power and enable or restrict the choices that people can make.

(Continued)

Table 4.1 (Continued)

Type of power	Description
Economic and material power	Having the means to obtain not only valued possessions and services, but also to pursue valued activities, e.g. types of education, employment, leisure activities or housing.
Ideological power	The power to create beliefs, propagate stereotypes about certain groups, have control over the interpretation of experiences and over meaning, language and agendas.
Interpersonal power	All types of power operate through relationships. Specifically interpersonal power refers to the power to protect, look after or not protect someone or groups of people.

These forms of power do not necessarily require intentional acts by individuals to have effects as they operate through structures, institutions, organizations, physical environment, media, education and social and family relations. It may be easier to identify the visible forms of power, such as the hierarchy in an organization. However, the less visible forms of power are equally potent with people self-policing or "code-switching" to conform to dominant cultural ideas and practices to gain more social acceptance, or access to power (McCluney et al., 2021; Wright et al., 2022). Code-switching as a concept emerged in linguistic studies to describe language fluency or the use of multiple languages within a single conversation. The term has recently been extended to represent an impression management strategy where members of the global majority adjust their self-presentation to achieve desirable outcomes (e.g. perceived professionalism) through mirroring the norms, behaviours and attributes of the dominant group in specific contexts. Examples of code-switching behaviours include adjusting style of speech, name selection or aspects of appearance in order to conform to the dominant cultural norms. This is a relevant concept for coaches to consider as it is a strategy that could be suggested to gain professional progression, although employing this approach can incur social and psychological costs for the individual involved (McCluney et al., 2021).

Ideological power also operates in the forms of knowledge that are deemed acceptable, such as beliefs about what constitutes professional practice. The coaching profession, along with other forms of psychological science, largely draws on a knowledge base that is culturally homogenous, being based predominantly on European or American theories and approaches to psychological health. While there is a growing awareness of the challenges that this presents, most current coach training is still based on concepts aligned with Western cultural values and ethics (Lane et al., 2023). For example, some coach training draws on the theories and techniques of cognitive-behavioural therapy (CBT) which has been widely recognized as an evidence-based approach (Corrie & Lane, 2021; Gray et al., 2016). However, most CBT research has historically focused on European Americans (Hays, 2019). When transferred to the coaching context, approaches drawn from CBT often emphasize concepts that are based on Western values, such as personal independence.

This bias towards Western notions of self marginalizes other approaches and supplants alternative narratives regarding the challenges a client faces and the potential solutions. These individualistic cultural norms can lead people to blame themselves for failing to meet certain standards and coaches and their clients may fail to recognize the impact of the elements of identity and power (Johnstone & Boyle, 2018).

As with all interactions, power is a factor in any coaching relationship and process. The coach and client's positionalities will be influenced by their relationship to the different forms of power. This network of power relations in which people are embedded and the resources which they can therefore access will play a major role in the coach's formulation, and how the client can respond to any coaching intervention. The challenge for the coach is to ensure that they have considered their own position in relation to power and how this is reflected in their formulation along with any differences to the client's experience of power.

The Importance of Context

The elements of social identity and power are intertwined with the third strand of positionality, context; that is, the circumstances and conditions in which an individual exists, such as an organization, community or nation. The way in which individuals make sense of their position in the world is shaped by interactions, the interpretations of experiences and the effects of positioning (Kezar & Lester, 2010). The process of meaning-making does not develop in a cultural vacuum as every person is surrounded by broader cultural narratives that encode various social norms. These norms are learned from infancy and are updated throughout life to reflect the changing narratives of a particular culture (Johnstone & Boyle, 2018).

Evaluating these norms reveals how context and power are inextricably linked. The dominant narratives reflect the current economic and structural relationships and embody the current ruling ideas (Johnstone & Boyle, 2018). Within professions these narratives inform and impact on the practices adopted. Culturally specific beliefs are developed through social interactions imbued with power relations. These social norms and discourses can be difficult to identify as they make up the very fabric of existence (Hagan & Donnison, 1999), forming a backdrop that operates outside conscious awareness. Italian philosopher and political activist Antonio Gramsci (see Hoare & Sperber, 2016) referred to these broadly accepted beliefs as *senso comune*. Although there is no direct English equivalent of this term, it is loosely translated as "common sense", that is, the accumulating body of unquestioned knowledge and assumptions about ourselves, others and how the world works. The Italian *senso comune* is a more neutral term than its English equivalent, referring to the collective knowledge of a culture, the ways in which it becomes accepted as beyond question, and by whom. What becomes *senso comune* is usually the result of institutions and producers of knowledge promoting a particular view of the world (Crehan, 2016). For example, one of Gramsci's major contributions was his argument that political power ultimately depends upon making one's ideas commonplace within society. When an idea assumes the status of being "normal", it ceases to become a legitimate topic for discussion and debate and acquires the status of a factual reality. In essence, it becomes immune to challenge (Corrie, 2020).

In the case of coaching, there is indirect or direct exposure to a range of influences that may make up the dominant narratives about coaching. Drawing on the work of Mohan (1996), Corrie and Lane (2010) have previously argued that these influences can be identified at three levels:

1 Influences at a local level: for example, the beliefs, values, processes and priorities operating in the context in which the coaching is being delivered (e.g. an organization)
2 Influences at a national level: for example, the priorities of the political system in power, economic trends, the dominant views of human nature, and current social and cultural norms
3 Influences at a global level: for example, concerns that affect the global community as well as the international trends in coaching and applied psychology

Local influences shape a coach's thinking both explicitly (through a requirement to adhere to practice guidelines or codes of conduct) and implicitly (through values, assumptions and ethical frameworks). These local influences also shape what types of questions or goals are appropriate for coaching, what the client expects from the coaching and what form the coaching may take.

National influences also inform how coaching practitioners think and operate. As with local influences, there are implicit beliefs and assumptions that form the social norms shaping how a client's needs are presented and formulated. For example, the extent to which the culture within which the coach is working is inclined towards individualism or collectivism will influence how the coaching purpose is framed. Additionally, traditional and social media have a role in raising awareness of issues and trends, in turn influencing how the public views the coaching field and the role that it plays in addressing prevailing concerns. National influences also play a central role in informing the ethical expectations that emerge between a coach and their client as the coaching proceeds. The ethical underpinnings of the coaching represent more than reference to a particular professional code. They are how coaches underpin their relationships with clients, the communities that are served and the planet itself. Increasingly, coaches may be asked for evidence of ethical practice, from how client data are protected to policies on diversity and inclusion, and the environment.

Global influences are those broader trends, opportunities and threats which shape how coaches conceptualize their role. At the time of writing, some of these influences impacting the coaching industry include:

- Increased awareness of inequalities between people as a function of gender, race, culture and geographical location
- The ongoing threat of current and future pandemics, including a pandemic of antibiotic-resistant bacterial infections
- The urgency of addressing the impacts of climate change and the experience of climate change-related natural disasters

- Ongoing changes to the nature and culture of employment, with hybrid ways of working changing the needs of employers and employees
- The opportunities and threats of technology, such as artificial intelligence (AI) and social media platforms
- The increasing polarization and fragmentation in global societies, driven partly by the use of social media and the internet to spread disinformation
- Demographic changes in attitudes to work and employment
- The ideology of individualism that dominates Western society

An appreciation of local, national and global contexts encourages coaches to work creatively with the major issues facing clients in their own local, national and global communities and to understand how the formulations we construct as coaches have consequences at different levels. In doing so, coaches become better able to understand their offer to clients and how that offer might be relevant to their needs.

Understanding Identity, Power and Context in Action

The three strands of positionality are interwoven and the intent in describing them separately is to provide a framework that can assist coaches in their reflective process. Articulating positionality ensures a coach understands the ways in which positionality is influencing how they see themselves in relation to the client and the formulations that they develop.

The starting point for any reflection is to consider the key aspects of identity and articulate the influence that this has had on an individual's life. This includes considering how it positions the person in relation to power, identifying the values that are intrinsically attached to these identities and the interpretations of events or interactions resulting from this positionality. As an example, cisgender women see the world through the eyes of individuals who are, and have been treated by others as, women. The relationship to power is such that in many situations they have less power than men and that they have experience of the historical and ongoing fight for equality (Jacobson & Mustafa, 2019).

The next stage of reflection is to consider what emotions are tied to the details of the individual's identity. To continue the example above, women are often warned to be cautious in order to avoid being assaulted when walking alone at night, which implies that the woman has a responsibility to avoid being attacked. This experience significantly informs how some women approach the world – as cautious women, which in turn may impact how others interact with them and how they position themselves in certain situations and interactions (Jacobson & Mustafa, 2019). Additionally, their experiences of inequity may mean that they feel a sense of anger and injustice in their treatment. On the one hand the woman is cautious about how she approaches the world, and on the other she is frustrated by the treatment she receives on a day-to-day basis. Even in the case of a cisgender woman, this one aspect of their identity and its relationship to power and context can be complicated. The relationship between gender identity as one strand of an individual's social identity and the other aspects of positionality become even more complex for those who identify as agender, bigender, gender fluid, transgender or are gender non-conforming.

The relationships to power and privilege are far from straightforward, especially when considering that elements of social identity are interdependent and indivisible from one another, interacting to create differential social positions (Christoffersen & Emejulu, 2023). However, institutions and policymakers often consider elements of identity separately, which leads to greater levels of social disadvantage for already marginalized groups. Crenshaw (1989) coined the term intersectionality to describe how Black women's experiences are marginalized by practices that treat race and gender as mutually exclusive categories. When different aspects of identity, such as race or gender, are conceptualized as separate and independent, there is a tendency for the most powerful members of the marginalized group (e.g. white women or Black men) to universalize themselves and their experiences and position themselves as the only legitimate representatives of the group as a whole (Christoffersen & Emejulu, 2023). Coaches should be aware that the impact of interdependent elements of identity can lead to profoundly different lived experiences at the intersection of social locations such as race, gender, sexuality and class. For example, the relationship and access to forms of power would be significantly different for a Muslim Black woman and white middle-class woman, and therefore any coaching between the two would need to consider the impact of the distinctly different positionalities.

While elements of identity position an individual either closer or further away from power resources, there is also the need to understand what this position means for how a person behaves to gain more power, or to reinforce, resist or change current power relations. Some examples might include:

- Leaders from minoritized groups who code-switch to adopt what are traditionally considered dominant cultural norms and leadership traits to be considered for promotion
- An organizational leadership team that uses their power resources (e.g. interpersonal and ideological power) to redefine leadership to be more inclusive of different styles and cultures and encourage promotion of candidates from minority groups
- Training as a coach generally requires economic, interpersonal or material power to access training, limiting the choices of some groups to pursue coaching as a profession
- Using interpersonal power (perhaps through a social network) to secure work as a coach, therefore potentially retaining, increasing or decreasing economic and interpersonal power

Recognizing the relationship between identity, power and the impact that these elements have on a person's experiences and life is a key step in the recognition and reflection on how positionality can impact a coach's work. Yet, context factors are also highly relevant. Consider the positionality of a white coach working in a predominantly white organization with someone from a minoritized group. The differences in positionality between coach and client have the potential to impact the coaching. For example, given the coach's racial identity, does this position them as having more power than the client in that organizational context, and how would this compare to working with a white client in the same organization? The key point is to recognize the effect of positionality and the relationships to privilege and power in a particular context. While this can be extremely difficult, it is important as it is in the areas where we have access to power and privilege that we have the least knowledge about the lives of people without the same position. This can unwittingly lead to bias in the way coaches approach their work (Hays, 2019). There is also the risk that the coach reinforces and reproduces the beliefs, stereotypes or power dynamics of the wider societal context in the coaching relationship.

The combination of the elements of identity, power, and context constitute the means to shape an individual's experience and position in the world. Our general sense of who we are is something we bring to every interaction and shapes how we behave. However, the interaction between identity, power and context also means that our positionality in one context may be different in another. For example, the leader who is in a position of authority at work may acquiesce in a domineering relationship at home. A useful analogy here is that of the chessboard. A pawn on a chessboard is considered safe or dangerous, powerful or weak, according to its relation to the other chess pieces (Alcoff, 1988).

The Influence of Positionality on Coaching Formulation

A coach's positionality has shaped how they see the world in general, influencing their approach to their practice more broadly. However, people are positioned differently and take different stances in different contexts, which for a coach means at the level of an individual formulation with a specific client.

Positionality and Purpose

A coach's identity influences how the purpose of their work in general is framed, such as the clients with whom a coach chooses to work, or the types of coaching that are pursued. However, their identity also influences how the purpose of a formulation for a specific client is articulated. At both levels the way a coach and client frame the purpose of the engagement will also be affected by the context in which they are working. All parties in the coaching will be influenced by the implicit beliefs about coaching prevalent in both society in general and the specific context of a coaching encounter, such as an organization.

Attention also needs to be given to how power relations can influence the way in which the purpose of the coaching is defined. In some contexts, coaching can be used as a means of coercing one person to conform to the will of another under the guise of improving performance. This can be difficult for a coach to resist if a purpose defined in this manner conforms to their beliefs about the use of coaching as a means to maximize performance (Hawkins & Smith, 2006). This is only one example of how, without a sufficient understanding of their positionality, coaches risk making assumptions and exhibiting biases towards their clients' needs and the purpose of the coaching.

How Positionality Influences Coaching Perspectives and Process

In terms of influence on the perspectives on which a coach draws, positionality impacts the types of training that is selected, the approaches that are considered valid and how evidence-based practice is conceptualized. Therefore, how a formulation is constructed, or even whether formulation is considered to be a valid approach, is a result of the coach's positionality. As already discussed, most of the current coach training available draws on Western knowledge and perspectives, which may be appropriate for many contexts. However, there will also be contexts where these perspectives are not as useful, such as when working cross-culturally or where there are major differences in the client's and coach's positionality and ethical stance (Lane et al., 2023). Kinouani (2021) has argued that the current Western psychological models lead to a focus on the mind and the cognitive, marginalizing other aspects such as the body and spirituality. This positioning can marginalize people from other cultural backgrounds such as those of African descent (Kinouani, 2021). Additionally, there is the potential for cultural influences on a client's behaviour to be framed as negative by the norms of the perspectives on which the coach is drawing. These perspectives may also fail to take into consideration culturally related stressors, which include discrimination, living in unsafe neighbourhoods or inadequate housing or health care, legal problems or exposure to trauma from disasters or wars (Hays, 2019). Equally, these perspectives might not consider the positive aspects of cultures and approaches that could be useful to support the coaching, such as extended families, religious communities, traditional celebrations and rituals and storytelling activities (Hays, 2019).

The process that the coach adopts is also influenced by positionality, making some processes more likely to be considered than others. Aspects of the coaching process that can be influenced by the coach's preferences may include:

- Which stakeholders are consulted and whose views are given priority
- The data collection processes that are considered
- The lines of enquiry which a coach pursues
- Which psychometric instruments are deployed, or if they are used at all
- The interventions that the coach considers and employs with the client
- The information that the coach chooses to share with the client and when
- How the coaching success or progress will be measured
- What information is shared with the key stakeholders and when

The preceding section has illustrated the potential influence of positionality on formulation, and Box 4.1 contains an example. In this instance, the 40-year-old female coach is white, British and from a middle-class background. She is university-educated with a psychology degree and master's degree in coaching psychology.

Box 4.1   The impact of positionality on coaching

Female Gender

The coach is motivated to help female leaders, influencing not only the choice of clients but also how the purpose of the coaching is defined. Her gender may also influence which stakeholders she chooses to involve, such as those most supportive to her female clients, and she may potentially ignore data that is not aligned with her view of the client. There is a risk of bias towards and over-identification with cisgender female clients. She recognizes the role of systemic factors in the success or challenges of female leaders and incorporates these systemic factors into her formulation.

University-Educated, Psychology Training

She considers formulation a useful and valid approach, favouring an evidence-based approach, drawing on concepts from the psychological literature such as cognitive and behavioural principles and methods. She constructs formulations based on the psychological theories with which she is familiar and tends to see her clients' challenges through the lens of these theories.

White, British, Middle-Class

She often frames coaching purpose towards progression, achievement and personal success. She favours an individual perspective with beliefs around personal change based on education and effort. The formulations she develops are predominantly individually focused while also considering the systemic factors that may be barriers to success, which need to be navigated, or that could be enablers of a leader's success. She may not recognize the additional intersectional, systemic issues that people from minority groups may encounter in pursuing their careers.

She is based in the south of England and provides executive coaching to clients who are predominantly leaders within corporations and government organisations. Prior to becoming a full-time coach she worked in the human resources function of a major multinational organization. Examining just a few elements of her positionality illustrates how much potential influence on formulation this can have.

What is evident from the example above is that the influence of different elements of positionality interact and overlap, creating a unique set of influences for each individual. While individuals may share aspects of positionality, their experiences and background will also influence their work, resulting in both formulations and approaches to coaching that are unique to them.

Working With a Client's Positionality

So far, this chapter has focused on the coach's positionality and its influence on for-mulation. However, the client's positionality and the interaction between the coach and client are also important considerations that need to be reflected in any formula-tion. Once a coach has articulated their own positionality there is greater potential to identify what may be shared with a client and what will be different, and there-fore where they may need to direct attention to appreciate the client's perspective. There are also overlapping and/or differences in social identities that create power dynamics in a relationship, which can impact a client's openness to discussing cer-tain topics. This may hamper the ability to gain a full picture of the client's perspec-tive. Even where elements of positionality are shared, for example gender, these commonalities do not necessarily mean that the coach and client make sense of the world in the same way. There are too many intertwined factors to assume that a client's perspective is understood simply because of a shared aspect of identity.

Throughout this book the importance of recognizing and privileging the client's perspective in any formulation is emphasized. However, part of our function as coaches is also to challenge the perspectives of our clients and the current narra-tives that they hold about their situation. This creates a tension between privileging the client's story and challenging their perspective so that they can move forward. A coach's role is to ensure that while the client's perspective is fully considered, they are also encouraged to critically reflect on their perspective (Shoukry, 2017). Nonetheless, there is potential for this approach to alienate the client and therefore requires that the coach develops an understanding of how strongly held the current perspective is and whether other approaches to working with the client's perspective are more appropriate. For example, in Personal Construct Psychology the difference between core and peripheral constructs is considered (Bradley-Cole et al., 2023; Horley, 2012). The former are more resistant to challenge and change. Consider, for example, a young Australian-born client of Chinese ethnicity who comes to coach-ing with the aim of changing their career from their current role as an accountant to pursue a career in acting. The client currently lives with their parents and siblings and the family are resistant to any discussion about the client's desired career change. Formulating from a dominant Western perspective, the coach may conceptualize the issue as needing to challenge the authority of the parents and perhaps leave the fam-ily home in order to pursue their preferred career. This approach, however, would involve challenging culturally based beliefs regarding the nature of responsibility towards family and respect for elders embedded in Chinese culture and may cause the client to feel that the coach has little understanding of their cultural context lead-ing the client to terminate the coaching relationship. Alternatively, the client may be open to pursuing these alternative perspectives, in which case coaching may assist the client in navigating the challenges of pursuing their chosen career.

Coaches faced with such differences will need to assess to what extent the client wants to explore different perspectives. Making an assumption that clients living within a certain cultural context will prefer to abide by it implicitly denies them the right to resist such an identity and to define their own. Alternatively, in adopting an approach that aspires to empower the client, the coach may end up imposing their own "liberating" ideas on their clients (Shoukry, 2017).

In some instances, even if a coach believes that they can understand the client's perspective, there are some concepts that are impossible to comprehend if an individual is not raised in a specific culture. As an example, Indigenous Australian scholar Tyson Yunkaporta (2019) articulates why it is impossible to describe for non-Indigenous people the Indigenous notion of time:

> Explaining Aboriginal notions of time is an exercise in futility as you can only describe it as non-linear in English, which immediately slams a big line across your synapses. You don't register the non-, only the linear: that is the way you process the word, the shape it takes in your mind. Worst of all it is only describing the concept by saying what it is not, rather than what it is. We don't have a word for non-linear in our languages because no one would consider travelling, thinking, or talking in a straight line in the first place. The winding path is just how a path is and therefore it needs no name (Yunkaporta, 2019, p. 21).

This example highlights the need for coaches to fully engage with the client's positionality and ensure that their perspective underpins any formulation. While a coach might believe that their skills and competences enable them to work with people from all backgrounds, as the example above illustrates, there are limits to their understanding of how their client sees the world.

Conclusion

The concept of positionality is likely to be unfamiliar to many coaching practitioners. This chapter has introduced and explored positionality through the lens of the three elements of identity, power relations and context and, in so doing, has sought to make a complex topic easier to grasp and apply in practice. The value of articulating positionality for the coach is to fully understand the impact that the combination and interaction of these elements has on their work with clients. It is not possible to escape the influences of positionality. However, by taking a critical and reflexive stance, it is possible to reduce bias and understand how the ways in which coach and client experience and see the world is applied in a specific coaching engagement.

Questions to Consider

Taking the time to reflect on positionality provides a way not only for coaches to see themselves more fully but also provides an opening to seeing the client as they are rather than simply as the issue they bring.

- What are the key elements of your social identity and what impact do these have on your worldview?

- How are you positioned in relation to the different forms of power described above?
- How does your positionality impact how you define the overall purpose of your work?
- Thinking about a current or recent coaching client, in what ways are/were you positioned differently to your client? How do/did you take these differences into consideration in the coaching formulation?

Chapter 5

Formulation and the Purpose of Coaching

One of the initial aspects of coaching assignments generally and of formulation specifically is agreeing a purpose for the work that will follow. This chapter explores how, in using formulation to conceptualize the encounter, clients can learn to define the purpose of the work not just in terms of an agreed outcome but also as a learning journey that will build knowledge and understanding for future use.

A key part of coaching is the way in which decisions are reached concerning the work that is to follow (Jansen, 2023). Exploring the different purposes that coaching might serve and when it is not the most appropriate approach provides a way to help both parties, and potentially other stakeholders, understand the primary concerns in a way that makes sense. A rush to define a goal can derail effective work, as goals cannot always be defined at the outset (David et al., 2013). A period of reflection and conversation with stakeholders might first be necessary to deciding on the focus of the coaching; thus this phase becomes a search for meaning from an encounter. The search involves understanding the context within which the journey is to take place and the relational framework that helps to define it as a worthwhile endeavour. While this chapter explores particular contexts to illustrate this, regardless of the place and space within which coaches work, encompassing a broad understanding of the prevailing context enables the emergence of a purpose that is worthwhile to each party involved. Defining goals prematurely can inhibit the process of building expertise as part of the journey.

This chapter will outline the range of influences that could be part of the decision-making process and which will impact the coaching journey that follows. The end point will be a greater understanding of how defining the purpose of the work creates the potential for a meaningful experience.

Towards Defining an Individual Purpose

Every child comes to understand that they are part of something greater and they exist in a socially constructed world. They learn how to deal with that world. There is increasing evidence on the relationship between adult outcomes and childhood skills. For example, social skills – learning to relate to others – is linked to later mental health and wellbeing (Goodman et al., 2015). Children are social beings and

DOI: 10.4324/9781003174585-8

as such forming and maintaining relationships matters both to the child and society (Lavis, 2016). The quality of those relationships impacts on the development of the brain (National Scientific Council on the Developing Child, 2004, updated 2009). While healthy relationships and a feeling of being supported can enable a sense of security, a long-lasting negative impact can be the result of unhealthy relationships (NSPCC, 2024 cited in Bentley et al., 2020).

There are different ways a child can learn to navigate their relationships (Barden, 2021). This might be by getting along with others to meet their own needs (consensual). Alternatively, they might learn that the world is hostile and experience themselves as excluded (conflictual). How they come to understand the world, their needs and the stance they take in meeting those needs is shaped by others. If they later come to be leaders in various fields such as education, industry or the military, it seems that the stance to the world they developed as children will be highly influential on the way they deal with the issues faced as leaders. In researching successful leaders, Barden (2021) found the idea of "navigational stance to the world" as central to the way that leaders solved problems.

As social beings, individuals learn to cooperate for a purpose – to meet their needs. Similarly, to lead an organization, it is necessary to be able to build from individual perspectives and create a shared concern. Employees may embrace the purpose of an enterprise because it meets their individual needs (Hakimi, 2015; Murray, 2017; O'Brien & Cave, 2017). The degree of embrace may be purely transactional – that is, they receive a wage. The embrace may be philosophical – the employees believe in the enterprise and its values. Alternatively, the degree of embrace might be transformational, perceived as changing some part of the world and themselves as part of it. In a study of over 900 organizations conducted by Rajan & Lane (2000), this range of perspectives was present. In some organizations, employees reported being proud of who they worked for and its standing in the world. They talked of its environmental and community commitments, its commitment to customer service and quality and care for employees. They expressed pride. For others the conversations were quite different. They simply saw this as a job with no sense of commitment to the organization or its purpose, (Rajan & Lane, 2000). More recent studies point to similar conclusions, namel, that pride in their organization inspires individuals and teams to achieve more (Hastwell, 2022; Segal, 2021).

The Concept of Purpose in Organizations

Every organization, service and enterprise is faced with the fundamental question, "What is our purpose?" Any answer to this question immediately raises further questions that essentially come back to the same concern – what makes this endeavour purposeful to self and others? For example, the entrepreneur starting a business has a sense of what they want to achieve, but unless that is shared by customers, the business will fail. If the business grows, the need for concerns to be shared means that staff will join customers in defining purpose, as perhaps will other stakeholders.

Towards Defining an Organizational Purpose

Those who study society from Marx, Weber, Durkheim, to more recent theorists such as Giddens, Piketty, Zuboff or Lent have different approaches to purpose. Thus, purpose might be consensual, seeking to work with others for a greater good or conflictual, seeing only competition to be overcome. The operational structures used will reflect each of these ways of organizing. Traditionally, many organizations have had a hierarchical structure of command and control (O'Donovan, 2014). Others encourage active engagement so decisions are made at a local level. For example, Seddon (2003), comparing the historical approach to production at Ford and Toyota, pointed to the top-down approach at Ford and the local decision-making at Toyota. As the world becomes more complex and interconnected, organizations increasingly discover that perspectives that worked in the past (particularly command and control) are not a sustainable basis for success (Seddon, 2003; Uhl-Bien, 2021). Purpose provides the reason for an enterprise to exist, a sense of direction and motivation. It also encompasses how it should exist; that is, its ways of being or operating. These are sometimes expressed as values or a mission. How the organization partners with its staff, customers and wider society reflects that fundamental purpose – it is what makes its activities meaningful.

Defining Purpose

When someone has a sense of purpose this is seen as giving them a direction and a motivation to achieve. Increasingly, organizations have understood purpose in a similar way. In a study for the Chartered Management Institute (CMI) (Ebert et al., 2018) based on interviews with 14 major corporates, purpose was understood as:

- A transcendent, meaningful reason to exist
- An enduring attribute of the organizational identity
- Aligned with long-term financial performance
- A clear context for daily decision-making
- Unifying and motivating for stakeholders

While the authors of the study view this as a recent trend, they argue that it is becoming mainstream for businesses. The CEO of Blackrock called his annual letter to chief executives "A Sense of Purpose" (Fink, 2024), and the Centre for Social Justice (2021) estimated that this sense would become all-encompassing in UK business by 2026, a position supported by the advisory panel to the UK Government's Mission-led business review (Gov.uk, 2016). Other recent articles and position papers within the global business community make similar arguments (Brower, 2021; Ebert & Hurth, 2022; McKinsey, 2020).

If establishing a clear purpose is so important, why is it only just now emerging? How can the justifiable cynicism from middle managers, also noted in the CMI study that it is just another management fad, be addressed?

Defining a Clear Organizational Purpose

The emergence of purpose as a key question arose at a much earlier stage than the current interest in the literature. As Checkland (1989) argued, the success of the mission to land a man on the moon and return him safely led to considerable interest in applying the same systems-style thinking (that is, Systems Engineering and RAND Corporation Systems Analysis) to solving problems in society, particularly within education and health. Such methodologies rely on a search to find the best means to achieve an agreed purpose (a desirable end). The application of these system ideas to schools and health was found to be inadequate. Part of the issue, according to Checkland, was that while all parties could agree on the purpose of the moon mission (place a man on the moon and return him safely), all parties could not agree on the purpose of education or health systems. This is contested space. There are multiple discourses in play (Gray et al., 2016). Purpose, as soon as you move from the simple to the complex, is a more difficult concept and one that organizations find problematic as it involves true collaborative thinking and learning in order to succeed (Gray et al., 2016). It cannot be top-down but has to be built across many levels of discourse. As has been argued (Boulton et al., 2015; McFee, 2023), a top-down process does not work in a complex world. The need in these contexts is to move beyond a structure in which a purpose is defined by senior management. Typically, core values are subsequently defined together with a mission statement. These are filtered down the organization into statements of behaviours, objectives and key results. Finally, they are then interpreted by departments and individuals. The arrows on the organizational chart work one way. The appeal is to the "orthodoxy" and certainly creates the impression that management is in control. Yet, as Boulton et al. (2015) argue: "In turbulent and fast changing environments there is unlikely to be sufficient information at the top of any organization to enable a largely top-down strategy to be effective" (p. 162).

The role of purpose increasingly features in the literature, with many calls to embrace the concept (Hurst, 2014; McKinsey, 2020). Yet, if purpose arises in a contested space, how might an agreement emerge? Unless the question of how purpose can emerge within a contested space is addressed, then the charge of just another "fad" becomes cogent and the cynicism of middle managers, identified in the CMI study, is justified. To do so, it is necessary to understand the spaces not just those who occupy them. As Boulton et al. (2015) contend, employees have heard many stories before as numerous initiatives have found their way into organizations. Mission statements, competencies, business process re-engineering and positivity ratios are just some of the ideas to which employees have been expected to commit only for those initiatives to fade away and be replaced by the next new idea.

Defining a purpose for coaching encompasses more than establishing a specific goal. If a person or organization is asked to define a fundamental purpose, that is, what makes its activities meaningful, that purpose will likely incorporate both values and a sense of what is fulfilling. In life coaching a person may incorporate work issues as part of the concern they wish to address, but the coaching might also incorporate broader relationships and concerns. Thus, the coaching might focus primarily on the self in relation to significant others. In organizations the coaching may relate to achieving an organizational purpose. It might still be achieved through people but is more likely to be expressed through the concept of role. As Kahn (2014) has argued, the shared interests of the individual and organization are expressed though the roles that people play. The individual does not leave behind the concerns as "self" but rather seeks to find ways to express these in how they perform the role. Coaching can be seen as one way to enhance the potential for a role to be performed well or exceptionally. In finding a purpose for coaching the individual (their sense of self), the relationship through which a role is performed and the wider organizational mission need to encompass a shared concern upon which they can act. Coaching might focus on developing capabilities to perform an activity, ensuring the quality of the performance, or transforming the way the concern is conceptualized so that it now forms part of a bigger perspective that ensures a purpose meaningful to all is achieved. The agreed performed activity might thereby look very different to an initial assumption about a specific goal.

Learning and Identity in Coaching: How Purpose Emerges

Coaches have a role in helping clients look at their life-long learning and the formation of their identity in the work context, as discussed in Chapter 2. As Lo (2005) argued, identity arises in sites of action; thus in organizations it is shaped by the engagement with the client in the context of their work. Negotiating that moving agenda is part of the task coaches increasingly face. In this sense, the learning process can be understood as a narrative in which a person continually negotiates their identity with others in a social context, commonly career or work context. It could also be in relation to a couple, a family or as a result of a difficult event such as redundancy. Yet, each of these represent, as Lo (2005) contends, a site of action.

In considering identity through the narratives coaches create, it is helpful to consider the notions of reflexive and relational narrative identification (Chappell et al., 2003). Reflexive identification refers to the way a person can construct their own identity through a process of self-narration. So, for a coach, a series of events may be involved in the way they plot a narrative of their identity. They have a sense of who they are as a person and as a coach. When a coach starts an engagement with an organization, this pre-existing narrative provides their entry point. However, as the coach works with people in the organization, a re-negotiation occurs. Each person will have their own definitions of the coach and there are also organizational definitions. These impact the identity of the coach as the process of relational narrative identification unfolds in each interaction. A similar process happens for clients. They start with a self-narration (the reflective process in the Kolb cycle, see Chapman, 2023, for a detailed exploration of this) that gradually evolves into a relational narrative. A narrative will be constructed between coach and client as the characters take shape in the emerging story (Corrie & Lane, 2010). What it is to be a coach or client in an organization is co-constructed as a process of relational narrative identity. It is in this relational process that adult learning emerges in the context of coaching. Hence, purpose is defined through engagement in each and every relationship. We are always, as Kahn (2014) points out, achieving understanding across a relational axis between the players in an organizational story.

Coaching is therefore an engagement of relatedness more so than the deployment of a particular method or skill. Central to this notion is the fundamental principle that the sponsoring organization and the individual being coached are equitable clients. Kahn (2011), therefore, insists that, "successful approaches to business coaching incorporate significant consideration of the relational dynamics between the triad of coach, individual client and organization, and focus on the coaching relationship and its systemic interface with the business environment" (p. 194).

The work of Kahn and others (e.g. Cavanagh & Grant, 2006; Gray et al., 2016; O'Connor & Cavanagh, 2013) is based on the fact that organizational environments consist of complex relational systems, overt and covert. Furthermore, a person's ability to deliver value in such an environment is largely dependent upon the extent to which they are able to create relationships with others, which, in turn, facilitates the conversion of their talent into real outcomes that meet an agreed purpose. In this view, coaching interventions create relational bridges (axis) that facilitate learning through an intersubjective story-making process. This process delivers value because it facilitates learning through the creation of a shared success story; "a story that emerges from a meeting of meaning between the individual and the organization that is based in a sense of mutual responsibility for the business" (Kahn, 2014, p. 6). Here the entire organization is seen as "the client" in as much a way as the individual, and neither organization nor individual can be approached as separate entities. Ultimately this means that learning in the context of coaching, even when deeply intrapsychic in nature, is always embedded in relationship and emerges as a course of the interpersonal experience of organizational, marketplace, family, community or professional/occupational life.

Defining the Purpose of the Organization

Given increasing numbers of studies pointing to the importance of purpose and the cynicism noted by CMI that "fads" come and go, what might be the difference between values or purpose or mission and vision? If the five points in the CMI definition noted above need to be included in a purpose statement, then terms such as "maximize shareholder value", "to be best quality lowest cost provider of financial platforms" and "to be the best and be seen as the best in our industry" do not convey enough information to guide action. The purpose statement has to be meaningful – it tells everyone why an organization exists, but must also reveal some enduring identity that provides a guide for how decisions are made and how it might generate a sustainable future that motivates all stakeholders to believe in the organization (Ebert et al., 2018).

Defining Purpose in a Complex World

It is now common in the literature to see discussion of the world as more Volatile, Uncertain, Complex and Ambiguous (VUCA; see, for example, Giles, 2018). The increasing interest in ways to operate in these challenging times together with the increased consideration of purpose-led organizations (Hurst, 2014; Murray, 2017; O'Brien & Cave, 2017) has led to an emerging interest in complexity theory as a way to understand turbulence (Boulton et al., 2015). Lane and Down (2010) have argued that in turbulent times purpose provides a linking theme which enables the possibility of a rapid response to change as there is a higher value to guide decisions when events are uncertain. These themes are:

- The level of agreement on purpose: For an organization this encourages dialogue to find shared values to underpin and guide behaviour as in the case vignette (Box 5.1). For the individual in a coaching encounter, it enables exploration when faced with critical dilemmas to lift the conversation from short term goals to the persons core sense of self, others and their place in the world – what they want to be, not where they are now.
- The predictability of outcomes in pursuing goals to achieve that purpose: Thinking beyond short timescales for organizations and individuals helps to ensure we do keep the end in mind rather than become too distracted by immediate demands that drive out the focus on what really matters to us.
- The narratives people declare that focus on the end purpose: The stories provide a sense of where an organization is heading without the need for specific short-term goals.
- The interest in purpose, predictability of outcomes and narrative: This enables people to focus on how stories emerge from complex and turbulent contexts which lead to agreements around a new purpose.

How to define a shared concern (Lane, 1990) that reflects the integrity of the individual's purpose in the context in which they live or work and the organizational purpose is central to the process of formulating in coaching. Box 5.1 provides an example.

Box 5.1 Changing direction to stay true to a purpose

An entrepreneur, Silvana built a successful company in commodities trading. Her company was so successful that it was bought by a larger company and became a stand-alone division with the entire staff employed by the acquiring company. Initially, the take-over was successful and new business was secured. However, some tensions emerged between Silvana and the director of the acquiring company who had oversight of the division. The situation became even more difficult and was presented by the director as "Silvana's attitude problem in not understanding that she was part of a larger entity and no longer the Queen Bee". Silvana was referred for coaching.

Some initial discussion around the issues took place but it gradually emerged that she was unhappy in her new role not because she was no longer in charge but through a sense that the way the organization operated was not right. She also began to explore her relationship with the director. Conversations in the coaching about what she wanted to do with her life led her to realize that while she had set out to build a successful business and make money she was not satisfied and felt more was needed. Silvana tentatively started discussions with colleagues in the division who had joined with her and found similar concerns. She initiated a dialogue and it emerged that many colleagues felt a sense of loss caused by the change and they began to realize they had lost their sense of direction.

The dialogue gradually focused on the question of their purpose in being part of the organization. They realized they had never defined a shared purpose in the previous business but there was a latent feeling that they shared some underpinning values that were no longer apparent. They decided to try to create a narrative to express a sense of purpose. Out of many discussions between Silvana and her coach, and with her colleagues, that narrative emerged. They created a purpose that they then wanted to share with the wider organization to consider how to improve the business in a way that better served themselves, their customers and the larger organization. Their task became how to initiate those conversations.

For both Silvana and her colleagues the change represented a sense of loss but they were unable initially to define that experience. Gradually, through dialogue, a purpose emerged. The exploration enabled Silvana to consider the question, "What makes this worthwhile?" This led to further exploration with colleagues as to why that purpose was meaningful to her, the team, the organization, the community and society.

Defining Purpose to Explore the Work With Clients

Chapter 4 examined positionality and highlighted that individuals have multiple, fluid and overlapping identities that are contextually bound. As coach and client work together to define the purpose of the encounter, recognition of this intersectionality is important. The client may want to examine just one aspect of their life, such as in the case of a specific situation that they wish to address. Consequently, it will be necessary to understand how they see just that part of their experience; a fuller exploration of how they see the world will be unlikely as part of developing a formulation. The focus could be on the present and objectives for the future. If the situation they describe forms part of a pattern of relating to others, a deeper understanding might be sought. Hence, an exploration may necessarily include a sense of who they are and the origins and implications of that pattern for how they relate to self and others. The areas they wish to explore may involve fundamental and more complex challenges. In this case a more detailed exploration of how they see self, others and their position in the world is needed. Consideration could include how as a person they see and are seen and make meaningful connections between past, present and their sense of the future. Without this it will be difficult to develop a formulation that is comprehensive enough to enable change.

Similarly, for the coach the degree of separation between their own narrative of self as person and as a practitioner and that of the client in front of them will vary depending on whether they are working with a situation, pattern or the whole person/case (see Chapter 6). The more challenging and complex the issue, the more the coach will be drawing upon their own sense of self and being in the world.

When working with a straightforward, situationally based issue, it is possible for the encounter to be transactional in nature. Coach and client can agree the issue they will work on and how they will do so. Where the issue to be explored potentially challenges central aspects of a client's identity, aspects of coach's identity might also be challenged. The important task is one of the coach and client working together to build a relational narrative of how they see the work and the challenges they face. This helps to ensure an effective working alliance that can be sustained when faced with resistance or any ruptures along the way.

Building and maintaining this relational narrative will be enabled by the coach having developed an understanding of their own positionality and how they conceptualize their role as a practitioner. In seeking to define a purpose for the work, being able to find a shared concern to form the basis of a contract for the encounter matters and may not be simple. If the coach struggles to relate to the multiple intersecting identities of the client, or those identities challenge core elements of the coach's own way of being in the world, then it may be that they are not best suited to work with each other. Coach and client need to agree that the purpose of the work is one to which they both feel committed. Seeing the world differently does not make the work impossible. An effective working alliance can be built between diverse clients and coaches, but it cannot be taken for granted and will require ongoing reflection and attention to maintain it. The work of agreeing a shared concern to form the basis of the purpose of the encounter will inevitably engage the power relations within the contract they agree. Their own and their client's access to power and resources to enable their current and future options for change is part of how understanding of the purpose of the work emerges. This leads directly to a consideration of context.

As discussed previously, meaning-making does not develop in a cultural vacuum. The work to be undertaken will be influenced not just by what happens in the coaching session but by the relationships experienced day by day. An individual's context shapes their sense of self from infancy and the story of their life changes, or does not, to reflect the changing narratives of a particular culture and the individual's experience within it. Understanding the context for the work is part of defining the purpose agreed. This raises the question of the different ways we come to understand our self and the world and the narratives used to make sense of it.

There are a number of ways we build the narratives of our life and in particular how we construct stories to inform case formulation (Corrie & Lane, 2010). In thinking about purpose, specifically, three ideas are considered here. Bruner (1990) identified two primary modalities of cognitive functioning. One concerns abstract knowledge that enables us to solve practical problems using data and logic. Clients will draw upon this modality as they describe the concern they are bringing to coaching. However, Bruner also refers to another way of making sense of the world, the narrative, which is rich in context and idiosyncracies. The stories clients tell us as we seek to define our purpose in working together will be full of such narrative thinking. We have to pay attention to both, otherwise our understanding will be partial.

From the perspective of cognitive psychology, Teasdale and Barnard (1993) explored propositional and implicational levels of meaning. The former is concerned with ways of knowing that can be expressed in words and be evaluated as true or false. The implicational refers to more holistic ways of knowing. It is more difficult to express this sense, and certainly it cannot be done as if it were propositional knowledge. Lane and Corrie (2011) make the point that while therapy and related fields to include coaching have multiple ways of dealing with propositional levels of meaning, there is much less on the implicational. Use of imagery, art, vision, poetry, metaphor and dance provide potential ways into understanding the implicational level of meaning, but given that narration is the primary way people make sense of their world, attention to both levels is important in seeking to define the purpose for the work.

The idea that there are ways of communicating that can be described and explained and those that we are unable to describe and explain was explored by Rowe (2021). Similarly, Gendlin (1996) has talked about the latter as a felt sense. From the perspective of coaching Rowe (2021), and from the perspective of therapy Gendlin (1996), have both provided ways to work with this. When considering this in working to define the purpose of the work between client and coach it is important to pay attention to these different ways of understanding. The richer the narrative, the more informed will be the coach's understanding. However, that which cannot be expressed in words but only experienced as a felt sense cannot be ignored. It can be held but not described as the formulation emerges. The coach can validate the client's felt sense and ask them to hold that and return as the work proceeds as a way to reflect upon progress in working towards the achievement of the purpose. The client can check if movement is felt to be happening and the coach can value feedback on that sense as a way to know that the formulation arrived at seems appropriate as a narrative at the different levels of ways of knowing.

Purpose as a Shared Concern Arising From the Relational Narrative

Traditionally we think of professional practice as being in service of a client and based on a codified body of knowledge acquired through training and practised within a code of conduct controlled by an autonomous body. However, coaching is not a traditional practice. There are multiple associations, different codes and no agreed body of knowledge. Hence, what evidence can support such variety? How might we use the different ways of knowing discussed above to agree a viable purpose for the work with the client and in a way that we can justify as a professional practice? Should we be evidenced-based using propositional knowledge that can be tested or do we need to draw upon much richer ways of seeing to reflect the narrative the client brings? As we listen to the client's story and attempt to work with them to define the purpose of the work there are a number of questions that might be asked. It is not suggested that all of those questions listed below be asked, only those most relevant to the context:

1 As you listen to the client's story what do you want to find out to fully understand them to help define the purpose of the work?
2 How can you fully capitalize on existing skills and knowledge to understand different ways of knowing that might underpin the story the client wants to be able to tell?
3 What opportunities are available to notice different ways of knowing in the client's account?
4 What do you need to understand, in what format and from whom?
5 Given the account the client presents, are you in a position to influence and evaluate change (necessary to make the decision about whether you are the right person to be working with this person)?
6 How can you ensure that you are not unduly dependent on one source of knowing to make sense of the client's account?
7 What is your own position in relation to the purpose – why does it matter?
8 What is the position of the client in relation to the purpose – why does it matter to them?
9 What is the position of significant others in relation to the purpose – why does it matter to them?
10 What makes this meaningful and worthwhile as an encounter for the client, you as coach and others who may be impacted by the journey that enables you to justify this work as a viable practice in coaching?

In thinking about purpose, a number of supplementary questions arise.

• What is your fundamental purpose in being a coach?
• What is the purpose in working with this client question/concern at this time? Who is or needs to be involved and what are the expectations?
• What is the wider context that will influence the work and which gives it meaning?

This requires you to be reflexive: reflexivity is a key practice which includes self-criticism and alerts the individual to the human subjective processes involved in undertaking coaching.

Conclusion

As the coach and client work, together, they explore what matters to them both. They define the purpose of the encounter. This may be a relatively swift process or a lengthy procedure depending on the constellation of the key elements involved. These elements can include the theoretical approach of the practitioner, issues that arise in the management of the case, the stakeholders and how they define their engagement, and the type of agreement reached on the concerns to be explored. Each of these will influence and privilege the information they seek, their decision-making and the choices they make. An understanding of the factors that inform the coach's choice will inform the basis of the work that follows. Purpose is central to this decision and will help to ensure the approach to formulation is capable of dealing with the complexity of the work that may emerge.

Questions to Consider

Given that purpose is so central to understanding the work undertaken with the client, reflection both prior to and during coaching is critical to success.

- As a coach how do you help the client develop a sense purpose?
- How do you explore expectations of key stakeholders?
- How do you negotiate the role that each stakeholder will play?
- How do you explore the context for the coaching that generates meaning for the activity?
- What makes coaching a worthwhile activity for you?

Chapter 6

Formulation From an Individual Perspective

As will be evident from the previous chapters, a formulation can take many forms. The content and structure, as well as the way in which it is developed, will vary as a function of the positionality of the coach, the purpose for which it is constructed and the perspectives that are brought to bear on the issue in hand. The aim of this chapter is to focus on one particular perspective: the factors relating to the individual and how a coach might approach the task of formulation when developing an understanding of a client's needs through this lens. This chapter considers the types of information commonly sought when approaching formulation from an individual perspective and introduces Corrie and Kovács' (2019) Levels of Formulation as a guide to application. A case vignette illustrates the form that each of these levels might take, and guidance is provided on how to decide which level to use. The strengths and limitations of formulation from the individual perspective are also examined.

Formulation Approached Through an Individual Lens

Many of the theories that coaches use to inform their practice adopt what is essentially an individually focused approach to conceptualization and change. We term this stance the individual perspective. When working from the individual perspective, the source of understanding and change is located within the client themselves, and thus the formulation that underpins the approach taken will privilege internal experiences, such as thoughts, emotions and physical reactions, behavioural repertoires and relevant factors from the client's personal history, as well as their values, character strengths and the stories that the client holds about themselves and others (see Table 6.1). Working from this perspective will also include relevant external factors, such as relationships with others or wider environmental influences. However, these will be explored from the vantage point of the individual; that is, how these external factors might represent enabling factors and opportunities upon which the client might capitalize, or constraining factors that the client will need to decide how to manage or resolve.

The individual perspective has a long tradition within applied psychology (see Bruch, 2015, for a review) and remains a dominant perspective in the way in which approaches to change have emerged. Within the psychological professions, many

DOI: 10.4324/9781003174585-9

Table 6.1 Potential Areas of exploration when approaching Formulation from the
Individual Perspective

Category of exploration	Examples
1 Emotions	Mood states, specific feelings and general tendencies towards positive or negative affectivity.
2 Physical sensations	Particular, situation-specific sensations, levels of energy, fatigue or pain, general body state.
3 Cognitions	Situation-specific thoughts, assumptions, standards and rules for living as well as deeply held beliefs about self, others, relationships and life and the world in general. This also includes relevant mindsets and tendencies towards optimism and pessimism.
4 Cognitive processing	How the client tends to perceive and interpret the situations in which they find themselves; patterns in attentional or interpretive biases, as well as heuristics; attentional capability and the functioning of working memory and long-term memory. The influence of schema.
5 Behavioural repertoires	Typical action tendencies, adaptive and maladaptive, in specific situations as well as typical daily routines. Also, ways of coping such as efforts at creating a balanced life, including typical responses to everyday stressors and methods of relaxation as well as strategies used to manage more significant episodes of challenge, positive and negative, active and passive.
6 Strengths	Character strengths, areas of personal resilience, knowledge and skills, lessons acquired through life experience and personal values.
7 Personality	Traits and characteristics, where the client positions themselves within the so-called "Big Five" personality traits of openness to experience, conscientiousness, extraversion, agreeableness and neuroticism.
8 Resources	Resources at the personal, interpersonal and systemic levels that are potentially available to the client, and which might be utilized by them to enable desired changes.
9 Obstacles	Personal, interpersonal and systemic level factors that appear to represent obstacles to the individual exercising their personal resources or that undermine their attempts at actualizing themselves or their goals.
10 Aspirations	Intentions, hopes, goals, aims and vision that the client has for themselves, their life and career (if relevant), both short term and longer term.
11 Personal history	Key life events, character-defining moments or experiences. Also, perspectives on the world informed by cultural background, religion, family background and socioeconomic status, political factors and perhaps gender roles and identity.

(Continued)

Table 6.1 (Continued)

Category of exploration	Examples
12 Education	Learning history, educational experiences including attainment and the frustration of attainments. Also, any special education needs identified or missed in early life including neurodivergence.
13 Work history	Work and career history, experiences that were most and least rewarding for the client, challenges encountered in the workplace and how the client managed these, current stage of career and expectations of the future.
14 Life stage	Issues associated with life stage, including competing priorities and pressures arising from trying to balance work and family demands.
15 Relationships	History of relationships, past and present, experience of self in relation to others, as well as beliefs about others and relationships.
16 Health	Current health status at a general level, any diagnosed conditions (e.g. health conditions that might be relevant to the client's circumstances and needs and which might impact the content of coaching or how the coaching needs to be delivered).
17 Spirituality	Beliefs about what lies beyond this world; highest ideals and sense of connection to something beyond the individual self. The experience of being part of a religious or spiritual community if applicable.

of the approaches which claim an evidence-based status have been grounded in ways of working that privilege the individual perspective. Consider from within the field of clinical practice, for example, cognitive behaviour therapy (CBT), itself a broad family of therapies that collectively seek to help individuals achieve desired change in their lives through targeting profiles of thinking, feeling and behaviour. The many empirical studies and reviews of the literature that have endorsed the effectiveness of CBT (see Roth & Fonagy, 2005; Hofmann et al., 2012; David et al., 2018) have been used to determine national guidance, such as that provided by the National Institute of Health and Care Excellence concerning which interventions are effective for specific disorders and which should, therefore, be prioritized by commissioning bodies for the treatment of specific mental health problems.

Within coaching, approaches that privilege an individual perspective to formulation include cognitive and behavioural models, psychodynamic models, solution-focused models and narrative approaches, as well as compassion-focused approaches and acceptance and commitment therapy (ACT). At its most beneficial, a coaching formulation constructed from the individual perspective yields a detailed understanding of the client's experience that can be used to design an intervention that is likely to map onto the client's needs and aspirations for change.

Content Areas of Relevance to the Individual Perspective

When working from the individual perspective, a wide variety of content areas are likely to be of interest and represent valid areas for discussion. Depending on the coach's prior training, experience, confidence and emerging hypotheses about a client's needs, areas of exploration that are likely to inform the development of a formulation include (but are not limited to) the following (see Table 6.1).

The areas of exploration summarized in Table 6.1 are not offered as a checklist of items that must be covered in order to arrive at a comprehensive formulation, but rather as areas that are useful to hold in mind as avenues of potential exploration. Those areas that a coach and client choose to explore together will depend upon a variety of factors, including what is experienced as most pressing or significant by the client and also the coach's own positionality. As noted in Chapter 4, no area selected for exploration can be understood in a truly impartial way but will always be interpreted through the concepts, theoretical principles, models and general worldviews which reflect the preferences of the coach as well as those of the client. For example, the relevance and impact of specific cognitions and cognitive processing will be conceptualized differently when delivering cognitive behaviour coaching as opposed to when working within narrative or psychodynamic frameworks. Equally, repertoires of action and inaction on the client's part will be understood differently when interpreted through a behavioural lens as opposed to a solution-focused approach.

Thus, while different domains of a client's experience enable the coach and client to begin the task of identifying areas of relevance, the ways in which these experiences are identified, interpreted and addressed as part of any coaching intervention cannot be considered in isolation from the range of perspectival lenses that the coach and client have available to them. In this context, the individual perspectival lenses selected might include the following:

- Specific coaching theories and/or models that inform the coach's thinking
- Theories, models, constructs and principles drawn from literature indirectly related to coaching, such as those from applied psychology, leadership and management, and neuroscience
- Data from a variety of assessment tools (which themselves will be informed by specific theories, models, perspectives or coaching approaches), including psychometric and other 'diagnostic' tools
- Observational tools
- Knowledge of relevant research that addresses questions of theoretical, conceptual and practice-based significance to coaching as well as the evidence base relating to coaching outcomes
- The coach's prior experience of what has been more and less helpful in working with clients with similar issues
- The coach's ability to listen to the client's self-told story, identify relevant narrative threads and extract central themes for the purpose of hypothesis testing
- The client's domain-specific (i.e. context-specific and discipline-specific) expertise

Levels and Types of Formulation From the Individual Perspective

Depending on the agreed focus of the coaching and the theories and models that are privileged, it is possible to approach formulation using the individual perspective at different levels. From an adjacent perspective in the clinical field, Corrie et al. (2016) have distinguished four types of commonly used formulations, which, in a slightly adapted form, are also highly relevant to coaching. These are: (1) the generic models, largely used to construct a detailed description of a particular dilemma; (2) the problem-specific models, which offer an in-depth understanding of a specific area of concern; (3) the transdiagnostic approaches, which seek to identify factors that are relevant to and common across areas of concern; and (4) the multidimensional models, which prioritize a search for interactions between multiple factors in the onset, development and maintenance of the client's primary concern over time.

In coaching, an equivalent approach has been offered by Corrie and Kovács (2017, 2019, 2021) and Kovács & Corrie (2021) who propose that approaches to formulation can be understood as ranging on a perspectival continuum from the micro to the macro. While a micro formulation will be concerned with a specific need as might be the case when a client requests coaching for a focal area of concern, the macro perspective is concerned with developing a broader perspective that is likely to take account of a wide variety of factors that impact the client and their coaching needs. Thus, at the micro end of the continuum, the focus is on a specific situation. Moving towards the middle part of the continuum, the meso level, the emphasis will be on patterns, themes and trends in the client's experience that are identified as worthy of consideration. Finally, the coach may take a more macro perspective, choosing a person/case level formulation where a broad range of individual or systemic factors may have relevance (see Figure 6.1).

Regardless of any preferred theoretical orientation, Corrie and Kovács (2019) advocate that coaches always need to make a choice about whether to begin formulation at the level of the situation, pattern or person/case. Each of these levels provides a unique vantage point from which to explore the issue of concern and will yield different forms of information and lead to the design of different types of intervention. To illustrate these perspectival differences, Corrie and Kovács (2019) use the metaphor of a rice farmer assessing the health, output and possible future of

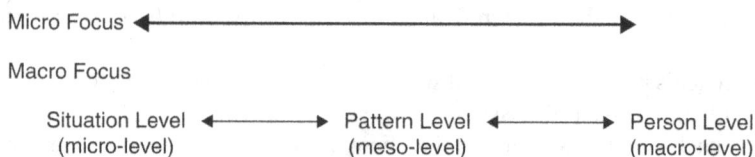

Figure 6.1 Corrie and Kovács' (2019) Levels of Formulation

Box 6.1   Case vignette – Li Jing

Li Jing works for a Western multinational with approximately 3,000 employees. Aged 30, Li Jing is Chinese-Singaporean and transferred to London on completion of her MBA a year ago. She has worked in the organization's finance team for eight years and is currently leading a team of 15 people.

Li Jing has been selected for coaching as part of the organization's talent programme, which aims to develop a diverse talent pipeline for senior leadership positions. She has been assessed as having high potential and has been assigned a coach to assist her with her development. No specific goals have been proposed by the organizational sponsors.

The coaching programme is to consist of eight sessions over six months, with a three-way conversation scheduled with Li Jing's manager after the first session and at the end.

Although the coaching agenda is open, Li Jing expresses concerns about her ability to deliver a forthcoming presentation to the executive leadership team (whom she is hoping to impress). In particular, she finds herself procrastinating on her preparation and time is running out. She asks if you could work with her on addressing her procrastination in the context of this pressing commitment before you consider any other coaching goals.

---

his rice field. How this metaphor might be applied to coaching is illustrated below using the case vignette of Li Jing (see Box 6.1).

Formulation at the Level of the Situation (the Micro Perspective)

For the purposes of the metaphor, if the (imaginary) rice farmer was to approach formulating the health and yield of their rice field from a micro perspective, they would direct attention to an individual rice plant. This perspective enables them to ascertain whether this single plant is thriving or withering and to identify potential reasons for this occurrence. The farmer's focus may be one of addressing the needs of that rice plant in isolation, or as part of a broader process of detecting patterns such as the extent to which this single plant is typical of the apparent experience of other rice plants in the field; that is, a detailed analysis of the needs of a single plant might be used to generalize conclusions to the needs of the other plants in the field.

Applying the analogy to coaching, the micro lens enables a detailed focus on the minutiae of any specific situation of interest, including specific emotions, physical sensations and cognitions and their connections to subsequent action. An example of this is provided in Figure 6.2.

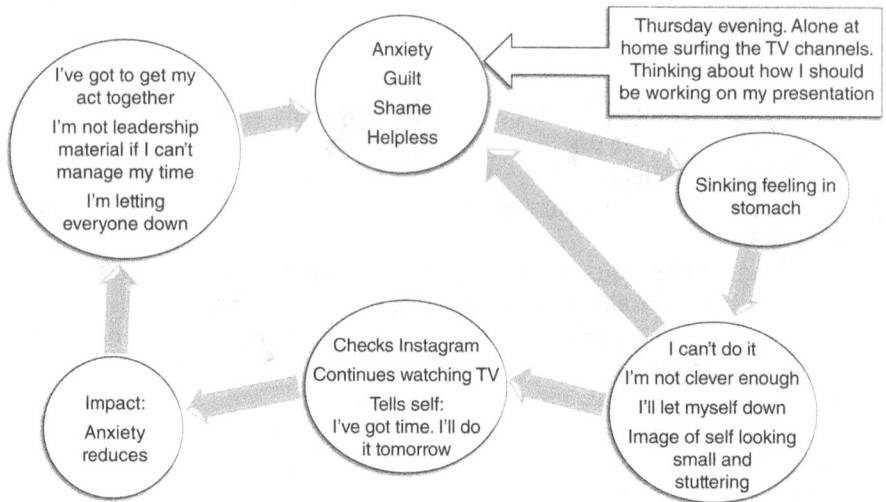

Figure 6.2 Formulating Li Jing's procrastination at the situation (micro) level

Working at the micro level can be particularly useful where: (1) there is a specific situation that warrants scrutiny; (2) the client's coaching goals can be optimally met through exploring and intervening in a specific situation such as a forthcoming event; and (3) the coach and client believe that the factors that are maintaining an issue in the here and now, or which need to be enabled for the client to achieve their goals are not the same factors that led to the development of an issue initially. A situation level formulation might also be preferred where those factors that are of immediate relevance are embedded within specific situations that can themselves be improved or modified in some way that is advantageous to the client. In essence, a formulation at the micro level enables a detailed analysis of the factors of influence that can themselves be the target of change.

In order to work at this level, the client needs to be in a position to recall specific and recent examples of the situation of interest. Alternatively, if the situation concerns a future event, then what is necessary is the ability of the client to anticipate the factors that are likely to be influential in creating a problematic and desired outcome. Examples of requests for coaching that might lend themselves well to a formulation at the situation level include the following:

- Where a client wishes to prepare for a forthcoming internal job interview that would lead to a desired promotion (a specific event)
- Where a client seeks help in preparing for a forthcoming presentation to key stakeholders (a specific event)
- Where a client is procrastinating on revising for a forthcoming exam for a professional qualification (recent, specific instances of procrastination in relation to

this event can be identified and there is a clear future event towards which the client wishes to work)

- Where a client is wanting to prepare for a difficult meeting with a direct report in which a performance issue has been identified (there is a clear future event which the client wishes to explore)
- Where a client wants help in negotiating a pay rise or challenging the outcome of their performance review (there is a specific desired outcome with identifiable factors that need to be considered in order to achieve the goal)
- Where a client wishes to analyse, in detail, a recent situation or event that did or did not have the desired outcome to see what might be learned (a recent, specific event can be mined for information that might yield beneficial learning for the future).

Working at the micro level, Li Jing and her coach construct the following visual formulation of the factors that appear implicated in triggering and maintaining her procrastination (see Figure 6.2).

Formulation at the Level of the Pattern (the Meso Perspective)

If the (imaginary) rice farmer introduced above was to approach formulating the health, yield and future of their rice field from a meso perspective, they would be interested in identifying broader themes, patterns or tendencies that can inform their decision-making. Here, the focus may be on the relative health of the rice plants in their entirety and how to ensure that the rice field can be planted and harvested in ways that ensure an optimum yield. Questions to guide the exploration might include, how does the farmer get the most from this particular rice field and what might support or inhibit its productivity? If the field is sub-optimal in its yield, is this because of overplanting, poor harvesting or other factors as yet unidentified?

Applying the analogy to coaching, the coach may decide that rather than look at a single situation, or a series of separate, sequential situations, the most productive focus would be to identify and explore similar reactions that the client exhibits across contexts. Patterns explored may take the form of repertoires of responding that have been proved beneficial in the past and which a client could usefully capitalize upon and generalize to the current area of concern. Alternatively, the patterns explored might identify ineffective patterns of response that would benefit from modification as they prevent the client from achieving the goals of the coaching contract and may result in future difficulties. Thus, at this meso level, the coach would seek to uncover themes within the client's emotional or physical state, recurrent patterns of mindset, thoughts and ways of processing information, behavioural repertoires (active and passive), including methods of coping, character strengths and recurring themes in relationships.

Working at the meso or pattern level can be particularly useful where the client experiences similar types of challenges that span situations or time. Equally, this level of formulation is beneficial where a client has been able to achieve desired outcomes in the past or where they have performed at a consistently high level as these occurrences suggest the influence of more enduring positive patterns of thinking, feeling and action that, if identified, might be utilized for the purposes of pursuing current goals.

In order to work at this level, the client needs to be in a position to recall and reflect upon situations in the past that were consistent in terms of what was experienced, or the outcomes obtained, and to be open to exploring their own contribution to what occurred. Working at the pattern level can also illuminate missing skillsets, as well as overdeveloped or underdeveloped repertoires of coping that might themselves represent a valid focus of the coaching contract. For example, procrastination when it is an engrained response can reflect a fear of failure, a fear of negative evaluation, the inability to plan effectively or a use of experiential avoidance (i.e. engaging in maladaptive actions to avoid experiencing aversive internal states such as unpleasant thoughts or uncomfortable emotions or physical sensations). Examples of client issues that might lend themselves well to a formulation at the pattern level include the following:

- Where a client appears to hold unrealistic or otherwise unhelpful standards or assumptions or has rules for living that seem to be undermining their progress towards a desirable outcome and/or that others are finding problematic
- Where a client has perfectionistic tendencies that are impacting their quality of life and professional performance
- Where a client has a history of unhelpful reactions to setbacks or perceived failures
- Where a client engages in repeated repertoires of behaviour that undermine their efforts to achieve their goals
- Where a client is engaging in behaviours that appear to have a compulsive element to them (e.g. an unhealthy pursuit of physical fitness in the form of excessive exercise with a related difficulty in coping with low levels of stimulation)
- Where procrastination is an engrained response to multiple situations
- Where the client has difficulties regulating their emotions in particular types of situations or with particular types of people
- Where a client is experiencing consistently high stress levels
- Where a client experiences high, maladaptive levels of anxiety in the presence of particular kinds of people (e.g. perceived authority figures)
- Where a client has patterns of attitude and behaviour that have been positively utilized to bring about past successes and which might be drawn upon to address the current aims of coaching
- Where a client notices a tendency for others to react to them in a particular, undesired way and does not understand why

Returning to the case vignette, through exploration in the coaching sessions, supported by some between-session assignments, Li Jing and her coach identified the following patterns and themes that they hypothesized were implicated in increasing

- Procrastination has been a significant issue for me since adolescence.
- When I look back over my life, I realize that my procrastination is usually driven by fear of making a mistake.
  - I operate according to the rule that "It's better to be safe than sorry".
- I don't think my procrastination is linked with problems with motivation or missing life skills such as underdeveloped planning and time management. I have a track record at work that suggests I am good at these things.
- My procrastination only really happens at work.
- I tend to procrastinate when the outcome is important to me or when the stakes are high such as when there is the chance for me to impress the senior leadership team and I tell myself that it's important I get it right.
- Over the course of my life, I now realize that I have acquired and conduct myself according to the following rules for living which I have never truly examined. These rules are:
  - I must always appear capable and intelligent to be liked.
  - I must always appear capable and intelligent to do well.
  - I must always show respect to senior people.
  - I must defer in my judgement to those more senior than myself or else I might upset them.
  - If I make a mistake, people senior to me will think badly of me.
  - If I make a mistake, it means I have failed.
- At times I can fall into using patterns of avoidant coping, burying my head in the sand when I feel anxious about what is to come and my ability to deliver.

Figure 6.3 Formulating Li Jing's procrastination at the pattern (meso) level

the likelihood of episodes of procrastination in the here and now. Although collaboratively constructed, the patterns are captured in Li Jing's own words to encourage her ownership of the process and the themes identified (see Figure 6.3).

Formulation at the Level of the Person or the Case (the Macro Perspective)

Finally, there is the option of approaching formulation from the macro perspective – that is, the perspective of the person in their entirety (or the case as a whole taking into account broader systemic factors, depending on the coaching context). This requires a holistic understanding of the client, their circumstances and personal history, and the range of systems in which they are embedded. This broader and deeper level of formulation may draw on relevant theories of life stage development (e.g. Kegan & Lahey, 2009) to help conceptualize a client's current priorities as well as, where necessary, identifying and formulating the impact of significant existential questions relating to life purpose, what is authentically meaningful and what is possible in the context of advancing years.

Returning once more to the analogy of the rice farmer, the macro perspective entails a focus on the rice field in its broader context, that is, as a case. Here, the health and yield of the rice field is considered in terms of its relationship to the farmer (e.g. whether the farmer depends on the field for income, whether the field has personal significance to them as a family-owned business for several generations and whether the field has tended to yield a high, low or inconsistent quality product). From this perspective, its relevance to the local community might also be considered. For example, does the field enable the local community to feed their families? Does the employment provided by the farmer form a vital part of the local economy? If so, are these priority considerations for the farmer? The macro perspective also takes account of the wider contexts that are of relevance to the future of the rice field: is there a high level of sustained market demand for the product? Is there significant competition emerging? Would there be any benefits – personally and for the community – of selling the field to a property developer who wishes to build a luxury hotel in the area? The farmer will need to identify those factors that will be most impactful in making a decision about the future of the field in light of their priority outcomes.

In the context of coaching, working at the level of the person entails developing a detailed, longitudinal formulation of the client's background, their personal and professional history in context and how these relate to the client's current circumstances and the aims of coaching. At the level of the case this would additionally include the broader context and stakeholders that need to be considered. This would potentially entail an exploration of any or all of the areas identified in Table 6.1 depending on the hypotheses that coach and client were developing and interested in testing. Figure 6.4 illustrates Li Jing at the whole-person level.

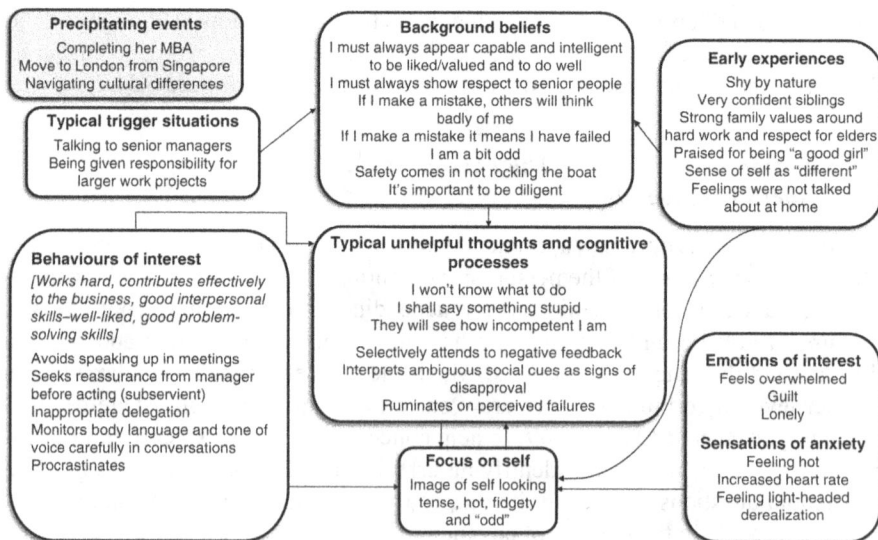

Figure 6.4 Formulating Li Jing's needs at the person (macro) level

Considerations When Deciding Which Level of Formulation to Use

Each level of formulation, situation (micro), pattern (meso) and person (macro) affords the coach and client particular benefits and operates within specific constraints. For example, the situation level remains closely tied to the data collected and therefore enables a detailed analysis of relevant factors that can afford a high degree of accuracy. Nonetheless, by definition, it considers situations in relative isolation from their broader context and thus relies on a potentially limited dataset. Constraining the range of data drawn upon can be helpful if the coaching contract is brief, where the coaching is organized around a SMART goal (Doran et al., 1981) and where the range of factors of influence are easily identifiable. However, it will be less useful if the coach and client suspect that underpinning the client's current needs are recurring themes that can either be drawn upon to enable growth or will likely represent obstacles to growth.

Working at the pattern level enables greater depth of perspective, supporting a process of identifying themes that are potentially central to the client's sense of identity and self-worth. However, working at this deeper level can involve greater perceived risk-taking as the client is encouraged to consider embedded ways of relating to self and others that have enabled them to survive in the world thus far. As such, this requires a greater level of self-awareness and ability for reflexive and reflective thinking than is required of formulation at the situation level. It may also require a greater level of sensitivity and tact on the part of the coach.

Working at the level of the person or case has the potential to identify a very rich dataset upon which to base the design of a coaching intervention. Yet it can also take time and is more effortful to develop as the coach may use a wide range of methods of data gathering. The benefits of investing the time and energy that are needed must be considered alongside what will be most useful for the client in light of both the coaching contract and any practical constraints; formulation at this level requires a consideration of the balance between depth and efficiency. This is important to hold in mind as working at the person level can hamper the identification of a clear coaching focus (there are, after all, many possible points of intervention). Deciding on what is possible to change is a necessary consideration, and the formulation may uncover more areas of potential concern for a client than the coaching could ever hope to address.

Finally, working at this level requires considerable clarity of thinking and decision-making as there may be occasions when a coach feels compelled to enquire about areas whose relevance may not be obvious to the client and which could be experienced as a boundary violation. Working at the level of the person does not give the coach permission to go on an unfocused meandering through the client's personal history and so the ethics of exploring different areas of a client's life need to be considered.

When the Individual Perspective Might Be More or Less Optimal

As noted in earlier chapters, there is no single, correct approach to formulation and no "one size fits all" solution. Rather, each perspective offers just one lens on the client's needs which then enables a specific type of journey. Understanding the strengths and limits of each perspective enables a coach to make an informed decision about which approach to use (and why) with each individual client. As a guide, however, the individual perspective is most likely to be useful when:

- The main issue of concern for the client is clearly defined and easy to operationalize
- The main factors of relevance appear to be directly under the client's influence or control
- There is an established theory or knowledge base that provides a compelling reason for working from an individual perspective (e.g. there is an empirically supported intervention available for the particular issue that the client wishes to address)
- The focus of the coaching contract entails a consideration of specific factors in the client's current functioning
- The focus of the coaching contract entails a consideration of specific factors in the client's personal history that are relevant to making changes (as in the case vignette in this chapter)
- The client's concerns have been present across time and context, even where interpersonal and systemic factors have changed over time
- The issue of concern is not occurring in contexts that are so complex that a systemic perspective is essential to inform the approach taken
- Issues are relatively static and stable as opposed to circumstances that are couched with complex environments or situations that are rapidly changing

Some of the advantages of using an individual perspective for formulation are as follows:

- It offers an account of the client and their circumstances and needs that can promote self-awareness and self-knowledge that is not only relevant to the current coaching but has potential implications for choices in the future.
- This type of formulation can facilitate a sense of agency for the client that is experienced as highly empowering.
- It locates the journey of change within factors that are potentially under the influence of the client, which can promote a sense of agency and personal control.
- It provides a degree of clarity on relevant factors that enables a clear sense of direction and focus for the work that is to take place.
- The factors of influence are potentially more amenable to intervention than other levels (e.g. interpersonal and systemic factors; see Chapters 7 and 8).

- There is a wide range of theories, models and approaches that the coach can draw upon to support their decision-making and intervention planning.

Potential disadvantages of using the individual perspective for formulation, in comparison with interpersonal and systemic perspectives, are that:

- This perspective locates the issue of concern and its resolution in the individual. While factors in the wider context are likely to be identified, this perspective does not provide a means of conceptualizing these issues directly or of designing an intervention that targets them.
- The individual perspective does not provide an easy route into formulating factors of relevance and interest beyond the individual. As noted above, the individual perspective does not ignore interpersonal and systemic factors, but they are seen through the prism of the individual client's needs, resources and capabilities which will limit the extent of focus on interpersonal and systemic factors.
- It may be of limited value for coaching in contexts of complexity.
- It is most useful when seeking to understand factors that are relatively stable and static and might be less relevant and helpful in understanding the factors of influence in situations that are rapidly changing.

Conclusion

This chapter has examined one specific approach to formulation, namely, formulation based on the individual perspective. Approaches to formulation from this perspective can be understood as ranging on a perspectival continuum from the micro to the macro and can operate at different levels: the situation, the pattern and the person. A case vignette has provided an illustration of some of the different forms that this can take, and the strengths and limitations of formulation from the individual perspective have been reviewed to help the reader reflect upon and better understand the relevance and value of this perspective to their own coaching practice. The individual perspective has traditionally been dominant in coaching practice generally and in relation to formulation specifically. However, alongside this perspective, interpersonal and systemic perspectives have also emerged and offer significant benefits for making sense of clients' needs. The interpersonal and systemic perspectives are, therefore, the subject of the next chapters.

Questions to Consider

Having read this chapter, consider what emerges in relation to your own practice. For the purposes of formulation, you may find it helpful to consider the following questions:

- To what extent is your positionality (see Chapter 4) consistent with an individual perspective in your work with clients?

- To what extent are your preferred coaching approaches (theories or models) anchored within an individual perspective as outlined in this chapter, or would they be more consistent with an interpersonal (Chapter 7) or systemic (Chapter 8) perspective?
- Of the potential areas of exploration described in Table 6.1, which feature – always, frequently, rarely or never in your own explorations with clients? What is the rationale for your choice? Are there any areas that you might like to experiment with exploring more explicitly in your coaching practice?
- Select a client with whom you are currently working or have recently worked. Consider how you have attempted to make sense of their needs – did you broadly adopt a situation, pattern or person-level approach to formulation? What were the implications of your choice for the work that followed?

Chapter 7

Formulation From an Interpersonal Perspective

Individuals are embedded in relationships. While many of the dominant perspectives in coaching originate from the individual perspective that was introduced in Chapter 6, most forms of coaching will include at least a consideration of the interpersonal contexts in which a client's actions occur and in which their needs are embedded. Indeed, this perspective is consistent with the many ways in which coaching is now delivered. For example, as group and team coaching have emerged as major areas of activity, ideas from decision-making in teams have become influential and group and team process research has informed the way that change can happen in an interpersonal space (see Chapter 13). These developments point to a recognition that the behaviour of any individual cannot be adequately understood without appreciating the contexts in which that behaviour occurs and the importance, in Gestalt terms, of adopting a "field perspective".

This chapter explores some of the factors that are important when approaching formulation from an interpersonal perspective. The chapter begins by positioning coaching itself as a relational encounter. The impact of relationships on human experience, wellbeing and functioning is then examined. This provides the basis for understanding the impact of the coaching relationship on coaching outcomes. Some specific theoretically and culturally informed ways of making sense of the interpersonal factors that shape how coaching unfolds are considered. Finally, the chapter provides suggestions for when an interpersonal perspective might be beneficial for formulation to enable the reader to reflect upon the relevance and value of this perspective for their own practice.

The Case for Coaching as an Interpersonal Encounter

Coaching typically takes the form of an interpersonal encounter between a coach and a client. A significant amount of the client's learning and development is embedded in and enabled by a relationship that is genuine, supportive and adaptive. Coaches cannot control outcomes, but they can influence the process through agreeing a contract of aims and objectives, adopting a focused but flexible and responsive approach and ensuring that empathy, authenticity and validation of the client's worldview lie at the heart of the work. Where relevant, an interpersonal

DOI: 10.4324/9781003174585-10

focus also entails conceptualizing and addressing any interpersonal challenges that arise, including ruptures. Coaching, then, can be understood as a relational change process.

The value of conceptualizing coaching as an interpersonal encounter becomes clear when considered alongside the evidence pertaining to the impact of relationships on personal and professional life more broadly. There is convincing evidence for the fact that relationships are of central importance to all aspects of life, wellbeing and functioning. Human beings are social animals and throughout their lives will occupy a variety of social and occupational roles that are lived out in and through relationships with others. Opportunities to create meaningful and rewarding relationships are, therefore, vital to a rewarding life for many (Baucom et al., 2020).

Relationships not only add to the quality of our lives but also serve vital survival and developmental functions. Much of our social and cognitive development occurs through relationships with others who facilitate learning and socialize us into the norms of our culture and communities. The quality and experience of our early relationships are also the basis for a secure sense of self. We learn about ourselves and our sense of worth through the reactions of those close to us and it has been consistently evidenced that those unable to form secure and reliable attachments are more prone to psychopathology in childhood and adulthood (Dagan et al., 2022; Madigan et al., 2016).

Healthy and secure relationships contribute to health, happiness and longevity, and provide psychological and emotional protection against the challenges of life (Shafran, 2020). Conversely, relationship distress is associated with negative outcomes for both physical and mental health (Baucom et al., 2017; Markman et al., 2010; Sandberg et al., 2012; Whisman & Bruce, 1999; Whisman & Uebelacker, 2009), with relationship distress having direct, negative effects on individuals' cardiovascular, endocrine, immune and neurosensory systems (Guan & Bingxue, 2013; Kiecolt-Glaser & Newton, 2001).

Couple satisfaction has also been shown to predict work satisfaction (Sandberg et al., 2012) and the link between relationships and wellbeing also extends to the workplace. Moreover, in the workplace, positive working relationships have been shown to promote employee wellbeing (Day et al., 2016; Gehlert et al., 2013). There is evidence of a relationship between leader behaviour and employee behaviour and performance (Judge & Piccolo, 2004; Lai et al., 2020; Nielsen et al., 2018) and wellbeing and safety in organizations (Kelloway & Barling, 2010). Leader behaviours and leadership styles along with the relationship between leaders and their employees have also been associated with employee stress and emotional wellbeing (Skakon et al., 2010).

There is, therefore, a good rationale for positioning coaching as a relational change process, a perspective that is evident in the expanding literature investigating a diverse range of interpersonal phenomena and their impact on both the process and outcome of coaching. This literature includes studies that have examined connections between the coaching relationship and coaching outcomes (e.g. De Haan et al., 2013, 2016, 2020; Erdös et al., 2021; Gessnitzer & Kauffeld, 2015;

Molyn et al., 2022); the impact of client and coach characteristics including matching factors (Gehlert et al., 2013; Law et al., 2007); the impact of the self and self-awareness of the coach (Bachkirova, 2016; Corrie & Kovács, 2021); and the use of "critical moments" in the coaching relationship (Cox & Bachkirova, 2007; Day et al., 2008; De Haan et al., 2010).

Additionally, clients' aspirations, needs and contexts as well as the expectations of other stakeholders are now widely recognized as emerging within a landscape of interdependencies. The development of relationship coaching, team-based coaching and coaching interventions aimed at large-scale organizational change have all necessitated approaches to working that are sensitive to the interpersonal characteristics and processes which increasingly shape how we all live and work. Within this context, being able to devise formulations from an interpersonal perspective is an important capability of the effective coach.

Although the case for conceptualizing coaching as an interpersonal encounter might be compelling, the ways in which the relational domain are understood are multiple and diverse. This is not surprising when it is considered that the definition, nature and scope of coaching itself remain contested (O'Broin & Palmer, 2019). Thus, while the interpersonal can be framed at a very broad level, referring to complex and multiple interdependencies at the systems level (explored in Chapter 8), or more tightly framed in relation to team functioning (see Chapter 13), it also takes the form of more local and personal, dyadic relationships that are central to the client's life, such as a relationship with a line manager, business partner or life partner. Additionally, as the coach–client dyad is central to most forms of coaching even in the context of team coaching (Egan & Hamlin, 2014), the interpersonal domain of interest might be defined in terms of the rapport, connection and relative alignment of characteristics and style between coach and client that inform the reciprocal exchanges that occur. When considering formulation from an interpersonal perspective, then, relevant questions become:

- Who is the "us" to which this coaching assignment needs to attend?
- Whose perspectives are to be included and privileged in the work that takes place:
  - The coach and client alone?
  - The client's line manager?
  - The client's life partner?
  - The client's organizational sponsor?
  - The views of the team/s, which the client leads or participates in?
  - The views of additional stakeholders internal or external to any organization that has commissioned the coaching?
- Who has a role in determining the focus of coaching and any goals agreed?
- How is the agreed purpose of the work most likely to be achieved? Is it through:
  - Privileging the emerging story co-constructed through the interpersonal process that unfolds as the coach and client work together?

- Examining the relationship between the client and other invested parties such as a life partner or line manager?
- Adopting a team or group perspective?

When undertaking formulation using this perspective the interpersonal is not, therefore, predetermined but needs to be defined. For the purposes of this chapter, we focus primarily on the most discrete relational "unit" that the coach can use as the basis for a formulation, namely, the relationship between coach and client.

The Coaching Relationship and Coaching Outcomes

As noted by Egan and Hamlin (2014), despite ongoing debates as to whether coaching can claim a unique professional identity or a distinct knowledge base and methods of practice, coaching has been identified as offering a level of "developmental richness" (p. 244) that other forms of performance enhancement do not offer. They hypothesize that the growing popularity of coaching is likely due to the uniquely tailored opportunity for growth that the coaching relationship provides. Yet, a comprehensive understanding of the coaching relationship across clients, formats and models of coaching remains elusive (O'Broin & Palmer, 2019). According to Peterson (2011), a positive coaching relationship is "characterised by trust, acceptance, understanding, open, honest communication, and other interpersonal factors that support learning and development" (p. 537). Nonetheless, approaching formulation from an interpersonal perspective raises many questions as the coaching relationship comprises a range of interpersonal factors that may exert differential effects on the process of coaching and the outcomes obtained.

Given the variety of organizational, professional and personal contexts in which coaching is delivered, the expanding models employed alongside the diverse views of coaching as a skills-based, performance enhancement, developmental or transformation-focused intervention, it is perhaps unsurprising that there is a lack of consensual understanding concerning the precise nature of the coaching relationship, its role in the coaching process and the way in which it can leverage positive outcomes for clients. Nonetheless, from the 1990s onwards, there has been a growing awareness of the impact of the coaching relationship on both coaching process and outcomes and, accordingly, research examining the coach–client relationship has emerged as a distinct area of scholarly interest.

There is reliable evidence to suggest that the effectiveness of coaching is significantly impacted by the quality of the relationship established between coach and client (Baron & Morin, 2009; Boyce et al., 2010; De Haan et al., 2011; Turner & Goodrich, 2010; Wasylyshyn, 2003). Indeed, an early study conducted by McGovern et al. (2001) found that in 84% of their participant sample, the relationship was reported by clients as central to the success of their coaching. Similarly, previous studies, summarized in Graßmann et al.'s (2020) meta-analysis, have consistently demonstrated that the coaching relationship impacts coaching outcomes, at least when measured by the Working Alliance Inventory (Horvath & Greenberg, 1989).

Resonant with Cox and Bachkirova's (2007) view that, "It is the coach as a person, rather than the application of particular techniques or methods, that makes a difference in coaching practice" (p. 141), De Haan et al. (2011) proposed that a positive working relationship is likely to be of greater significance to coaching outcomes than any specific technique or method. In their study of 71 executive clients shortly after starting coaching, and 31 of that same sample six months later, De Haan et al. (2011, 2020) found that clients identified the relationship and the interpersonal qualities of the coach as being central in determining the helpfulness of coaching. This led De Haan et al. (2020) to conclude that the main predictor of effectiveness is the coaching relationship as experienced by the client. Nonetheless, in a more recent review De Haan and Nilsson (2023) modified this position. It seems that while the relationship has an overall impact, session by session it does not determine outcome. The way the working alliance is structured session by session may therefore need further consideration and involve more subtle forms of influence than any simple, direct connection between relationship and outcome. However, the research reviewed by De Haan and colleagues makes clear that investing effort in developing the relationship adds significant value.

In complementary fashion, negative working relationships are likely to predict unsatisfactory outcomes (Thompson et al., 2008). In their analysis of negative coaching outcomes in academic institutions and industry, Gehlert et al. (2013) identified one factor of influence as a sub-optimal pairing of the coach and client. This appeared to echo the earlier work of Jarvis et al. (2006) and Thompson et al. (2008) who found that 65 per cent of those who ended their coaching prematurely did so because of the client's perceived mismatch between themselves and their coach. Effective coach–client matching has also been shown to enable the development of a strong relational connection that is conducive to coaching and is most likely to be achieved through ensuring complementary personalities and interpersonal styles, as well as additional characteristics such as experience, the coach's abilities to meet the client's needs and coach credibility (Boyce et al., 2010).

Different elements of the coaching relationship may exert varying levels of impact. In his exploratory study of 49 coaching dyads, for example, Grant (2013) examined which of four elements of the coaching relationship were most associated with measures of coaching success: (1) autonomy support; (2) the extent of client satisfaction with the coach–client relationship; (3) the extent to which the coaching relationship was similar to an "ideal" coach–client relationship; and (4) a goal-focused coach–client relationship. His results found that client satisfaction with the relationship did not predict successful outcomes but that positive outcomes were moderately predicted by autonomy support and proximity to an ideal relationship. However, the strongest predictor of positive coaching outcomes was a working relationship that was goal-focused. Grant (2013) concludes that his findings draw attention to the crucial importance of goals as an aid to the coaching process. He also highlights the crucial point that the coaching relationship is not a single phenomenon and that different aspects of the relationship are more influential than others on the coaching outcomes obtained. This may explain some of the more recent findings of De Haan et al. (2023) described above.

Schema-Focused Approaches and Helping Roles

When using an interpersonal perspective for the purposes of developing formulations, a major contributing factor is the ability to reflect on interactions through a dyadic lens. In the context of an effective coaching relationship, this dyadic lens enables both parties to consider how the multifaceted, dynamic process between coach and client is unfolding in ways that are creating a strong relationship. Where a conversation or relationship is not unfolding as hoped or expected, adopting a dyadic lens can support a stance of curiosity in both parties and prevent any tendency to locate the "problem" in one individual who is then judged as needing to change. For example, a session that is experienced by the client as sub-optimal can be interpreted as the poor performance of the coach on that day ("He couldn't seem to find the right questions to ask me in this session"), more generally ("I'm not sure how good a coach he is"), the self on that day ("I was distracted so I couldn't get the best out of the session") or more generally ("I am not smart enough to get what he was encouraging me to explore"). Alternatively, it could be conceptualized dyadically ("That coaching session was not as helpful as the others I have had. I found it tricky to express what I needed today. It is possible that my lack of clarity confused my coach who then struggled to know how to respond so we ended up in a conversation that did not seem that productive").

The ability to think in relational terms, also termed relationship schematic processing (Baucom et al., 2020), is a critical component of effective relationships. Moreover, enhancing the capability for relationship schematic processing is an important way of strengthening relationships. It can also be used for coaches wishing to increase their understanding of the unfolding relationship dynamics occurring with a particular client. For example, schema-focused approaches (e.g. Young et al., 2006) aim to uncover individuals' deeply embedded emotional, cognitive and behavioural responses that fuel interpersonal tendencies and shape functioning, including in the social world. In an interpersonal context, schema typically elicit complementary "schematic pulls" in the other person. Consider, for example, the following case vignette where the coach uses his understanding of schema theory to conceptualize difficulties in his working alliance with his client.

Box 7.1   Formulation of the impact of Michel's unrelenting standards on his coaching relationship with Jon

Michel had been offered coaching to help him modify his uncompromising and demanding leadership style that was judged by his line manager to be negatively impacting the performance of his team. Michel was also noted to be highly demanding of himself. Jon, his coach, found himself feeling uncharacteristically edgy around Michel. He sensed Michel's irritation with him, especially when Jon put a time boundary around their coaching sessions and on his availability to him outside of their scheduled meetings.

Jon hypothesized that Michel had developed an unrelenting standards schema which was impacting the relationship between them. To guide his thinking about how to approach the issue with Michel, and drawing on knowledge accrued from earlier coaching sessions, Jon developed the following tentative formulation of the interpersonal process unfolding between them:

Michel's cognitive and behavioural tendencies: Difficulty owning his past successes, tending to forget or dismiss them; over-valuing hard work and persistence at the expense of other needs such as rest, sleep and exercise; neglecting relationships at work in pursuit of organizational results.

Michel's potential beliefs about coaching: "I need to get the most out of Jon to make this coaching a success for me and my team; coaching needs to deliver results; I need more time with Jon than he is currently giving me; he should be more available to me so I can get what I need".

Jon's beliefs that he saw as relevant to working with Michel: "I work hard for my clients; I am a good coach; I will not let Jon transgress my boundaries; Jon is overly demanding and lacking appreciation for how hard I am working for him".

Jon then considered how these tendencies and beliefs might be giving rise to the following interpersonal process:

Schematic Activation

Michel wants more from Jon and pushes Jon for greater contact and longer coaching sessions.

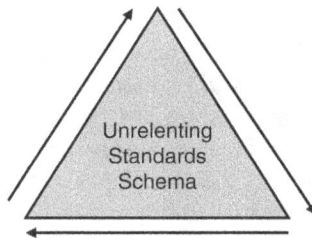

Schematic confirmation for Michel	Schematic "pull" in Jon
Michel feels misunderstood and irritated.	Jon feels irritated by Michel's demands.
Michel pushes Jon for more time together.	He feels slightly bullied by Michel. He becomes more inflexible in his approach, including in his availability to Michel.
Michel becomes more challenging and combative.	

An additional approach that can support the development of an interpersonally focused formulation is the work of Hawkins and Shohet (2012) who, in their work on training supervisors, describe the value of first raising awareness of the variety of helping relationships that trainee supervisors have experienced and the differing expectations and transactions associated with each. Among the helping relationships typically identified by trainee supervisors are that of doctor (to whom a person takes symptoms and expects a diagnosis or treatment), teacher (to whom a person takes questions and a lack of understanding and expects answers and knowledge) and friend (to whom a person can take their own self and expect acceptance, understanding and validation).

The parallel to coaching lies in a recognition of the variety of roles that a coach and client might adopt – consciously or less consciously – that then unfold as part of an interpersonal dynamic. In particular, without the necessary self-awareness of personal tendencies, Hawkins and Shohet (2012) propose that individuals tend to revert to styles of interaction that reflect other forms of relationship and which result in collusive, crossed or named transactions. For example, if a coach and client implicitly (or explicitly) construe the relationship as one where the role of the coach is to impart knowledge, the conversations may drift into a style of interaction where the coach increasingly provides information, knowledge and answers. On one level this may feel satisfying for one or both parties, but this relational process renders the client a passive recipient rather than active agent in the coaching process. This would be an example of a collusive transaction. Alternatively, if the client reverts to a role expectation of friendship, seeking acceptance, understanding and validation, but the coach reverts to the role of doctor (offering a "diagnosis" or explanation of the issue at hand and proposing potential remedies), a crossed transaction occurs, with the potential for a rupture in the coaching relationship arising from frustrated expectations. In contrast, where coach and/or client can name the patterns that are occurring and the roles, expectations and transactions that underpin them, it becomes possible to reflect upon them, observe their consequences and make informed choices about how to proceed.

Schema theory and helping roles are just two approaches that can be used to uncover, conceptualize and explore interpersonal tendencies and styles that are relevant to achieving the purpose of the coaching. Yet, these approaches may support an understanding of some of the moderating factors concerning how, when and why the coaching relationship influences the outcome of coaching itself. For example, Graßmann et al. (2020) have hypothesized that the working alliance may in fact reflect less of an interpersonal process than a stable personality trait denoting the client's predisposition towards developing effective working relationships. This has important potential implications for an approach to formulation that adopts an interpersonal perspective as it highlights that stable individual characteristics must also be considered. However, an emphasis on the individual may be incompatible with many cultures that adopt a more collective view of the world. Exploring coaching within Islamic, African, Asian and South American cultures, Lane et al. (2023) point to the importance of the individual as part of a community and argue that to operate outside of that worldview creates misunderstandings of the nature of change. Approaches to formulation from beyond the Western perspectives in which the term emerged is considered next.

Interpersonal Formulation Beyond Western and Individualistic Worldviews

In their critique of coaching and drawing on the postmodern perspective of Gergen and Gergen (2006), Gray et al. (2016) differentiate the reflexive identity (i.e. the self-narrative that we create about ourselves and the services we offer to clients) and the relational identity (i.e. the narrative that coach and client co-create or which emerges from the relational process) of the coach. Gray et al. (2016) claim that any reflexive identity and individually defined sense of our coaching offer will ultimately be shaped by the relational identity that is formed as the work unfolds. From this perspective, there is a shift of emphasis from bringing to the work a pre-formulated narrative concerning what coaching will look like and what the coach can offer (the reflexive identity) to a co-constructed way of working whereby we join with the client as co-author of an emerging story.

The recognition that an individual needs to be understood within an interpersonal context is present in a number of Western theoretical traditions. However, there are also older and richer perspectives from within African, Asian and Islamic cultures. Ratele (2019), for example, working from the perspective of developing an African Psychology, argues that unless we are prepared to listen to and work directly with communities, we will not ultimately be able to understand the whole person who requests our help. This plea is also present in the call from Whybrow et al. (2023) for a collective and collaborative journey as part of a pilgrimage with nature to address the need for an ecological and climate-conscious coaching. In a search for meaning, the divergence between a Western individualistic worldview and an Eastern collective is noted by Lent (2017). Hence, in considering the role of formulation in coaching, it is necessary to recognize that for many, an individually focused approach would sit uneasily with their worldview. It is important to note that the approaches that follow do not necessarily use the concept of formulation, but in seeking to explore the issues presented they emphasize the individual in a relational space. A formulation within such frameworks would, therefore, seek to conceptualize how the context informs the patterns of behaviour observed or other needs arising.

Following Ratele's (2019) perspective it becomes necessary to ask the question, "what does the world look like from here?" From an African perspective, it is important to recognize that it is not possible to speak of a single, unified African culture. That said, the concept of Ubuntu (meaning "I am because we are") is present in many languages and cultures (isiZulu, isiXhosa, isiNdebele, SiSwati and several others). Thus, to be fully human entails valuing all of humanity collectively and not focusing on the superficial or learned differences that seek to separate. The collective is privileged over the individual. In the dance between the reflexive and the relational, Ubuntu is inherently a relational practical guide to co-existence that goes to the heart of ethics in coaching, neutralizing most power bases to enable everyone to safely share their ethical stance without fear of judgement. A formulation from this perspective would have to include the person as part of their community in the spirit of the maxim, "we are therefore I am" (Lane et al., 2023; Stout-Rostron, 2019a).

In contrast, Ershad is an approach to coaching based on Islamic principles (van Nieuwerburgh & Allaho, 2017) which describes the coach as a guide to help the individual grow towards their desired capacity and degree of accomplishment. However, this has to be delivered within a framework of Islamic beliefs about God, self, others and the world. The principles of discovery, intentions, pathways and effort are used to guide the coaching process. Essentially, we are asked in coaching to align our lives with the deepest goals we find in ourselves – these are considered gifts from God. In exploring our life and discovering the areas on which we want to work the intentions we form need to reflect our relationships with self, others, the world and God. The pathways we choose are not individual but aligned to these beliefs. Our formulations represent the intentions and pathways we choose arising from our discovery process but which are also embedded as part of a community of belief.

Older and richer assumptions about the self in relation to others are also present in the teachings of Confucius, which remain influential in many Asian cultures (Waley, 2000). The importance of relationship in this philosophy has particular relevance for coaching, with the emphasis on coach and client having a role in creating a harmonious and righteous nation. Hwang (2012) explored this in terms of key features of the dyad, including benevolence, which refers to the closeness/distance of the relationship of the dyad; righteousness, which refers to the choice of appropriate rule for social exchange, and propriety, which dictates the proper behaviour for social interaction in the dyad. Emphasis is placed on understanding the relationship in coaching and perhaps preventing misunderstanding that might arise through adopting a Western lens. An example of this is in the concept of face. We are familiar with the idea of "saving face", which is an individual reaction. The Chinese concept relates to "giving face"; that is, the individual is understood not as the unit of analysis but as "individuals-in-relation" (Ho, 1994). The difference lies between the Western emphasis on individuality – the self-reliant and self-oriented individual – and an Asian (especially Chinese) focus on the importance of the collective good of the group. "Giving face" is an interpersonal not an individual process.

Formulation from any of the above perspectives cannot be understood outside of the interpersonal relationship between coach and client, which is also emphasized in perspectives such as Gestalt, Constellations, Ontological and Social Constructionist thinking. For example, central to the Gestalt approach (e.g. Denham-Vaughan & Gawlinski, 2012; Spoth et al., 2012) is the emphasis on working from a relational stance. While goal-focused approaches are often favoured in workplaces, Gestalt coaching adopts a more emergent and phenomenological route in which goals are held lightly. A goal is a figure of interest that may evolve into something else

(Spoth et al., 2012). The client-focused emphasis of many coaching approaches is replaced in the Gestalt approach by a relationship-centred focus. Consequently, the emergent, contextual and relational nature of change and the intersubjective nature of relationships forms the basis for constructing a mutual process. For the Gestalt coach, the relational field includes self, other and the coach as well as the environment (Spoth et al., 2012).

In some ways similar to the Gestalt approach where the self is seen as part of the field, the Constellations approach (Farr & Shepheard, 2018) sees the notion of self and behaviour as dependent on the environment. Hence the sense of self shifts as a result of the different spaces that individuals occupy. The concern is with the pattern of relationships and the contexts in which they take place. The aim when working with a Constellations approach is to reveal the hidden or obscured to enable all parties to find their place within the system. In our terms, the formulation emerges as coach and client work together to identify the parts of the system related to the issue at hand so that the areas that are actionable become clear. In a similar way to the earlier distinction between reflexive and relational narratives, the client comes with their own story and the coach works with them to place it within a broader system-informed story.

In an Ontological approach the emphasis is on both the coach and client's "way of being" (Sieler, 2020). Of particular interest is the idea that our way of being is the central driver of our behaviour, but this always occurs within a cultural and historical context. As Sieler (2020) states, humans are relational and conversational beings interacting with the world from their way of being to take care of what matters deeply to them in the different areas of their lives. Coaching effectively to a way of being requires a sound working familiarity with how language, moods and the body can be utilized to support clients in generating their own perceptual and behavioural changes. In working together coach and client are looking for shared understandings of the issues to be explored in a relational engagement. Of central importance, the approach recognizes that different cultures reflect different ways of being, providing a frame of reference to both understand and behave in diverse situations. These cultural narratives inform members of a community how to respond. The coach needs to listen deeply to the social norms and practices in play to build the relationship. Understanding the interpersonal is a core feature of any formulation within an Ontological approach.

Similar to the Ontological approach with its interest in cultural narratives, the underlying principle of Social Constructionism is that social reality is situated in particular cultures and societies at specific points in time (Misra & Prakash, 2012). As a radical challenge to the empiricist worldview, Social Constructionism refutes the notion of any external objective reality. Rather, what is perceived as reality – by individuals, groups and societies – is understood to be the product of culturally and historically situated social norms and customs. These include values, beliefs and rules of conduct, culture, institutions and hierarchies, rituals such as marriage and education, and gender and language, among others. The concept that we need to interpret the world as it is too complex has a long history in philosophy and has been framed as the idea that we socially construct reality (Berger and Luckman, 1967). Gergen (1985) as a response to the crisis of rationality within science (see Chalmers, 2013, for an overview) proposed Social Constructionism as a way to advance a range of disciplines, including the social sciences and philosophy of science. For the purposes of formulation, what it offers is a recognition that human experience is crafted through a dynamic process of interaction and construction that occurs within communal conventions and narratives in which the coach and client are embedded. A formulation underpinned by Social Constructionism recognizes that meaning is co-constructed in and through dialogue. It is those constructions that form the basis of a shared sense of meaning that enable possibilities for action.

Considerations for Use of an Interpersonal Perspective

A theory, framework or perspective provides what Corrie and Lane (2010) termed "a range of convenience" (p. 91) that offers guiding parameters for developing a formulation. What, then, does the interpersonal lens offer that the individual lens cannot? Regardless of how it is defined, any robust consideration of the interpersonal domain will shift thinking away from linear perspectives on cause–effect relationships (e.g. if the coach introduces intervention A, it is predicted that the client will produce response B) towards reciprocal patterns of influence in an unfolding process of dialogue, action and reaction. Coaching is not a one-sided, top-down process, but one in which both parties are co-creating understandings and making decisions throughout. Akin to the systemic perspective introduced in Chapter 8, the interpersonal perspective illuminates how the individuals involved in coaching (including the coach) are shaped in their thinking and behaviours by the interpersonal and interactional fields in which they operate. How these fields are conceptualized will vary as a function of positionality, context, the purpose of the coaching that is subsequently agreed, and the theoretical perspectives adopted, which determine the factors of influence to be considered. Yet, collectively, they require the coach to move beyond a focus on the characteristics, beliefs, behaviours, needs and aspirations of the individual client (the individual perspective) towards the factors that contribute to forms of knowing and growth that emerge from the coach–client dyad. Understood through this lens, coaching becomes conceptualized less as a task-focused endeavour and more as a partnership-based framework for exploration and change. Below are some considerations for determining when an interpersonal perspective might be a useful basis for formulation.

When the Interpersonal Perspective Might Be Advantageous

The interpersonal perspective is likely to be useful as a basis for formulation when:

- Dyadic features appear to be strongly implicated in the agreed focus of the coaching.
- There are aspects of the interpersonal encounter between coach and client that are not working smoothly or that are perplexing for one or both parties.

- There are aspects of the coaching relationship that are working too smoothly (i.e. the process has become too comfortable for meaningful change to take place).
- The client's concerns appear to occur in some interpersonal contexts but not in others.
- Working directly or indirectly with "a significant other" (professional or personal) is predicted to enhance the likelihood of achieving the desired coaching outcome.
- The context for the coaching involves interpersonal factors that must be navigated for the coaching to be effective.
- The agreed purpose of the coaching has the potential to create a ripple effect across other relationships that may require anticipation and management.
- The context and client's situation are changing rapidly with many moving parts and understanding, and managing relationships with specific others is likely to be crucial to an effective response.
- The client is embedded in relationships where interpersonal power and influence need to be more fully understood and managed.
- A significant relationship in one domain of the client's life is negatively impacting their ability to achieve results in another.
- The focus of coaching takes the form of a developmental rather than a skills-based journey, and the emphasis is on who the client is becoming as part of a process of transition.
- An interpersonal perspective is consistent with the culture, values and beliefs of the client's worldview.

The interpersonal perspective is less likely to be useful as a basis for formulation when:

- The agreed focus of the coaching is on the acquisition of a discrete skill.
- The coaching is very brief or short-term in nature.
- The client is highly target driven and this mindset is consistent with the values of the wider organization.
- The client is highly focused on goals and behaviourally defined outcomes that can be acquired through the effective use of the client's own individual resources.
- The client (or the coach) is not sufficiently able or willing to engage in the process of reflection on the self, and their contribution to the coaching process.

Conclusion

This chapter has examined some of the factors that need to be considered when approaching formulation from an interpersonal perspective. It has also examined how an interpersonal perspective for formulation can help coaches identify, conceptualize and capitalize upon specific opportunities for change. However, the interpersonal is a very broad domain that does not come predefined. Thus, the interpersonal perspective adopted might take the form of stable personal characteristics such as schema that create cognitive, emotional and behavioural reactions or tendencies to engage in particular helping roles. Alternatively, the client's positionality, context, culture and worldview might necessitate a broader interpersonal perspective that engages with the intersubjective nature of relationships and the collective community from which any meaningful understanding of the individual cannot be isolated. Yet, regardless of how the interpersonal is defined, the formulation is conceptualized as emerging in and refined through a dialogical encounter between client and coach who work together as a dyad to construct different accounts of the client's experience that can give rise to new perspectives and possibilities for action.

Questions to Consider

Having read this chapter, consider what emerges in relation to your own practice. For the purposes of formulation, you may find it helpful to consider the following questions:

- What form of relationship does your coaching approach tend to favour? What would the implications be of adopting an interpersonal focus if you do not do so already?
- An interpersonal perspective may adopt the form of a search to understand more fully the client in their context. How might such a search impact your usual approach to working?
- The concept of the interpersonal implies that both coach and client come with their own narratives, which they then explore and adapt to arrive at a shared concern and formulation of that concern. How might adopting an interpersonal perspective impact how you approach your practice?
- The coach and client can be conceptualized as two separate individuals/units or as a dyad. How would you approach understanding the interpersonal dynamics at play in each case?

Chapter 8

Formulation From a Systemic Perspective

In recent years, coaching has been applied to a wide range of contexts, and the traditional focus on individual change has expanded to include a growing interest in coaching aimed at systemic change. As a result, theories from systems thinking, complexity and chaos theory have begun to influence coaching practice, bringing ways of thinking about coaching as a complex process embedded within systems which are messy and difficult to predict. These perspectives recognize that cause and effect can be distant in time and space and that the complexity of causal relationships makes it difficult to identify direct connections. These concepts have important implications for how coaches approach formulation, given that outcomes cannot be predicted and that it is not even clear where change will emerge within the system.

This chapter introduces some key concepts of systems thinking – from simple to complex – and illustrates how coaches are constantly learning to work in multiple ways across many systems. How coaches understand and approach these systems will have an impact on how change is approached as the coaching unfolds. This chapter explores what these perspectives can bring to the coaching engagement and the implications for how formulation is approached when coaches and clients are grappling with an understanding that the world is unpredictable.

What Are Systems?

Systems can take many forms, including physical (e.g. river systems), biological (e.g. the human body), human-designed (e.g. computer systems), abstract (e.g. systems of philosophical thought), social (e.g. a team) and systems of human activity (e.g. a quality assurance system). Humans exist in a world of systems and spend most of their lives interacting in a constantly shifting network of systemic relationships (Oshry, 2015). However, many of us do not readily notice the multiple systems in which we are embedded: the family, a neighbourhood, a city, a team, an organization, nations, global citizens and organisms in the ecosystem. When we talk about systems, what then do we mean? A system can be defined as a complex whole, the functioning of which is dependent on its parts and the interaction between these parts. It is these interactions that give rise to the whole system; once the system has emerged, it gives meaning to the parts and their interactions. As an example,

DOI: 10.4324/9781003174585-11

consider an organization. The whole organization and its activities emerge from the interactions between all the people and systems that make up that organization. The organization as a whole gives meaning to the individual parts such as the leaders and individual roles. Without the organization the individual leader has no role and without the people the organization would cease to function (Jackson, 2003).

The Evolution of Systems Thinking

During the 1950s multiple systems theories emerged as scientists experienced the limits of reductionism in solving complex problems. Problems rarely come neatly contained within one domain or discipline; rather they are richly interconnected problem situations (Jackson, 2003). Solving complex problems requires thinking about how a specific issue is connected to other issues rather than breaking down a problem to its constituent parts. While originating in other scientific fields, systems approaches have been applied to human systems, such as organizations, to assist people in understanding the context in which they operate and expanding their problem-solving capacity through applying a systemic lens (Capra & Luisi, 2014; Lawrence, 2019, 2021a).

Early applications of systems thinking, such as General Systems Theory (GST) (Von Bertalanffy, 1968), often referred to as hard or first-order systems thinking, offered managers a way to optimize the performance of a system and were focused on efficiency. From this perspective it is assumed that the world is made up of systems that can be objectively observed and modelled. The primary task of a leader in these approaches is to be in control of the direction of the organization, reduce uncertainty and increase stability and predictability so that the purpose of the organization can be achieved (Stacey, 2007b). A challenge to this way of viewing organizations emerged early in the field of Soft Systems Methodology (SSM) in which Checkland (1981) argued that social systems were too complex to be modelled mathematically as proposed by GST. SSM recognizes that people have contested purposes and contradictory perspectives. Rather than using mathematical modelling, SSM proposed that people come together to model the problem in the forms of systems and use this model to generate questions and identify potential solutions (Checkland, 1981; Lawrence, 2019).

Arising at a similar time to GST, the theory of systems dynamics was being developed by Forrester (1958) and was later popularized by Senge (1990). According to systems dynamics, there are multiple variables in complex systems which become interrelated in feedback loops. These feedback loops also interact, creating the structure of the system (Jackson, 2003). Adopting this approach to understanding organizations enables managers to see the less obvious cause-and-effect relationships that exist in complex systems (Lawrence, 2021b).

Complexity Theory

As the limitations of first- and even second-order systems thinking (e.g. SSM), for understanding more complex systems, became evident, complexity theory arose as an alternative approach. While there are many different complexity theories, one that has garnered interest in leadership and coaching fields is that of Complex Adaptive Systems (CAS) (Lawrence, 2021b).

A CAS has been defined by Boal and Schultz (2007) as consisting of "aggregates of interacting sub-units, or agents, which together produce complex and adaptive behaviour (hence the term 'complex *adaptive* systems'" (p. 413). Simple cause-and-effect relationships cannot explain the emergent, dynamic and non-linear actions and properties of a CAS. A CAS adapts to the environment in an unpredictable pattern, with no individual agent controlling the whole system and the way that it evolves. In this way CAS are considered to be self-organizing, with the patterns of behaviour emerging from the interactions between the individual agents in their local context, with no explicit co-ordination. However, these interactions still lead to the emergence of collective order (Stacey, 2007a).

The non-linear nature of relationships and interactions within a CAS contribute to the unpredictability of the behaviour of a complex system. For example, small changes in the initial conditions of a system can have disproportionate effects on the final state as the non-linear relationships within a CAS can amplify small changes into very different outcomes (i.e. the butterfly effect), making long-term prediction in CAS impossible (Stacey, 2007a).

Complex Responsive Processes

While complexity theory can provide a useful metaphor for illuminating the behaviour of complex systems, Stacey (2010) has argued that we cannot simply apply the theories of CAS to human beings. Humans are not the same as the digital agents used to model complex systems or as agents in other natural systems. Humans are conscious, self-conscious, emotional, often spontaneous and they are born into societies with long histories, all of which influence how they respond to interactions with other people and systems. Instead, Stacey (2010, 2012) proposes that the appropriate term for applying the concepts from complexity science to social systems is complex responsive processes (CRP). Stacey (2010, 2012) argues that rather than seeing the interaction between people as a complex system, it is in fact a temporal process, the outcome of which is simply further interaction and nothing more. What is important in how things are achieved are the local interactions and the ongoing and everyday conversations (Stacey, 2010, 2012).

As discussed in Chapter 4, which introduced the concept of positionality, in social systems, individuals' co-construct patterns of power relations through their interactions. The interactions between people also reflect the other aspects of positionality (the norms and values that infuse their thinking, their social identity), which in turn are reflected in how they choose to act. What is produced by CRPs is population-wide patterns of interaction that are collectively termed societies, constitutions, industries, organizations and groups. As individuals in local interactions form these social patterns, they are at the same time formed by population-wide patterns (Stacey, 2012). There is a generalized tendency for large numbers of people to act in similar ways in similar situations. This is what enables people to develop some capacity to predict the consequences of their interactions. Despite there being some general patterns to how groups of people in a society will respond, it is still very difficult to predict how a specific interaction will evolve (Stacey 2010, 2012; Stacey & Mowles, 2016). Thus, the CRP perspective offers a different view on how change occurs. Organizational – or indeed any – change emerges from the interplay of individual choices and interactions in a way that no one can control. In this context it is very difficult to claim that an outcome was caused by a particular intervention, or to plan out a large-scale change process (Stacey, 2010, 2012; Stacey & Mowles, 2016).

Systems Perspectives in Applied Psychology

Systems perspectives have been influential in applied psychology since the 1950s when a different way of conceptualizing psychopathology emerged. From the systemic perspective the concepts of symptoms, defences, character structure and personality can be understood as describing an individual's typical response to a particular interpersonal context that contains multiple complex systems (Bavelas & Segal, 1982; Jason & Bobak, 2022; Masten et al., 2021). For example, the sociocultural perspective takes the view that people and their social worlds require each other (Markus & Hamedani, 2007). Therefore, to understand behaviour or psychopathology, both the individual and their social world need to be considered (Olthof et al., 2023).

Another example is Family Systems Theory (FST) (Bowen, 1978; Baptist & Hamon, 2022), which also illustrates how a systems perspective shifts the focus from individuals to the dynamics within a social system, in this case the family. The focus of FST is mapping the patterns that develop in families in order to defuse anxiety. The goal of any intervention is to facilitate awareness of how the emotional system operates and increase individuals' abilities to make self-directed choices rather than reactive responses and thereby forge an alternative role within the family system (Brown, 1999; Kim-Appel & Appel, 2021). These ideas have also been explored in relation to work issues and coaching in family businesses (Kramer & Kramer, 2021; Shams & Lane, 2011).

Concepts from systems thinking are evident in some of the FST approaches to therapy. For example, FST draws attention to patterns of interaction such as "triangulating"; that is, the dynamic of drawing a third person or entity into a dyadic relationship in an attempt to relieve tension and anxiety (Kim-Appel & Appel, 2021). Another pattern that is considered in FST is the use of a multigenerational lens, which goes beyond the view that the past influences the present, to a model that considers that patterns of relating in the past continue in the present system. This encourages clients to consider the connections between the current situation and how previous generations may have dealt with similar issues, again situating a problem outside of the individuals concerned in order to consider broader influences (Kim-Appel & Appel, 2021).

Additionally, later developments in FST have introduced a multi-contextual lens, which includes exploration of broader systemic factors that would influence how a family would respond to stress or life changes. These developments acknowledge the significance of gender, ethnicity or class on the dynamics of a family and draw attention to how wider socio-political issues of power and hierarchy can be played out in family systems (Baptist & Hamon, 2022; Brown, 1999).

These examples demonstrate how systems perspectives have influenced approaches in applied psychology. In the next section we explore the implications of assuming a systemic perspective for coaching.

A Systemic Perspective in Coaching

Working from a systemic perspective introduces a number of important differences in the way that a coach approaches their work. The importance of this perspective has been emphasized by Cavanagh and Lane (2012) who argue that given that, as coaching operates in complex contexts, a systemic approach is necessary. Its value has also been explored by Lane and Down (2010) in terms of leading in turbulent situations and by Kuhn and Whybrow (2019) in relation to coaching at the edge of chaos. Lawrence (2019, 2021a, 2021b) has considered the different forms of systemic perspective based on the evolution of systems theories summarized above and how these different perspectives can be reflected in both individual and team coaching. Coaches may draw from multiple systems theories in their work, based on their preferred perspective on systems (Lawrence, 2019, 2021a) or create a systemically integrated approach (O'Connor, 2020). Coaches may also integrate individual and systemic perspectives, such as the systems psychodynamic approach, which emerges from a combination of individualized psychodynamic thinking and open systems theory (Roberts & Brunning, 2018).

A Holistic, Multi-Systemic View

Taking a systemic perspective has the potential to reveal many layers of complexity and multiple paths for the coach and client to consider, particularly if using a complexity theory lens (Lawrence, 2019). As previously discussed in relation to applied psychology, the systemic perspective holds the view that individuals are shaped by the interactional field in which they operate. This requires the coach to take a broader perspective, one that removes the focus solely from the individual and turns attention to the many layers of interacting systems which may impact the individual and the coaching (Hawkins & Turner, 2020; Lawrence, 2019, 2021a).

The coach may also pay attention to the systems in which the coaching could create a ripple effect of change (O'Connor & Cavanagh, 2013). For example, is the coaching aiming to create change beyond the individual who is the immediate client, and if so in what way? Even if this is not a stated intention for the coaching, taking a systemic perspective assumes that changes in the way an individual interacts with the systems in which they are engaged has the potential to create changes that cannot be predicted (O'Connor, 2020).

In practical terms the coach cannot hope to fully map the complexity of all the systems and interactions. Therefore, focus will likely be on those factors that the coach hypothesizes will have most relevance to the coaching purpose, while drawing on the systems theories best suited for the coaching purpose or with which they are most familiar (O'Connor, 2020). For example, working with an organizational client, the coach would spend time in understanding the culture of the organization, systems with which the client interacts (such as a performance management system or rewards system), patterns of interaction with others or relationship dynamics. However, they might also extend their attention to consider what the systemic context requires of the coaching, such as the needs of organizational sponsors, local communities or the global environment. In this way the coach listens to the client but also to the systemic contexts and the relationships between the two (Hawkins & Turner, 2020). Unlike coaches working from an individual perspective, the systemic coach is making an assumption that individual changes will also impact the systems of which the client is part, and therefore considers how the needs of both the individual and systemic contexts may be best served (O'Connor, 2020).

A systemic coach may work with the client to identify the systems of influence on the client. A sense of these systemic influences can be gained by listening and observing how the client's world is reflected in their communication and behaviours as they interact with the coach. Hawkins and Turner (2020) understand the world as systems nested within larger systems that are, in turn, nested within them: "We live in the world and the world lives within us" (p. 29). Individuals are part of their families, their communities, and their organizations; however, these cultures also exist within them and are exhibited through the language they speak, the way they communicate and how they think and behave. In essence what is being referred to by Hawkins and Turner (2020) is the impact of the client's positionality, portrayed through a systemic lens.

While some systems theories (e.g. GST) imply that it is possible to take an objective stance and plan how to "change the system", complexity theory argues that this level of objectivity is impossible (Lawrence, 2019). As soon as coaches begin to interact with clients, they become part of the system and their involvement will begin to change that system, or themselves, perhaps in ways that were not anticipated. Additionally, coaches also bring to the coaching all of the systemic influences from their positionality that shape their perspectives and inform how they approach the client and the coaching. We can only relate intersubjectively. Systems are not what we are looking at, but where we are looking from and how we are engaging in the work (Hawkins & Turner, 2020).

Formulating From a Systemic Perspective

Agreeing a coaching purpose remains an initial task of the formulation and becomes even more important when working in an environment of unpredictability and instability. However, there are some potential differences in how the purpose may be agreed. Rather than being agreed solely between coach and individual client, the purpose may encompass the perspective of many stakeholders. This might include engaging with representatives of the systems in which the coaching is taking place; that is, holding in mind the question, what does the systemic context require of this individual's coaching, including all the systems of which they are part (Hawkins & Turner, 2020)? Yet, in agreeing the coaching purpose with multiple parties, there is the potential for conflicting views and the coach may need to stay in dialogue with stakeholders until an agreed purpose emerges.

Once the purpose is agreed, rather than formulating what is happening solely at an individual level, coaches working from any one of the systems perspectives shift the view from individuals to relationships or interactions, and from events to patterns (Hawkins & Turner, 2020). These patterns and interactions may be taking place at many different levels and in different domains. Complex systems are unpredictable, but from the interactions between people and systems patterns will emerge with which the coach can work. Patterns can take many forms, such as the themes emerging from conversations across an organization or community, patterns of group dynamics, patterns of behaviour, patterns of process or outcomes, and patterns of motivation or mindset (Stacey, 2012; Hawkins & Turner, 2020).

At the interpersonal level, one key set of interactions is between the coach and the individual client as discussed in Chapter 7. There may be useful patterns that emerge from the coach–client interaction that can inform the formulation, such as the themes that emerge from the conversation, the patterns of interaction of the client and the dynamics in the relationship. For example, how does the interaction make the coach feel, act or think? Similarly, the client will also have a perspective on the interaction that can be explored. Another area to consider is how to bring to the surface assumptions that both the client and coach are making about the client's dilemma, and the formulation may therefore include patterns of thinking in the form of assumptions, beliefs and stories (Hawkins & Turner, 2020). Each relationship develops a systems "dance" (O'Neill, 2000) and identifying the type of dance being enacted can provide information about how the client interacts with others.

A systems perspective formulation is likely to consider more than the interpersonal interaction only. The coach, while listening to the patterns that are showing up through that interaction, will also consider what these patterns tell us more broadly about the systemic context of the client, their background and the world in which they operate (Hawkins & Turner, 2020). This might include an exploration of the "initial conditions" of the client. In complex systems a small difference in initial conditions can be amplified over time (Cavanagh, 2013). Therefore, coaching needs to consider the past, not just in terms of actions, but also in terms of how the client has been thinking about the issue over time. They may also consider how social influences have been involved in how the client came to face the current dilemma. What influence have factors such as the client's own background, upbringing, experience or social norms had on the current situation?

Another way of considering initial conditions is in identifying any individual client characteristics that may act as antecedents to positive outcomes. There is a growing literature in the coaching field that attempts to identify characteristics that are most likely to support positive outcomes. These include proactivity and learning orientation (Joo, 2005); the personality traits of openness, conscientiousness and extraversion (Athanasopoulou & Dopson, 2018); and self-efficacy, commitment and coaching readiness (Pandolfi, 2020). A formulation could consider how these characteristics are to be determined or measured and whether these factors are likely to impact the success of the coaching. Subsequent coaching may focus initially on developing greater commitment, for example, before tackling other aspects of the coaching.

In some cases, the client may have the opportunity to intervene in systems to shift patterns, such as a story people in an organization continue to tell, which is now a barrier to change. In order to create a ripple effect, the client may need to consider the networks of which they are a part, which could form a vehicle for change (O'Connor, 2020). In this case, the formulation may also identify significant connections and relationships that can be leveraged for positive change. Deciding what should be included in the formulation will be guided by whether these factors are likely to have an impact on the achievement of the purpose of the coaching. The coach and client would also consider whether systemic factors will be included to enhance awareness in order to enable the client to navigate more effectively the systems in which they are embedded (O'Connor, 2020).

The following case vignette provides an example of some of the elements described above in a formulation from a systemic perspective.

Box 8.1   Example of formulating from a systemic perspective

Adam is an experienced executive coach based in Hong Kong. He had recently accepted an assignment to work with a newly promoted audit partner, Kai Lee, in a global professional services firm. The stated purpose of the coaching was to assist the client with her transition to partnership, including the mindset shifts needed to go from director to partner. Gathering some feedback from the sponsor on what they and other key stakeholders needed as outcomes, the key elements that arose were:

- Make the mindset and behavioural shift to partner. Currently Kai Lee is still operating more as a director. Specifically, her interactions with other partners seem to indicate she still sees herself as a subordinate rather than a peer.
- The firm is a large network of partners, and relationships across the firm are essential for success. Kai Lee's network is rather small and confined to people she has worked with in the past. This is hampering her ability to bring in revenue to her practice.

With the coaching engagement underway, Adam noticed that a pattern of interaction between Kai Lee and himself was emerging:

- I ask a question; Kai Lee gives tentative answers and then asks for his opinion.
- Kai Lee doesn't make eye contact and tends to sit in her chair in a way that I read as lacking in confidence, almost as if she is trying to make herself small so that she goes unnoticed.
- This creates a reaction in me that I feel that I should step in with answers and give advice, or step into a "rescuer" role.

Hypotheses:

- Kai Lee interacts with others in a similar way, creating the impression that she sees herself as a subordinate to those with whom she interacts.
- Interacting with those she sees as having higher status than her activates beliefs or patterns of thinking that lead her to interact in a way that positions her as a subordinate.

Having observed their interactions, Adam and Kai Lee formulated some of the wider systemic influences at play that may reinforce the pattern of interaction or of which she may benefit from greater awareness:

- In the organizational culture the Hong Kong office dynamics were overlayed with global cultural aspirations. However, local cultural elements were often dominant, including paternalistic leadership norms, respect for elders/experience and lack of female representation at senior levels.
- The local organizational culture reflects some of the social norms from Hong Kong and mainland China, which reinforced the local culture.
- Adam and Kai Lee's interaction was also impacted by the historical context of Hong Kong as a British colony, as were her interactions with other Westerners. Kai Lee was raised in Hong Kong and her early childhood was spent in a British-ruled Hong Kong. Her parents respected the colonial government.
- Norms of communication and interaction differed between Kai Lee and her Western colleagues who formed the majority of her global counterparts. She was frequently talked over and found it hard to get attention in large groups where she was often the only Asian female.

These additional systemic issues gave Kai Lee greater awareness of some of the challenges that she faced and allowed her to begin to come up with solutions that might aid her and also create a ripple effect within the broader organization.

Further Implications of Formulation From a Systemic Perspective

Recognizing the unpredictability of coaching in complex systems has implications for some of the foundational or traditional approaches to coaching. As an example, consider the role of goal setting in a systemic coaching perspective. In many coaching models, goals are seen as central to the process and are clarified early in the encounter (Grant, 2018). This leads to the development of action plans and setting metrics to measure progress and goal achievement. In general, these goals are individual goals, with very little consideration of the systemic context. In fact, these contextual factors may be seen as sources of confusion and tension with individual goals (Cavanagh, 2013). Rather than specific goals, the range of possible outcomes and the potential effects on the broader systems should be considered. While actions may narrow the range of possibilities, they are unlikely to determine outcomes, as there are many systemic factors that may either amplify or block the effects of individual outcomes (Cavanagh, 2013; Kuhn & Whybrow, 2019).

As a coach and client working from the perspective of CAS it is useful to consider that there are outcomes that can be seen and those that can be imagined. However, given outcomes emerge from the interactions of a CAS, there are some that cannot even be imagined (Cavanagh, 2013). Given the potential for the emergence of unforeseen outcomes, any actions should be introduced as small experiments, listening to and monitoring systems for a reaction and adjusting ongoing actions in response (O'Connor, 2020).

Understanding that it is difficult if not impossible to predict the outcomes of the coaching interventions or the actions that the client may take as a result of coaching conversations, coaches need to be comfortable with the ambiguity and associated anxiety of not knowing. It is possible to be drawn into seeking a resolution for the issues that the client brings to coaching out of a desire for closure. Instead, what is required is to stay focused on the moment-to-moment interaction with the client and be attuned to what is happening and what is called for next. This requires tracking how well the formulation is serving the client as the coaching unfolds, in each moment as well as across the conversation and the coaching process (Drake, 2018).

Working from the systemic perspective has implications for the formulation process, which from this stance is considered a collaborative, emergent process. Much of the formulation process takes place within the coaching conversation as the client and coach make sense of what is occurring and what should happen next. This is in contrast to positioning a formulation as the coach's understanding of the situation, which privileges the role of the coach as an expert. Instead, formulating is conceptualized as an ongoing process that reflects the evolution of the coach and client's thinking as the coaching progresses (Kovács & Corrie, 2021). It is likely that a systemic formulation evolves as the client makes changes in their patterns of thinking and behaving. These changes evoke responses in the client, and the people and systems with whom they interact, and so represent additional information that might change the formulation or confirm the existing hypotheses. The coach may also reflect on the existing formulation before or after a coaching session.

This may reveal new ideas and avenues to explore that the coach may decide to raise in subsequent sessions (Kovács, 2016; Kovács & Corrie, 2021).

There are also implications for the capabilities of the coach of assuming a systemic perspective. For example, developing a systemic formulation may involve gathering data from multiple sources and interpreting information from disparate systems with which the client is engaged. This can result in the coach needing to synthesize large amounts of data leading to both the coach and client beginning to feel overwhelmed by the number of factors that are being considered. The coach will need to devise a process that helps identify and synthesize the information to gain the most valuable insights (Hawkins & Turner, 2020).

When the Systemic Perspective Might Be Advantageous

Given the need to synthesize large amounts of data, it is useful at this point to consider when a systemic perspective to formulation may be most useful, and the benefits and potential downsides of pursuing one. A systemic perspective would appear most relevant in situations such as team coaching or coaching in a family-owned business where both family and organizational dynamics are at play. In both cases the coach needs to navigate multiple and disparate systems. However, a systemic perspective also brings a useful lens to individual coaching as it offers the potential for both the client and coach to see the client's dilemma in a different light. Some of the key factors for selecting a systemic perspective are:

- The coaching involves multiple people, such as a team coaching assignment.
- The client's concern occurs in some contexts, but not in others.
- The issue that the client wishes to resolve appears to involve multiple factors, only some of which are directly under the client's influence.
- The context for the coaching involves multiple interacting people or systems creating a complex environment for coach and client to navigate.
- The focus of the coaching contract has the potential for creating a ripple effect across interconnected systems.
- The context and client's situation are changing rapidly with many moving parts.
- The client holds power and influence and can impact multiple people and systems through their decisions and behaviour.

There are a number of advantages to adopting a systemic perspective. Specifically:

- It provides a perspective on the client's dilemma that is not centred on the individual but includes multiple interacting factors, some of which are in the systems in which the client is situated.
- It provides a framework for conceptualizing the factors involved, providing an opportunity for the client to frame the problem differently and to consider interventions which address factors located in other systems or in the interactions or connections between systems.

- Where there is a limited knowledge base or theoretical model to guide the coaching, and many potential outcomes, the systemic formulation can provide a framework for keeping track of hypotheses, experiments and outcomes.
- In a rapidly evolving and uncertain situation, a systemic perspective focuses on possibilities of outcomes rather than linear cause-and-effect relationships, creating more comfort with uncertainty and potentially broadening the range of options.

There are also disadvantages to utilizing a systemic perspective in developing a formulation:

- With many factors involved, the amount of data collected may seem overwhelming for the coach and client.
- Consistent with the above, the formulation could identify many possibilities to pursue requiring the coach and client to work through multiple options before moving to action.
- The formulation may reveal elements that are beyond the client's control, which could lead to increased frustration regarding their situation.
- It may be difficult to link a direct relationship from the formulation to the outcome.
- This approach may be more demanding for the coach as it requires additional skills and an understanding of systems theories and systemic approaches.
- While there is a growing interest in the application of systemic approaches to coaching, there is still a limited theoretical base, and therefore fewer tried and tested methods, tools or approaches on which to base the formulation and subsequent intervention.

Conclusion

This chapter has provided an introduction to systems concepts, outlining the value that a systemic perspective can bring to coaching formulation. The implications for formulation of applying the core concepts of a systemic perspective have also been considered.

The systemic perspective can capture considerable complexity within a coaching formulation, which presents some challenges for the capabilities of coaches who wish to adopt this approach. However, it has the potential to create new possibilities for change, for an individual client and the wider systems in which the client and coach are embedded. This provides a valuable perspective in a world that is increasingly interconnected and complex, a world in which coaching can have an important role in helping individuals, organizations or communities solve the challenges presented by increasing levels of complexity.

Questions to Consider

Reflecting on your practice in the light of this chapter, here are some questions to consider:

- In what contexts would the adoption of a systemic perspective be of benefit to your practice?
- Which systems theories are included in your perspective and how are they applied in your formulations?
- Considering an existing client, what additional insights might be gained by adopting a systemic approach?
- With which systems does your coaching work interact and what might be the potential impact of your coaching practice on these systems?

Chapter 9

Formulation and the Process of Coaching

In this chapter we examine some different approaches to designing a process and the impact that our formulations have on the coaching that follows. A formulation essentially offers the potential to change the worldview taken by the participants and thereby opens directions for change that would not otherwise be possible. Hence, a formulation provides not just a way to conceptualize the change process and devise an intervention plan but also a way to evaluate its progress.

This chapter examines the links between formulation and coaching interventions, illustrating how the chosen approach to formulation provides a framework for the overarching tasks and approaches to the coaching. The chapter introduces some approaches to the process of formulation and provides an example of how a co-constructed process facilitates data gathering and decision-making. In considering process, we also explore how formulation is not only an outcome (a noun) but also how it is an ongoing process of making sense of the client and their world (a verb).

What Functions Does the Process Serve?

Before introducing examples of process, it is useful to consider why a process is necessary; that is, how it aids the formulation and the associated coaching. The following section explores the main functions that a process serves, including its role in: (1) facilitating the coach and client in reaching an agreed "story" (the formulation) that is compelling and useful; (2) assisting the planning and execution of data gathering; and (3) supporting decision-making and reducing impact of cognitive biases.

One of the functions of any process is to enable the coach and client to explore the client's story in a way that is constructive and offers the potential for change (Corrie & Lane, 2010). Humans have an innate inclination to represent themselves through the medium of storytelling, and the capacity to tell stories is part of our evolutionary and cultural heritage (Drake, 2018). However, without a process or structure the story may lack the narrative arc that leads to a satisfactory conclusion. A compelling story has a structure that contains elements that sustain engagement with the narrative while ensuring that information is delivered in a way that is

DOI: 10.4324/9781003174585-12

memorable (Boyd et al., 2020). The work of 19th century scholar Gustav Freytag identified a framework that contains three key processes in the unfolding of a story (Freytag, 1900). The first is describing the context and setting the scene for the story. Once the stage is set, the action between characters unfolds with a focal point of the story being the central tension or conflict that must be resolved. Once the peak of the narrative is reached, the characters transition towards the denouement and resolution of conflict or cognitive tension (Boyd et al., 2020). This narrative arc (or what is also known as a story grammar) of context setting, plots progression and cognitive tension is found in a wide range of narratives across genres (Boyd et al., 2020). Corrie and Lane (2010) have previously proposed that drawing on story grammar may provide an effective process for creating compelling stories (formulations) that engage clients and have positive implications for change.

For example, using story grammar can enable the events of a story to be sequenced in such a way as to promote a clearer understanding of the connections between events (Corrie & Lane, 2010). Similarly, narrative coaching approaches such as those of Drake (2018), Law (2019, 2020) and Stelter (2013) specifically draw on the principles of narrative structure and offer ways in which the story can be heard and re-storied as a means of creating change.

Other evidence-based approaches offer processes that, while starting with the client's story, provide a theoretical perspective that is used to guide the enquiry (Corrie & Lane, 2010). Many models and frameworks fall into this category; however, the following three examples are rooted within a psychological approach, drawing upon a body of theory and research evidence (Tee & Passmore, 2022). The SPACE framework (Edgerton & Palmer, 2005) is an evidence-based model grounded in a cognitive-behavioural perspective. PEAK (O'Moore, 2012) is a performance coaching model drawing on psychological theories that underpin performance and wellbeing such as self-efficacy, goal setting and self-determination. The DEFINE process (Lane et al., 2018) draws on adult learning theory to provide a process to develop objectives for coaching, construct a formulation and intervention plan and provide a basis for evaluation. These approaches provide the structure for the client to tell their story in a way that enables the coach to offer an empirically supported intervention that has been shown to be effective with clients with similar aspirations or challenges (Corrie & Lane, 2010). Even at the level of a coaching session, frameworks such as GROW are designed to act as a guide to the coach, delineating specific phases of the coaching (for example, the beginning, middle and ending phases of a coaching session) and preventing the coaching from straying into a conversation that has no clear purpose (Grant, 2011).

The process used also has the potential to provide a framework for collecting data that will inform decision-making. When working with the potentially complex issues clients may bring to a coaching engagement, it is useful to have a "road map" which assists the coach in organizing and making sense of varied forms of evidence (Corrie & Lane, 2013). Coaches can collect a wide range of data from multiple sources, such as the client's self-told story, input from a range of stakeholders, observational data, outputs from the client's self-monitoring tasks or the results of diagnostics or other psychometric and profiling tools (Kovács & Corrie, 2021). The structure offered by a process will draw attention to potential gaps in data and assists in deciding which data are most useful in the construction of a formulation. Processes derived from different perspectives will prioritize different approaches to data gathering as well as the data that are considered to be useful. As an example, a process based on a form of story grammar known as canonical story structure (Corrie & Lane, 2010) will look to ensure that the story includes data in the form of event categories: the setting, the initiating event, internal response, the goal, actions, outcome and ending. The structure enables the coach to ensure that data are gathered for each category. Working from a different perspective, the cognitive-behavioural approach represented by the SPACE framework (Edgerton & Palmer, 2005) directs data collection efforts towards the five elements of the framework – social context, physiological, actions, cognitions and emotions – in order to inform the coaching.

In addition to aiding the collection of data, a process may be a useful support to the coach in making decisions throughout the coaching process. As the coaching progresses, decisions will be made such as selecting the focus of the work or developing a plan for any techniques or interventions that may be applied (Corrie & Lane, 2013). Within a coaching session, decisions are made that influence which material or topics to attend to, what questions coaches choose to ask, and what aspects of the client's story they choose to respond to (Berry, 2020). These decision points and judgements all have the potential to influence the direction of the coaching and ultimately the effectiveness of the coaching (Berry, 2020). Despite the importance of understanding decision-making in the coaching context, there is little in the existing coaching literature that covers the topic (Berry, 2020; Corrie & Lane, 2013). Decision-making is also largely absent from the competence frameworks that have been developed by professional bodies such as the International Coaching Federation (ICF) and the European Coaching and Mentoring Council (EMCC), although it is implicit in other competences included in the frameworks (Berry, 2020). For example, one of the EMCC's competences requires that a coach can demonstrate that their approach is adapted in response to client information. However, the antecedent mechanism, that is the decision-making that would lead to the adaptation of the approach, is missing from the competence framework (Berry, 2020).

The limited studies that have been conducted to understand coaches' decision-making indicate that many coaches draw on intuitive judgements as they work with their clients (Berry, 2020). Yet, without a process on which to base their decisions, coaches run the risk of falling prey to many potential cognitive biases, heuristics (Berry, 2020; Corrie & Lane, 2013) or self-deception (Bachkirova, 2015). Given the paucity of literature in the coaching field, it is necessary to consider findings in related fields. Lane and Corrie (2011) have identified a framework to provide a "MAP" (Mission Attitude Process) of decision-making. This may be particularly helpful for understanding the impediments to decision-making of counsellors and psychotherapists, which could have a similar utility for coaches (Corrie & Lane, 2013).

Attribution theory is one useful framework for exploring the potential biases present in a coach's decision-making. Attribution theory (Heider, 1958) attempts to make sense of the factors involved in perceived causation in relation to an individual's behaviour and proposes that attributions fall into either internal or external categories. Internal attributions link the reason for a person's behaviour to a quality or characteristics that they possess, whereas external attributions infer that situational factors are influencing the person's behaviour (Heider, 1958). In a coaching relationship both the client and coach may hold a bias towards either attribution pattern. One source of this potential bias is the training and theoretical perspectives of the coach. Drawing on research conducted in the field of psychotherapy, it has been hypothesized by Segers and Vloeberghs (2009) that coaches trained in psychoanalytic and cognitive approaches are highly likely to privilege factors internal to the client. Coaches whose perspective draws on behavioural or systemic approaches may be more likely to pay attention to the impact of environmental factors and seek to make changes to the situation.

A second framework that aids understanding of how decisions are made is the field of heuristics (Corrie & Lane, 2013; Kahneman and Tversky 1972; Lane & Corrie, 2011). Heuristics are rules of thumb or mental shortcuts (Kahneman, 2011) that provide a means of reducing the complexity of the information involved in a decision and are used as an alternative to a systematic approach to decision-making. The framework of heuristics was developed by Kahneman and Tversky (1972) and includes biases such as representativeness, anchoring and availability heuristics. There are different perspectives concerning the role of heuristics in helping or hindering judgement. Heuristics can speed decision-making and reduce mental effort and may even be necessary when there is a lack of complete information. However, they can also be a source of cognitive bias, both perceptual and interpretive (Corrie, 2009; Ramanayaka et al., 2023). Scholars from both sides of this debate do agree that rather than deem heuristics an acceptable approach, decision-makers should develop an awareness of the limitations of heuristics, make adjustments to mitigate potential biases and review decisions based on feedback, research and new knowledge (Kahneman & Klein, 2009).

If as Berry (2020) argues coaches make many decisions intuitively, there is a risk that their decisions are subject to multiple sources of bias. Therefore, any coaching process should enable the coach to evaluate their decision-making and provide an opportunity for reflection and metacognition (Berry, 2020; Collins et al., 2016).

Process and Coaching Models

Many coaches are trained in a particular approach that recommends a specific coaching process, which is often represented and visualized systematically as a coaching model. These coaching models provide the basis for what happens or will happen in both a specific coaching conversation and the overall coaching journey (Stout-Rostron, 2014). For many coaching approaches, these models also include tools and techniques that may be applied as an integral part of the coaching process. Stout-Rostron (2014) makes a useful distinction between models and frameworks (most coaching models are defined by her as frameworks, that is, an architecture that structures the work) and the tools and techniques used. She defines tools as instruments used to produce certain results, such as assessments, questions and reframing of statements. Techniques are skills and competences that a coach has developed to use tools effectively. For example, completing a series of stakeholder interviews and providing a debriefing report are coaching tools. The techniques include the skills to gather the information, write a compelling report and facilitate the coaching conversation about the feedback provided. Listening is also a tool, and the technique is skilful active listening. In designing a coaching process, the coach might decide to represent their own approach as a model that can be easily explained to a client, or they might simply use it as a process to guide their own thinking. Coaches may have one process or model that they adhere to in all coaching engagements, or they may integrate several and apply the process flexibly to each client based on their needs (Stout-Rostron, 2014).

Any approach to coaching will come replete with several models, tools and frameworks, which may already provide the basis for a robust process that will aid the coach in developing a formulation. Alternatively, it may be the case that these frameworks can be adapted and refined to co-create compelling formulations or the context may make it more appropriate for a coach to design their own process.

Selecting a Process That Is Fit for Purpose

The selected process should be consistent with the other elements of the 4P Framework. The aim is to identify a process that best meets the purpose of coaching within the constraints of the coach's and client's positionality and the perspectives from which the coach typically works or reflect the perspectives of the client.

When developing a process for the work that is to take place, there are multiple decisions that must be made about the type of information needed, how to gather data and where the focus of the work will be. Choices will also need to be made regarding how the information that is obtained will be synthesized into a meaningful account that has implications for change. There are a number of considerations to bear in mind when beginning to identify the process that best fits the purpose of the work within the constraints of the perspectives chosen. For example, Corrie and Lane (2010) have identified the following:

- How does the coach deploy coaching models, tools or techniques to ensure the coaching purpose is met?
- Are there specific frameworks that are favoured by the perspective from which the coach works?
- What frameworks, tools and techniques are generally not included or sanctioned in the perspectives in which the coach is trained?

The answers to these questions are a starting point for identifying a process that is aligned with a coach's positionality, purpose and perspectives. The following sections introduce examples of processes that are designed from specific perspectives to achieve a clearly articulated purpose.

Process Examples

This section outlines two examples of processes that have been designed to support a coach not only in achieving a defined coaching purpose but also in providing a framework for formulation. These two examples are evidence-based and clearly articulate the purpose for which they were designed and the perspectives on which they are based. The first process introduces a framework underpinned by the theory of personality and the possibility of personality change in terms of thinking styles, actions and emotions (Martin et al., 2014), and the second was developed for the specific purpose of supporting leaders in transitioning to more senior roles.

A Step-Wise Process of Intentional Personality Change

The use of coaching to facilitate personality change is a relatively unexplored area. Yet, Martin et al. (2014) have argued that personality change, in terms of adapting ways of thinking and behaving, can (for participants without psychopathology) be achieved in the coaching context (Martin et al., 2014). The purpose of this approach is clearly articulated as accessing the potential benefits of personality change, such as increased wellbeing and positive outcomes in life domains such as interpersonal relationships and employment (Martin et al., 2014). The process was designed to facilitate personality change based on several psychological perspectives: intentional change (Boyatzis, 2006), personality theory, motivational interviewing (Rollnick et al., 1999) and a range of coaching psychology tools and techniques.

The step-wise process aims to develop an understanding of the current situation and the desired personality change in the first six steps of what is a ten-step process. From the perspective of developing a formulation, it is at this stage that an initial formulation would be developed that identifies an individual's current personality profile, gaps between ideal and current self, clear coaching goals, attitudes to change and a proposed coaching plan.

Box 9.1   A step-wise process (Martin et al., 2014)

Step 1: Assess personality and client values.
A personality profile and a questionnaire on client values are administered as a data-gathering process.

Step 2: Discover current self.
The results from personality and values profiles are shared and discussed with the client.

Step 3: Explore gaps between current and ideal self.
In dialogue with the client the gaps between current and ideal self are identified and the potential facets of personality that would be targeted for change are explored.

Step 4: Choose personality facet change goals.
A shortlist of targeted changes is agreed and alignment with client values is discussed.

Step 5: Assess attitudes towards change.
The client's attitudes towards change are assessed, any ambivalence is managed and changes made to the final coaching goals.

Step 6: Design and implement coaching plan.
The interventions that target the desired changes are identified and a coaching plan is agreed.

Step 7: Re-assess and revise coaching plan.
The personality assessment is administered a second time to evaluate progress. The coaching plan is adjusted, if necessary, based on the results.

Step 8: Remaining coaching sessions implemented.
The coaching continues according to the agreed coaching plan.

Step 9: Re-assess, review and maintain.
The personality assessment is administered a third time and the progress towards the agreed goals is evaluated. A maintenance plan is developed to reinforce changes.

Step 10: Follow up, review and refinement.
After a three-month interval the personality assessment is readministered and, if required, changes are made to the maintenance plan.

With the formulation in place, the coach and client continue the coaching process with the remaining four steps being a means to monitor progress, revise the coaching plan and agree on a maintenance programme to embed change. A final assessment is conducted at step 10, three months after the coaching has concluded, in order to revise the maintenance programme if needed.

Transformative Transition Coaching (TTC) Model

The TTC (Terblanche et al., 2018) was designed for coaches to enable transformative learning in managers who are transitioning to more senior or complex roles. This purpose is underpinned by three key theoretical perspectives: leadership transition theory, transition coaching and transformative learning theory (Terblanche et al., 2018). Transformative learning forms a substantive part of the coaching process and is based on the work of Mezirow (1994). The theory of transformative learning refers to a process whereby previously uncritically accepted assumptions, beliefs, values and perspectives are questioned and therefore become more amenable to change (Cranton, 2005). The TTC operationalizes aspects of this approach by assisting the client to identify and transform perspectives that may be a barrier to a successful leadership transition. The TTC model guides the leader through five stages that form an iterative process of reflecting on the current perspective and undertaking action learning to test and challenge this perspective (Terblanche et al., 2018). These stages are not tied to a specific number of sessions. Instead, the coaching model includes a means of measuring transformative learning based on three criteria: (1) depth, that is, the magnitude of impact on the individual's life; (2) breadth, which refers to the number of contexts in the individual's life that the change manifests; and (3) stability, that is, the change needs to be permanent to be considered transformative (Hoggan, 2016). Clients progress through the five stages based on whether these criteria are met.

Box 9.2   The TTC (Terblanche et al., 2018)

Stage 1: Initiate.
The coach explores the context for the coaching, agrees the coaching contract and the leader identifies the key challenges that they are facing in the transition and new role.

Stage 2: Understand.
The client completes a perspectives questionnaire to identify the key perspectives they currently hold.

Stage 3: Identify and design.
From the perspectives identified in the previous stage, the coach and client identify the one that may be the biggest barrier to success in the new role and discuss the potential impact of this perspective on the transition. The desired new perspective is articulated, and behavioural experiments designed to facilitate transition to the new perspective.

Stage 4: Reflect and redesign.
Using the Hoggan (2016) criteria, the client and coach reflect on the progress towards transformational learning. Further action learning and behavioural experiments are designed to deepen learning.

Stage 5: Complete.
When the transformation learning is achieved (as assessed by the above criteria), a maintenance strategy is agreed. The coaching is either complete or is repeated to achieve additional learning relating to another perspective.

A Flexible Framework for a Formulation-Based Coaching Process

The two process examples above articulate an approach that is designed to meet a specific coaching purpose, underpinned by specific perspectives, and can be adopted by coaches who are working to the same specific purpose. In this section we introduce a flexible framework that can be adapted by coaches working in different contexts as a process for developing formulations. In developing the formulation this framework uses a hypothesis formation and testing approach to supply evidence on which to base the coaching interventions and so is likely to be most suited to those adopting an empirical approach to formulation (Corrie & Lane, 2010). An empirical approach starts with the client's story but also draws on the evidence base with which the coach is familiar to guide the enquiry. This process is based on the PAIR (Purpose, Account, Intervene, Reflect) Framework that was developed by Kovács (2016) as part of her doctoral research project (see also Kovács & Corrie 2017b, 2017c).

The PAIR Framework is not intended to be a step-by-step linear process for developing a coaching formulation. Instead, it acts as a guide by articulating an approach to developing a formulation and identifying its relationship to the coaching that follows. There are four components (Purpose, Account, Intervene and Reflect) which inform and influence each other in an iterative process as the coaching progresses, both supporting the development of the formulation (noun) and the ongoing act of formulating (verb). The following sections outline these three components, describing each element and identifying the primary activities of each one.

Articulating Purpose

A coach applying the PAIR Framework will likely already have an overall purpose for their practice, such as developing leadership capability or improving wellbeing. However, for each client, the first step in this approach involves agreeing a specific purpose for each client in their context. This sets the individual coaching assignment within a set of boundaries that provide enough scope to explore the complexity of the client's situation while ensuring that the work remains sufficiently focused on, and organized around, the intended aims. The "purpose", as understood within the PAIR framework, clarifies broad objectives rather than specific goals.

Developing the Account

In this phase, the aim is to develop a formulation that can inform the coaching that follows. Outlined below are the three activities that are involved in the development of a coaching account: (1) exploration of the client's situation, background and coaching needs; (2) a process of idea generation; and (3) articulating the coaching approach.

1   Exploration: As soon as the coach is engaged with the client or a sponsor of the coaching in an organizational context, the process of formulation begins. As the

coaching proceeds, more information is uncovered, ideas are tested, actions or interventions occur and the results are evaluated. As a result, the formulation is continually revised, with the process of exploration being an iterative one. How broadly the client's background and situation are explored or what information is considered will be largely guided by the positionality and preferred perspectives of the coach and client.

2   Generating ideas: As information is gathered, ideas are generated about the client, their situation, and the approach that might be adopted. It is not uncommon for coaches to begin to develop their hypotheses and mini-theories about a client from the earliest stages of the coaching engagement. In developing a formulation, the coach makes these emerging hypotheses explicit and, therefore, open to discussion and testing. Testing these hypotheses might involve a simple discussion of the ideas or involve asking additional questions to confirm or refute an idea. Hypothesis testing may also include the use of specific diagnostics, tools or techniques. All of these actions will provide more information that can be incorporated into the formulation and may confirm or challenge the initial ideas.

3   Designing the coaching approach: At this stage the potential coaching approach is mapped out, including any tasks, tools, techniques or interventions that are being proposed. Approaching the formulation and associated coaching process with a view of hypothesis testing provides the coach and the client with some structure while allowing for new information and a change in circumstances to be integrated. The approach taken needs to remain flexible to adapt to changes as they arise throughout the coaching. This is particularly useful where there are many potential interacting factors to consider and where the situation is in a state of flux.

When designing the coaching tasks and approach there are several critical considerations:

- What approaches are most appropriate in this context and for this client?
- How involved will the client want or need to be in designing the coaching approach?
- What measure or feedback mechanisms will assist in monitoring progress?
- Does the client have needs that may require services beyond the scope of the coaching offer (e.g. therapeutic or medical services)?

Intervene

In this phase, the coach continues to gather information that can be used to update the formulation and to further refine a shared understanding of factors relating to the agreed purpose of coaching. As the intervention phase continues, the formulation is also a support to evaluating the barriers to success and whether additional perspectives are needed to support change. If the coaching is progressing as expected, the formulation can be used to capture insights into the effectiveness of interventions in a specific context or in relation to the outcomes achieved.

In an environment with many shifting factors, the formulation is unlikely to be a static account. Rather it becomes a useful tool for capturing ideas, noticing patterns and keeping track of hypotheses, interventions and changes. Throughout the coaching it is to be expected, therefore, that the formulation will change as more information comes to light and as changes are made. The formulation will also be updated as a result of the reflective processes that are an essential underpinning of this approach.

Reflect

What connects the different elements of the formulation and coaching process are the reflective practices of the coach. The formulation remains a central support throughout the coaching assignment and is an important aid to reflective practice. The process of reviewing and updating the account serves to deepen the coach's thinking about the client, the coaching approach, the factors implicated in the extent of its effectiveness and the coach's own learning. The formulation can also provide a useful framework for reflection with the client; a co-constructed understanding of relevant factors enables the client to collaborate on developing solutions that enhance the likelihood of the client owning the work that unfolds. The reflection process is an opportunity to review hypotheses and consider the client and their situation from different viewpoints, for example, through the lens of alternative theoretical perspectives if necessary. It is also a chance to consider the coach–client relationship and dynamics, which can be a source of insight as well as a point at which to consider whether supervision is needed.

Example questions that a coach may use as a prompt to reflection include:

- How is the positionality (of coach and client) impacting the formulation, the hypotheses that are being developed and the ongoing coaching? What assumptions, beliefs and potential biases might be reflected in the formulation?
- What perspectives are predominantly being considered in gathering information and developing hypotheses?
- In using these perspectives, what is being omitted and what other perspectives might be useful?
- In working with a particular client, how do the interactions make me feel? What does this tell me and how can this be reflected in the formulation?
- What progress is being made based on the agreed measures of success? What factors might be barriers to success? What factors can be leveraged to support further progress?
- Are any selected interventions supported primarily by the formulation, or are they driven by previous experience or intuition?

As the coaching progresses the coach will move between the four spaces of Purpose, Account, Intervene and Reflect as they develop the formulation, implement their coaching plan and reflect on the outcomes, their own actions and responses to the client material.

The three approaches presented above are some of the evidence-based processes that can be adopted by coaches if applicable to their practice. However, a coach might wish to develop a process that is personalized to their own specific professional context and aligned with their positionality, purpose and perspectives. The next section presents some ways in which this can be approached.

Approaches for Developing a Process

For coaches wishing to develop a process that is consistent with the other elements of the 4P Framework, a question arises as to how this can be done in a rigorous way. There is scant literature that identifies methodologies and methods for developing coaching models and many existing models are not validated and tested in the coaching field (Stout-Rostron, 2009). Nonetheless, there are several approaches drawn from research that could be adapted by coaching practitioners, namely, action research, grounded theory and a coaching specific approach that combine these two, the Coaching Model Derivation Process (CMDP) (Terblanche, 2020).

The term action research is generic and has been used to describe a wide range of activities and research methods (Adelman, 1993; Gray, 2009; Strauss & Corbin, 1990). However, in essence it is an approach that focuses on action and research simultaneously with the aim of intentionally merging theory and practice (Coghlan & Brannick, 2004). The underpinning principle of action research is that practitioners can create knowledge by critically reflecting on their experiences, formulating generalizations and then testing the concepts and ideas in different situations. Thus, new concrete experience can be gained and is applied in the next cycle of experiential learning and knowledge creation (Zuber-Skerritt, 2015). There are four major phases in an action research cycle: planning, acting, observing and reflecting, which are repeated in a spiral of action research cycles (Gray, 2009). Action research aims to solve real-world problems and sees the researcher and the participants working in partnership (Strauss & Corbin, 1990) much as a coach and client work together.

Grounded theory is a qualitative research methodology that aims to develop theory from a process of systematic data collection and analysis (Strauss & Corbin, 1990). While the original aim of grounded theory was to generate an actual theory, the same approach can be used to construct a conceptual picture that emerges from the data (Charmaz, 2014). In the case of a coach developing their proprietary process, the aim is to identify key concepts and elements that could be included in a coaching model (Terblanche, 2020). In classical grounded theory the researcher does not start with a clear hypothesis or research question (Gray, 2009). Later approaches adopt an "informed grounded theory" approach where existing theoretical frameworks are used to generate insights from the data collection process (Charmaz, 2014; Terblanche, 2020).

An informed grounded theory approach is applied in the CMDP (Terblanche, 2020), which was used to develop the TTC model (Terblanche et al., 2018) presented above. The CMDP is a five-step process that combines grounded theory and action research and can be used by researchers to derive empirically grounded coaching models (Terblanche, 2020). The five steps of the CMDP are: (1) delineation of the coaching space; (2) a foundational research phase using an informed grounded theory approach; (3) production of a draft coaching model based on the findings of step 2; (4) an application phase using action research to evolve a draft coaching model; and (5) the production of the final coaching model that satisfies the needs of the coaching space identified in step 1 (Terblanche, 2020).

Coaches do not need to instigate a full research project to engage with CMDP. Rather, the principles of these approaches can be used in order to develop a personalized process. For those coaches wishing to adapt an existing process, an approach based on action research may be useful. If the coaching space in which a practitioner is involved is a new application of coaching, the grounded theory or CMDP approaches might provide a useful framework.

Box 9.3 provides a case vignette of a coach developing their own approach to formulation drawing on action research and using existing knowledge and models.

Box 9.3   A personalized process

Christina has been coaching for several years and her services are offered to those with serious or chronic illnesses and their workplaces. She articulates the purpose of her coaching as helping her clients continue or return to work with confidence while influencing workplaces and managers to provide appropriate support for their staff. Her coach training was based on the GROW model and tools and techniques such as active listening and reflecting, action planning and reviewing progress. While she found these useful for some coaching engagements, she found that she needed a process which provided greater opportunity for the client to tell their story, for stakeholders to be engaged and to formulate with the client the current situation and an ideal future scenario.

Having reviewed her practice and current models of working, Christina began a process grounded in action research principles, engaging her clients in the process of forming a more effective coaching process. Clients provided her with ideas and feedback during the coaching and she conducted her own reflective processes. She refined the approach over a period of six months to arrive at a final process which met the needs of her clients. Her coaching process is outlined below.

Client story: In the initial stages of the coaching, active listening is used to gather the client's story and their experience of both their illness and the organization's responses so far. The data gathered includes both the medical information that the client wants to share as well as the current support and resources at home and work. This data forms the basis for a formulation of the current situation.

Ideal state: The next stage in the process involves identifying what the ideal state would be for either a return to work or continuing at work. This would identify the current support both inside and outside work and what else would be desired. It might also include the client's understanding of the organization's expectations as well as what additional support from people or organizations outside work is required. The coach also enquires into mental health needs and support and referrals to other professionals are made if necessary.

Engage organization: With a formulation providing clarity on the current and ideal state, the client and coach engage with the organization, generally meeting with the client's manager and representatives of the HR team. The coach facilitates the conversation with the client and their organization. This session ends with agreement on specific goals that the organization and client will seek to achieve to ensure the client feels supported and is able to meet the organization's needs and performance expectations. Given the specialist nature of the coaching, the coach also provides resources to both the client and their employer, some of which the coach has developed herself.

Monitor progress, review and adapt: Ongoing coaching sessions monitor progress towards the stated goals. Given the unpredictable nature of serious or chronic illnesses, goals may need to be restated, or action plans and resources adapted to meet the changing needs of the client.

Coaching closure: Depending on the nature of the client's needs, the coaching may be a short-term intervention to assist in return to work or a longer-term assignment to support the client manage a chronic illness. In either case, in ending the coaching the coach and client review progress towards the agreed goals, identify what worked well and what still needs improvement, and an ongoing action or support plan is finalized.

As can be seen in the case vignette above, using an action research approach does not have to be a complicated endeavour in order to develop a new process. Starting with common coaching tools and techniques can be a useful way of creating a personalized process. Likewise, while the use of formulation may seem complicated and could potentially require additional skills in collecting and synthesizing data, this example demonstrates that the process does not need to be complicated to effectively achieve the purpose of the coaching.

Conclusion

This chapter has provided several examples and approaches to selecting or developing a process that aligns with the 4P Framework. A well-designed process should facilitate the development of the coaching formulation in conjunction with the client and enable the client to fully collaborate in the construction of solutions. There are many decisions that coaches make as they work with their clients, and the process should help the coach in making these decisions, while helping mitigate the effects of cognitive biases and decision-making shortcuts. As illustrated in the examples above, the process does not need to be complicated and can be adapted from current coaching approaches. Many coaches will find that in assessing their current practice, there is already an inherent process embedded in the way in which they work. The approach taken in this chapter is to ensure that the process is explicit, delivers the coaching purpose and is aligned with the positionality and perspectives of the coach.

Questions to Consider

It is valuable to reflect on the current process (or processes) you use in your work with clients. This can include the current preferred approach, consideration of how that aligns with your purpose and how you adapt process to meet specific needs.

- What processes are currently embedded in your approach to coaching?
- How do the processes you use align with the purpose of your practice and the perspectives on which you draw?
- Thinking about a current coaching client, what process did you use and how did you measure its effectiveness?
- If you modify the process for each client, on what do you base the decision to do so?

Part 3

Applying Formulation and the 4P Framework to Different Coaching Contexts

This section of the book provides a series of illustrations of how formulation generally and the 4P Framework specifically can be applied in different coaching contexts. Drawing on areas of practice selected for their likely familiarity to readers, the areas of focus for the chapters in this section are health and wellness coaching, executive coaching and leadership development, teams and systems coaching and coaching in education.

DOI: 10.4324/9781003174585-13

Chapter 10

Formulation for Health and Wellness Coaching

The need to improve the health of the population has become an increasingly pressing social agenda. There is now widespread recognition that many aspects of wellness and ill health, including a number of chronic health conditions, are life-style-related, and that improvements in population health require the implementation of changes in behaviour (Birkenbach et al., 2023; Campaign for Social Science, 2017). In this context there has been a growing interest in the role that the social sciences might play in improving health, not only for individuals but also in terms of the types of interventions provided, models of service delivery, the environments in which states of illness and wellness occur and the policies needed to positively impact population health over the longer term. The rapid expansion of health and wellness coaching (HWC) represents one important response to the changing landscape of services and interventions designed to promote health and prevent disease.

This chapter explores how formulation can assist coaches who are working with clients confronting health and wellness issues. Coaches working in this field often have to make sense of multiple interwoven issues that cross boundaries between physical and mental health, between biomedical and psychological approaches to treatment and between condition management for the individual and broader systemic factors that inform the decisions of policymakers. This chapter illustrates how coaches can use formulation to understand and untangle some of these issues in order to agree an approach that can make sense of and address the needs of the individual client.

The Context for Health and Wellness Coaching

It is now widely recognized that the rapid escalation of many health conditions is closely connected to lifestyle behaviours, which are implicated in at least 80 per cent of long-term health conditions (Armstrong et al., 2013). Additionally, regardless of origin or cause, advancements in medical and surgical technology have transformed a number of diseases from terminal diagnoses to chronic medical conditions that require ongoing management. This ongoing management often includes behavioural adaptation. However, helping individuals change their behaviour in order to manage, resolve or indeed prevent health conditions has proved challenging. For example, the significant benefits of healthy eating habits,

DOI: 10.4324/9781003174585-14

maintaining an optimum weight, physical exercise and sufficient rest and sleep are widely known, as are the benefits of avoiding smoking and alcohol consumption. Yet, these healthy lifestyle choices fail to be adopted by many who would benefit from them. Although information is widely available, this does not, in many cases, result in lifestyle modifications and the advice provided by experts has also consistently proved insufficient to enable behaviour change (Campaign for Social Science, 2017).

The escalation of health conditions in the global population as well as the challenge of helping individuals make sustainable behavioural changes calls for a paradigm shift in how states of health and ill health are understood and how wellness is conceptualized and enabled. In response to this and as examined below, there has been a growing interest in offering interventions that are developmental, supporting individuals in acquiring the knowledge and skills they need to manage their own health and wellness. Additionally, the current zeitgeist of knowledge coproduction and the involvement of experts by experience in all aspects of health care design and delivery has led to a growing emphasis on individuals' agency in the management of their own wellness. In this context, alongside the rising costs confronting the health and social care sector, HWC has emerged as a means of empowering individuals to implement more healthy lifestyles.

Challenges and Debates in Health and Wellness Coaching

HWC is an emerging, rapidly developing and highly diverse field. Originating early in the 21st century (Cosgrove & Corrie, 2020), coach training programmes emerged in North America in 2002 and grew rapidly, such that by 2016 more than 53 programmes had trained over 20,000 health care professionals (Kreisberg & Marra, 2017). As is typical of emerging disciplines, HWC has been characterized by debates concerning definition, the scope of its practices and how it differentiates its theories, models and practices from other health care professions (Cosgrove & Corrie, 2020). However, for the purposes of this chapter, HWC is understood as:

> a patient-centered approach wherein patients at least partially determine their goals, use self-discovery or active learning processes together with content education to work toward their goals, and self-monitor behaviors to increase accountability, all within the context of an interpersonal relationship with a coach (Wolever et al., 2013, p. 52).

Based on Wolever et al.'s (2013) definition, certain core features of HWC emerge. The first is that HWC takes the form of a client-centred, collaborative intervention where coach and client work together towards clearly defined health and wellness-related outcomes. The second is that the goals are client-determined, albeit with coach input. The third is that, consistent with the view of the National Board for Health and Wellness Coaching (n.d.), client agency and accountability are elevated to the heart of the coaching process; the client is positioned as the expert on their own life with the consequent choices and responsibilities that such expertise confers.

Although it is beyond the scope of this chapter to provide a comprehensive review of the HWC outcome literature (the interested reader is referred to Cosgrove & Corrie, 2020; Sforzo et al., 2017, 2019), as a rapidly developing coaching specialism the field is noteworthy for its application to a growing range of health-related challenges and lifestyle issues. There is growing evidence for the effectiveness of HWC for weight and nutrition management (Kennel, 2018), pain management (Rethorn et al., 2020), the management of chronic health conditions such as fibromyalgia (Hackshaw et al., 2016) and type 2 diabetes (Sforzo et al., 2017) and as part of a cancer recovery journey (Sforzo et al., 2017). HWC has also provided benefits for people living with ADHD (Ahmann et al., 2019), workplace health promotion (Chapman et al., 2007), addressing the mental health needs of college students (Bleck et al., 2023) and as an intervention to support healthy ageing (Maxwell et al., 2022). HWC has also been proposed as a promising means of developing health literacy – that is, the ability to assess, understand, evaluate and apply health-related information and guidance (Ahmann et al., 2020).

As evidence for its effectiveness has accumulated, there appears to be good reason to concur with Stark Taylor and Blair Kennedy's (2018) conclusion that HWC is an intervention that holds great promise. Nonetheless, definitive conclusions about the effectiveness of HWC remain elusive. In their compendium of the existing literature, Sforzo et al. (2017) note some of the challenges of evaluating what is currently a highly disparate collection of studies. In particular, different studies are underpinned by diverse definitions of HWC, reflecting the fact that the concepts of health and wellness are challenging to define. The variety of models and approaches hamper conclusions about effectiveness and efficacy as studies do not compare "like for like" in terms of the interventions evaluated. There are also complexities relating to the nature of the workforce delivering HWC. Studies include the delivery of coaching interventions by different professional groups as well as lay helpers, giving rise to questions concerning who is best qualified to be a health and wellness coach. Should HWC be delivered solely by health care professionals who subsequently train in coaching or coaching professionals who choose to specialize in health and wellness, and when might there be a role for lay helper coaches (Stark Taylor & Blair Kennedy, 2018)?

A further challenge to establishing its effectiveness is how to isolate the effects of HWC from those of other interventions. The frequency of comorbidity alongside the fact that many health conditions are managed through multicomponent interventions creates challenges in isolating the impact of HWC from other inputs, biomedical or psychosocial. Moreover, for some health conditions, biomedical treatments remain the primary intervention (Campaign for Social Science, 2017), which themselves cause significant short- and long-term side effects that can confound the benefits that HWC might otherwise achieve. Thus, there are significant challenges associated with establishing a robust evidence base for HWC despite studies which indicate its beneficial effects. There are also challenges in developing best practice guidance for the use of HWC for particular aspects of health and wellness – health promotion, illness prevention, and the management of long-term conditions. In such circumstances, ensuring that practice is informed by a formulation enables the coach and client to navigate these complexities through: (1) co-creating an understanding of the client's idiosyncratic needs; (2) agreeing goals that are meaningful to the client and that foster a sense of agency; and (3) supporting a process of decision-making about how best to assist the client in working towards their goals.

Applying Formulation in HWC Using the 4P Framework

Having identified some of the broad complexities confronting the delivery and evaluation of HWC, the chapter now considers how formulation might be supported through use of the 4P Framework, to structure key areas of exploration.

Positionality in HWC

The elements of positionality introduced in Part 1 are proposed as relevant to all forms of coaching. However, there are some elements that arise specifically when working in a health and wellness context which may distinguish coaching in this setting from other applications. Maintaining an awareness of these elements can support a process of client-focused goal setting, increase the likelihood of designing an effective approach and, where necessary, help synthesize the inputs of different health care professionals who are working together to deliver a multicomponent intervention.

An initial priority is considering the definition and meaning of health, illness and wellness for the client. Health and wellness cannot be determined as present or absent in any categorical way; that is, individuals cannot be meaningfully categorized as either wholly healthy or wholly unhealthy. Nor are health and wellness states of being that lend themselves easily to objective, measurable definitions. Diagnostic criteria exist for diseases and many long-term conditions. Yet, health and wellness exist along a continuum, and individuals move along that continuum as a function of the accessibility of external protective factors such as a caring life partner, social support and financial stability, as well as internal factors such as the individual's resilience, coping style, problem-solving skills and mindset (Corrie & Parsons, 2021).

Additionally, health is now recognized as a state that is distinct from and more than the absence of disease or illness (Stelter & Anderson, 2018). In the principles that form part of their Constitution, the World Health Organization (WHO, n.d.) illustrates this clearly in their definition of health as, "a state of complete physical, mental and social wellbeing and not merely the absence of disease or infirmity". Indeed, WHO goes further in how they position the consequences of health, elevating it to the status of a necessary condition and fundamental right of individuals and societies.

In the same way that health and illness are distinct, health and wellness are also different if overlapping states of being. Complementary to the WHO's positioning of health, the National Wellness Institute (NWI) emphasizes wellness as the ability to function optimally within one's environment and as a "conscious, self-directed, and evolving process of achieving one's full potential" (n.d.). As a holistic, multi-cultural and multidimensional state of being, wellness is positioned as a state that encompasses lifestyle, mental and spiritual wellbeing and the wider environment. Derived from the work of Hettler, one of its co-founders, the NWI identifies and seeks to promote the following six dimensions of wellness: emotional, physical, intellectual, occupational, spiritual and social. The proposition is that by exploring and enhancing wellness in each of these dimensions, individuals can be supported to arrive at an idiosyncratic understanding of a "whole person" approach to wellness, one that is affirming and which contributes to opportunities for living a healthy life.

The positions of both the WHO and NWI are not offered as definitive descriptions of health and wellness. However, they do provide an important starting point for engaging a client and others involved in the client's care journey in a comprehensive and nuanced exploration of what might be possible and desirable for a particular client at a specific point in their life. This then makes it possible to establish a purpose for coaching that places the client and client agency at the heart of the coaching journey.

Establishing a Purpose for HWC

Given the issues raised above, an important focus of exploration that will inform the purpose of any coaching offered is the client's understanding of health and wellness, what forms these might take in the client's life and how these interpretations might inform the development of any coaching objectives. This task might be relatively easily completed if: (1) a client regards themselves as already having good health and is simply seeking to refine their health-promoting habits; (2) the client has a focal area of concern; or (3) where desired changes are clear and agreed by all parties (e.g. where a client is motivated to stop smoking to improve their heart disease following a recommendation from their cardiologist). Alternatively, this phase of the work might require a lengthier exploration if: (1) the client is undergoing biomedical treatment for a diagnosed health condition; or (2) where the necessary course of treatment itself gives rise to distressing or life-limiting symptoms (e.g. the onset of neuropathy following radiotherapy).

One useful framework for guiding the development of purpose is salutogenesis, a theory which seeks to elevate a focus on health (*saluto*) promotion (*genesis*) over the traditional tendency to privilege alleviating *dis-ease*. Introduced into the literature by the medical sociologist Aaron Antonovsky (1979, 1987, 1996), salutogenesis is a valuable framework for describing a complete state of health where approaches that protect and promote the health of individuals can co-exist with those aimed at preventing or treating disease. Salutogenesis proposes that even in states of tension, distress and dis-ease, individuals can maintain and even enhance their health and wellness through building and accessing generalized psychological, social, and material resources (Antonovsky, 1979). Rather than classifying states of health or disease in a dichotomous way, a salutogenic orientation favours a continuum of health. This continuum focuses not on reducing risk factors and treating pathology, but rather on promoting the identification and use of resources to support health in the context of adopting a holistic view of the person and their needs (see Mittelmark et al., 2021, for an overview of current thinking in salutogenesis).

Central to salutogenesis is what Antonovsky termed a "sense of coherence". In its original form (broader interpretations have since followed), sense of coherence refers to an orientation of confidence in one's capabilities to manage the situation and one's environment and to maintain a realistic optimism. It is a sense of coherence through which individuals come to see the world and the events that happen to them as understandable, manageable and having meaning. Salutogenesis is therefore interested in the interplay between personal, social and environmental resources and learning through an engagement with life stressors how these resources can be applied. How an individual learns to develop and utilize their resources to arrive at a sense of coherence is a lifelong process.

Salutogenesis does not deny the presence of pain and suffering. Nor does it seek to undermine the value of a biomedical perspective where effective interventions for conditions exist. Rather, its contribution lies in offering a framework for identifying options that might promote a client's sense of agency. Thus, by drawing on salutogenesis as an organizing worldview, questions to explore with a client as a basis for shaping the purpose of coaching might include the following:

- What might health and wellness look like for you at this point in your life? How would you like things to be, given your circumstances/the stressors you are facing?
- What factors – internal and external – are influencing your position on the health continuum at this point in your life?
- How, to date, have you learned to develop and use your resources to help you manage your circumstances?
- (Drawing on the three components of a sense of coherence: comprehensibility, manageability and meaningfulness) How have you (or could you) come to view the stressors in your life as understandable, manageable and meaningful?
- What ideas might you have about how coaching could enable you to develop and use your resources to support your sense of coherence? How might you create meaning from your experiences as well as grow in confidence that you can manage whatever occurs?

To date, salutogenesis has had limited impact on coaching and is rarely mentioned in the coaching literature (see Corrie & Parsons, 2021; Stelter & Anderson, 2018, for exceptions). Nonetheless, it is consistent with the positioning of health and wellness offered by both the WHO and the NWI. It also has implications for the perspectives that HWC might adopt, as considered next.

Perspectives of Relevance to HWC

Health and wellness coaches draw on multiple perspectives to achieve the purpose of the coaching and to inform any aims, objectives or goals agreed. These may draw on the personal, interpersonal or systemic perspective depending on whether the focus of change reflects actions that are under the client's direct influence or control (e.g. increasing exercise) or wider systemic factors (e.g. advising a team, organization, or policymakers on the use of the social sciences to inform health care initiatives or policy). Even when undertaking formulation from an individual perspective, the area of interest might range from focusing on a particular behaviour to addressing holistic lifestyle changes (Stelter & Anderson, 2018). An important starting point is, therefore, to decide which and whose perspectives need to be considered. Is the client's perspective alone sufficient for the coaching to take place or do the perspectives of others also need to occupy a place in the work that is to follow?

In general, the theoretical perspectives that underpin the practices of HWC are broad, often combining the insights from psychological theories concerned with motivation and behaviour change (Cosgrove & Corrie, 2020; Jordan & Livingstone, 2013; Mettler et al., 2014). In deciding on the perspectives that will inform an intervention tailored to the client, HWC will then likely draw upon fields as diverse as motivational interviewing; self-determination theory; transtheoretical models of change; positive psychology; cognitive-behavioural principles and methods; social cognition; theories of emotional intelligence; mindfulness; and neuroscience (Dossey et al., 2014; Jordan, 2013).

An additional perspective that may prove relevant for some clients is post-traumatic growth (PTG), a theory introduced by Tedeschi and Calhoun in the mid-1990s that seeks to explain how many individuals who endure suffering as a result of adversity subsequently experience positive growth. Where those who experience traumatic events not only survive but also process what has occurred in ways that lead to beneficial changes, the result can be a new sense of possibility for themselves, their lives and how to relate to others, which can crystallise personal priorities. PTG has been noted as occurring in five areas in particular, namely: a sense of new possibilities; human relationships; strength; appreciation for life; and spirituality (Tedeschi & Calhoun, 1995). For example, individuals who have faced major life crises can develop a sense that new opportunities have emerged from the struggle, opening up possibilities for one's life that were not present before. Relationships can also change, either with specific others or through an increased sense of connection to all those who suffer. For some, PTG is associated with an increased sense of one's own strength ("If I lived through that, I can face anything") or a greater appreciation for life in general. Finally, some individuals experience a deepening of their spiritual lives, whereas for others, PTG can trigger a significant change in religious or spiritual beliefs.

In deciding which perspectives to select, the areas of focus proposed by the NWI might provide a useful orientation to what is needed to enable a holistic experience of wellness for an individual client. Adapted here for HWC, the following questions can be used as a source of reflection prior to a coaching session or in conversation with a client to support the development of a coaching process:

- Given your desired purpose for coaching, what perspectives (e.g. theories, models, frames at the individual, interpersonal or systemic levels) might be optimally suited to enhancing your self-awareness, self-management, interest and motivation in pursuit of your personal definition of health and wellness?
- Given your desired purpose for coaching, what perspectives might support you in identifying and strengthening the beliefs and values that will provide an empowering view of the world and your choices within it?
- What perspectives might support empowered choices in relation to self-care, whether at the physical level (e.g. regular physical activity, nutrition) or the psychological level (e.g. a sense of strength and vitality)?
- What perspectives might facilitate your engagement with enriching life activities, both at work and at play?
- What perspectives might help you connect to your talents and abilities and identify how you could share them with others?
- What perspectives might be relevant to considering how you engage with your social networks for the betterment of self, others, your community and your wider environment?

(adapted from NWI; available at: https://nationalwellness.org/resources/six-dimensions-of-wellness/)

Devising a Process for HWC

The diversity of approaches and perspectives that currently underpin the practice of HWC raises important conceptual and technical questions about how to design a process for the work that is to follow. In their work on formulation, Corrie and Kovács (Corrie & Kovács, 2019, 2021; Kovács & Corrie, 2017b, 2017c, 2021) propose that approaches to formulation can be usefully considered as ranging along a continuum from "micro" (a narrow focus as might be the case when a client presents with a single, clearly defined area of concern) to "macro" (a broad perspective that includes a variety of factors of influence). They recommend considering how formulation might take place at one of three levels: (1) the situation; (2) the pattern; and (3) the person (or case, depending on the coaching context). This approach has been described in detail in Chapter 6 with this chapter considering the form this might take in the context of HWC.

Formulation at the level of the situation. Formulation at the level of the situation directs the attention of coach and client towards a micro-level analysis of elements relevant to a specific growth area. Factors of interest typically include specific emotions, physical sensations, cognitions (e.g. thoughts, predictions, images) and cognitive processes (e.g. perception, attention and interpretation) and how these internal experiences shape subsequent behaviour. Often, this level of formulation involves analysing the sequence of internal and external events that result in sub-optimal reactions, as a basis for designing an alternative, more adaptive response.

A (fictitious) example of a situation level formulation would be where a coach and client wish to better understand the factors involved in the client's difficulty with adhering to their medication regimen following a diagnosis of type 2 diabetes. Analysing a specific instance where the client did not take their medication at the required time highlighted how, being absorbed in an engrossing and challenging task, they felt a sense of elation and achievement. These internal reactions were pleasurable, resulting in a desire to continue with the task rather than pausing to take their medication. Moreover, the need to take medication signified to the client a sense of being different, frail and flawed. As a result, the client engaged in justificatory thinking, including, "My medication can wait until later – I'm on the brink of a breakthrough with this task". Identifying the details of the client's experience in this situation enhanced the ability to empathize with the client (relinquishing a rewarding experience to engage in one that has unpleasant connotations is difficult) and also gave rise to further avenues of exploration (how the client could change their relationship to their diabetes). It might also lead the coach to search for other similar examples as the basis for exploring whether there are patterns in how the client is responding to their recent diagnosis.

Formulation at the level of pattern. A formulation organized at the pattern level is concerned with understanding the factors that are implicated in similar types of reaction across situations. An accumulation of situation level formulations may alert the coach and client to a recurring theme that limits the client's choices, or which represents an area of resourcefulness that could be built upon to enhance wellness. Working at this level can help uncover limiting or enabling mindsets (including assumptions, standards and beliefs) as well as information about internal and external resources and behavioural repertoires. For example, following a cardiac bypass procedure, a client might work with a health and wellness coach to reduce excessive alcohol consumption. As coach and client work through a series of situation level formulations it becomes apparent that episodes of excessive drinking are typically preceded by feelings of frustration and anxiety and a series of permissive thoughts ("One more drink won't hurt me; I will start over tomorrow"). By looking in detail at this pattern, the coach begins to suspect that the client has not yet had the opportunity to develop robust effective problem-solving and emotion regulation skills, and so alcohol consumption is currently the client's only way of self-soothing. Identifying this pattern generates ideas for resources that the client might usefully acquire during coaching (e.g. enhanced problem-solving and emotion regulation skills).

Formulation at the level of the person. There will be occasions when developing a more detailed understanding of the client's background and personal, educational and professional history is vital to devising an effective coaching process. This will likely result in formulating at the level of the whole person. In HWC, this might well be the approach of choice when operating using the broad definitions of health and wellness offered by the WHO and the NWI, which emphasize a complete state of wellness and an evolving process of achieving one's full potential, respectively. The use of salutogenesis would also most likely direct the coach and client towards formulation at the level of the person. An example of formulation at this level might occur where an individual is seeking to find meaning and purpose following treatment for cancer. The challenges – both physical and psychological – of cancer survivorship have given rise to a recognition of the importance of working with existential needs (Carlson, 2017) that include imbuing the experience of the cancer journey with meaning. Meaning can be attained through small, daily pragmatic actions, or through reflection on the client's core values, sense of purpose and personal priorities. They can evolve organically or be supported through deliberate, in-depth reflection. Thus, HWC at this level often entails providing a client with the opportunity to explore what holds most significance and to support them in living with greater intentionality in line with their life purpose. Interventions arising from this level of formulation might include self-reflection tasks that aim to foster a deeper understanding and connection with meaning and purpose, finding a way to narrate one's story, clarifying goals that are truly significant to the person, planning one's legacy (either for family members or more broadly in the case of social justice) or, in the case of advanced cancer, life story books, audio or videotaped messages and memory boxes. Depending on the client's circumstances, needs and preferences, the approaches used at this level of formulation are many and varied, and potentially more exploratory than the other levels of formulation (see also the case study below).

Deciding on the Level of Formulation Needed

As noted in earlier chapters, there is rarely a right or wrong level of formulation. Yet, different levels of formulation will result in different types of explanation with implications for the direction that the coaching subsequently takes. It is important, therefore, for the coach to be able to decide which level might be most appropriate for the client at the point at which coaching is sought. One approach that can inform decisions about whether to focus a formulation primarily at the level of the situation, pattern or person is the Health Awareness Tool developed by Corrie (2019).

Inspired by a salutogenic orientation to health and wellness, the Health Awareness Tool (Corrie, 2019) helps coaches and their clients consider the intersection of two broad domains – resources and functioning – and to consider whether the client is high or low on each of these as a basis for deciding where the client might want to make changes. It can also be used as a basis for deciding whether coaching is likely to be a helpful intervention for the client (see Figure 10.1), especially where they are undergoing simultaneous biomedical interventions.

In its original colour-coded form, the top right-hand quadrant (flourishing) appears in green. The bottom left-hand quadrant (struggling) appears in red. The adjacent quadrants (existing and managing) appear in amber. The original

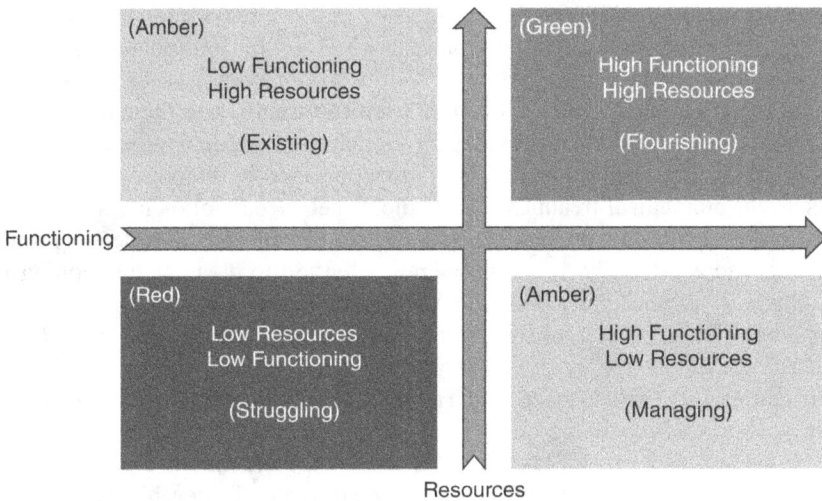

| (Amber)

Low Functioning
High Resources

(Existing) | (Green)

High Functioning
High Resources

(Flourishing) |

Functioning →

| (Red)

Low Resources
Low Functioning

(Struggling) | (Amber)

High Functioning
Low Resources

(Managing) |

Resources

Figure 10.1 The Health Awareness Tool (Corrie, 2019)

colour coding was intentional. Like a system of traffic lights, the quadrants are coloured red, amber or green as a function of whether an individual needs to stop (red) to reconsider what form of intervention is required, whether they can proceed with caution (amber) or whether coaching can proceed with confidence (green).

Where a client is high in both resources and functioning, there are grounds for confidence that coaching is a potentially helpful intervention. This is akin to the client having a strong sense of coherence. In contrast, if a client is well placed in neither their resources nor their functioning, this is likely to place them within the red quadrant, the zone of struggle. Although there might well be a role for coaching, the red zone suggests that alternative or additional forms of support or intervention will likely need to be considered. Where a client is high on one dimension but low on another, they might be considered as being in the amber territory. Here, the client may be managing daily life or simply existing but will not currently be in a position to flourish. Attention may need to be given to ways of enhancing either functioning or resources before the purpose of the coaching can be pursued with confidence. In salutogenic terms, the client's sense of coherence could benefit from being strengthened in areas that can be clarified during the contracting phase of coaching.

The purpose of the Health Awareness Tool is to provide a framework that enables dialogue rather than categorization. Consistent with a salutogenic perspective, it recognizes that we are rarely exclusively in one quadrant and certainly not in any static sense. In preference to diagnosing, therefore, the Health Awareness Tool seeks to build up a shared picture of a client's level of wellness and type of need based on a person-centred and holistic approach to care planning. Its use is intended to be flexible. For example, used as a framework for facilitating discussion, the coach and client can consider which of the four quadrants most accurately reflects the client's current overall position and any factors contributing to that position. Alternatively, it can be used to visually plot the client's current resources and/or needs that provides a rationale for introducing particular methods or skills. The Health Awareness Tool can be used by individuals undergoing concurrent biomedical treatments, to explore their needs following a biomedical intervention or to support and refine methods of self-care in order to promote wellness more generally. It can also draw attention to areas of functioning that could signify the onset of compassion fatigue or burnout and in this context has been applied to a process of supporting coaches' own self-care practices (Corrie & Kovács, 2021).

In summary, the processes to which a formulation can give rise in HWC are multiple and varied. Depending on the purpose of the coaching and the perspectives adopted, the process might take the form of focal interventions organised around SMART goals (that is, goals are Specific, Measurable, Achievable, Relevant and Time-Bound; Doran et al., 1981) or take the form of a broader intervention that locates wellness in the quest for a connection to the client's values, purpose and meaning.

Case Study

Keira had recently completed active treatment for breast cancer involving surgery, chemotherapy and radiotherapy. Medically, her treatment had been successful. Her regular visits to hospital had ended with Keira now transitioning to follow-up appointments for ongoing monitoring. Everyone was delighted with this outcome, except Keira who was struggling to embrace what her consultant had assured her was good news. At the age of 35, with a good relationship, two young children and a rewarding career as the founder and director of her own business, Keira believed that she should be embracing life fully in view of what she described as a "wake up call". However, emotionally she said she felt worse now than when she had been undergoing active treatment. It was this disclosure to her oncologist that precipitated a referral to the health and wellness coach within her multidisciplinary team.

At their first meeting, Keira presented her coach with the following concerns:

- A fear that she was "falling apart" as she felt low and irritable most of the time
- Finding everything an effort. Beyond going to work she was doing little else with her partner or socially
- Confusion over why she felt worse now than when she had been undergoing treatment
- Difficulties following through on medical advice for long-term health, such as engaging in regular exercise and healthy eating patterns
- No longer seeing herself as strong and capable. She reported feeling frightened by how vulnerable and weak her cancer journey was making her feel

A purpose for the coaching was swiftly established. Keira said that more than anything, she needed to regain a sense of control over herself and her life. Exploring this further enabled the purpose of the coaching to emerge as supporting Keira in reconnecting to a sense of herself as strong and capable, a central part of her identity that had been threatened by this stage in her cancer journey. It was anticipated that this would facilitate a sense of agency that could subsequently empower her to make informed decisions about desired changes in other areas of her life.

In order to co-create a formulation that would provide the basis for designing an intervention plan, her coach began with some psychoeducation about the cancer journey to help Keira better understand aspects of her current experience that were puzzling to her. Here, the coach introduced the concept of cancer survivorship and the stages of adjustment that individuals typically pass through during a cancer journey to aid exploration of Keira's subjective sense of not coping. They also explored how the end of treatment might prove more psychologically threatening than earlier stages. For example, when undergoing active treatment, Keira had focused on managing the immediate challenges confronting her and her family (exercising her effective problem-solving skills) while attending multiple hospital appointments (feeling reassured that her condition was being carefully monitored). Now the intensive contact with her oncology team had been withdrawn Keira was left feeling vulnerable. In addition, without any immediate challenges to address, her thoughts and feelings had taken on a new form that was less amenable to her usually effective problem-solving strategies, as Keira began to process at a deeper level the meaning and implications of all that had occurred.

The psychoeducation offered by the coach allowed Keira to put her difficulties in a wider context, which helped her feel less afraid of what she was experiencing. She was encouraged to share this information with her partner and the coach offered to meet with Keira and her partner to talk through what they might expect from this stage of Keira's cancer journey and how they could work together as a couple to support this next stage of Keira's recovery.

Through their initial conversation and psychoeducation, Keira realized that her current experiences did not negate her strengths and capabilities or her many skills and resources. Using the Health Awareness Tool, the coach then worked with Keira to identify some of the many resources she had available to her that she could draw upon to address her current concerns. To her surprise, Keira realized that many areas of her life were progressing well, with evidence of high functioning and high levels of resource. For example, she recognized that she had always had an ability to solve complex problems and make effective decisions in situations of ambiguity, which had enabled her to establish and lead her own business successfully while also raising a young family. A high threshold for tolerating uncertainty along with a clear sense of her own values had been important anchors during times of change. She also described strong protective factors in the form of a supportive partner and family, a network of good friendships and social relationships and stable financial resources. Identifying these resources and locating them within the green quadrant of the Health Awareness Tool (see Figure 10.1) helped her identify what was potentially available to her in designing a way forward. Keira began to reconnect to a sense of herself as strong and capable and as someone who could exercise choice during this new stage of her cancer journey.

Purposes, Perspectives and Processes Beyond the Coach–Client Dyad

So far, this chapter has focused principally on forms of coaching that occur in a dyadic relationship between coach and client, with the client establishing their coaching goals with relative autonomy. Yet, HWC often takes place in multidisciplinary teams which position any intervention within a particular set of conceptual and technical frames and where any formulation developed will reflect the views of multiple stakeholders operating from different disciplinary perspectives.

Overall, it would appear that clinicians are positive about working with health and wellness coaches (Sforzo et al., 2017). Coaching has the potential to bring fresh perspectives and approaches to working with health and wellness concerns that elevate the client's agency to the heart of their relationship with services. Nonetheless, depending on the setting in which a health and wellness coach is operating, and as noted previously, coaching might be just one element of a complex, ongoing, multicomponent intervention.

In order to work effectively with clients in this field, health and wellness coaches need to be cognizant of the conditions with which their clients are living and able to incorporate current thinking about best practice into their coaching conversations (Sforzo et al., 2019). Although specialist knowledge may be advantageous for most forms of coaching, particular forms of knowledge are likely to be needed by health and wellness coaches working with clients who are living with specific long-term conditions and/or the consequences of invasive treatment. For example, coaches working in the field of oncology need an understanding of the distinct challenges that arise from surviving cancer. For some, treatment may be ongoing or individuals can be left with pain resulting from nerve damage caused by surgery, radiotherapy or chemotherapy. Chronic health conditions, including heart or lung damage, infertility and cognitive impairment, which themselves might be severe or life-threatening, can be caused by late effects of cancer treatment. Thus, surviving cancer can negatively impact quality of life. How wellness is understood by the oncology team and the role of coaching in enabling wellness needs to be carefully considered in light of a knowledge of the cancer journey.

As each health condition will give rise to different types of need, health and wellness coaches will likely require disease or disorder-specific knowledge alongside in-depth knowledge of behaviour change in order to "meet" the client wherever they are and co-design an intervention that can prove effective. However holistic in their approach, it is important that the coach understands the condition, the likely consequences for the individual – short and longer term – the treatment provided (and by which professionals) and the potential consequences of that treatment, the likelihood of recurrence and/or the need for ongoing treatment.

Formulation and Its Relevance to Population Health: An Emerging Proposition

Although a currently under-researched area of HWC, formulation has the potential to contribute to initiatives aimed at improving population health, where it is recognized that the health and social sciences have a significant role to play (Campaign for Social Science, 2017). Models of formulation already exist for complex contexts (see, for example, Gosling, 2010; Lane, 1978, 1998) where myriad factors and the perspectives of multiple stakeholders need to be included in any decision-making process. In examining the use of formulation in working with children and young people at risk of exclusion, for example, Gosling (2010) highlighted the challenges of agreeing a purpose for casework due to the multiple stakeholders involved and how an understanding of context gives meaning to any formulation that is ultimately agreed and sets parameters for what is possible to achieve.

There are parallels between the approaches of those such as Gosling (2010) and the complexities encountered in HWC. As noted at the start of this chapter, the global recognition that both an ageing population and an increase of long-term health conditions have major implications for the design and delivery of health care has resulted in a range of innovations aimed at improving health. For example, the principle of integrated care has been introduced to develop connections between clinical, organizational and policy initiatives as well as informing approaches to funding and delivering health and allied services (Department of Health & Social Care, 2022). Yet, as Hughes et al. (2020) have observed, operationalizing, delivering and evaluating the impact of integrated care has proved complex. In consequence, they conclude that integrated care is currently best understood as an emergent set of varied practices that will be shaped by setting and likely include multidisciplinary case management and strategic partnerships. Effective formulation at this level is, therefore, likely to be tied closely to an understanding of the location for the work, the narratives that different stakeholder groups bring to the enquiry and the focus of any intervention subsequently agreed. A knowledge of the availability of local resources in addition to HWC, such as psychological therapies, fitness programmes and service user and carer networks will also be important in shaping how a purpose that is meaningful for all stakeholder groups can be agreed.

Of further relevance to future thinking about health, as well as the design of health systems, health sciences and training of the health care workforce is the WHO's concept of functioning (see Stucki & Bickenbach, 2017). Introduced to facilitate a paradigm shift that enables the bridging of individual wellness and societal welfare, functioning represents a third, vital indicator of human health that complements the existing indicators of morbidity and mortality (Bickenbach et al., 2023). Functioning combines both the physical functioning of the human body's systems and the performance of everyday and desired actions in the individual's physical and social environment, thus unifying biological health with health as it is lived by the person within their environment (Bickenbach et al., 2023). The call is to create health care systems that focus on enhancing functioning (Stucki et al., 2018) to provide a fuller and richer understanding of human health that can promote individual wellness and improve population health.

The introduction of integrated care and functioning as a third indicator of human health creates significant opportunities for the delivery of HWC in holistic and person-centred care. Formulation at this broader level requires health and wellness coaches to consider their skillset in new ways. Rather than tools, techniques or methods aimed at improvements for an individual client, the task will involve using these skills to bring together different stakeholders to enable conversations that support mutual understanding, build trust and ensure that all of the relevant voices have input into the creation of a shared narrative around the health and wellness area of concern. In accordance with Gosling's (2010) proposition, it is through the processes of guided sharing and discovery that it becomes possible to develop and test hypotheses about potential factors of influence against multiple sources of evidence. The skillset of the coach, including the ability to create the conditions for meaningful conversations, is a vital element in the development of the multidisciplinary and transdisciplinary research, practice and knowledge generation that is needed to improve the health and wellness of the population in the years ahead (Academy of Medical Sciences, 2016).

Conclusion

HWC is a rapidly expanding form of coaching provision, offering the basis for a paradigm shift in how the experiences and needs of those living with health conditions or those seeking to improve their health and wellness can be understood. Although the dominant approach to treating many health conditions remains the biomedical model, more holistic notions of health and wellness provide the basis for individualized pathways of care and support that place client agency at the heart of the journey, even where a biomedical intervention is necessary. Formulation is a vital part of this endeavour. Using formulation in the service of social change and policy development is an emerging proposition, but one that is likely to be of growing interest and which is consistent with the WHO's claim that health is a fundamental right of individuals and societies. Regardless of the perspective on health and wellness that is adopted, however, HWC seeks to position clients as active partners in both the formulation and any intervention that follows. This creates multiple opportunities for coaching to make a positive difference to the lives of individuals and societies.

Questions to Consider

Having read this chapter, consider what emerges in relation to your own practice. If you work as a health and wellness coach, you may find the following questions useful:

- Who are the stakeholders that need to be involved in deciding upon the purpose, perspectives and processes of any coaching you offer your HWC clients?

To what extent are their views on the nature of health and wellness aligned with yours?
- To what extent do biomedical accounts, treatments and their consequences feature in your formulations?
- Given your professional context, does your coaching tend to adopt a goal-focused, behavioural approach, or do you tend to adopt a wider, more holistic exploration of values, purpose and meaning? What factors inform your choice in different cases?

Regardless of whether or not you work in HWC, you might find it useful to consider your own positionality in relation to health and wellness:

- How would you define health and wellness for yourself at this point in your life? Where would you locate yourself on a health continuum at this time, and why?
- (Drawing on the three components of a sense of coherence: comprehensibility, manageability and meaningfulness) How have you (or could you) come to view any stressors in your life as understandable, manageable and meaningful?
- Select an area of your health and wellness that you would like to understand better or improve. Try applying the Health Awareness Tool to consider the quadrant in which this area might sit and what your options might be.

Chapter 11

Formulation in Workplace and Executive Coaching

The use of coaching as a means of development for managers and executives has evolved from being an activity on the fringes of mainstream learning and development to one of the central elements of leadership development. Coaching and mentoring are becoming the norm in many corporate organizations and are widespread in the public and not-for-profit sectors (Chapman, 2023; Gray et al., 2016; Gorrell, 2023, Lai & Palmer, 2019). The growth in the use of coaching is a response to the demands of today's workplace with leaders facing a broad range of issues and an unprecedented level of volatility and complexity. Leaders within all sectors are faced with an environment of continuous change, with demands coming from an influx of new technology, globalization, shifting demographics and the impact that the Covid-19 pandemic has had on working conditions (Schermuly et al., 2022). Additionally, the use of coaching has gained support as a means to improve the transfer of training and sustain behaviour change (Dixit & Sinha, 2023). For these reasons, organizations are deploying coaching in a range of forms, including external executive coaches and internal workplace coaches, and training leaders in coaching skills and techniques.

Developing leaders and leadership capability is a complex task requiring coaches to consider individual factors, the needs of the organization and how to develop leaders in line with the needs of wider society. This chapter explores how formulation can support workplace and executive coaches to work collaboratively to develop formulations that not only assist their clients in meeting their immediate goals but also act as a vehicle for their ongoing development.

The Context for Workplace and Executive Coaching

A study conducted by IBM with senior executives in 2010 found that the biggest challenge they faced was the level of complexity that senior leaders were required to navigate. The same study found that 50% of those executives who recognized this challenge did not believe that they had the capability to manage it effectively (IBM, 2010). Since this study, levels of complexity have continued to grow. Organizations have had to deal with the impacts of the global pandemic with the years following the Covid-19 pandemic posing serious challenges for leadership, which the majority of leaders struggled to meet (Kaiser et al., 2023). Poor responses to

DOI: 10.4324/9781003174585-15

the impact of the pandemic demonstrated that many leaders were unable to work adaptively when the situation was evolving rapidly (Uhl-Bien, 2021).

The challenges facing leaders are many and varied and include waves of social unrest; rapidly evolving technology such as generative AI; changing customer and employee demographics; shifts from hierarchical to team-based structures; and demands for organizations to deliver business results, while also having a positive impact on the social and physical environment (Deloitte, 2019; Kaiser et al., 2023; Tarry, 2018; Whybrow et al., 2023). The impact of working in the current environment is not restricted to the leaders of organizations but is increasingly felt by all employees who are dealing with constant change, uncertainty and the effects of the global pandemic on their personal and work lives. In the UK context, it is estimated that one-sixth of workers have experienced a mental health issue and almost half of lost time is caused by the health impacts of stress, anxiety and depression (Deloitte, 2021). The sense of wellbeing in the UK was deteriorating prior to the pandemic, and measures of life satisfaction worsened in the year following the onset of Covid-19 (Deloitte, 2022). Workplace wellbeing has yet to improve, with nearly half of both executives and employees struggling with fatigue and poor mental health (Deloitte, 2023). Similarly, presenteeism is on the rise as employees attend work even when they are unwell and consequently are working at reduced levels of productivity. People may choose to come to work (in-person or remotely) because of the stigma associated with mental health concerns (Deloitte, 2022). Similarly, leavism is increasing with employees being unable to switch off, leading to burnout, a situation that is fuelled by the increase of remote working enabled by technology (Deloitte, 2021).

Coaches are being affected by the same transformations as other knowledge workers with AI already finding its way into workplace coaching (Graßman & Schermuly, 2021) and internet-based companies connecting clients and coaches through virtual platforms (Schermuly et al., 2022). While AI coaches may have a more extensive role to play in the near future, coaching in organizations is a demanding task requiring coaches (internal or external) to synthesize multiple sources of data and manage multiple stakeholders and their expectations, while meeting the specific needs of both the client they are coaching and the organization. A more complex working world is likely to give rise to more diverse coaching topics (Schermuly et al., 2022) and coaches need tools to navigate this complexity. Formulation offers a way in which the coach and client can capture, synthesize and make sense of the information and work together to achieve the agreed coaching purpose (Kovács & Corrie, 2021).

Applying Formulation in the Workplace Coaching Context

Having considered the context of coaching in organizations, examined next is the impact of positionality on workplace and executive coaching, exploring how the purpose of coaching in this context is framed and the relevance of different perspectives. Examples of the types of processes that might be used in formulation in this context are given and a case study to illustrate the key points is provided.

Positionality in Workplace and Executive Coaching

The broader aspects of positionality that have been discussed in earlier chapters are equally relevant and useful to consider in the context of coaching in organizations. However, there are some elements that arise specifically for coaches in the workplace. For example, given that coaches working in organizations may be internal or external, an explicit insider–outsider dimension of positionality is introduced into the relationship. From the perspective of positionality theory, an insider means that the coach has similarities with the client, whereas an outsider, who does not have a shared identity or background with the client, may misconstrue culture or practices (Bayeck, 2022). Either position has implications for the coaching, the relationship with the client, and the connections to the broader organization.

An internal coach is positioned as an insider, bringing the benefits of intimate knowledge of the business, the organizational culture, people and policies (Baldwin & Cherry, 2019). However, issues of confidentiality and trust may arise as well as the potential that organizational knowledge can influence the coach's objectivity (Frisch et al., 2019).

Alternatively, a coach working independently and brought into an organization to work with specific clients will be positioned as an outsider. Coaches in this situation offer the benefit of having experience across multiple organizational contexts and may bring alternative perspectives to the coaching. While the external coach may be seen as more independent, they may take time to understand the nature of the organization, the business challenges and culture. There is some evidence that clients are more open with external coaches, likely due in part to the perception of increased confidentiality (Jones et al., 2018). Insider–outsider positionality is not a simple binary of whether the coach is internal or external. Aspects of shared identity will be a factor, as will the background of the coach. A coach who had an executive career prior to training as a coach is more likely to be seen as an insider, whereas a coach with a psychology background may be seen as an outsider. This may become even more specific by industry, with coaches without experience in a specific profession or industry being positioned as outsiders.

Entering into any relationship brings with it a network of power relations. In any workplace or executive coaching engagement, there is always the possibility for covert and explicit power dynamics to manifest between stakeholders. The most obvious form of power is that of the organization over the coach who is seeking to make their livelihood from coaching within that organization (Jackson & Carter, 2007). Similarly, a manager coaching someone in their direct reporting line has an overt position of power over the person being coached. There are other, less obvious forms of power involved in a workplace coaching relationship. For example, coaches can be asked to work with clients who are more successful than themselves in their careers. This can give rise to feelings of insecurity and inadequacy in the coach and as a way of compensating for this situation they may seek to exert power in the coaching relationship (Welman & Bachkirova, 2010). Ways of dominating the coaching include holding on disproportionately to the coaching process, application of a forceful pace or extensive use of structured activities, thereby denying the client their share of control. Coaches who are acting as representatives of an organization can develop a sense of being more powerful than their clients due to the interpersonal power this position gives them (Welman & Bachkirova, 2010). They may identify with the needs of the organization to an extent that they put inappropriate pressure on the client and coaching becomes a tool to control the client's behaviour (Lai & Turner, 2023). The use of formulation itself, if applied inappropriately, has the potential to create a power imbalance. The coach may believe they have power because they have a deeper understanding of the client and their situation than the client themselves and may choose to withhold or give their insights as a means of exercising power over the client.

Those being coached also have covert ways of exerting power over the coach. They may underplay all positive outcomes and experiences of the coaching when discussing their experiences with other stakeholders or may undermine the coach's credibility by reporting unfavourably on the work or attributing the failure of the coaching to the coach (Welman & Bachkirova, 2010).

The above are just some of the ways that power can impact the coaching. As with other elements of positionality, one of the keys to managing the effects of power relations is to increase self-awareness. This self-awareness may include moment-to-moment awareness of the power relations in a specific coaching relationship, but also a deeper reflection on the coach's attitude towards power and the effect this has on their coaching, and their relationships with clients and organizational stakeholders (Welman & Bachkirova, 2010). It may also be necessary for coaches to broaden their education from psychological models and to integrate other disciplines that provide insight into topics such as culture and context, power and morality (Louis & Fatien Diochon, 2018).

With multiple stakeholders involved in workplace and executive coaching engagements there is the potential for people to hold different positions and ideas about the nature of coaching and what it should deliver (Kahn, 2014). Being clear about the position that the coach holds and enquiring into the views of the other stakeholders become essential as these views will impact not only the expectations of the client and the organization but also the perspectives and process that they will sanction. Workplaces will often have their own processes for development, existing leadership models, commonly used frameworks and tools, and these may need to be integrated into a coaching engagement and reflected in the coach's formulation. Engaging with the organization at multiple levels in order to understand how coaching is viewed and deployed is essential to a successful engagement (Hawkins & Turner, 2020; Kahn, 2014).

Identifying the Purpose of the Coaching

Articulating a clear purpose for the services being offered is as important in the workplace and executive coaching domain as in other fields of coaching.

There will likely be multiple stakeholders involved in the commissioning of coaching services, whether with an internal or external provider. The ability of the coach to articulate how they define the purpose of their offering enables all stakeholders to understand the likely focus, direction and approach that will be adopted. Coaches often need to act as mediators to ensure alignment on the coaching purpose between client and the organizational sponsors (Lai & Smith, 2021). For internal coaches, the purpose may be directed by the organization and there may be less scope for the coach to define it for themselves, or as with an external coach, negotiation with the organizational sponsors may be needed (St John-Brooks, 2014; Lai & Smith, 2021).

In the workplace and executive coaching field, some definitions focus the purpose at an individual level, e.g. improving leadership skills, developing high potential candidates for future roles or helping people transition to new positions (Athanasopoulou & Dopson, 2018; Terblanche, 2022). The purpose may also include performance-related changes to behaviour, enhanced self-awareness or personal growth (Wang et al., 2021). For coaches adopting a systemic perspective, the purpose of coaching turns from the purely individual to the broader system. For example, Hawkins (2021), in defining systemic coaching, expands the purpose beyond the individual and their organization to consider how leaders co-create value with and for all the organization's stakeholders and the wider business ecosystem. In essence, Hawkins and Turner (2020) see the purpose of systemic coaching as being in service of the relationships that connect and weave between all parties, not just the individual development of the client. Similarly, O'Connor (2020) has argued that the purpose of a coaching engagement could include creating change in the organizational system.

The subject of wellbeing is not specifically mentioned in the examples above, although executive coaching has been shown to have a positive impact on wellbeing (Grant et al., 2009; O'Connor & Cavanagh, 2013; Wang et al., 2021). Given the increasing demands placed on today's workforce, for some coaches there may well be an argument to give wellbeing more prominence when discussing the purpose of their services. Grant (2017) is a proponent of this perspective, arguing that coaching needs to broaden its definition to meet the demands of the contemporary workplace. For Grant (2017) workplace coaching should focus as much on development and wellbeing as individual effectiveness and on culture change as much as organizational performance. Wellbeing can also be considered from the systemic perspective as there is some evidence to suggest that developing the positive leadership capabilities of executives has a positive impact on the wellbeing of the organization and other key stakeholders (Addison & Shapiro, 2023; Boniwell & Smith, 2018; O'Connor & Cavanagh, 2013).

As discussed in earlier chapters, how a coaching purpose is defined has implications for the perspectives on which a coach is likely to base their practice. Some of the perspectives that are applicable to workplace and executive coaching are considered next.

Perspectives in an Organizational Setting

Coaches working in organizations come from an ever-widening circle of backgrounds (Jones et al., 2016), including psychology, business, sport, law, academia, management consultancy or human resources (Joo, 2005; Kahn, 2014). Consequently, workplace and executive coaches draw on a range of perspectives, based on their beliefs about human change and development, their training, background and the purpose of the coaching.

Kahn (2014) has argued that while perspectives drawn from psychology and counselling are important to coaches working in organizational contexts, they need to be balanced with perspectives suited to that setting. Workplace coaching is taking place within the culture of the marketplace and coaching is simultaneously aiming to help both the organization and the individual leader achieve success. Coaches also need to understand the culture of business in general, and that of the organization specifically, while taking a systemic perspective in order to align individual and organizational needs.

In the business world there is a cultural assumption that in order to survive in a fast and reflexive marketplace, leaders do not have time to prove something before responding (Kahn, 2014). Leaders are often required to make decisions without all the information, and they frequently use a combination of intuition and analysis when facing complex problems (Okoli, 2020; Hallo & Nguyen, 2022). In using intuition leaders draw on their experience and their ability to recognize patterns, which is particularly useful when there is limited time, high levels of complexity and data are scarce. Given that multiple perspectives and a focus on viability are embedded in the business culture, it has been argued that no one theory fits, but that an eclectic or integrative approach is best suited to a commercial context (Hardingham, 2021; Kahn, 2014; Passmore, 2007; Turner & Goodrich, 2010).

The terms eclectic or integrative are often used interchangeably, and while some overlap exists between the two, there are also some key differences. Integrative approaches draw together different theories and models in a considered way (Passmore, 2021), seeking synthesis between multiple schools of thought to create a new model (Hollanders, 2014). Eclecticism also draws from multiple sources; however, it is a pragmatic approach that aims to apply the most appropriate tool or technique for the person in their context (Hardingham, 2021; Hollanders, 2014).

Using eclectic or integrative frameworks relies heavily on the coach to select or develop an appropriate approach to the client (Hardingham, 2021). While there is some indication in the coaching literature that the application of diverse techniques can be helpful (De Haan et al., 2013), there is currently little research to guide coaches in selecting what techniques work best for specific clients or which theories could be integrated. In practice, coaches will make decisions on the approach to be used based on their professional training and experience (Hardingham, 2021). This reliance on the coach emphasizes the importance of both formulation and a grounding in reflective practice for an eclectic or integrative coach. Formulation can provide the basis for decision-making and for providing a rationale for the choice of approach at any point. It is also a useful aid in reflective practice. Through the reflective process the experience of working with a specific client becomes integrated into the coach's approach to their practice, informing future coaching engagements (Hay, 2007; Kovács & Corrie, 2017a).

Leadership Perspectives

Given that workplace and executive coaching are frequently used as an intervention to develop leadership capability (Anthony, 2017; Korotov, 2016; Passmore, 2015), there is an argument that those who work in this field need a robust engagement with the literature related to leadership theory and development (Otter, 2018). However, there are two main challenges for coaches in engaging with the leadership field. First, multiple definitions make it difficult for coaches to develop familiarity with the full range of leadership perspectives (Otter, 2018). While some of the coaching literature mentions theoretical models of leadership (e.g. O'Connor & Cavanagh, 2013; Passmore, 2015; Watts & Corrie, 2013, 2022), much of the literature focuses on the theories that inform the coaching process such as theories of adult development, communication, psychology or human performance. There is relatively limited engagement with the theory of leadership or leadership development, compounding the challenge for coaches of integrating these knowledge bases in practice (Otter, 2018). Second, common practice in organizations adds complexity. Despite the existence of a large number of leadership theories and models, development is often undertaken haphazardly in organizations and is not explicitly connected to any theoretical model. Coaching is simply one of a number of interventions (e.g. assessments, leadership training, digital content, experiential learning) that the organization uses (Day et al., 2021). While coaching may be offered to support other initiatives, it is also offered as a stand-alone development activity which may or may not be linked to the organization's perspective on leadership.

Rather than adopting a theoretical perspective, organizations often adopt competency models as they provide bundles of knowledge, skills and capabilities that appear to simplify the complex construct of leadership into discrete and concrete variables (Day et al., 2021; Salicru, 2020). Competency frameworks often provide a generic set of skills and behaviours, which implies an assumption that those who excel in the same role display the same behaviour (Bolden & Gosling, 2006). This is problematic in several ways. Studies have demonstrated that leaders achieve the same results using entirely different approaches and the generic nature of these models fails to consider individual differences or the context in which the leader is embedded (Day et al., 2021). Additionally, the behaviours or capabilities contained in these frameworks often focus on present rather than future requirements. Leadership cannot be disconnected from the broader social context and, therefore, the competency model may not aid the understanding of what is required for a specific leader to be effective in the present or emerging context (Bolden & Gosling, 2006; Salicru, 2020).

Given the complexity and emerging nature of the field of leadership development theory, familiarity with the full range of perspectives is unrealistic (Otter, 2018). However, models are useful frameworks and heuristics for development conversations, and coaches working in organizations should engage with a number of models so that they can adapt to suit the individual, culture and context in a specific situation (Passmore, 2015). How the approach is selected can be a function of the formulation that the coach and client develop. Coach, client and key stakeholders may hold different perspectives on leadership (Otter, 2018) and the formulation can also be a vehicle for making sense of these different perspectives and integrating leadership and coaching theories.

Having considered the perspectives that might be useful in workplace and executive coaching, the matter of process is considered next.

Frameworks and Process for Formulation in Executive Coaching

A number of conceptual frameworks have been developed to articulate the workplace and executive coaching process, most of which have an input–process–output structure. These provide a useful guide and form the basis of practice for a number of coaches. While many frameworks have been developed by transferring a single model from its origins in therapy to a coaching context (Passmore, 2007), a number of integrative coaching models have been developed. Laske (1999) has proposed an approach which integrates constructive developmental psychology, family therapy and theories of organizational cognition. Grant (2006) integrates goal-setting, self-determination and personality theories to provide an evidence-based, integrative executive and workplace coaching framework. Chapman's (2018) Integrated Experiential Coaching model is grounded in the metatheories of integral and experiential learning theory and was later updated to include a synthesis of additional perspectives, including complex responsive processes, the physiology of learning and neuroscience (Chapman, 2023).

An overview of Passmore's (2007, 2021) holistic model for coaches working within the business world is provided, as it was developed specifically for executive coaching. Passmore's approach also provides an example of the integration of approaches from individual, interpersonal and systemic perspectives, including humanistic, psychodynamic, behaviourism and cognitive-behavioural traditions.

The integrative coaching model (Passmore, 2007, 2021) consists of six "streams" that are involved in achieving the desired outcomes. These streams flow together, with the coach moving between them as they respond to the client. The first two streams are concerned with the coach–client relationship:

Stream 1: Developing the coaching relationship draws on the humanistic tradition to establish a successful partnership (interpersonal perspective).

Stream 2: Maintaining the relationship. Once the relationship is established, the coach needs to work to maintain trust and respect, again drawing on concepts from the humanistic perspective.

These form a ring around the next three streams, providing a safe space for the coach and client to work together. Streams 3–5 draw on approaches that are underpinned by the individual perspective.

Stream 3: Focusing on behaviour change, which Passmore (2007) describes as being at the core of executive coaching. The aim of this stream is to support behaviour change through problem-solving and planning.

Stream 4: Conscious cognition draws on cognitive-behavioural coaching approaches, the aim of which is to increase the client's awareness of the links between thoughts and behaviour.

Stream 5: Focusing on unconscious cognitions and deepening a client's awareness of aspects of thought and motivation that may be inhibiting their effectiveness. This stream draws on psychodynamic tradition, but also coaches may use specialist approaches in which they are trained to target unconscious cognitions.

The sixth stream surrounds the other five and represents the systemic perspective.

Stream 6: Drawing awareness to the context in which the coaching is taking place. One of the tasks in this stream is to help the client understand the wider systemic influences at work and how they affect the client's behaviour. The coach and client might include the perspectives of other stakeholders into the coaching process. They might also consider how changes in the client's behaviour may impact the wider context, creating a ripple effect through the organization.

While Passmore's (2007, 2021) model was developed to provide an integrative frame for the coaching process, it can also be used in parallel as a framework for formulation. The resulting formulation would integrate elements from the three perspectives explored in previous chapters. The level of attention and focus devoted to each stream in the formulation will be a function of the purpose of the coaching.

Passmore's (2007, 2021) model may be best suited to coaches who have some training in the psychological approaches that underpin this approach. However, as workplace and executive coaches come from a wide range of backgrounds, one alternative for those coaches without such training is offered in the form of the Universal Eclectic Model of Executive Coaching (Hardingham, 2021). While originally drawing on psychological theories, Hardingham (2021) argues that this model is an intentionally inclusive framework that can be expanded to include tools and techniques drawn from organizational and management theory, as long as there is some evidence for their effectiveness.

A further alternative is the PAIR framework (described in Chapter 9), which was developed within an executive coaching context and also supports those working with an eclectic or integrative approach. The flexible nature of the process that this framework outlines enables coaches to collect and integrate data from a wide range of sources as well as supporting an approach that draws on multiple perspectives. The case study provided below illustrates how this framework can be used to support a formulation that considers individual, interpersonal and systemic perspectives. This framework also supports the reflective processes that are necessary for an effective use of eclectic or integrative approaches.

Executive Coaching Case Study Using the PAIR Framework

Sue has recently been promoted to her first executive level role, now reporting to Christine, the CEO of a global multinational that is headquartered in London. Sue is based in Ireland, where she moved during the pandemic, while most of the people reporting to her are based in offices around the world. Married with two school-aged children Sue predominantly works from home, which assists her in maintaining a work–life balance.

Angus, a London-based coach, is an eclectic practitioner who selects the tools and techniques he adopts for each client based on his formulation. He predominantly draws on cognitive-behavioural, adult developmental and systemic approaches. Underpinning his approach to leadership development is the perspective of developing leadership versatility as a key to leading in complex environments (Kaiser et al., 2023).

Purpose: Angus has been asked to work with Sue as Christine, and Sue's peers, have perceived that the transition to this more senior role is not going as smoothly as they had expected. Specifically, there is a perception that there is a lack of communication in all directions – to Christine, Sue's peers and the managers reporting to her. While the day-to-day work of her department is being delivered, it is not clear to any of her stakeholders if she has determined the key issues that need to be resolved in her department and if she has a strategy to address them. Sue has recently received this feedback from Christine and has become even more withdrawn as a result. Angus has met with Christine, the head of HR, and Sue individually. After discussions with each, the purpose of the coaching has been agreed as accelerating Sue's transition to executive leadership and that specific aspects of feedback, such as improved communication, will be addressed.

Account: Angus begins data gathering by spending several hours with Sue, hearing her perspective on the transition to her new role. They also agree that Angus will interview Sue's direct reports and several of her peers.

Based on the data from these conversations, Angus and Sue develop an account of potential factors at both individual and systemic levels.

- Sue is over-reliant on email and other electronic forms of communication. She has not met with her peers or Christine in person since her promotion.
- Previous psychometric results have indicated that she is an introvert and she stated herself that she is reluctant to do any public speaking, and minimizes in-person interactions.

- Sue has high standards and rather than delegating and coaching her team, she spends time improving their work.
- Being criticized by Christine was a painful experience and she is avoiding meeting with her.
- She wants to be a good mother and spend time with her children as well as pursue an executive career. Her high standards apply at home as much as they do at work.
- Her partner is also working in a senior role and has an equally demanding job.
- The organizational culture is highly collaborative with the expectation that people will be consulted about issues that affect them and that there will be consistent and regular communication between leaders and the teams that work for them.
- Peers expect to be consulted and updated regularly with a high value placed on the relationships between peers. It is not a competitive peer group, rather they seek to work together to achieve the overall organization's goals.
- Sue's direct reports work in different time zones and it is difficult to find a time when everyone is available to meet.
- The organization is going through a major transformation project and Sue's team have yet to deliver on several key objectives.
- Sue is not demonstrating high levels of leadership versatility, largely basing her leadership on a directive style, which is focused on operational delivery, rather than a more strategic and empowering approach.

Based on the data gathered, Sue and Angus develop a number of hypotheses:

- Sue's high standards mean that she finds it difficult to delegate, both at home and work. This leaves little time for meetings to communicate and collaborate.
- Underlying cognitions include:
  - If everything is not perfect, I shall be seen to be a failure.
  - If I am criticized, it is best to withdraw and not communicate until things are right.
  - It is better to over-deliver and be judged by my results, rather than what I say I am going to do.
  - My time is best spent doing the work, rather than attending "pointless" meetings.
- There is a mismatch between Sue's more introverted style and the preferred ways of working of her peers on the executive team.
- Sue's team is highly capable but is unclear about Sue's priorities. They are becoming dependent on her to help them deliver their work as they are becoming conditioned that Sue will correct it if it doesn't meet her standards.
- Sue's reluctance to travel and meet in person has widened the gap between her and her peers, and has affected her relationship with Christine.
- Sue has a clear plan for delivering the aspects of the transformation but has failed to communicate her strategy to the key stakeholders.

- Sue is not demonstrating the required leadership versatility to lead in this context. A more empowering style would free up her time to strengthen her relationships and improve communication.

Intervene: Based on this formulation a number of these hypotheses are tested through interventions.

- Sue makes several trips to London to present her strategy to Christine and her peers, immediately gaining support and offers of help where it is needed.
- Sue works with the coach on managing how her high standards impact herself and others.
- Sue and the coach work to identify cognitions and beliefs, testing strategies to reduce their impact on her behaviour and gradually shift her patterns of thinking.
- Sue commits to empowering and delegating to the managers who report to her, reducing the amount of time spent in refining their work. This creates more time for other activities, such as informal meetings with her peers.
- Sue enrols in the organization's "manager-as-coach" programme and Angus helps her apply what she has learned to embed her delegation and empowering style.
- Sue worked with her direct reports to develop a schedule of meetings for regular updates and discussions, building a more collaborative and supportive team to support Sue.
- Sue works with her partner to find a more equitable share of the childcaring work and to find additional resources to support them and the children.

Reflect: Angus and Sue regularly reflect on the coaching process and the progress being made. Sue received several positive pieces of feedback from Christine and was successful in building more effective relationships with her peers.

The combination of cognitive-behavioural, leadership perspectives and shifts in the way Sue interacted with the organizational system were having a positive impact. The team were beginning to demonstrate their full capability and Sue was beginning to be more comfortable in her communication, realizing that effective stakeholder management was a key part of her leadership role. It was more challenging to tackle some of the underlying beliefs, but Sue was gaining greater awareness in how they were impacting her behaviour.

Angus recognized how the collaborative nature of the organization also affected his relationship with key stakeholders. There were more requests for updates, offers of help and additional feedback than he felt were necessary. Angus struggled to manage the balance of what was appropriate for the coaching and what the organizational system expected. Angus reflected that, in hindsight, more contracting on what was expected or required from the stakeholders would have been useful. However, even with this additional understanding, the organizational culture may lead to these agreements being disregarded.

This case example demonstrates a pragmatic approach to working with the client. Based on the data collected and the hypotheses that were developed, interventions were designed and implemented, addressing specific behaviours as well as underlying cognitions. While these interventions were primarily at the individual level, the effects of these behaviour changes had impact across teams and a network of relationships.

Challenges in Applying Formulation in Workplace and Executive Coaching

There are a number of challenges that may arise in applying formulation in a workplace and executive coaching context. Firstly, formulation is not well understood outside the fields of applied psychology and psychological therapy, and the term itself may be perceived as having a medical or clinical tone. Coaches working in organizational contexts may choose to use an alternative term, such as story or account.

Another challenge is that in the fast-moving world of organizations, there may be some resistance to taking the time to develop a formulation. Given the tendency for leaders to act quickly on their intuition (Kahn, 2014; Okoli, 2020), some clients may want rapid solutions to their issues. Therefore, coaches will need to ensure that they engage the client in the formulation process and ensure some early wins are identified with the client. Internal workplace coaches may feel less comfortable taking the time to develop the formulation as they are often providing coaching as a secondary task to their main role, with time already being in short supply. It may be useful to position the formulation process as a form of analysis that balances the intuitive decision-making in the same way that leaders make other decisions for the business (Hallo & Nguyen, 2022).

Conclusion

Despite the potential challenges outlined above, formulation has a critical role to play in supporting the effectiveness of workplace and executive coaches. In this chapter we have considered how the elements of the 4P Framework, and other models, can support the use of formulation in this context. Coaches in organizations are required to manage the demands of multiple stakeholders, synthesize data and deliver results. This needs to take place in an environment of increasing uncertainty and volatility and developing a practice grounded in formulation can assist coaches in navigating their way.

Questions to Consider

For coaches working in organizations, consider the following aspects of your practice:

- In working with multiple stakeholders, how can the expectations of different stakeholders regarding the purpose, perspectives and coaching process be aligned?

- When considering a coaching engagement, how would the impact of potential power relations be identified and managed?
- How will the effectiveness of the coaching be measured in an environment that is characterized by ongoing change and volatility?
- In selecting perspectives on which to base coaching in an organizational context, how well aligned are they to the commercial business culture?
- What leadership and leadership development perspectives do you currently integrate into your coaching practice?

Chapter 12

Formulation and Coaching Teams and Systems

Teams are central to the effectiveness of modern organizations, and Hawkins (2021) has argued that teams have greater potential than individuals to rise to the challenges of navigating a complex world. Given the importance of teams, it should be no surprise that there is a global trend for the increasing use of team coaching (Clutterbuck, 2020; Hawkins & Turner, 2020). The rise of team coaching is also driven by the "fourth industrial revolution", bringing concepts such as distributed leadership and agile teams, which require faster levels of decision-making at the team level rather than dictated from above.

Despite this increase in practice and interest from scholars, there is limited evidence on which to base practice, and there is as yet no empirically validated theory of team coaching (Clutterbuck et al., 2019). Likewise, while the professional bodies have produced competencies or accreditation processes (e.g. Association for Coaching (AC), 2023; Association for Professional Executive Coaching and Supervision (APECS), 2024; EMCC Global, 2023; International Coach Federation (ICF), 2020), research that identifies the competencies needed to be an effective team coach is also lacking (Jones et al., 2019).

In this chapter team coaching is explored and some of the challenges of working with teams and systems are discussed. The benefits of using formulation to support the co-creation of an overarching purpose of a team is considered and perspectives that may support an understanding of team dynamics are introduced. A range of processes that can support the coaching and formulation are presented, followed by a short case study illustrating group and team coaching formulation, which concludes the chapter.

Group Coaching or Team Coaching?

While the field of team coaching appears to be a new and evolving area, there is a long history of group-level interventions on which to base practice. In the field of psychological therapy, the use of groups began at the beginning of the 20th century (Brabender et al., 2004). Organization development (OD) consultants have been utilizing group interventions as part of change initiatives since the 1950s (Brown & Grant, 2010), and they have been widely deployed in various sectors (National

DOI: 10.4324/9781003174585-16

Fire Chiefs Council, 2024; Local Government Association, 2024; NHS, 2024). Proponents argue that the group represents a microcosm of the environment that the individuals inhabit, and that the processes that emerge in this setting assist individuals in developing awareness, alignment and accountability as well as developing systems thinking (Brabender et al., 2004; Brown & Grant, 2010). There is also a detailed literature on the influence of groups on decision-making (Baron & Kerr, 2003; Gorell, 2022; Kerr & Tindale, 2004; Lane & Corrie, 2011; Tindale & Winget, 2019). Given the history of group-level interventions it is unsurprising that in both the coaching literature and in practice there is a lack of clarity concerning the differences between group interventions, group coaching and team coaching.

The approach used for a group as opposed to a team engagement can vary substantially (Hawkins, 2021), making it essential to clarify into which category the group falls. The following definition identifies some of the key elements that distinguish a team from other groups:

> A team can be defined as a) two or more individuals who b) socially interact (face-to-face or increasingly virtually); c) possess one or more common goals; d) are brought together to perform organizationally relevant tasks; e) exhibit interdependencies with respect to workflow, goals, and outcomes; f) have different roles and responsibilities, and g) are together embedded in an encompassing organizational system, with boundaries and linkages to the broader system context and task environment (Kozlowski & Ilgen, 2006, p. 79).

The factors that distinguish a team and a workgroup are at the level of shared goals and the interdependencies between the team members. A team requires a collective endeavour that can only be achieved by working together and for which they hold shared accountability (Hawkins, 2021).

There have been some attempts to further identify the distinctiveness of team coaching and its place within the range of group interventions. For example, Jones et al. (2019) offered a definition based on their review of the team coaching literature that identified the focus of team coaching on learning together, team performance and the achievement of a shared or common goal.

Other definitions also focus on the outcome as being team performance but set the coaching in the context of the wider system (e.g. Widdowson & Barbour, 2021). Hawkins (2021) has further extended the definition to consider coaching teams of teams, while setting the coaching in the broader eco-system in which the teams operate. Eco-systemic coaching sees the team as co-evolving in a dynamic relationship with its ever-changing eco-system of interconnected teams, with which it co-creates shared value. According to Hawkins (2021), the strategic dialogue of the coaching process:

- Involves its wider stakeholders (coaching strategizing processes),
- Develops a team-based culture within an organization, and
- Across a network of enterprises (coaching networks), or

- Partnerships that bring people and organizations together in pursuit of a common goal (coaching partnerships).

What Team or Group Coaching Aims to Achieve

Teamwork has become such an important topic because it is argued that effective teams can drive enhanced performance and is particularly important when facing complex problems (O'Neill & Salas, 2018). In a volatile, uncertain, complex and ambiguous (VUCA) (Barber, 1992) world, even the notion of performance is challenging, as a high-performing organization today could disappear tomorrow. As organizations deal with rapidly changing situations, an idea that is gaining acceptance is that uncertainty and ambiguity cannot be resolved but instead need to be managed. Leaders are making decisions in a world of readily accessible information, yet the value of that data deteriorates as situations rapidly evolve.

Leaders must make decisions without the predictability that they previously sought (Crevani et al., 2021). Top-down strategy, goals, tasks and controls lose value, and adaptive solutions are found through collective creativity processes and alternative distributed models of leadership, which have been linked to enhanced team performance (De Brún & McAuliffe, 2020).

The nature of teams is also shifting. Technological advances, accelerated by the Covid-19 pandemic, mean that organizations are changing the composition of teams from those who are inside formal organizational structures to loosely connected members of a larger community, such as the virtual employees of large companies. Increasingly, organizations are relying on fluid teams, enabling them to remain agile and respond quickly to opportunities and market changes (Benishek & Lazzara, 2019). The gig economy also means highly skilled workers sell their services and become temporary team members with the specialized skills needed for a specific project (Larson & DeChurch, 2020).

An increasingly proposed alternative leadership approach that meets the needs of today's VUCA environment is the idea of establishing a common purpose, as explored in Chapter 5. Where groups of people understand the essence of what they are trying to achieve, it is possible to think creatively without command-and-control structures. The principles of effective teamwork proposed by Hawkins (2021) and Clutterbuck (2020) centre on the idea of a shared purpose that teams understand, which makes sense to their stakeholders and themselves, and is focused on learning in real time.

However, coaches encountering any team, but particularly self-organizing or agile teams, will recognize that formulating a common purpose "does not just happen – you need to look at how it would work for you and why it matters" (Gorell, 2022, p. xiv). The team need a story; a narrative of who and why it is, and the practices to match. The use of dialogic conversation facilitates a new expanded understanding of what is possible and encourages the changes necessary to generate new knowledge (Stelter, 2019; Tsoukas, 2009). The purpose explored in this process can be unique and appropriate to the context, system and the people involved; new stories emerge, but the person and team changes according to each story. Thus, dialogic conversation becomes a joint inquiry of giving and receiving, while sharing and learning from practices. It enables an openness to the uncertain, and the willingness to know. Such processes are increasingly seen, not just in team coaching, but in fields such as dialogic OD as a means to transformational change (Bushe & Marshak, 2015; Hastings & Schwarz, 2022; Maxton, 2021; Schein, 2015).

Transformation in a VUCA world presents significant challenges for team coaching at an ethical and professional level. Businesses, along with the leaders and coaches who work in them, can be instrumental to the transformations necessary to promote flourishing and address the issues facing the global community (MacKie, 2023). Leadership in the context of responses to these complex challenges requires very different approaches to traditional models of strategic planning and leadership. It requires teams to think wider, deeper, taking different perspectives, embracing more complexity (Lane & Corrie, 2011) and using emergence to enable adaptive responses (Uhl-Bien, 2021). Consequently, a wider perspective is also needed when considering the capabilities for team coaching.

Capabilities for Team Coaching

While the literature on the competencies of an effective team coach is limited, the existing research has identified some key themes:

- Team coaching requires advanced coaching skills such as considering multiple perspectives, observing and interpreting interactions and creating a strong sense of safety within the team (Jones et al., 2019).
- Team coaches need to be adaptable, changing their shape and form to meet the needs of the team (Hauser, 2014).
- Coaches must be able to manage uncertainty throughout the coaching process (Ghosh, 2020).
- Coaches must be able to make decisions on how to respond to the team's needs in any given moment (Ghosh, 2020).
- Coaches need to be able to take an eclectic approach, drawing on a wide range of approaches and disciplines (Ghosh, 2020).
- Coaches need to be able to use a systemic perspective to help the team see the broader system and the interactions between the team and the wider context (James et al., 2020).
- Coaches need to understand group dynamics and group-based dialogue processes (Brown & Grant, 2010).

These capabilities are consistent with those that leaders also need as they navigate the challenges outlined above.

The 4P Framework Applied in Team Coaching

Given the potential complexity in navigating a team or systemic coaching engagement, formulation can provide a flexible means of co-creating and capturing the emergent properties of the team and the coaching. This section illustrates how the 4P framework can be used within this context.

Positionality

In the case of teams, positionality concerns the position of the team or group in the world. As the world becomes more challenging and the factors influencing organizational success become increasingly complex, multiple diversities need to be considered. Traditionally, this has been viewed through the lens of ethnicity, gender, sexual identity, ability, neurodivergence, class, education and cultural background. However, there is no simple relationship between these identities and how individuals view their own place in the world or the narratives that organizations create to position themselves in relation to others. Stout-Rostron (2019b) discusses the idea of "common diversity attributes", which have differing impacts on group performance:

- Readily detectable versus less observable
- Surface level versus deep level
- Highly job-related versus less job-related
- Task-related versus relations-oriented
- Role-related versus inherent.

As team coaching is adopted by more organizations as a way to improve productivity it is possible to consider how diversity within the group can become a productive asset, especially in terms of areas featured in the literature, such as diversity and creativity, team performance, cooperation and conflict, competition and collaboration (e.g. Horwitz & Horwitz, 2007; Hundschell et al., 2022; King et al., 2009). As Stout-Rostron (2019b) suggests, the research is mixed, with some studies showing positive and some marginal impacts. What it does underline is the importance of taking positionality seriously.

Purpose as a Narrative for Change

In Chapter 4 we considered the Chartered Management Insitute (Ebert et al., 2018) research, which identified five features of an effective purpose statement. A shared purpose, which is agreed with the team's internal and external stakeholders, provides direction, a guide to decision-making, and the motivation to commitment. Creating a team narrative around this purpose provides the higher-level perspective that validates specific goals and tasks, a basis for evaluation against the core purpose and a focal point for continuous learning. Reviewing Hawkins's (2021) features for effective teams (discussed below), the importance of the team's needs for a real but shared sense of itself and how it delivers its purpose to enhance effectiveness is clear.

While team coaching may have a shared purpose as a starting point, coaching groups requires a different approach to addressing the concept of purpose. Group coaching may be established with a broad purpose in mind prior to the formation of the group. For example, group coaching has been used to support people with long-term health conditions (Whitley, 2013), maximize health and wellbeing (Nacif, 2021; Wolever et al., 2024), foster transformative learning (Peters & Göhlich, 2024) and support newly graduated doctors (Malling et al., 2020). Similarly, when working internally in organizations the overarching purpose may be established between the coach and organizational sponsor. Individuals then pursue their own, usually work-related, goals, which are linked in some way to this overarching purpose of the group coaching. Regardless of the context, clarity on the purpose is an essential first step to any coaching or formulation.

Perspectives for Group or Team Coaching

Multiple perspectives may be required to develop the eclectic approach needed to assist the team or group in achieving the purpose of the intervention (Ghosh, 2020; Gorell, 2022). Individual, interpersonal and systemic perspectives may all be useful in working with teams and groups. For example, systems psychodynamic approaches (Lawlor & Sher, 2021) blend constructs drawn from the fields of psychoanalysis, group relations and sociotechnical and complexity theories, resulting in a complex interweaving of concepts that are brought to bear in a group setting. Some existing team coaching models also draw on all three perspectives, such as the coaching approach adopted by Robinson and Yanagi (2019), which focuses on raising awareness at the individual, relational and systems levels. Pavlović (2021) also adopts all three perspectives in her framework of team coaching, adopting personal and relationship constructivist, systemic and solution-focused approaches.

While all three perspectives may be used, familiarity with systemic perspectives is particularly useful as team and group coaches often work within and across different systems. As discussed in Chapter 8, there are multiple systems theories with each bringing a different perspective on the work with the group. A first-order systems approach may focus on diagnosing and intervening in the functioning of the team, while a meta-systemic coach who sees the team as part of a broader, dynamic social network focuses on patterns of interactions and emergence of team behaviour and performance (Lawrence, 2021b). This latter approach is consistent with the contemporary view in the team development literature, which is considered next.

A Dynamic Systems Lens on Teams

There is an existing body of knowledge and research regarding teams and team development on which coaches can draw (e.g. Costa, 2024; Grote & Kozlowski, 2023;

Rapp et al., 2021). Much of the contemporary literature takes a systemic perspective, which conceptualizes teams as complex dynamic systems that develop as members interact over time, evolving and adapting as situational demands unfold (Rapp et al., 2021). Individuals comprise the team, which becomes a collective entity that, in turn, also serves as the social context that influences the individuals (Delice et al., 2019; Kozlowski & Ilgen, 2006). Interactions between the broader system and the team are reciprocal. As the team operates and performs tasks, the outputs from the team meet demands from the organizational context while also changing the state of the system in some way (Kozlowski & Ilgen, 2006).

Understanding the team as a system of interactions, rather than a collection of people, provides a novel understanding, giving rise to insights into patterns of dynamics, both within and outside the team, which unfold as the team interacts both internally and with the wider environment (Delice et al., 2019; Fyhn et al., 2023; Kozlowski, 2018). Many team-level phenomena have their origins at the individual level; however, through interaction and exchange with other individuals these phenomena have an emergent nature (Kozlowski & Bell, 2020).

While the dynamic and complex nature of team interactions may be difficult to capture in real time, they yield emergent states and patterns that represent echoes of repeated interactions (Kozlowski & Ilgen, 2006). A formulation, therefore, may include patterns of interactions and emergent states as a means of identifying areas of strengths and those that can be improved. To engage the team in this process, it can be helpful to have a framework that guides the identification of relevant patterns. Scholars have made numerous attempts to categorize the states that can emerge from team interactions (Rapp et al., 2021), and there is good evidence to support the usefulness of the Attitudes, Behaviours, Cognitions (ABC) Framework (Kozlowski, 2018; Kozlowski & Ilgen, 2006; Rapp et al., 2021), which is summarized below in Table 12.1.

The ABC Framework is not intended to be a linear checklist, as there are many potential interactions between the different factors (Salas et al., 2015). Psychological safety is key to team learning (Edmondson, 1999), which in turn underpins other cognitive states such as shared mental models. Lane (2013) considered psychological safety as a basis for teams to be able to adapt to changing states, moving quickly from an existing game plan to responding to game moments and being game changers. Similarly, the level of trust in teams is both developed through and impacts on behaviours such as communication, coordination and the team's ability to tolerate conflict (Costa et al., 2018; Kozlowksi & Ilgen, 2006). While not a checklist, this framework is useful to hold in mind when formulating where the team should focus in order to improve performance. The formulation can be updated as the coaching proceeds and as team dynamics change over time, with emergent states increasing and decreasing as the team works together (Fyhn et al., 2023).

The systemic perspective also offers an alternative view on team performance, which is conceptualized as a behavioural process rather than as being assessed against outcomes. Performance is not seen as a static achievement evaluated in retrospect, but as an ongoing dynamic process. The team members take action

Table 12.1 Attitudes, Behaviours and Cognitions Framework

Category	Emergent states
Attitudes *What team members believe or feel. Affective states likely to play a role in creating the glue that bonds the team together.*	**Psychological Safety:** *Shared perception that the team is a safe place for interpersonal risk-taking.* **Trust:** *Trust can help team members tolerate conflict over task-related issues without it spilling over to destructive relationship conflict.* **Cohesion:** *Three potential areas of team cohesion: task, interpersonal and group pride.* **Team efficacy:** *Shared belief in the team's collective capability to organize and execute the course of action required to produce goal attainment.* **Group potency:** *A generalized sense of the team's viability and capability (team efficacy is more task or goal specific).*
Behaviours *What the team does.*	**Communication:** *Patterns of communication between team members, and with the broader systems.* **Coordination:** *The combination and synchronization of disparate team members' actions and effort.* **Conflict:** *Understanding how to handle conflict is useful. Conflict is not monolithic and may relate to tasks or interpersonal relationships.* **Leadership styles:** *Application of appropriate leadership styles within and outside the team.* **Team regulation:** *A multilevel construct at both individual and team level that is related to the team's ability to regulate effort and resources towards agreed goals.*
Cognitions *What team members think or know.*	**Team learning:** *Acquisition of knowledge, skills and performance capabilities through interaction and experience. More than just a pooling of individual knowledge.* The other cognitive concepts are emergent states that develop from learning as a dynamic process. **Team climate:** *A shared climate that captures the strategic imperatives which are reflective of the team's core mission or purpose.* **Transactive memory:** *Knowledge of who knows what in the team.* **Shared mental models:** *Knowledge that the team holds in common regarding the key aspects of the team, the task and role systems and the environment.*

Adapted from Salas et al. (2015) and Kozlowski and Ilgen (2006)

towards goals, they resolve task demands, they coordinate effort and adapt to the unexpected: this is what constitutes team effectiveness (Delice et al., 2019; Kozlowski, 2018; Kozlowski & Ilgen, 2006).

There is also a temporal dimension to consider, with performance conceptualized as a cyclical and episodic process. For each task or goal the team undertakes, they begin a discrete cycle, potentially having many cycles at different stages running simultaneously. These task or goal cycles have three stages: (1) preparation; (2) task engagement; and (3) disengagement/reflection (Kozlowski, 2018; Kozlowski & Ilgen, 2006). At each stage, the importance of different behavioural aspects will vary. During the preparation stage, setting goals and developing strategies is important, whereas in the engagement phase, monitoring discrepancies between current actions and desired outcomes is more important. At the disengagement stage, there is an opportunity to reflect on processes and how they can be improved. An understanding of these stages and relevant tasks may be particularly important in contemporary organizations where teams are being formed quickly and changing shape during their short lifespans (Mayo, 2022).

Process Frameworks for Establishing Team Coaching

Having considered the perspectives with particular relevance to team coaching, attention can be given to what process or processes can be implemented to enable the team to achieve its agreed purpose. There are several models available, including: the PERILL model (Clutterbuck, 2020); stages of team development (Peters & Carr, 2013); transformational coaching (Stout-Rostron, 2019a) and Hawkins's (2021) model of high value creating teams. Each of these models is reviewed briefly, starting with the work of David Clutterbuck, who has pioneered team coaching.

Five Pillars (Clutterbuck, 2020, 2023)

Clutterbuck (2023) has developed his model (PERILL) based upon 20 years of research on team performance and dysfunction. The model identifies five contexts that can impact how well a team functions, along with the moderating influence of leadership; each of these contexts is described below:

- Purpose and motivation: Clutterbuck (2020, 2023) identifies purpose as a key context for effective teams. This may be generated as part of a wider organizational purpose or one from within the team itself. From this shared purpose collective energy flows, indicated by the clarity of the vision, goals and priorities that the team articulates.
- External processes, systems and structures: These cover the interrelationships between the team and its stakeholders, and its access to resources such as information and finance. Success indicators include reputation, environmental awareness of markets, technology, competition as well as performance against targets.
- Relationships: How people work together is essential to effective teamwork, including levels of respect, honesty and enjoyment in working together. Success indicators include the level of satisfaction and psychological safety.
- Internal processes, systems and structures: How a team manages its workflow, support for each other and the quality of communication provides an internal mirror. Success indicators include role clarity and decision-making quality.

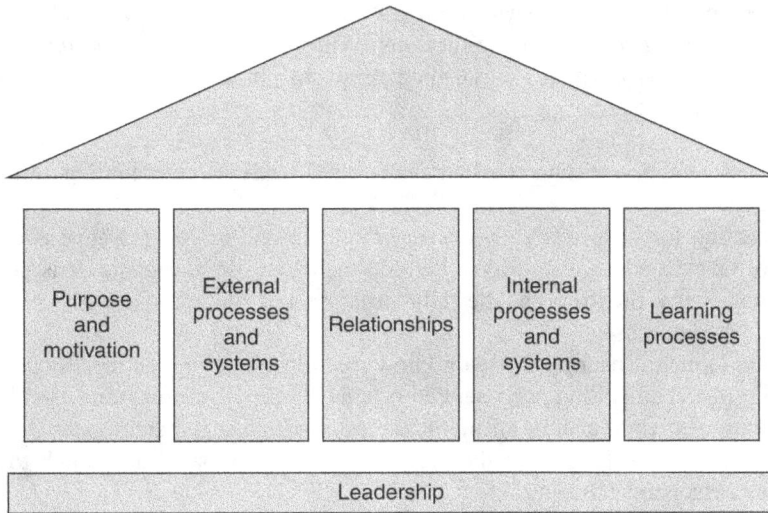

```
                    ┌──────────────────────────────────────────────┐
                    │                                              │
             ┌──────┐  ┌──────────┐  ┌──────────┐  ┌──────────┐  ┌──────────┐
             │Purpose│  │ External │  │          │  │ Internal │  │          │
             │  and  │  │processes │  │Relationships│ │processes │  │ Learning │
             │motivation│ │  and    │  │          │  │   and    │  │processes │
             │       │  │ systems  │  │          │  │ systems  │  │          │
             └──────┘  └──────────┘  └──────────┘  └──────────┘  └──────────┘
                    ┌──────────────────────────────────────────────┐
                    │                 Leadership                    │
                    └──────────────────────────────────────────────┘
```

Figure 12.1 The PERILL model (Clutterbuck, 2023)

- Learning: A key emphasis is placed on learning as a basis for continuous improvement and growth. Success indicators include being able to change in response to the team environment. The clarity of the team's learning objectives and their relevance to changed circumstances is also featured.

These five pillars represent the contexts impacting team effectiveness. The moderating factor is the team leader's qualities and behaviours. Given the vast literature on leadership, and differences in perception between cultures, prescribing what leaders should or should not do is difficult. Instead, it is the system of which the leader is a part, not solely their personal competencies as a leader, that should be considered. In using this approach, the exploration of these pillars and the questions generated in the coaching process take the coach and team through the thought process to formulate impactful solutions.

Stages of Development (Peters & Carr, 2013)

The focus on high-performing teams that featured in Clutterbuck's (2007) earlier work was further explored by Peters and Carr (2013), who investigated teams in both private and public institutions. Peters and Carr (2013) define teams in terms of three stages of development: the beginning, midpoint and ending, with different coaching functions related to those stages. These functions include the need to define and initiate, review and realign, and research and integrate. This emphasis on the developmental stage of the team and the related functions provides a core set of principles that enable the practical steps required to develop team performance. A sense of team safety is emphasized as an underpinning for the other functions. With this at the core, the team stages and functions as outlined above then relate to six components (see diagram below), which cover:

- Assessment: Examining whether the team is ready to meet the conditions for success.
- Coaching for team design: Ensuring the team and its leaders have addressed core team conditions and have defined their purpose and goals. It is possible to consider if the team has the right structure and talent in place to achieve the identified purpose.
- Team launch: Ensuring the team know the rules under which it will operate to underpin a compelling purpose. Peters and Carr (2013) recommend establishing a team charter to ensure all members are working together towards the same agreed purpose, leading to the organization of a formal team launch to build team safety and cohesion.
- Individual coaching: Peters and Carr (2013) advocate the need for individual coaching to support members especially at the beginning stage to ensure a successful start.
- Ongoing team coaching: Subsequent coaching is designed to reinforce the team's actions and agreement. Peters and Carr (2013) advocate a wide range of approaches, including peer coaching, which they increasingly see as a key driver of engagement.
- Review learning and success: Peters and Carr (2013) make the point that review and learning are critical at the final stage of the team's work and central to success throughout the project. Outcomes such as individual engagement, developing team capabilities and relationships and quality outputs can follow from the six components set within a safe team.

Their approach is highly structured and provides both steps to establish and run effective teams but also a set of activities to support the different actions. As for Clutterbuck (2021), there is a strong emphasis on purpose and learning.

Transformational Coaching (Stout-Rostron, 2019a)

A key issue for team coaching is the way in which diverse thinking is incorporated. This was the focus of the work of Sunny Stout-Rostron (2019a) whose interest is in transformational coaching to enable leaders to effectively lead culturally diverse teams.

The model developed by Stout-Rostron (2019a) includes many of the issues raised by Peters and Carr (2013). However, considerable emphasis is placed on both diversity and cultural awareness. Working in the context of coaching in Africa, Stout-Rostron draws upon the concept of Ubuntu, the importance of shifting cultures in organizations and the agility necessary to work within a VUCA world.

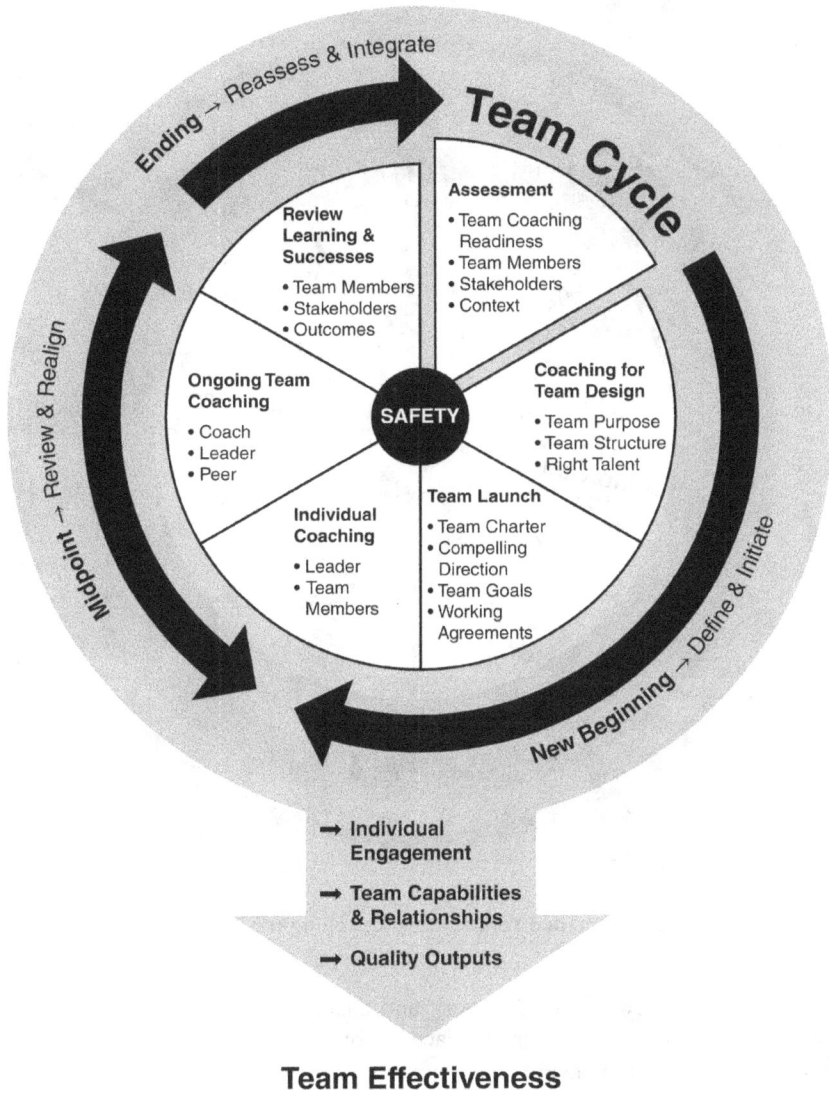

Team Cycle

Ending → Reassess & Integrate

Midpoint → Review & Realign

New Beginning → Define & Initiate

Assessment
- Team Coaching Readiness
- Team Members
- Stakeholders
- Context

Review Learning & Successes
- Team Members
- Stakeholders
- Outcomes

Ongoing Team Coaching
- Coach
- Leader
- Peer

SAFETY

Coaching for Team Design
- Team Purpose
- Team Structure
- Right Talent

Individual Coaching
- Leader
- Team Members

Team Launch
- Team Charter
- Compelling Direction
- Team Goals
- Working Agreements

→ Individual Engagement

→ Team Capabilities & Relationships

→ Quality Outputs

Team Effectiveness

Figure 12.2 Peters and Carr's (2013) model of team coaching

As illustrated in Figure 12.3, Stout-Rostron's (2019a) high performance relationship coaching model consists of four concentric circles.

- The inner hub is the relationships that are built in the course of team coaching.
- The second hub provides for seven stages starting with contracting for the work and assessment of the team. This is followed by diagnosis and design, which

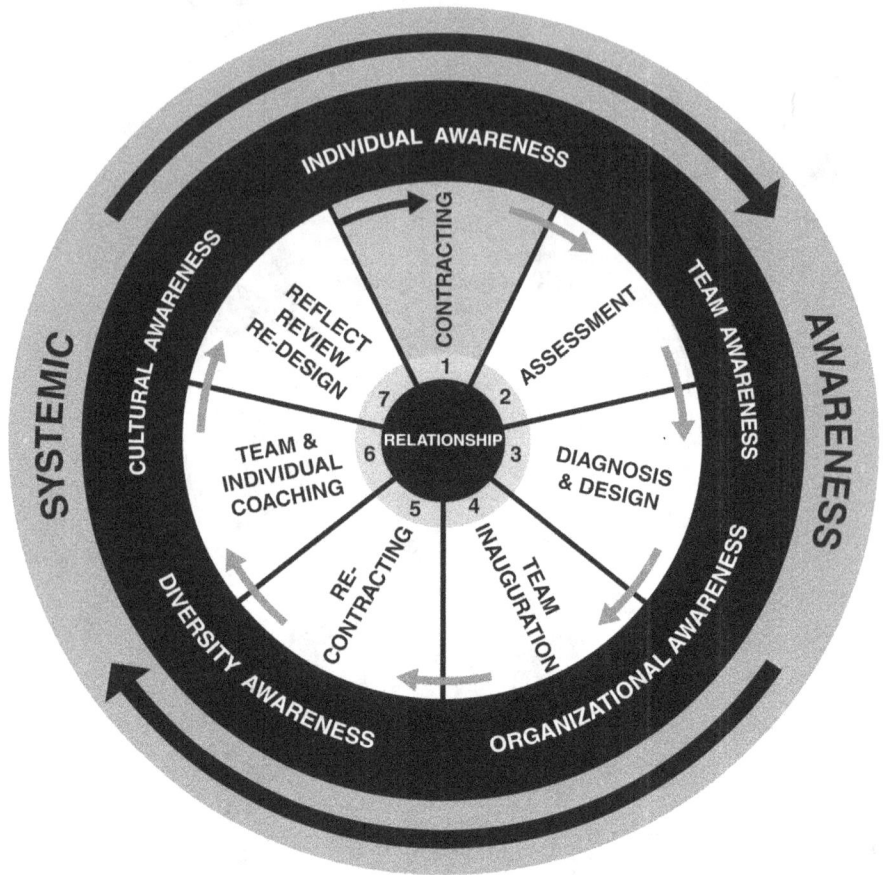

Figure 12.3 High performance relationship coaching model

creates the framework for the work and ensures organizational buy-in to the project. With this agreement in place, a formal team inauguration process is advocated. This step ensures the team is fully oriented to each other, the tasks at hand, team boundaries, roles and norms and leads to a team charter covering how they relate together and achieve their work. Individual and team coaching follows with the final stage of reflection and review.

• The third circle through the coaching process leads to increased individual, team, organizational, diversity and cultural awareness.
• The outer circle is concerned with deepening systemic awareness and an ever-widening reach.

In presenting this model Stout-Rostron (2019a) provides a strong emphasis on a structured model to work through the stages in establishing effective coaching with teams. Additionally, Stout-Rostron clarifies and endorses the importance of incorporating cultural awareness and building on diverse thinking and experiences to ensure the potential for transformational coaching.

Capacities for High Value Creating Teams (Hawkins, 2021)

Finally, we consider the work of Peter Hawkins (2021, first developed in Hawkins, 2011), which argues for a central role of continuous learning if teams are to prosper. Hawkins identifies five capacities for highly effective teams:

- Commissioning: Why are we here and who do we serve? This leads to ensuring a clear commission and purpose for the team and contracting on its deliverables.
- Clarifying: What exactly is the team? Creating shared identity and shared purpose, goals and objectives, roles and processes.
- Co-creation: How we are going to work together and make this happen; interpersonal and team dynamics, and culture.
- Connecting: Spreading enthusiasm and key messages beyond the team, engaging and partnering with all critical stakeholders.
- Core learning: The capacity for the team to grow and learn collectively by coordinating, consolidating, reflecting and integrating learning.

Central to Hawkins's (2021) model is the work that the team needs to undertake in order to understand its purpose both internally and externally, the constant

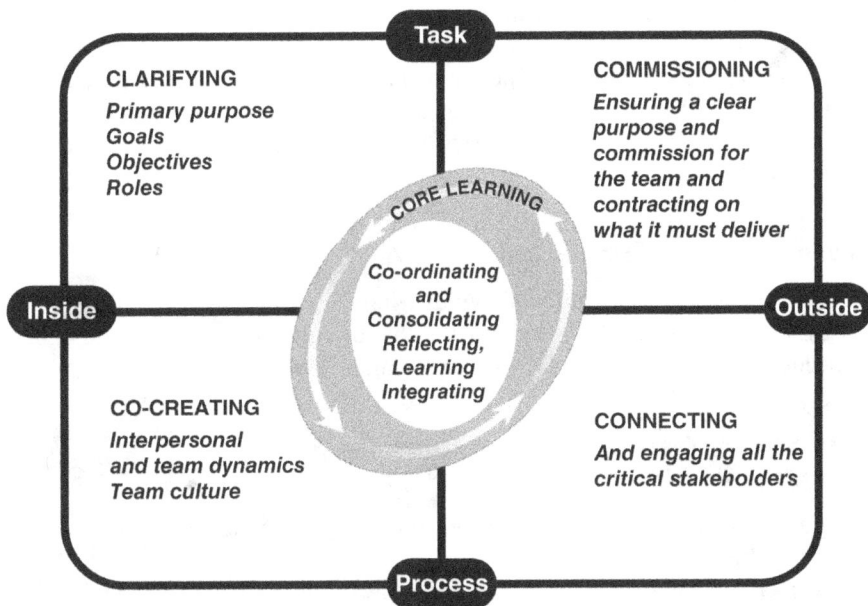

Figure 12.4 Capacities for high value creating teams (Hawkins, 2021)

monitoring and learning within the team and with the external stakeholders, and for members to be clear about how they need to be in order to deliver their purpose.

Summary

Taking these ideas together with the earlier discussion of positionality and decision-making, it can be appreciated that each part of the system holds fragmented knowledge, parts that have potential but do not become meaningful until enacted in a performance united by a shared purpose. Success requires the team to enter into a dialogue to establish a core purpose, shared internally between its members and reflecting the wider stakeholders. Each part of the system holds differing perspectives to inform the justification for the agreed purpose with each fragment of knowledge having a potential influence. Where those fragments are acknowledged and shared, an agreed purpose can manifest. Where those fragments are ignored or marginalized, they become latent influences that might work against the shared purpose. Where a shared purpose emerges, this can only be sustained by learning, so that adjustments can be made to ensure the potentialities are shaped through feedback to become continually fit for purpose.

Systems include not just people but also technologies and physical elements, which again have potential but only contribute to purpose when in use to enact performance. The diversity of the potentialities, human and otherwise, within a system provides for high levels of redundancy, which can be activated as needed to meet emerging needs. That activation is dependent on ways of seeing and thinking that are equal to the system diversity. This shared sense of the purpose of the team, the perspectives it brings to understand and define its position in the world, creates potential for a process of action that is fit for purpose. Taken together, the team narrative concerning what the team is, why it exists and what makes its existence worthwhile provides the shared sense, a formulation, that guides the work that team members do together.

Processes and Formulation

A coach can embed formulation activities within any of these team coaching processes. Table 12.2 provides an example of the formulation activities that might be embedded within the Hawkins (2021) coaching process.

Case Study: Team and Group Coaching Within One Organization

This case study takes two brief examples of a group coaching and a team coaching process within the same organization.

An international food and agriculture research organization was undertaking funded research and providing technical services to industry. There were groups devoted to specific disciplines and client sectors. While parts of the organization

Table 12.2 Formulation activities

Coaching model stage	Description	Formulation activities
Commissioning	Gaining a clear commission of the role and purpose of the team, agreeing on how team effectiveness will be measured, and by whom.	• Information gathering by both coach and team members • Identifying the dominant narratives about the team that its members and stakeholders hold • Identifying risks and threats to success • Forming, refining and documenting hypotheses in conjunction with team members and stakeholders
Clarifying	Clarifying the team purpose, vision, strategy, core values, key collective priorities and goals, standards and behaviours.	• Information gathering • Clarifying team purpose and purpose of the coaching • Identifying core values, patterns of behaviour • Capturing the key narratives the team holds regarding the vision for the future for the team • Identifying and documenting the ideal behaviours for the team
Co-creating	Exploring how the team works together to achieve and surpass the team targets. Identifying the team dynamics and culture that will enable the team to perform. The team explores new ways of working and specific coaching interventions to ensure identified needs are implemented immediately in team sessions.	• Synthesizing data, identifying patterns and key themes or narratives • Capturing patterns and themes that emerge through the dialogue • Forming, refining and sharing hypotheses in conjunction with the team • Designing and agreeing the coaching process, exploring and outlining key team development goals and interventions • Updating formulation based on the outcomes of the exploration and experimentation of the team, or coaching interventions

(Continued)

Table 12.2 (Continued)

Coaching model stage	Description	Formulation activities
Connecting	Identifying and improving how the team collectively interacts with key stakeholder groups. Assisting the team members to integrate their membership and their contribution to the team with the responsibilities of their formal leadership role.	• Capturing patterns and themes of interaction between the team and its stakeholders • Identifying narratives the team holds regarding stakeholder groups, and vice versa
Core learning	Developing the team's collective and individual capacity through learning together, often as part of the other activities.	• Identifying learning styles of the team and hypotheses regarding how to assist the team in their collective learning • Reflecting and review formulation process, content and form • Noting outcomes, results of actions, updating hypotheses • Capturing key learning points for the team and the coach • Formulating approaches the team can use to sustain learning after the team coaching is completed

were outwardly focused on industry clients, other sections provided services to internal clients. These were seen as cost centres rather than as profit centres. Following a major review, it was decided that all parts of the organization should become profit centres selling services to both internal and external clients. This created a major learning challenge for all. Neither the existing profit centres had experience of buying internal services nor the cost centres of selling their services. Internal and external markets were created to address this.

A number of technical specialists grouped under a titular head of division, but all working to different clients and drawing on varied expertise, decided they wanted to engage in a learning process to work within the new setup. However, they also wanted to address climate change impacts on food supply. There was a real interest across the group in how new technologies could create opportunities and production capabilities. As a group they all had a different purpose and there were few overlapping dependencies between them. The failure of one would not impact on the success of the other. However, they did have a shared interest in climate, food and technology and a shared need to learn to work within the new organizational structures. For them the purpose that emerged was how they could support each other to work in new ways but also to consider what joint projects might be developed for the future around climate, food and technology.

As they were all working to their own clients and using different expertise and perspectives on the world, they decided that a process was needed which enabled them to share ideas, understand each person's own purpose and explore how together they could learn new skills which could then be directed to a different purpose. Thus, the formulation centred on each defining a purpose for their engagement together, outlining the perspectives they were working with and where they felt the gaps in their knowledge were located. This ensured each member could gain a sense of their colleagues' position in the world of client relationships. The initial discussion was led by a coach to help them understand how to explore together (given that this process was a new experience for them) and on the basis of the narratives they shared to decide on an approach that would best support their learning. Over an initial three sessions they explored together their understanding of their needs and, guided by the coach, looked at alternative ways to enable their journey.

The formulation suggested that they needed a process where they could each have space to explore their concerns, with their colleagues engaging in a number of steps to support them. These included ensuring everyone understood the need they were expressing, checking out what would or would not be an appropriate way forward, then supporting learning experiments to change the way they interacted with clients. Roleplay between them was one suggestion they explored. They decided to find a group coaching process that would work for them. They eventually decided that an Action Learning Set (Revans, 1982) would be a process that would meet the need. The coach ran three sessions on how to manage a learning set, and thereafter the group coached each other, with each taking turns to chair the group. The coach was available to be called if needed. The coach was called back towards the end of the process to help them evaluate the work and gains made.

A separate section in the organization worked to provide bioinformatics to internal clients. They researched data, created and tested models and ran search services for the whole organization. In developing a formulation, they recognized that while each had an individual role within the section, they were interdependent to meet the overall section purpose, so individual tasks had to be integrated to meet stakeholder needs. This led them to conclude they needed a team coaching process. They were now faced with considering how to charge internal clients, remain competitive (given that those clients now had the option to buy services in the market) and find new external clients for whom they could develop and provide products.

For this group they quickly realized they had to find a new team purpose, clarify the roles they needed to play in the team and explore their relationships with stakeholders. They decided team coaching (with an external coach) would be focused on defining a purpose statement for the new world, deciding how much effort to place on services to internal or external clients and creating continuous feedback loops to assess how well they were doing in meeting needs. Given this initial formulation they choose to use the "capacities for high value creating teams" model outlined above. The work they undertook was similar to that in Table 12.2, adapting the Hawkins (2021) framework to meet their needs.

Conclusion

Formulation can provide a means to assist a coach to navigate the complexities of developing teams for sustainable performance. Before commencing a formulation, the coach needs to establish if the engagement is team or group coaching, with the emphasis on the interdependency of the members being a feature of the former. Group coaching has the longer history and offers benefits to enable people to come together to share a learning journey around common or diverse objectives. For teams it is the shared purpose that binds them into a joint endeavour. As with other coaching contexts there are multiple perspectives on which coaches can draw to develop a formulation. However, given the nature of team coaching, the systemic perspective may provide a useful lens on which to base a formulation and examples of how this may be used have been provided. This chapter has outlined a number of frameworks drawn from the team coaching literature and which can also be adapted to support a formulation in team and group contexts. The place of diversity has been underlined as a means for understanding team dynamics and the enablers and barriers to team effectiveness. Teams are central to the effectiveness of modern organizations and formulation is offered as a useful support to assist team coaches and the clients in addressing some of the challenges inherent in the team coaching context.

Questions to Consider

Consider the material presented in this chapter and reflect on its application to your own practice or the case study above.

- Based on the material in this chapter or one of the specific models outlined, what might need to happen to set up a group coaching process?
- To set up a team coaching engagement what process might be useful?
- The process frameworks for team coaching outlined above privilege certain information. How would they differ if applied to different coaching projects?
- What information is required before you begin any team or group coaching engagement?

Chapter 13

Formulation for Coaching in Education

With its emphasis on promoting, learning, resilience and wellbeing, as well as helping facilitate psychological problem-solving, interventions derived from the fields of coaching have potentially much to contribute to educational settings. The emerging role of coaching in educational contexts is introduced and examined. Within higher education, it is now well established that there are high levels of mental health and psychological morbidity in student populations. Higher education institutions are increasingly developing a range of offerings alongside the more traditional student support services to facilitate the student experience and contribute to enhanced wellbeing. This is an emerging field of practice designed to meet the needs of a new and distinct client group. The potential of coaching in this and other areas of education is considered. For example, the impact of lockdowns on the educational sector, including schools, as well as the challenges that have arisen for mental health, disclosures of sexual violence or broader discrimination all pose significant challenges. Coaching may also have something to contribute here in terms of changing attitudes and behaviours.

Coaching and Mentoring – A Long History in Education

Some of the earliest discussions about mentoring and coaching come from education. As Gray et al. (2016) discusses, this includes the experience of craft guilds, early use of coaching at Oxford colleges, the writings of Fenelon from the late 1660s, Caraccioli from the 1760s and Honoria from the 1790s. Her books reference various educational conversations (Gray et al., 2016).

By the 1980s peer mentoring in schools was strongly established (Topping, 1989) and later appeared in official recommendations as a way to transform teachers' professional learning (Bolam, 2008). Youth mentoring schemes became widespread in the USA and UK (Colley, 2003; Grossman & Tierney, 1998). A national framework for coaching and mentoring was established by the Department for Education and Skills (see Cordingley & Buckler, 2012) and is well established in schools. It is similarly well established in the USA (Devine et al., 2013). There is also evidence that coaching teachers can improve the performance of students (Ross, 1992; Shidler, 2009) and increasing evidence that it can improve the wellbeing of students

DOI: 10.4324/9781003174585-17

(Cosgrove et al., 2021). However, critiques on its effectiveness serve as an important caveat (DuBois, 2021; Garmezy & Masten, 1986). These include questions on ways to improve effectiveness, differences between immediate and long-term results, understanding of how they impact and variability between programmes.

Understanding Positionality

Coaching has historically been positioned as playing a role in education. All coaches are likely to have their own histories as pupils and perhaps as parents in the educational system, and some reflection on how that positions them is a necessary prerequisite for engaging with the sector.

The concept of formulation within educational settings often refers to system-level thinking rather than individual-level analysis, and managing the relationships between generalizable findings and idiographic problems presents particular difficulties (Miller & Frederickson, 2006). Miller and Frederickson (2006) also make the point that the richer the data and the more complex the understanding of the individual case, the harder it is to draw generalizable conclusions. The aim in much educational work is to formulate understanding in order to be able to generalize to develop policy and practice. Thus, the coach working in this context has to consider how they view the educational system and how they position themselves in terms of both supporting individual programmes and system-wide interventions. The position of the coach in education is as much about designing programmes as providing the intervention. Hence, the coach is likely to need programme design skills as well as coaching knowledge to operate in the sector.

What Can Be Learnt From Examples of Coaching Across Education

Purpose as Contested Space

There is a growing awareness that schools have an important role to play if we are to overcome persistent underachievement and non-attendance, address bullying and abusive cultures, enhance the potential of all students and their teachers and ensure we enable them to meet an increasingly challenging work experience (Commission on Young Lives, 2022). In studies in the UK, USA and Australia, in particular, coaching is increasingly seen as part of the offer that could make a positive difference (Devine et al., 2013; van Nieuwerburgh & Passmore, 2018). Hence, education is seen as having societal-level impacts and coaching has taken a role as part of such interventions. The question becomes one of considering the purpose for coaching an individual and coaching as a way to achieve the purpose of education at a system level.

What indeed is the purpose of education? Checkland (1989) raised this in relation to failed attempts to apply systems thinking to education in the USA because defining its purpose is contentious. The point has also been made by van Nieuwerburgh (2012).

The difficulties schools face in addressing issues that are contentious were raised in a Council of Europe project "Free to Speak Safe to Learn" (2022). As the project concludes, what is controversial varies greatly, as do views on what issues schools are expected to address. This raises the question of whether or not a shared purpose for education as a system can be defined or whether it is more appropriate to focus on how individuals define the purpose of education for themselves. In this context, is coaching in education an offer to help the individual student, teacher or leader achieve, or a means to assist an organization in delivering its agenda?

In 2005, Creasy and Patterson, for the National College of School Leadership, suggested that coaching was everywhere and had gained a high profile at national level. They argued that there was strong evidence that coaching both promotes learning as well as builds the capacity for developing change in schools. A number of studies (Cordingley et al., 2005; Cordingley & Buckler, 2012; Bell, 2017) support this view, and Creasy and Patterson (2005) highlight a clear value when teachers learn from each other. As Creasy and Patterson (2005) suggest, the Department for Education and Skills (DfES) pointed to the use of mentoring and coaching in schools. This resulted in the DfES commissioning the Centre for the Use of Research and Evidence in Education (CUREE) to collate work on the practice of effective coaching and mentoring within educational professional development (Creasy & Patterson, 2005). Studies generated by this initiative have appeared; for example, Lindon (2011) reported on its value in upskilling the teaching workforce. This raises the question of the use of formulation at the system or whole programme level.

Perspectives in Coaching in Education – Formulation and Intervention at a Systems Level

While much early work in education related to individual interventions often based on behavioural approaches (Miller & Frederickson, 2006), systems- and consultation-level work was identified as a way to deal with the complexity involved in educational systems. Across work in the USA and UK, they point to efforts to incorporate social constructionist and systems thinking to stimulate conversation that led to making a difference. Thus, problem analysis frameworks were developed that created hypotheses to be tested. Interventions were devised, then evaluated in order to create an integrated explanatory structure that informed practical action. In the terms discussed here, this is a formulation that offered ways to define potential interventions. In education these approaches have been defined as both four- (Gutkin & Curtis, 1999) and five- (Lane, 1988, 1990; Woolfson et al., 2003) step processes. This has led to the primary focus for coaching in education to be at the level of the whole school or national intervention.

There are many examples of these whole school approaches in education. Peer coaching is one area that has widespread application across primary and secondary schools. Examples of this include reciprocal classroom observations with coaching feedback on potential areas for enhancement. A common use of coaching in primary schools is as part of continuing professional development (CPD) for teachers and teaching assistants (Jarvis et al., 2017). However, peer coaching may include teachers as peers coaching each other (van Nieuwerburgh & Barr, 2016). The Jarvis et al. study (2017), in particular, looked at the power of reflection and feedback in triad teams of teachers supporting each other as coach, coachee and observer.

In her "how to" guide for peer coaching, Robbins (2015) formulates a set of guidelines that begins with the understanding that planning, implementing and sustaining a peer coaching programme so it becomes an integral part of school culture requires persistence. Next, leaders must clarify the vision of peer coaching for staff by identifying what peer coaching is, and what it is not; for example, its non-evaluative, confidential, supportive nature; its emphasis on collegiality; and choices regarding participation should each be clearly communicated to all staff, preferably in written guidance materials and resources. Time and space need to be made available for staff to ask questions and discuss concerns, eliciting input from teachers on aspects that can be tailored for individual school sites. Finally, appropriate support for peer coaching must be marshalled if it is to be both successful and sustainable. This support includes responding to the emotional side of change (individuals experience disruptions in past practices as new expectations being shared), and to the behavioural side of change. As is clear from both Jarvis et al. (2017) and Robbins (2015), coaching offers value at an individual, interpersonal and systems levels; however, it must be targeted to the need and context.

A further key component of these approaches is the emphasis on evaluation so that adjustments can be made. Evaluation is a critical part of the formulation process. There are several examples of schools reporting on their own practice in coaching which point to the value they see in its use based on their evaluations. A few are briefly referenced but many more could be identified. They have been chosen as examples where the schools stressed the importance of evaluation and to cover interventions at different levels, but also for the specific links they make between coaching and the purpose they set for the programmes.

The Communities Education Trust reported (in May 2021) on a project undertaken at Windmill Primary School in which children coached each other to generate improvements in their work or own performance. Children aged 5 to 11 years were given basic training in coaching skills to use when another child felt stuck. The project used laminated cards with coaching questions on them emphasizing asking not telling. Positive impacts were reported, particularly with children having more difficulties and those with special needs who grew significantly in confidence. Other gains for the children included less anxiety, more resilience, more reflection on their own performance and greater teamwork and collaboration. Specifically, coaching helped both the child being coached and those offering the coaching.

In another example, Lanesend Primary School on the Isle of Wight has produced a coaching policy (2020) which is evaluated and reviewed every two years. This programme was built on a clear purpose for coaching based on the teachers' own learning in the belief that this would underpin school improvement as well as being a means to raise achievement and attainment. The school took the view that development based on an assessment and understanding of children's learning enables teachers to adapt their practice, leading to valuable differences in outcome for the pupils. The school specifically linked teacher learning and impacts on children. There is a clear commitment to monitoring and evaluating the impact of coaching, which is formally reported to the Trustees via a Teaching and Learning Group. A notable feature of the work at Lanesend is the link between teacher development and children's learning. This concept finds its way into many educational leadership programmes. It reflects the aims of many to make a difference to people's lives. As van Nieuwerburgh (2012) points out, educational leadership is particularly challenging, involving learning, the leadership of people, dealing with a complex organization and with responsibilities to the community. Additionally, leaders are governed by a series of changing regulations, directives and guidance from governments determined to shape education to their agenda. An example might be the sudden abandonment of the highly successful "Every Child Matters" programme instantly upon a change of government (Jones, 2012). The purpose of education can be highly contentious and is certainly subject to political influence.

The complexity surrounding the education system has made education a flourishing place for coaching and mentoring to take hold. Because there is no single way to be a successful educational leader, the idea of formulating an approach that works for the particular context and leader has relevance. As Creasy and Patterson (2005) contend, coaching in education is driven by a desire to make a difference to the students' learning.

At the secondary school level just one of many possible examples is a collaborative project at Sittingbourne Community College. This large secondary school explored the impact of coaching for students trained as coaches as well as for those coached (van Nieuwerburgh et al., 2012). The school was also an active participant in the Social and Emotional Aspects of Learning strategy (SEAL), which embedded emotional intelligence in the curriculum. Year 12 students (16 to 17 years) were selected for three days of training plus three reflective practice sessions over the six-month coaching assignment. They provided support to year 11 students (15 to 16 years) to enhance their standards of attainment. As a research pilot, 11 matched pairs in coaching were compared to students offered alternative support. Evaluation looked at changes in confidence and achievement. The school found that those providing coaching increased in confidence, their understanding of others and in using a range of study skills. Those coached reported that the sessions built confidence and resourcefulness and several then wanted to become coaches. A few felt they did not fully understand the benefits. Overall, it enhanced students' examination results.

Students as peer coaches schemes have been tried elsewhere at school and college level (Eriksen et al., 2020; Well-Being Ambassadors, 2023). Using coaching in pre-kindergarten to enable staff to enhance outcomes for children from deprived backgrounds has shown benefits across a wide range of measures (Ernest & Strichik, 2018). Coaching for peers, teachers and parents has been happening on a global basis, and while some studies are difficult to interpret overall, the effectiveness of coaching in these contexts has been established (Oberholzer & Boyle, 2023; van Nieuwerburgh & Barr, 2016).

In a specialist service within the former Inner London Educational Authority Schools Psychological Service, coaching was offered as one part of a range of supports to staff within the service, staff within referring schools and pupils receiving services. The service worked across the age range nursery, primary and secondary with children seen as at risk of exclusion and teachers and others providing services within schools. Evaluations including long-term follow-up showed that it significantly reduced exclusions, improved achievements and greatly reduced levels of delinquency (Lane, 1990). Multiple examples of the successful use of coaching are reported by Lofthouse et al. (2010), including with pupils seen at risk of exclusion.

The use of coaching to develop leadership in education covers all levels from primary through to higher education (van Nieuwerburgh, 2012; van Nieuwerburgh & Passmore, 2018). Used to support aspiring and new head teachers and college leaders a UK National College for Leadership was established (NCSL, 2013), although its functions were subsequently moved into the DfES in 2018. An important emerging role for educational leaders is as coaches or mentors to others. A key part of developing an effective coaching programme in many of the schemes outlined above is the process of developing an understanding of the particular issues faced in the context and ensuring the purpose is clear – in effect, a formulation.

There are many more examples from education at primary, secondary and university level available in the literature (see, for example, chapters in Passmore & Tee, 2021; Watts & Florance, 2021), and it is clear that coaching now has a central and valued role in achievement for the organization, its leaders, other staff and students. In some cases, the engagement of the wider community is also seen as a core part of the offer. Consequently, coaching in education has to draw upon a wide range of perspectives as well as deal with the purpose of education being contested. This is made more difficult as education is seen to play a role in dealing with mental health.

Perspectives in Education – Formulation, Coaching and Mental Health

Mental health problems have been identified as one of the main disease burdens worldwide (Whiteford et al., 2015). The *Mental Health of Children and Young People in England, 2023* report (Newlove-Delgado et al., 2023) found that 20.3 per cent of 8–16-year-olds had a probable mental disorder. Among 17–19-year-olds, the proportion was 23.3 per cent, while in 20–25-year-olds it was 21.7 per cent. Mental health problems have been identified as one of the main disease burdens worldwide (Whiteford et al., 2015). The issue has become particularly prominent since the Covid-19 pandemic (Theberath et al., 2022).

Impacts of bullying, including sexual molestation, have been identified since the 1980s (Tattum and Lane, 1989) and the role of the internet has reduced safe spaces and exposed children to aggressive and demoralizing images (NSPCC, 2024).

This raises the question of balancing individualized formulations and interventions (important as they are) with system-level approaches to change the context in which this happens. Schools have a critical role to play in terms of formulating policy and practice. Key to this is establishing between all of those involved in education clear partnerships to create a basis for effective leadership, as a review of 63 studies has shown (Leithwood, 2021). At the university level a set of league tables has been established, which show the difference they can make to students (Phoenix, 2023). Coaching is one of the intervention possibilities that can promote prosocial rather than antisocial behaviours as well as enable those impacted to survive and thrive. However, we need to formulate programmes at the system level, which requires community effort and initiatives such as Thrive London (2023), which brings together key agencies in partnerships to tackle underlying causes of difficulties as well as building support services.

The role of coaching in mental health and wellbeing is an emerging area of interest (Corrie & Parsons, 2021). Traditionally, while emotional wellbeing was seen as part of the role of the coach, mental health was considered to be the preserve of the therapist (Buckley, 2007). Yet as Tehrani and Lane (2021) contend there is a role for coaches, different to that of therapists, but valuable to supporting the development of skills to thrive in difficult circumstances such as trauma. They, as do Corrie and Parsons (2021), make clear that there are boundaries and that coaches need to know when to refer to a mental health specialist. However, as has been evident throughout this chapter, coaching in this context is not exclusively concerned with one-to-one coaching but also addressing the systems within education. As in the example at Sittingbourne Community College above, coaching was one part of their work and they were also involved in school-wide initiatives such as the "SEAL" programme to develop social and emotional aspects of learning across the curriculum (Humphrey et al., 2010). Coaching is one part of an intervention to address mental health in education. However, although there is an expanding workforce to meet these complex problems, the nature of the workforce delivering them has changed and is facing tighter government expectations alongside the deprofessionalization of service provision (Corrie & Lane, 2015).

The question of who should intervene in mental health is much more difficult to answer than it might have been a generation ago, and at the same time we have rising rates of concern. Indeed, Duncan et al. (2021) have argued that if we are to make a significant difference to mental health it is in education where we must place the focus. Coaching in education they claim moves away from a medical orientation towards enabling the person to achieve goals, attain enhanced wellbeing and achieve optimal functioning. The place of education to intervene before issues escalate is of particular value. They point to the cost of unaddressed mental health issues in terms of absence from school, greater likelihood of being on welfare as adults and increased criminality. At university level they point to increased numbers who have either disclosed a mental health issue or left early because of one. Given, as they suggest, official statistics show that 50% of mental health issues are established before the age of 14, intervention at school level becomes even more important. They point to various case studies and interventions where coaching has a role to play both for the individual pupil, for staff members and as an intervention at a systems level. They contend that there is an emerging evidence base for the use of coaching to support enhancing mental health.

A longitudinal study conducted by Vanzella-Yang et al. (2023) followed a group of young boys living in a poor neighbourhood in Montreal who from 1984 received coaching for two years in social skills such as self-confidence and perseverance. Re-evaluation showed lifetime benefits in terms of outcomes for the participants and for society. These included reducing rates of criminality and social dependence while raising positive outcomes in employment, education, likelihood of marriage, charitable donations and spending on tuition. This, the authors contend, is the only long-term randomized trial of coaching with disruptive children that shows substantial benefits in adulthood at the individual and social level.

The Role of Formulation in Coaching in Education – Building a Process to Address Complexity

As is clear from the previous discussion coaching in education is faced with a contested purpose, perspectives drawing upon the individual, interpersonal and systems level as well as interventions aimed at making a societal difference. Coaching has an important contribution to make in education, but it is a complex area. However, in considering developing interventions, as has been argued in this chapter, while it is necessary to formulate at the systems level and in terms of individual applications, it is also necessary to develop policy and practice. Formulation, particularly if developed as a collaborative process, therefore, has a very broad role to play in building coaching within the context of broad policy interventions. If considered at this level, by bringing together services within the community it is possible to link interventions in terms of mental health, wellbeing and a diverse range of social, economic and environmental factors (Corrie & Lane, 2021). The role of social disadvantage, risk exposure and social inequalities have been noted to play a fundamental part in mental health influenced by distributions of power and resources (Bell, 2017; Mezzina et al., 2022; Toleikyte, 2018). Education cannot resolve all of the issues but does have a central role to play. Coaching can contribute to ensuring that pupils and students have the skills to analyse events and thrive. Equipping teachers and related professionals who work with children with coaching skills will enable their own development and understanding of others. Formulation is the mechanism to pull these understandings together into a coherent narrative with implications for change. Coaching is, as Watts et al. (2023) contend, not about fixing people but enabling them to use their own resources. We need to begin to reflect upon how we develop a process of collaborative dialogue between key stakeholders so that we can formulate approaches to use coaching to address the challenges that educators are asked to address.

Adapting an argument by Lane and Corrie (2009):

- Formulation has a crucial role to play in development of focused interventions in coaching in education, particularly where the context is complex. Simple skills-based programmes can probably run on the basis of limited goals, but for more developmental tasks an analysis of the context is needed that reflects the position (positionality) of each player. Building this understanding is the place where formulation can have real impact.
- Formulation can help to identify relevant issues and the development of shared concerns and purpose as well as enhancing coach and client collaboration.
- The evidence base at present is limited and further knowledge is needed on the connection between the way issues are formulated and the effectiveness of the interventions subsequently offered.

It is clear from the increasing contexts in which it is used in education that coaching is seen as having a contribution to make at the individual and systems level. However, as illustrated by the range of authors cited so far, this contribution is not limited to one-to-one coaching sessions for pupils but offers a value to pupils, students, teachers, other staff and the communities served. Formulation, as Miller and Frederickson (2006) pointed out, is concerned with enabling policy and practice. Formulation can, therefore, be used as a way to understand the needs faced at the individual, team, school and university level and in wider community initiatives. Building on the work of Lane and Corrie (2009), it is proposed here that:

- In order to ensure that formulation has a role to play and is fit for purpose in developing coaching in education, the evidence discussed above indicates a need to develop frameworks consistent with client partnership to incorporate a variety of stakeholders.
- Coaching frameworks in education need to take account of a broader range of factors than an individual and internalized approach, otherwise the risk is seeing the individual as the problem in need of change rather than wider interpersonal and system contexts that are amenable to intervention.
- The ambition for formulating issues of concern needs to reach beyond limited goals to all contexts regardless of the objectives or theoretical position or process of coaching chosen. Values can act as a guide, but the vision developed cannot be limiting and marginal; it needs to be encompassing and expansive.

Case Study: Scripted Coaching for Managing Complex Encounters

Working with a group of six adolescents, classroom observations monitored by teachers had indicated difficulties that students faced in engaging appropriately with adults in educational settings. In discussing this with the students, they identified a range of situations in which they seemed to get into difficulties, whereas others could talk their way out of trouble. Although expressed differently, there was a shared interest in learning how to hold a conversation with those in authority in conflict situations. An initial formulation suggested a lack of specific social skills for dealing with such contexts.

A common approach in these circumstances is to examine the situations in which the difficulties occur, then identity skills that could more appropriately be displayed that would reduce the occurrence of conflicts. Once those are identified, they are broken down into small steps that can be learned and practised with feedback provided on observed performances. There were enough similarities for this group that it seemed that a group coaching programme for skills development for dealing with conflict situations was possible.

A potential way to approach this is through the use of scripts of situations with different outcomes. The participants work through a script of, say, a situation in class or a conversation on the street with a police officer that is going wrong. The group then explore the script to see where the conflict arose and suggest different ways that it could have been handled. They then write a new script and practise it, exploring what happened. Once they have a framework that they feel works, they each practice the new script and give each other feedback. This was the approach adopted with the group. The added feature was to engage the classroom teachers in providing feedback in the live context. This constituted a behavioural experiment that enabled students to both try out new skills and test out if in fact the skills did result in less conflict. Thus, there was feedback on the new script in the coaching group and feedback in situ. This provided an initial formulation and intervention agreed between teachers and students.

On evaluation of the intervention of the group, four found they could use the new skills in the practice sessions. One found that they could not, when confronted with a conflict, manage to use the skills and reverted to previous behaviours. One simply froze when trying to use the skills and said nothing. Back in situ, of the four who seemed to be able to manage, three found they were successful, and one challenged the teacher and did not effectively demonstrate the agreed behaviours. This raised the following questions:

- What might have gone wrong here in developing the social skills group?
- How might those who managed well reinforce their skills going forward?
- How might the behaviours of the two who did not manage the practice sessions be explored?
- How might the behaviours of the one who found it difficult in situ be explored?
- Based on the discussion of the existing formulation, how might it need to be changed and how might the situation be revisited?

Having thought about the questions above, it became apparent that while there was evidence for a generic programme of social skills training in that each of the pupils lacked those skills, factors governing their behaviours varied. It was necessary to move from a group programme towards individual formulations. For the group that responded well the emphasis became one of looking at other areas to which the skills could be generalized. Further scripted sessions were used to enhance this transferability. Of the two who could not manage in the practice sessions, two very different formulations emerged from further analysis. One showed strong social anxiety and a programme to work on that was instituted (Corrie and Lane, 2021). For the one who reverted to previous behaviours it was clear that this pattern was still being reinforced. He saw himself as strong when confrontative. "Being soft", in his words, did not work for him. A lot more work on contexts in which strength could be shown in different ways was needed. For the one who managed the skills well in the practice setting but did not in the classroom, an interesting picture emerged. She questioned the very basis of the approach, which she said meant that she was being required to conform with unreasonable and sometimes abusive behaviours by the teacher. There were behaviours that, she stated, this particular teacher used – such as publicly humiliating students about their stupidity, disabilities, sexuality or gender – which she felt were wrong. For her it required a more flexible approach to exploring when and how assertion might be the appropriate behaviour. A conversation with the head of department of that teacher also took place to address the concerns raised.

This example shows how a generic approach (social skills training) was used to formulate a programme, but how within this it can still be necessary to formulate an individual understanding so that the coaching works for the individual. The issues that arose with one student raised the question of whose agenda was being met – the school's agenda in seeking to establish compliance or the pupils' in developing skills to challenge.

Some Implications for Using Formulation in Education

Coaching is becoming widespread in education but often as a whole programme framework for an institution. This has value in that it can address organization-wide issues. Nevertheless, individual programmes or adaptions of system-wide interventions to meet specific needs are still necessary. As Devine et al. (2013) propose, coaching has a valuable contribution to make to individuals, but if the purpose is school improvement then it is necessary to work at a systems level. However, when using a systems view there is also a need to ensure that the individual perspective is not neglected. What is critical is understanding what makes a programme effective for which people in what contexts.

Any formulation has to reflect the development of policy and practices as a collective and collaborative learning culture. Coaching in education is already seen as a valuable individual intervention as well as a whole-system intervention for the school community.

Conclusion

The role of formulation in coaching in education is primarily about creating policy and practice to offer programmes of value across an organization. While individual coaching journeys happen, they do so within the framework of an organizational purpose. However, purpose is a contested area in education that has to be considered. It is clear that coaching is seen as a valued offer in generating change in educational settings. Through building an understanding of the issues faced in those contexts it is possible to formulate both policy and intervention practices. There is a critical role for coaching as a process of dialogue between stakeholders in these settings to identify concerns, explore causation, formulate an understanding, define a purpose, create a policy and intervention strategies, undertake and evaluate outcomes and enable adaptation over time on the basis of evidence. There are many examples of coaching programmes being built in this way and the benefits they bring.

The principle that it is important to follow is that a programme must make sense in terms of the individual experiencing and offering it as well as the context for the work. While a generic programme structure may be defined, ways to creatively adapt these to specific individual needs matters if the full benefit is to be achieved. Conversely, programmes that focus solely on individual change will be insufficient for the magnitude of the problems faced in education. System-wide initiatives are essential. In the same way that it has been argued that dealing with mental health issues needs to go beyond one-to-one interventions to involve schools and the wider community (Corrie & Lane, 2021, Thrive London, 2023), so is the case for coaching in education.

Questions to Consider

Given the breadth of potential interventions in education, questions at system and individual levels are worth exploring.

- When considering any coaching programme, how will you identify whose agenda is being served?
- How would you help an educational establishment identify their purpose?
- What might enable coaching to be a potential offer to meet that purpose?
- How will you help an educational organization distinguish between coaching to achieve their objectives and the objectives of individual students or staff?

Part 4

Developing Your Own Formulation Skills

This fourth and final section of the book takes a further and more in-depth look at how the 4P Framework for formulation can be applied in coaching practice. This section comprises a chapter that provides a detailed case example, a chapter offering guidance on how readers can develop their own personalized model and a final chapter that explores important considerations for how to approach formulation in the context of different worldviews.

DOI: 10.4324/9781003174585-18

Chapter 14

How to Develop and Apply Formulation in Coaching Practice: A Case Study

This chapter provides an example of how a formulation can be developed in coaching practice, using an application of the 4P Framework. As will be evident from previous chapters, there are many ways in which the 4P Framework can be applied. What follows, therefore, is best understood as simply one form of application in one specific coaching context – that of an executive coaching assignment. The purpose of the case study is for the reader to identify more easily the thinking and decision-making that sits behind the development of a formulation and to provide an illustration of some of the choices and decisions confronting the coach at different stages in the coaching process. The case study also provides a "step-by-step" account of how a formulation might be constructed, co-constructed and develop over the course of the coaching assignment as new hypotheses are formed and new information comes to light.

This fictitious case example concerns a coaching contract between Aaima (the coach) and Adesh (her client). Information provided in the main body of the text denotes information that emerged from the conversation between coach and client and that was, therefore, directly accessible to both parties. The information provided in the sidebars contains additional explanatory themes that reflect the thinking, hypotheses and decision-making points of the coach that are accessible, at least initially, to the coach alone and which shape her decisions about how to progress her conversations with the client.

Background Information

Aaima is a UK-based coach whose family originally comes from Pakistan. Aaima has lived in the UK all her life. In addition to working in the UK, she works in Europe, particularly with high-potential clients transitioning to more senior roles within their organizations. Aaima has a master's degree in coaching and her course provided training in a variety of theoretical perspectives, including cognitive, behavioural, psychodynamic and systemic theories, all of which she draws upon in her work. She regularly undertakes further training to expand her knowledge and has recently completed a course in neuroscience and neurodiversity.

Aaima has been trained in the 4P Framework by the authors of this book and had found it to be a helpful approach to honing her coaching offer, her practice and

DOI: 10.4324/9781003174585-19

her own process of self-reflection. She often uses the three levels of formulation – situation, pattern, person/case (see Chapter 6) – to help structure her thinking. Her positionality draws on her Pakistani cultural heritage and values from her Muslim faith. However, her view of the world also incorporates a number of Western values, including the right of autonomy, the importance of hard work and the pursuit of success. She does not experience herself as having been subjected to discrimination but does have an interest in working with marginalized groups, especially minoritized women. Although she knows little of the detail, she is aware that her grandfather, originally from India but subsequently forced to move to Pakistan, brought his family to the UK in the years following the partition of India in 1947.

The HR Director of the company who has worked with Aaima on many previous occasions has provided a significant amount of background information during their initial conversations. Specifically, Aaima is asked to work with Adesh, a 40-year-old minoritized male, in Rotterdam. Adesh has moved to Rotterdam from India. In coming to the European Head Office, he is currently a CIO but is considered a potential candidate for the role of CEO of the Asia Division. He has also been selected for an executive committee-level role within the next three years.

Adesh has a long-term physical health condition known to the company and believed by them to be under control. He has a very high work ethic. While he works hard and attributes his achievements to effort, success has come easily to him and he has always been both academically and professionally successful. This role is his first international experience – he has brought his family, wife and two children to Rotterdam. His children are in a private school paid for by the company. His wife is finding it difficult to adjust to her new environment and the family's relocation required her to give up her job.

Adesh has delivered high-impact projects in the past, having led the digitalization of significant parts of the business. It is his accomplishments in these roles that has led to him being considered as a potential CEO. He is seen as good with facts and figures but needs to develop his strategic understanding, which is why he has been brought to Europe for a placement prior to any promotion. Coaching has been offered as a way to help him understand how to transition to a new role with a clear objective of understanding and developing strategy. He is being given strategic projects to look at future directions for the company. These are mission critical for the organization and for its longer-term success. Adesh has not experienced coaching before but is a willing participant in the process.

Information Leading to a Formulation at the Level of Situation

At the first coaching session, following an initial chemistry session, Adesh started by disclosing to Aaima that he was living with a medical condition that was causing him concern. He said that he was unsure whether to raise this in coaching as it was not part of the agreed contract, but he decided to do so as he suspected that it could be relevant to their work and because he wished to be transparent.

Coach's internal process:

This is new information for Aaima. She feels pleased that Adesh has chosen to disclose this information and his stated reasons for doing so. His decision is consistent with her earlier impression of Adesh wanting to engage effectively with the coaching and to develop a positive and collaborative working relationship in which information can be shared openly. However, she also feels anxious – his disclosure is information neither expected nor planned. She is concerned that this condition may need them to reconsider whether coaching is the best option for him at this time or whether the input of another specialist might be needed. Aaima is aware of many thoughts, assumptions and predictions running through her mind at this point, rather than knowing the facts of his situation. She decides, therefore, to ask permission to learn a bit more about the challenges he is facing so she has some information to guide her decision-making.

Aaima thanked Adesh for sharing this information and reminded him of limits of her expertise; she is not qualified to give medical advice. Nonetheless, she asks for further information so they can decide how his medical condition might impact Adesh's aspirations for coaching.

Coach's internal process:

Aaima intentionally prefaced her request for more information with a reminder of the limits of her expertise. She believes that this is the most appropriate ethical decision. By doing so, she has also raised the possibility that they – or she – may need to decide to pause the coaching until other investigations are carried out or support of a more clinical nature is in place.

Adesh seemed relieved to be able to talk about his medical condition. He explained that he had a mild heart attack 12 months ago when he was still living in India. Since then, he had been under the care of a cardiologist who was based in India. Of medical significance was that he had a strong family history of heart disease, high cholesterol and high blood pressure. His father died at the age of 45 years old and his uncle at the age of 40, both from cardiovascular disease. His cardiologist had impressed upon Adesh the significance of his increased biological risk and been blunt about the need for ongoing monitoring and management to avoid premature death. Adesh knew that management of his condition needed to include medication to reduce his blood pressure, a change of diet to reduce his cholesterol and changes in lifestyle to include more exercise. Adesh admitted to being only partially compliant; he was erratic in taking his medication, had not altered his diet and took only occasional exercise. He was cross with himself for failing to follow medical advice but said that he often forgot his medication and did not like the side-effects. He also said that his job offered little thinking time for lifestyle changes.

Coach's internal process:

Aaima hypothesizes that there are multiple factors at play in this situation. She recalls reading some information about how individuals can be prone to depression following a heart attack, reading she undertook when her own father had a heart attack some years previously. She wonders if Adesh could be experiencing symptoms of depression. She is aware of her own personal reaction to his story and the need to "bracket" this sufficiently in order not to confuse Adesh's experience with her own. She also wonders if some of his difficulties with following medical advice reflect anxieties of an existential nature as he comes to terms with a possible genetic inheritance that he cannot directly alter or signal a pattern of avoidance. She wonders if avoidance is part of a broader pattern of response in his life. She remains unclear about whether Adesh might need an onward referral at this time.

Adesh continues his story, explaining that the company was aware of his medical history but was under the impression that the situation was well managed. Additionally, Adesh described pressure from his wife who accused him of failing to take his health seriously. She reminded him that their relocation from India had disrupted his family's life and that to further his career, she had sacrificed her own. She wanted him to discuss his circumstances openly with HR and occupational health and could not understand his reasons for failing to do so. However, while he felt guilty about what he described as "failing to honour my obligations to my family" Adesh was reluctant to disclose his current health situation at work. He predicted that his employer would conclude that he was incapable of managing the pressures of an executive role and find a way to dismiss him ("then uprooting my family will have been for nothing").

Coach's internal process:

Aaima starts to formulate some of the relevant factors in this situation that is clearly a priority for Adesh and which she also believes will need to be addressed before the original objectives of the coaching contract can be pursued. These factors are:

1   The uncertainty about Adesh's health future, perpetuated by his difficulty following medical advice.

2   A potentially avoidant coping style.
3   He and his family have undergone a major relocation, geographically and culturally. Major changes in life circumstances are well documented as psychologically disruptive and this may have triggered low mood and a sense of loss of control for both Adesh and his wife.
4   The reluctance to seek help might reflect a belief that help seeking is a sign of weakness or failure, giving rise to feelings of shame.

From these factors, Aaima developed the following hypotheses:

Hypothesis 1: Adesh, to whom success has always come easily, may have standards, expectations and assumptions about himself and life that are not consistent with the new set of circumstances he is facing.

Hypothesis 2: Adesh might not have the psychological problem-solving skills that are needed for complex, ongoing situations such as the management of a potentially life-threatening health condition.

Hypothesis 3: The way that Adesh told his story and outlined his own decision-making suggests that he is engaging in a number of cognitive distortions and information-processing biases that will prevent him from seeing his options clearly.

In view of the above, Aaima decides that her priority is to support Adesh in connecting to health care services that can assess his medical and lifestyle needs and to support Adesh in engaging with his employer to ensure that relevant information is shared.

As Adesh's heart condition appeared to be of sufficient magnitude to disrupt any efforts to work towards their original coaching objectives, Aaima suggested re-contracting around more immediate concerns which would represent some initial "groundwork" for their subsequent coaching objectives. Adesh seemed relieved at this suggestion. Following discussion, Adesh concluded that his immediate priority was deciding what information could be safely and usefully shared with his employer to allow access to the full range of services and support that might be available to him.

Coach's internal process:
   Aaima is pleased with Adesh's reaction, which suggests to her that he is open to seeking help but needs support in clarifying his options. She also suspects that he will need help differentiating actual "risks" to sharing

information with his employer from catastrophic predictions that may reflect the presence of information-processing biases. To achieve this goal and test her hypotheses, Aaima decides to guide Adesh through a cost–benefit analysis of disclosing more about his health condition to his employer. The purpose of this task is two-fold. First, in addition to exploring the potential consequences of different courses of action, it will enable the coach to learn more about Adesh's psychological problem-solving skills (his technical problem-solving skills were highly honed at work but his ability to engage in psychological problem-solving was less clear). Second, it was a means of learning more about Adesh's information-processing style and any interpretive biases that might be limiting his options.

The cost–benefit analysis revealed a number of potentially relevant factors:

1 There was no direct evidence that his employer would react to his disclosure negatively. Adesh appeared to be engaging in catastrophizing, which prevented him from establishing his options clearly.
2 There was direct evidence that the organization honoured its obligations to its employees – Adesh identified several colleagues, some of whom were in senior positions, managing ongoing health conditions, and overall the organization had been supportive.
3 Adesh had based his concern about the potential consequences of disclosure on one case where an employee with a health condition had subsequently had their contract terminated. However, he also knew that this individual was being performance managed. Thus, it appeared that Adesh had been selectively attending to information that seemed to confirm his worst fear.
4 He appeared to overestimate the level of threat to his position and discount the positive information relating to his reputation, career success and career prospects. This prevented him from considering the option that his employer might be invested in working with him to find ways of removing obstacles to his wellbeing so that he could excel in this new role.

Awareness of these factors supported Adesh in gaining clarity concerning what options might be available to him. As a first step, he chose to review the organization's policies so he was clear about the official position on supporting staff with ongoing health conditions. He also decided to share this information with his wife so that she could better understand why he had been reluctant to self-disclose. This promoted more effective couple communication and gave Adesh access to additional support and empathy.

After their second coaching session, Adesh decided to disclose his situation to HR who, in discussion with him, arranged a consultation with occupational health. One outcome was that a new health plan was put in place and his care was transferred to a local health care provider who could work with Adesh more immediately to examine lifestyle issues and the challenges he faced with medication compliance. By problem-solving with his cardiology nurse how he might manage the side-effects of his medication, Adesh started to take his medication regularly. At his nurse's suggestion, he also found a way to build exercise into his lifestyle by turning exercise into a weekly family activity. Adesh reported feeling brighter in his mood and more in control of his situation.

Coach's internal process:

Aaima notes that Adesh was able to engage in the cost–benefit intervention effectively and could use the results to construct a way forward. She concluded that Adesh could engage in psychological problem-solving but needed support with this – evident in both her conversations with him as well as the help provided by his cardiology nurse. Hypothesis 2 (above) did, therefore, seem to be confirmed. Hypothesis 3 was also supported: there was evidence of Adesh engaging in catastrophizing, mind-reading what his employer would think of him for seeking help, and selective attention as these were not supported by the evidence of his experience. Hypothesis 1 was yet to be tested, and Aaima continued to wonder about how Adesh's previous history of personal and professional success may have given rise to standards and beliefs about success that could be suboptimal for the next stage in his career development.

Formulation at the Pattern Level

Formulating at the situation level had hinted at broader themes that were hampering Adesh's development. It was evident that when anxious, he overestimated threats and catastrophized. Adesh also tended to ruminate, as apparent in his initial concerns about speaking with his employer. He would imagine himself dying of a heart attack and then repeatedly play over in his mind how his wife and children would have an unhappy life without him. When having to deal with work issues, his response was to retreat to the comfort of facts rather than try to problem-solve the issue itself. This suggested an enduring pattern which Aaima decided to explore using a pattern-level formulation.

Coach's internal process:

Aaima suspected that Adesh's rumination was a form of avoidance, a common and typically unproductive way of dealing with life's challenges. She suspected that Adesh was resorting to rumination when he was uncertain of how to respond and, while distressing, rumination enabled him to avoid the sharper discomfort of anxiety that he would feel if engaging in unfamiliar tasks. She formed two further hypotheses:

Hypothesis 4: Adesh had difficulty tolerating uncertainty and ambiguity.

Hypothesis 5: Adesh used rumination as a means of escaping uncomfortable thoughts and feelings (sometimes called experiential avoidance). At work, he would similarly attempt to escape the discomfort of new and people-oriented tasks by resorting to "the facts".

To test her hypotheses Aaima and Adesh discussed the possible pattern of over-estimating threats, rumination, avoidance and seeking the certainty of facts when presented with ambiguous challenges or uncertain situations. Adesh was asked to consider other situations where this pattern might be occurring. He was able to differentiate situations where he could deal with challenge and those where he could not. He was good at dealing with facts and figures but not so good at relationships. He said that he believed that people should understand evidence because "these are the facts not amenable to dispute". He ran his department in India on a strict hierarchical basis with clear targets and plans in place to meet them. He monitored staff performance closely to ensure projects were delivered on time and to budget. He expected staff to respect hierarchy and did not welcome being challenged by his direct reports. He confirmed that he became anxious when confronted with ambiguity and quickly sought linear explanations which could, at least in his head, resolve confusion. He had used this strategy as a way to manage any perceived threat.

Coach's internal process:
    Their conversation supported Hypotheses 4 and 5. Aaima thought that Adesh's reliance on rumination and resorting to the facts could be further evidence of his needing to enhance his psychological problem-solving skills as well as his professional relational skills. His quest for facts also made him reluctant to engage in unfamiliar tasks where he would experience anxiety and a temporary sense of being deskilled. Yet, this is what promotion would entail. Aaima decided that she needed to support Adesh in building his tolerance of uncertainty and ambiguity and that to do so, Adesh would need direct exposure to the very situations he was attempting to avoid. This line of thinking informed the next stage of the coaching conversation.

Adesh was already aware that the projects he was being assigned involved the need for effective cross-cultural communication, the ability to navigate multiple perspectives and a focus on bringing people with him. He also recognized that resorting to ruminating on issues of concern and anticipating disaster was counter-productive. He was asked to reflect upon what he had learnt when disclosing his health issue to the company. Adesh found this challenge difficult at first since he said the two issues were factually entirely different. He was asked to consider if, although the facts were different, there might be psychological similarities in his way of dealing with them.

> Coach's internal process:
> By asking him to consider similarities between how he had approached his health issue and how he might approach tackling his rumination, Aaima was testing his ability to generalize his learning from one context to another.

After much reflection Adesh identified a pattern that applied across different contexts but resulted in a common response, namely, he was focused on facts and figures at the expense of professional relationships. While he was respected for his technical capability, he found people difficult to predict and wondered whether he was perceived as distant and snappy. When he could not be all-knowing he felt unsure of how to act and resorted to avoidance and rumination. Aaima again asked if he could see a parallel way forward to that which he had adopted in addressing his health issue with the company. He recognized that he could seek feedback on his assumptions about how he was seen. He did so and found that while he was seen as prickly and distant he was greatly respected for his technical prowess and colleagues valued him as a source of information and advice. He also received feedback that his tendency to avoid challenge was not going to work well in the culture at the European head office.

At this stage, Aaima shared her hypothesis about the function of rumination for Adesh and introduced the notion of growth through exposure and response prevention; that is, in order to overcome his fear, he would need to engage proactively with the situations in which he felt anxious and deskilled and learn to accommodate the discomfort that these situations evoked in him, rather than fleeing from it. Given the other positive changes that he had experienced through coaching, and Aaima's clear and cogent account of his current predicament, Adesh said that he would be willing to engage in constructing a series of experiments that would help him discover what might happen if he engaged more proactively with new and relationship-oriented tasks. He now understood that initial discomfort would be an inevitable and indeed necessary part of his professional growth.

Formulation at the Level of the Whole Person/Case

As the coaching progressed, Aaima and Adesh expanded the perspective on the challenges that Adesh was facing in his new role and considered how some of his patterns were impacting different areas of his life. They began to construct a formulation at the level of the whole person as it related to a coaching purpose of being successful in his new role, developing a strategic perspective and ensuring that he and his family were successful in their move to a new country.

Coach's internal process:

Aaima was pleased with how Adesh's coaching was progressing. He had engaged effectively with his health care team, and she observed that he had lost weight, looked healthier and reported feeling more in control of his health. His relationship with his wife and family was also improving, even though this had never been an objective of the coaching. She was also gratified by Adesh's positive feedback on his progress. She was particularly pleased that he was learning how to pinpoint and modify cognitive distortions that trapped him into unhelpful predictions about his performance and the reactions of others. His psychological problem-solving skills were improving, although she noticed that he still required development to sustain him for future challenges. At this stage, Aaima wanted to extend the focus of the coaching to the level of person. Her rationale was to assist Adesh in formulating those aspects of his past and his positionality that might be evident in how he approached his new role and to identify those aspects that could be useful and those that might present barriers to his success. Aaima decided to use a range of perspectives to assist with this exploration, with an emphasis on the systemic – looking at systems of beliefs, cultural norms and the system dynamics of the organization and his family of origin.

As part of this formulation, Adesh recognized a dynamic that had been present throughout his life and career, namely, that he had always been praised for having the right answers. Indeed, in his previous role in India he had been seen as "the person who always knew what to do".

Coach's internal process:

As Aaima listened to Adesh recounting his tales of success and accomplishment, she noted that Adesh seemed to have had no real experience of struggle, difficulty or setback. As a result, she wondered whether Adesh had had the opportunity to acquire resilience in the face of challenges. His previous successes appeared to have helped create a mindset that "to experience difficulty is to fail". She wondered if this might partially explain why Adesh had not acquired robust psychological problem-solving skills – his personal history had given him little opportunity to do so. This gave rise to further hypotheses:

Hypothesis 6: Adesh equates difficulty with failure.

Hypothesis 7: Adesh's natural talents and capabilities, coupled with his work ethic and personal circumstances, have provided very limited exposure to challenge and setback. As a result, his resilience and skills in managing such situations is underdeveloped.

The coach and Adesh explored how this dynamic was placing him at odds with his current role and the organizational culture in a number of ways:

- The organizational culture, particularly at the senior levels, was one where all ideas were open for discussion and potential challenge, which had made him become defensive in some meetings. The coaching uncovered the belief, "If I am being challenged, it means that people think I am wrong and they are attempting to shame me".
- Adesh noticed that the above response occurred particularly frequently in meetings with his peers. He was able now to make a link back to his personal history and how, as the eldest in a family of three brothers, his relationships with peers/siblings was one where he expected that they should listen to him. He was seen as the most successful of the three brothers in his family and was not used to being challenged in this way by peers.
- His role involves making strategic decisions and developing solutions to long-term complex challenges and opportunities. Often there was no single, correct answer. He needed input from a number of people to craft a long-term strategy but was uncomfortable at not being able to provide all of the answers himself. This led him both to working long hours to try and absorb all the information at a detailed level and to him drilling down into the detail of the work of his direct reports. Thus, he resorted to his pattern of relying on facts which contributed to a perception by others that he was "prickly and distant".
- He was also reluctant to present ideas or a strategy until he believed that he had worked through all the potential outcomes and risks, pushing his direct reports to produce numerous versions of work. They were tiring of the additional hours and stress that he was putting them under and, consequently, were beginning to react against this approach. Adesh feared that he was losing their respect. However, he was potentially misreading this situation, fearing that his team was doubting his credibility for not having all the answers rather than witnessing

their unhappiness with his style of leadership. He was reluctant to engage his management team in a discussion about his leadership style as he feared that this would cause him to lose even more respect.

- Adesh also noticed the differences in cultural norms and his family dynamics in relation to hierarchy. He was not used to being questioned by those who reported to him. Although their relationship had by now improved, he was aware that his wife had challenged him over his non-compliance with medical recommendations and he had viewed this challenge as undermining him and his role as head of the family household.

Coach's internal process:

Aaima observed how Adesh was at this stage able to create links between his current challenges, his personal history and how the cultural expectations of leadership in the European head office contrasted with his experience of life in the India office. She interpreted this as a sign of Adesh's growing self-awareness and psychological mindedness. She decided that there was cause for confidence that they could progress with selecting areas of development in line with the initial coaching objectives and that Adesh would be able to generate, with increasing independence, opportunities to test and self-correct faulty assumptions, and engage in experiments with behaviour that would enhance his progress towards a more senior role.

While Adesh and Aaima identified several other cultural dynamics and behavioural patterns such as finding the direct nature of communication uncomfortable, they agreed that the focus of their work would be on enabling him to be more effective in his engagements with his direct reports and his peers.

With this aim in mind, they agreed on the following areas of development:

- To be more collaborative and open to challenge in coming up with both his strategic plan and in developing solutions to problems

  - This would involve continuing to modify some of the underlying beliefs and narratives that he held about himself and others, and his felt need to have all the facts and figures at hand.
  - Aaima and Adesh selected specific behavioural changes that he would implement including setting a broad direction and then allowing his team to come up with solutions; asking more open questions of his team and peers; adopting the role of facilitator of discussions rather than the expert advisor; and being open to feedback from his peers and direct reports.

- To develop a more agile and experimental approach to problem-solving in complex situations where there is no one right answer

  - This would require Adesh to reconsider his beliefs about problem-solving. Aaima offered to provide some frameworks and models for problem-solving in complex environments, which could support Adesh in learning different approaches.
  - The organization also agreed to support Adesh in attending a leadership development programme that focused on leading in a complex world.

- To take a more strategic viewpoint which involved looking at the overall strategic goals for the organization and aligning the technology strategy more effectively to these goals

  - Previously Adesh was focusing on the technology and what it could achieve. His development goal was instead to start with the strategy and then work with his team to develop technology solutions that would assist the organization in achieving its strategic objective.

During this stage of the coaching Adesh continued to make significant progress. In particular:

- Being able to articulate and identify the differences in cultural norms and ways of working enabled him to see that there were different approaches that could achieve the same thing and that could lead to better outcomes in the long term.
- Adesh asked more questions in meetings with his peers and listened to their suggestions, understanding this as collaboration rather than competition.
- His team gradually noticed that he was using their knowledge and skills more effectively and began to achieve some significant wins in projects and recommending technology solutions to support the organizational strategy. After a few months Adesh felt sufficiently comfortable to discuss his leadership style with his direct report team and to ask for their feedback.

Additionally, rather than working with his direct reports as individuals he started to bring them together to problem solve and develop strategy. He used an external facilitator to help his management team work together to develop the technology strategy for the next three years. This was a major step forward for Adesh as he had previously believed that he needed to do this himself. He recognized that the process was more enjoyable and the resulting strategy was creative and better met the organization's needs than the one he had been constructing alone. This was somewhat painful to acknowledge at first, but he was able to use the success to help him change the way he saw his role and challenge some of his outdated beliefs about what it means to be an effective leader.

Adesh also began to apply some of these changes to his role as a husband and father, helping his wife and children come up with solutions to the challenges they were facing in a new country rather than feeling that he needed to have all the answers.

Questions to Consider

Knowing that there is no universal agreement on how to approach formulation and, therefore, no definite way to approach this task, consider your responses to the following questions:

- What are your thoughts about how Aaima approached the formulation for this coaching assignment?
- What are your thoughts about how she used her formulation to structure her decision-making at different stages of the coaching process?
- Given that no formulation can be an exhaustive account of a client's life and circumstance, what do you notice about what Aaima chose to prioritize, and what was not considered?
- What was not present in this formulation or in Aaima's thinking but which might have been included? Can you identify other factors that could potentially have been relevant to understanding Adesh's needs to which Aaima did not pay attention?
- What decisions would you have made in her place?

You may wish to make a note of any observations or reflections you have had on this case as these might reflect aspects of your own positionality, sense of purpose, choice of perspectives and use of process. These will be useful in preparation for the next chapter, which considers how to develop your own personalized approach to formulation.

Chapter 15

Building a Framework for Formulation in Coaching

This chapter draws together the ideas discussed in previous chapters to enable the construction of a framework for incorporating formulation into coaching practice. A generic framework is first presented and then two examples are offered to illustrate how coaches might build their own approach.

The Generic Framework

Understanding Positionality – Where Do You Stand in Relation to Self and Your Role?

A starting point for any encounter in coaching is the position adopted by the coach and client to the work they are about to do together. This is not a neutral starting point as both parties come to the event with ideas about self, their stance to the world and the sense of what this encounter may involve. For the coach in particular, the sense of self as a person also includes a sense of self as a professional. What is it that they see as the offer they are able to make to potential clients? Corrie and Lane (2015) have previously referred to this as understanding brand, context and the type of contracts that practitioners prefer to enter into with clients. This idea has been considered in previous chapters as our positionality and also in terms of the reflective narrative that we each hold about self. It allows the subjective history in all its complexity to be understood and to inform our practice. However, coaching is not just a reflective practice; it is also relational. Therefore, part of the effort required is for the coach and client to share their narratives to ensure that they have a way to work together relationally.

In this book, we have presented a case for why coaches need to have thought about their own positionality statement and to understand how this might impact the coaching relationship and how they might enable their client to express their view of self and their world in a safe space for exploration. Psychotherapy trainees are typically supported in developing an understanding of their own selves and how they are positioned in the world, and this practice is also being embraced by a number of coaching and supervision training courses (Jackson, 2024).

DOI: 10.4324/9781003174585-20

As stated previously, a formulation process should include the work that the coach has done to understand their own positionality, how this relates to that of the client and its potential impact on the coaching purpose, perspectives and process. Hence, the key for the coach is ensuring that the client feels able to fully express their narrative, which is made easier if the coach has previously considered their own story. This makes possible an encounter in which coach and client can:

- Work to agree on a joint purpose
- Explore each other's perspectives
- Develop a shared process for working
- Work together to generate change
- Explore each other's moral stance and positionality and seek understanding
- Adopt a relational ethical stance agreeing what and how they make decisions throughout the coaching

This is not a one-off process at the start of coaching but an ongoing reflective stance that forms an important part of maintaining the working alliance. In Chapter 4, the following questions were offered as useful aids to reflection:

- What are the key elements of your social identity and what impact do these have on your worldview?
- How are you positioned in relation to the different forms of power?
- In what ways does your positionality impact how you define the overall purpose of your work?
- Thinking about a current or recent coaching client, in what ways are/were you positioned differently to your client? How do/did you take these differences into consideration in the coaching formulation?

This type of reflection places an emphasis on the elements of understanding that Drake (2010) considers key to the narrative of the work undertaken, namely:

- Person: An emphasis on: (a) self-knowledge for both coach and client; (b) creating an empathic container for awareness; (c) multiple sources of expertise and knowledge; and (d) attention to what they think is going on.
- Story: An emphasis on (a) foundational knowledge about narrative structure and psychology; (b) searching for openings for change; (c) the impact of the past, present and future; and (d) attribution of what they think caused it.
- Elements: An emphasis on (a) professional knowledge about work with the narrative material; (b) new opportunities that emerge from the interplay of the elements; (c) insights gained from assessing various streams of causality; and (d) action based on what they think they should do about it and why.
- Field: An emphasis on (a) contextual knowledge as found in the space between and around the coach and client; (b) a structure for new stories and behaviours; (c) a holistic view on what is possible now; and (d) anticipation of what they think will happen as a result.

We would encourage coaches to undertake this as an enquiry to better understand self as person and self as professional.

Purpose – Where Are We Going and Why?

The shared journey in any coaching endeavour begins as coach and client define the purpose of the work they will do together. How that endeavour was initiated, by whom and to what end is part of the discussion. Each party brings their own ideas on their purpose but will also seek to find a shared concern that makes sense to explore. Worthy starting points include questions such as: (a) What is our purpose in working together? (b) Where do we want to go? (c) What do we want to achieve? Thus, in building a formulation four areas need to be defined:

1   What are the questions/issues/concerns/objectives we wish to explore together?

    I   Is this an open enquiry which may lead to an unknown destination?

    II   Do the questions raised need a fixed point of resolution? Is there a problem that needs to be solved or a solution to be achieved that is recognized as appropriate by key stakeholders?

    III   Is it possible in this encounter to define in advance what an acceptable resolution would look like?

    IV   Has the purpose of the work negotiated between coach and client been agreed with relevant stakeholders?

2   What are our expectations about the work and those of key stakeholders?

    I   Is the intention of participants and stakeholders known and transparent?

    II   Are those who could impact on any outcome identified?

    III   Are there anticipated outcomes or results and how do these relate to the objectives of all involved?

    IV   What will be different as a consequence of achieving these outputs or results?

3   What role does each party want to play in this encounter?

    I   Who should (or does) play a role in identifying the primary objectives, data or hypotheses?

    II   What role does each party or stakeholder want to play?

    III   What investment of time, energy and resource will each party make, and how willing are they to commit?

    IV   How will each party be initiated into the journey to ensure a sense of partnership and ownership?

4   What is the context for the purpose and the way in which it has come to be defined?

    I   What does the client need to enable them to tell their story?

    II   Have coach and client been able to identify a shared concern that is appropriate to the boundaries of the contract and is best served by them working together?

III   Have they identified and understood the position of other stakeholders who might benefit from or be unnerved by the intervention?

IV   What makes this a meaningful encounter for coach, client and other stakeholders?

Perspective – What Will Inform Our Journey?

In formulating a coaching encounter, coaches are commonly faced with two possible approaches. The first is where the coach has a particular perspective such as cognitive-behavioural, Gestalt, solution-focused, or positive psychology. Here, the practitioner seeks to unlock the puzzle by privileging certain aspects of the client's story over others. This does not mean they cannot listen carefully or do excellent work. However, it does mean they need to be careful to work only with clients where their preferred approach has value and refer clients for whom their perspective may not be the best fit.

In the second approach the coach seeks to hear the client's story first and then explores with them the perspectives that might best work with them at that point in time. The coach and client seek to understand the goals or issues through multiple lenses as they work to construct, deconstruct and reconstruct the meaning of the encounter. The downside to this is a more complicated approach while being comprehensive.

Working with either of these two approaches involves the ability to maintain the balance between considerations that include the use of theory, the evidence base, responsiveness to the client's unique story and circumstances. Bruch and Bond (1998), in relation to the therapy alliance (but this could also describe the coaching relationship), refer to the importance of the client's construction of the world in which they work together to create a shared model. This enables them to consider experiments with behaviour they can try out, and thus the formulation becomes personalized to that client in those circumstances.

There are four areas to consider in relation to perspectives:

1   What perspectives inform the journey between coach and client?

   I   What perspectives are informing the coach's understanding of the encounter?
   II   What perspectives is the client bringing to understand the situation?
   III   How does the coach or client position themselves in the world and how is that influencing understanding?
   IV   What is the coach doing to ensure that the client is able to openly explore their beliefs, knowledge and competencies within the encounter?

2   What beliefs about models of practice are visible in the encounter?

   I   What beliefs about self and other inform the understanding of the puzzles we face as clients or the service we offer as practitioners?
   II   What perspectives based in personal theories of behaviour and change are informing the encounter?

  III What perspectives based in interpersonal theories and change are informing the encounter?

  IV What perspectives based in systemic theories and change are informing the encounter?

3 What beliefs relating to the nature of evidence are visible in the encounter?

  I What seems to count as evidence in the way the work is interpreted or undertaken?

    a Through the use of data which has a clear scientific basis

    b Through the use of a "what works" perspective such as a protocol or manual

    c Through action specific to the context and reflection

    d Through critical engagement with dominant discourses to challenge assumptions and power structures.

4 Who in the encounter decides what counts as evidence?

  I Who will benefit most or least by the decision on what counts as evidence?

  II What impact does the approach taken to evidence have on the client or coach where it conflicts with cultural expectations?

  III Who has the power to decide?

  IV What political, economic, social and environmental concerns are driving the choices made?

Process – How Will We Get There?

Once a purpose for the work is understood and the encounter has begun to explore influential perspectives, it is possible to decide on the process by which coach and client work together. For some, using a single theoretical model, the approach will reflect that, and it will have to be outlined to the client to gain their buy-in to proceed. For others, exploring the narrative more broadly, a framework for managing the storytelling process will need to be agreed. Corrie and Lane (2010), as discussed in Chapter 2, suggest there are five common discourses (to which here is added a sixth) in coaching practice likely to influence the process chosen:

1 A formulation derived from diagnostic classification – for example, the client has undertaken various psychometric tests or received 360 feedback which provides a classification that impacts decisions on the work.

2 A formulation based on scientist-practitioner models in which coach and client work together to identify hypotheses that can be tested to arrive at useful and accurate explanations.

3 A formulation based on a given theoretical position (either single or integrative) that will guide the encounter.

4 A strategic formulation based on a future orientation and the strengths people bring to the encounter.

5   A formulation as a means of social control based on actions and processes de-
    fined by those in power in an organization, which states that a given way of
    working is mandated and only predefined objectives are considered legitimate.
    This may sometimes include a requirement that any coach must be trained in a
    particular way.
6   A narrative formulation that explores the way the story is told and what is in-
    cluded or excluded from the account.

There are four areas to consider in relation to process when formulating an
encounter.

1   What process was used to ensure that the purpose was met given any constraints
    available in the work?
2   How did the coach and client structure the work?
3   What factors seemed to mediate the choices made?
4   What changed over the course of the work in terms of the definition of purpose,
    the perspectives employed or the process used?

In addition, the focus is on ensuring coherence between the process used with
the purpose of the work and the perspectives that inform it. How the participants
use the information gathered to develop their sense of the purpose of the work, the
factors that they have to take into account to understand the issues and the process
necessary to create a shared concern form the basis for the work they do together.
The formulation and intervention plan that arise from this provide the basis for
analysis. This is an important consideration for building a formulation.

A Personalized Framework for Formulation

As discussed above, any process has to be consistent with the other elements of the
4P Framework such as the perspectives on which the coach bases their approach. A
coach working from a solution-focused approach, for example, would be unlikely
to adopt a process that includes gathering data about a problem or a difficult situation. There should also be a means of measuring whether the process is effective in
supporting the development of the formulation and meeting the intended coaching
purpose. In the following section we provide some steps that can be used to guide
the adaptation of an existing model and develop a new personalized process.

1. Example: Guide the Adaptation of an Existing Model

Step 1: Review Current Approaches

The first step involves a review and reflection of current practice, the aim of which
is to identify key models, tools, techniques and approaches that are a foundation of
practice. In completing this part of the review, the coach's perspectives, knowledge

and skill are the key focus. The following questions can be used to assist in this reflective process:

- Which models are most commonly favoured and consistently used by the coach to ensure the coaching purpose is met? For example, is there a specific model learned in training that forms the basis for practice?
- What tools and techniques are most commonly used, and in which contexts? For example, is there a specific coaching purpose or context in which selected tools and techniques are commonly used?
- What tools, techniques or approaches are not currently used? Are there tools and techniques which are not sanctioned by the perspective underpinning practice?
- How are coaching outcomes measured? For example, in what ways is the achievement of the coaching purpose monitored?

Step 2: Capturing the Client's Story

Having summarized the key approaches currently used, the next step is to identify how the client's story is captured and how data are collected to inform the coaching journey. How this is done will depend on the coach's training and perspectives, as some approaches will favour particular data collection methods or approaches over others.

- What approaches, tools or techniques are currently used to ensure the client's story is heard?
- Based on the perspectives favoured, what aspects of the client's story are emphasized, and which are minimized?
- What types of data are typically gathered and through what means? This could include tools and techniques as well as diagnostics.
- How are decisions made about what data to include and what to exclude?
- Who is typically included in the data collection process and why?

Step 3: Identify Elements of Process

Having reviewed and summarized the insights from the first two steps, it may be possible to identify some process elements that are commonly used in current practice. Alternatively, it may be necessary to consider the logical elements or steps to a process that could be structured to deliver the purpose of the coaching.

- Are there steps taken in coaching assignments that are effectively a process which is commonly used but not necessarily articulated by the participants? For example, is there commonality in how the coaching commences? Or are a set of assessments used in every engagement?

- At what point or points in the coaching is it possible to develop a formulation? Is the formulation a natural outcome from the use of current approaches, or does the approach need to be modified?
- Are there measures for effectiveness included in the process? At what point and how is the outcome of the coaching measured?

Step 4: Articulate the Potential Process

From the completion of the previous steps, it should now be possible to articulate a process that can be consistently adopted. This may include a series of steps or, like the framework outlined earlier in this chapter, a series of elements used in a more recursive process. It might be an adaptation of a current model or a completely new process. Once the process has been identified, reviewing and refining the approach is ongoing. Coaches frequently continue their professional development, learning new theories, methods and assessments. In doing so, consideration needs to be given to how these approaches are consistent with or challenge the coach's current process.

2. Example: Developing a Personalized Process for Team Coaching

In addition to the processes described above, there is the option of the coach designing their own process. However, any such process needs to be justified through supporting literature or evidence derived from practice. Coaches might also incorporate a means to assess the extent to which it is efficient (the ratio of output to input to ensure best use of the resources available), effective (it achieves what it claims to do) and efficacious (it is worthwhile in producing the result intended). This would involve five areas for dialogue listed below.

Purpose

If we draw together the ideas in the literature we have referenced, and the models above, the common theme is the importance of a shared purpose. The team exists to meet that purpose, which is the rationale for them being and working together. Hence, the starting point for any team coaching process is establishing an understanding of how that team and its stakeholders understands its purpose. The dialogue starts within the team, its narrative about its purpose, the clients it serves (internal and external), the values it holds to inform its goals, the tasks needed to achieve them and the bond that holds them together. In building a team coaching process, the approach used to initiate and conclude this dialogue within the team provides not only an understanding of the level of agreement but also the beginning of insight into the worldviews that its members hold.

Below is an example of a personalized process devised by a coach working with a leadership team who have been recently formed as a result of a merger between two organizations.

STEP 1: CREATE A DIALOGUE TO ESTABLISH THE TEAM PURPOSE
AND EXPLORE PERSPECTIVES

- Check level of agreement and areas of difference. Try for a reflective and generative approach (rather than debate and discussion) to enable a bigger perspective on the purpose that can command agreement.
- Establish the extent to which this purpose includes the views of all internal and external stakeholders – has it been "socialized"?
- Agree a narrative that can be shared and to which the team feels accountable. This narrative will need to reflect the team's sense of brand, the context that gives it meaning (what makes it worthwhile, sustainable and ethical) and the contribution that the team makes.

Perspectives

The perspectives explored should cover those within the team, the relationships built and the wider context that informs how the work is viewed. The differing worldviews of team members and the varied stakeholders need to be explored and incorporated in a way that honours difference, and yet creates a bigger perspective that ensures the team purpose can be met.

STEP 2: SEEK TO UNDERSTAND HOW WE SEE THE CONTEXT IN WHICH
THE TEAM FUNCTIONS

- Discover the perspectives that are influencing how the team's purpose is viewed internally to the team and externally with stakeholders.
- Evaluate how each perspective might impact on the achievement of purpose.
- Define the means through which these impacts will be addressed or identify any emerging threats or possibilities.

Process

As introduced above, the process is concerned with how we work together to achieve the agreed purpose in a way that reflects the perspectives we take in the world. It includes how we incorporate the views of other stakeholders.

STEP 3: AGREE A BASIS FOR THE WORK TOGETHER

- Negotiate a contract that includes roles, goals, tasks and the relational bond or alliance that will hold all parties together.
- Create a structure for working together to fulfil the purpose.
- Determine how success will be measured.

Positionality

We have discussed the role of positionality in relation to how an individual views self, and also in relation to a shared perspective on how a team is viewed by others and understands the world in which it operates. As a team works to explore purpose, perspectives and process, this will raise questions on how individuals feel heard and choose to show up in the team. For the team, similar questions will emerge on how it is heard and chooses to present to the world. The questions need to be privileged in any dialogue and a process enabling them to emerge and be addressed needs to be devised.

STEP 4: ACKNOWLEDGE AND REVIEW THE POSITIONS OF ALL WHO ARE INVOLVED IN THE COACHING THAT WILL INFLUENCE OUTCOMES

- Notice inside; as the dialogue emerges notice how you feel inside. Do you feel heard and acknowledged? How will you present this to the team?
- Notice outside; as the dialogue emerges notice what it looks like outside yourself, in the team and the wider context. What do you observe being heard and acknowledged? How might you explore this as a team?
- Notice over time; as the dialogue emerges notice how things change over time, internally and externally. What process might you use as a team to acknowledge the positions of I, you and we over time?

Formulation

As the coach, consider how you will enable the team to complete this dialogue. This is never at an end point but is always a journey which will reach destinations along the way or take a totally different route to that initially envisaged. However, at various points it is possible for the team to agree a formulation – their narrative of who they are, why they are here, what they are intending, how they will achieve that and what makes it worthwhile. Creating a formulation provides a shared sense for the team that guides their endeavours and enables judgements to be made on what needs to change.

STEP 5: FORMULATE A NARRATIVE WITH THE TEAM THAT IS MEANINGFUL TO THEM AND ENABLES THE WORK UNDERTAKEN TO MEET THE AGREED PURPOSE

- Review all the work undertaken in the dialogue and draw together agreed themes.
- Craft together a narrative that encompasses the themes and provides a coherent sense for the team of who they are and what they contribute.
- Share and enact the narrative adjusting in the light of changing circumstances so that it remains relevant and tells a compelling story.

Conclusion

Adapting an existing approach to incorporate formulation or developing a personalized framework is not, as can be seen, a case of coaches simply doing whatever they want. Rather, it is about a considered process, reflection on the evidence and building a robust frame that is amenable to evaluation. It is also kept under continual review as new data emerge in the field of coaching. An ethical imperative is that as coaches we practise with integrity, respect for others, are responsible in the way we critique evidence and competently apply knowledge from the field to our practice. We find this an exciting and enriching endeavour. We hope we have shared some of that excitement and encourage you to explore ways to enrich your practice through exploration of these ideas on adapting and developing frameworks for formulation in coaching.

Chapter 16

Adapting Formulation to Respond to Different Worldviews

Many coaches will find themselves working with clients whose backgrounds are different from their own. This can introduce an added level of complexity to coaching engagements as differences of abilities (physical and neurological), age, class, ethnicity, gender, religion, sexuality and diverse experiences influence how a client may respond to a coach's approach. This can impact communication style, or any coaching tools and techniques that the coach may introduce. Having considered how do develop a formulation and create a personalized framework to meet specific needs in Chapters (14 and 15), in this chapter relevant models of diversity and worldview are briefly reviewed. While the challenges of working with people from diverse backgrounds are explored this is not an attempt to cover all forms of diversity in the detail they merit since this would be a book in itself. Rather, the aim is to look at some of the ways in which groups have been marginalized, to briefly mention some examples of practices that attempt to address concerns and to explore ways to adapt formulation to be more appropriate to different worldviews.

At the outset, it is important to recognize that the applied sciences and social sciences do not have a good record of dealing with diversity. Gould (1996) set out the ways in which people have been mismeasured and how racist stances have been promoted in psychology. The misdiagnosis and treatment of minorities in psychiatry (Suite et al., 2007), the distortion of cultures in anthropology (Blakey, 2020) and the marginalization of women as professionals (Opara et al., 2020) has been well established. The domination of white Western, largely male, thinking has distorted the way in which others are understood, which in turn shapes the services offered (Lane et al., 2023). Coaching, similarly, has relied heavily on the same sources of theory and practice. This chapter examines some of the ways in which this distorts thinking, and alternatives that have emerged or are emerging. The challenge is that until practitioners talk about the importance of equality and diversity but also act in ways that include all as a matter of course, marginalization and discrimination are perpetuated.

DOI: 10.4324/9781003174585-21

A Brief History of Distortion and Discrimination

There is a long history of discrimination and, as Gould (1996) states, "the mismeasure of man". This applies to the different ways that people are categorized. We explore this idea as preliminary to considering its role in formulation. For example:

> People are segregated because of being identified in terms of our own prejudices ... the ideal model is the white adult male ... middle class, handsome, sporting, witty ... the further away you are from this model, the more you are dehumanised and undervalued (Ruebain, quoted in Keise et al., 1993, pp. 189–199).

Keise et al. (1993) suggest that in this view the arguments in favour of special help are patronizing and founded in core segregationist beliefs. Before a rush to judgement on this quote or a felt sense of the need to defend professional services, consider the point made by Ratele (2019) in his thoughts on an African Psychology – *The World Looks Like This From Here*. What does the world look like from where Ruebain views it?

Let's take another look from here:

> As coaches we are asked to consider the importance of research to underpin our practice – as evidence-based practitioners. Yet for many communities the term is far from neutral.

Anishinaabe scholar Kathy Absolon (2022) writes about how the construction of Indigenous peoples in Eurocentric research has rarely been neutral and that research for Indigenous peoples and communities must be critically examined in terms of who is authoring the work and for what purpose, as colonial research on and about Indigenous people has not benefited Indigenous peoples. As she states:

> The observations, reports and documentations on and about Indigenous Peoples during early contact and colonization in North America entrenched stereotypes and justified colonists' agendas of civilize and Christianize leading to missionary presence and the Indian Residential School projects of cultural genocide. Much of what was written was from a colonial perspective and agenda to justify genocide and enact racist legislation to control and re-socialize Indigenous children and families (Absolon, 2022, p. 45).

Similarly, Suite et al. (2007) have examined historical interactions between African-Americans and the medical and mental health communities. This history includes medical experimentation, misdiagnosis and unauthorized sterilizations, which they contend contributes to a continuing mistrust within many communities and underutilization of services. The failure of practitioners to go beyond their traditional practices such as clinical history taking to encompass the broader cultural and historical perspectives, which they and their clients/patients utilize to make decisions, adds to that mistrust. Their view is that professionals can fail to acknowledge that our practice is culturally bound and informed by dominant ideologies. These ideologies can take a number of forms, a medical model used to justify intervention in another's life or psychological theory that provides a rationale for discriminatory behaviour. Or, as expressed by Ullman (1977), "The dominant paradigm provides a seeming explanation ... it permits intervention, especially for the target person's own good ... one may feel virtuous while acting tyrannically" (quoted in Keise et al., 1993, p. 194).

The latest example of this is perhaps found in the Infected Blood Inquiry in the UK, where medical professionals, policymakers and politicians failed to act ethically by claiming that people received the best possible treatment and refusing to accept that wrong had been done (Langstaff, 2024). It is clear from the report that a dominant paradigm was continually favoured over the experience of those impacted. In order to adapt formulation to encompass different worldviews, the role of dominant paradigms that shape practice needs to be constantly critiqued. Or, as Absolon (2022) put it above, "who is authoring the work and for what purpose". Lent (2017) proposes that we (that is, all of us as persons and as professionals) recognize that culture shapes our values, which in turn shapes our history. The enormous complexity of human cultures across time and space cannot be reduced to an assumption of a homogenous set of Anglo-American beliefs about how the world works. As Lent (2017) points out, the conquest of nature, the conquest of the world's peoples, and the decimation of Indigenous populations, philosophies and cosmologies, galvanized a pseudoscientific racist interpretation of history. This led to the grand narrative of the evolutionary progress of humanity from its origins in Africa and archaic peoples (Neanderthal and Denisovan) to the dominance of Western thought.

The challenge to this that Lent (2017) invites us to recognize is that the cognitive frames through which different cultures perceive reality, the implicit beliefs and values that create a pattern of meaning in people's lives, is a significant driver of our histories. Many of the approaches we adopt to the provision of services are driven by largely unchallenged cultural beliefs. Thus, a diagnostic instrument derived from one set of cultural values is applied to an entirely different culture. In trying to address this it is important that we consciously examine our own theoretical and cultural biases. However, we need to be conscious of not over-romanticizing other cultures and worldviews. We need to apply the same level of scepticism to all cultures and worldviews. We should not replace one set of unchallenged cultural beliefs with another. For example, the views taken of illness, difference, neurodiversity, the role of gender, and sexuality vary by culture and we cannot assume that the treatment of people is better is one culture rather than another. The importance of understanding diversity issues across a whole range of categories is vital, particularly as it impacts education (Christodoulou et al., 2022).

Let's take another view from here:

> For many Africa women and men, not only fluid, non-binary trans and genderqueer Africans, the term "African" itself, distinct from matters of gender and sexuality can be marked as a sense of loss, a sense of being unmoored, of rupture or rootlessness … Africanness can be for some people, bedevilled by feelings of unanchoredness and insecurity (Ratele, 2019, p. 132).

This reminds us not to frame our arguments in racially and culturally exclusive ways. It might be claimed that these are historical events that are no longer relevant, but the mistrust persists for good reason (Keise et al.,1993). This same pattern of underutilization is referenced by Corrie and Lane (2021) in the UK in the Increasing Access to Psychological Therapies programme (now NHS Talking Therapies). Multiple barriers to access services and to care are noted in recent studies in many places (Ahmadinia et al., 2022; Bignall et al., 2019; Knaak et al., 2017; Memon et al., 2016; NHS England, 2023). As a report from NHS Race and Health Observatory (2023) states:

> Ten years of anonymised patient data found that historically, people from Black and minoritised ethnic backgrounds have experienced poorer access to, and outcomes from, NHS talking therapies. Over this time period, compared to White British groups, they are less likely to access services, tend to wait longer for assessment and to access treatments (p. 1).

Clearly there is much to do.

Some Hopeful Signs in Coaching

Why does this matter in coaching? Essentially, coaching is largely based in assumptions about science and theories of behaviour that were established in American or European cultures and largely, although not exclusively, by white males (Lane et al., 2023). The implications of this narrow discourse seem not to be addressed. It is unusual to see a critical discourse approach where the underlying assumptions are examined in any coaching book (Gray et al., 2016). Diversity is integral to coaching, and being a good coach requires working from a diversity perspective, according to Baron and Azizollah (2019). This, they argue, is because acknowledging and working with difference is about maximizing each person's potential, yet sexism and racism still operate in organizations. The essential need is for the coach to consistently challenge themselves and provide a number of areas where change might be possible. In particular, their argument is to look at the difference between equal opportunities and diversity. The former focuses on overcoming the barriers and inequalities that people face. While legislation may identity areas such as disability, sexual orientation, religion, age, race and gender (Gov.uk, 2024), it requires coaches to understand how this works and the other factors that operate as barriers, such as social class, educational background and regional origin. This is not an add-on but central to our practice. Diversity is concerned with inclusivity and individuality (Kandola & Fullerton, 1998). A diverse workforce can improve creativity and innovation but also requires better management to prevent conflict or exclusion (Simons et al., 1999; Ely & Thomas, 2001).

In exploring coaching programmes to address diversity issues, Baron and Azizollah (2019) make the critical point that too often it is the individual who is seen as different who is the problem and in need of coaching. This echoes the earlier view of Ullman (1977), suggesting the response of others to that individual is not addressed. This same point was prevalent in earlier work on the way professional services operate. As Jackson states:

> since the onus of the problem is on the client, the professionals' mission is oppressively one of getting the client to adjust to the status quo, while the behaviour of those in power and the role they perform in creating and maintaining psychologically oppressive environments in which Blacks must function, are ignored (Jackson, 1977, quoted in Keise et al., 1993, p. 195).

As the NHS England (2023) study shows, these issues persist. Recent reviews of services to improve access to mental health care show long-standing inequities, and initiatives to improve the situation while having some impact have not delivered expected gains (Winsper et al., 2023). Baron and Azizollah (2019) go on to outline a number of areas to which the coach needs to pay attention. This includes self-awareness, knowledge and skills. Their framework deserves attention and the stance they take will add value to coaching practice both to help an individual value their own difference and to identify and work with negative diversity issues both in the client's mind and the environment.

All the coaching bodies have diversity and related statements to support appropriate practices or even the idea of intercultural competence. Nevertheless, what is missing from their stance is any challenge to the theoretical models used in coaching. Given that these mainly derive from counselling or therapeutic contexts, the earlier criticisms pointing to the negative effect of some counselling and therapeutic models is relevant (Gould, 1981; Jones, 1972; UNESCO, 1983, Wilkinson, 1986). According to Keise et al. (1993), most criticism has focused on psychoanalytic stances, but humanistic approaches have also featured. Alternative theories emerged during the 1970s to 1990s in these contexts from areas such as feminism, Black psychology, radical therapies, LGBTQ+ theory, social constructionism (Cedric et al., 1975; Hayes, 1972; Hayes & Banks, 1972; Kitzinger, 1986; Nicolson, 1986; Nobles, 1976; Ward, 1990; White, 1970). These ideas have been around long enough that you would have expected they would be influencing coaching theory. Yet recent standard texts (Cox et al., 2018; Palmer & Whybrow, 2018) in the field give little space to these critical theories.

Their importance is, however, seen as a matter of current concern for, as Shoukry and Cox (2018) argue, neoliberal values are embedded in the coaching discourse and can be used as a process of control. They further contend that if we understand coaching as a social process, it can become an enabler for change. Similarly, in dealing with racial bias, Orange et al. (2019) argue that there is an urgent need in coaching to enter the conversation ready to counter bias but also to actively refute a deficit approach and combat stereotypes. The deficit mindset has been part of a dominant paradigm for many years. Creativity and alternative abilities and ways to see the world have been marginalized (Pearson, 2017), and while professionals may start with good intentions to foster greater inclusion and creativity, rather than use deficit approaches, they can rely on premises that reify logics and practices that are exclusionary (Ziols et al., 2022). The deficit model has too often dominated approaches to the education of marginalized groups. Where help is offered it has appeared as a way to teach skills to make them succeed in Eurocentric ways of being rather than recognize the creativity that may exist in their way of seeing the world (Gerson, 2016).

The approach adopted for dealing with difference, as Roth (2017) argues, is not very broad and tends to divide between those who view culture through a societal or organizational lens and those who look at national cultures. Where research in the field is emerging, she identifies two ways in which this is seen. The first considers cultural issues in the client's world (Abbott, 2018; Rosinski, 2003) and the second looks at cultural impacts on the relationship between coach and client (Coultas et al., 2011; Milner et al., 2013; Plaister-Ten, 2016). As Roth's research suggests, the focus on national culture adds very little to our understanding of the individual. She rightly cautions that if coaches identify culturally rooted behaviours or expectations among their clients, they need to understand that this is about their perceptions and interpretation of something as cultural and hence contains the pitfall of cultural stereotyping. We can see this in many offers in the marketplace for cultural awareness training for executives placed abroad.

Nevertheless, there are many hopeful signs. There are increasing efforts to address culture, difference and diversity within the coaching and related literatures. There are examples of programmes that look at neurodivergence (Doyle & McDowall, 2023), promoting women in the workplace (Dzingwa & Terblanche, 2024), supporting disabled people in sports (Sports Coaching UK, 2014), parental coaching (Golawski et al., 2013), and drawing on a long interest in social justice issues in fields such as counselling psychology we have approaches to different sexual orientations (Milton, 2014a). As Milton (2014b) attests, sexuality cannot be viewed as a static experience. There are new phenomenon and debates occurring particularly in relation to technologically mediated patterns of relating, primarily online, which can further marginalize and abuse. These are not simply topics of interest to academics; they matter to the clients who approach us and the way we offer services in the contexts in which we work. However, it is important to recognize that individuals may have a number of different marginalized identities (Doyle & McDowall, 2023). Positionality may be complicated and working with people as a category rather than in terms of their entire narrative of identity is likely to be problematic. There is certainly a sense that diversity matters. As we think about the coaching offers we make, there is a need to formulate interventions with individuals that respect the totality of the story they want to tell.

By implication this requires us to avoid seeing a person as defined by a category rather than understanding their position in the world as they see it. In Chapter 4 the concept of positionality was introduced. That concept is relevant here. How the coach understands their position in the world personally and professionally will impact on the approach taken to different diversities. Similarly, the position taken by the client will impact on how they view any suggestions made by the coach. In coaching we seek to make and re-make our world sometimes in straightforward linear ways, but other times the coaching may involve a fundamental challenge to our worldview. This enables the possibility for us to reach beyond deterministic categories based on class, gender, abilities, sexuality and many more. How does the coach reach beyond deterministic categories to change their "ways of seeing", and how do they facilitate the client's similar endeavours to be different in the world? Formulation is at the heart of this in creating stories that make sense for this person in a given context.

Two Approaches That Try to Avoid Such Stereotyping

Where difference exists and there is a willingness to explore positionality, two common approaches to avoid stereotyping exist. One is to adapt current approaches to better respond to need and the other is to start from a different perspective, that of the client's world. Hence, there are examples in the therapy world of adapting cognitive-behavioural therapy to be culturally sensitive with ethnically diverse populations (Huey et al., 2023). Huey and colleagues (2023) suggest three different approaches, two of which share the approach adopted here, namely, the use of cultural adaptation strategies or personalizing the model to include diversity. (The third suggests a skills-based approach.) These two approaches are considered here using cultural diversity as the example, but the same principles apply to other areas of diversity – do we adapt what we have or reconceptualize our approach starting with the worldview of the person engaged in the journey with us?

Cross-cultural coaching has for the most part focused on preparing Western business executives to adopt a culturally sensitive approach (Law, 2011). However, working with Asian businesses, Law (2011) draws attention to the way these often operate across multiple generations and in different locations. So, while starting within one cultural context, later generations of the family may be running the business in a context very different from the founders. This raises issues of succession, governance, the generation gap and fragmentation of values. Below are some of the many examples of a culturally sensitive approach:

- Law (2011) advocates a framework that enables flexible and fluid responses where culture is a significant factor influencing the clients' values.
- Kreikamp (2017), in a study of a Chinese business operating in a European environment, makes the point that in our current fast-changing business environment

people from different national and organizational cultures and mindsets have to collaborate if they are going to deliver results.

- Yasargil and Denton (2011), in the context of working as coaches in family business in Turkey and the Middle East, ask the question: what comes first in a family business – family or business?
- Ramakrishnan (2011), working in the multicultural context of Singapore, argues for the central role of the coach as a trusted partner, as the cultural cross-currents are many and often hidden from those outside.

In the above examples, Western concepts such as narrative, competence, systems and constitution are adapted to function in a more culturally sensitive way. The argument is that while it is understood that leadership looks different culture to culture, there are similarities as well as differences and therefore a skilful coach working with a diverse team can leverage these synergies. Plaister-Ten (2016) identifies a series of lenses (a cross-cultural coaching kaleidoscope) through which we can explore cross-culturally. Largely (although not entirely) absent from the literature have been attempts to build models consistent with religious or cultural traditions. It is possible to start not with a set of Western assumptions and theories, which are then adapted, but to ask what principles and practices might emerge when working from within a different cultural stance (Lane et al., 2023). The same question can be asked within any diverse position – what principles inform the worldview of the client and what practices might emerge from working from those principles?

What Might the Approach Look Like When Western Coaching Models Do Not Feature at All?

Two examples of this approach are explored, drawing on concepts from African Psychology (Ratele, 2019) and Islamic coaching and approaches to research (Auda, 2021; van Nieuwerburgh & Allaho, 2017). The latter use the term Ershad, meaning guidance, to describe the role of a guide (coach) who develops and grows the individual into his or her desired maximum capacity and degree of accomplishment against a framework of Islamic beliefs about God, self, others and the world. Ershad echoes Islamic ideals of Discovery, Intentions, Pathways and Effort. These principles are used to guide the coaching process. Ratele (2019), in exploring the concept of African Psychology, asks us to consider what the world looks like from here:

> As an undertaking to psychologically understand the world from here, African Psychology also aims to liberate us from oppressive Euroamerican-centred psychology and to free psychology as a global endeavour from colonial-modern notions of being human in the world as it exists (Ratele, 2019, p. 206).

Stout-Rostron (2019a) argues for an integration of Ubuntu and coaching as a way to promote the idea of employers seeing all their people as an integral part of an interconnected system. As Ubuntu recognizes, we exist as a community and in belonging – it is a counter to the marginalization that we currently see: "It behoves us to shift from the individual focus of most dated Western individualistic business ideologies and adopt shared worldviews that place greater value on the collective, the community, the organisation, the environment, than the individual" (Stout-Rostron, 2019a, p. 92).

In coaching the individual leader this serves the greater good by enhancing each person's journey along the broader path of humanity (Stout-Rostron, 2019a). It is this shift of worldview which is central to approaching formulation from a diversity perspective.

What Does This Mean for Our Approaches to Formulation – Adapting Formulation to Respond to Different Worldviews?

As the concept of formulation is itself a cultural phenomenon, we need to ask:

- As formulation is itself rooted in Western psychological traditions, what does this mean for working with diversity?
- Is formulation a useful tool in working with diversity and what could be the pitfalls that we might need to consider if we were to use it?
- How might formulation fit with models of coaching from different cultures, or are we suggesting that perhaps it doesn't fit?
- How would the approach we are suggesting in this book (4Ps) enable a coach from a different culture to develop an approach to formulation that is appropriate for their cultural background and clients?

Chapter 2 examined different approaches to formulation, yet these are embedded in different, essentially Western, traditions such as diagnostic frameworks. The use of diagnostically led formulations is a useful example of the issues that coaches face. Narratives of disorder and disease (as discussed in our earlier consideration of health and wellness) are based on diagnostic criteria, which are separate from a person's experience of illness or wellness, whereas personal narratives around illness or wellness embed the understanding within meaningful relationships influenced by cultural systems (Nettleton, 2021). For example, Kleinman (1988) distinguishes between disease and illness. The first privileges practitioners' perspectives and biomedical reductionism, whereas the second looks at the lived experience of the person. Burchardt (2019) draws attention to the role of illness narratives as both a theory and method of working. This has implications for a number of the ways we conceptualize illness. For example, illness narratives might help people make sense of both acute and chronic experiences but also call into question their assumptions about the world. Each person brings a story to their medical practitioner, which means that any diagnosis can only be understood in terms of the particulars of that person's life. Telling a story is not just a way to present a sequence of events but shows how they are interconnected. Ochs and Capps (2009) describe narrative as fundamental and universal, emerging very early in our life as children as a way to make sense of the world. Absolon (2022) draws attention to the way Indigenous communities have often been separated from their stories, which are denigrated, and makes a strong case for a process to re-story away from colonial narratives so communities can recover their story. Similarly in relation to neurodiversity coaching, Doyle and McDowall (2024) point to the disability discourse and the way children hear narratives that force compliance with painful activities. Barden (2021), looking at leadership, explores how leaders do business with their world and identifies the role of early childhood experiences in shaping their response. As Barden states, understanding their "navigational stance" to the world is seen as essential for coaching.

If we think of this in terms of some of the issues our clients bring to coaching, we can understand how they seek to place events into a pattern of understanding of their lives. This includes their generic sense of the culture in which they are raised and the particularities of their own lived experience (Lane, 1973; Plaister-Ten, 2016; Roth, 2017). Corrie and Lane (2010) have explored this in terms of how we construct stories and see this narrative process as central to the way formulations emerge. Coaches can use diagnostic or theoretical formulation that privileges the perspective of the coach, but can also seek to privilege the story the client is trying to tell or decipher. It should be noted that this is not an argument to abandon Western technical or scientifically derived formulations in favour of a purely cultural stance. Rather, as explored in our earlier discussion on positionality, it is about understanding how these stances position us in relation to our clients.

How do we approach formulation to work with different worldviews? We are each formed by a range of influences that impact how we see ourselves, others and the world – our positionality. To effectively formulate an understanding when working with an "other" whose position is very different from our own, we have to first understand our own stance and how it impacts on the decision processes we use and the information we privilege. We then have to reach out to try to understand how our client positions themselves in the world and its impact on their decision-making process. In working collaboratively, we each seek to understand each other's perspective on the concern at hand and try to reach a bigger perspective that enables change. Recent approaches to wellbeing advocate interventions for whole populations, communities and individuals that reflect diverse needs, resources and views (NHS England, 2023). This approach moves away from a technological paradigm that implies our understanding of illness can be conceptualized separately from our relationships and values. Similarly, sometimes in coaching we can allow particular theories to lead us to act in ways that are context-independent. This is a particular danger when working with diversity, whether we are dealing with cultural, gender, ability, neurodiversity, sexuality or any other way in which we separate persons into categories.

In the two approaches to coaching mentioned above, Ershad and Ubuntu, coaching that separated clients from collective relationships and values would be to separate the storyteller from their story. The formulations created would become the practitioner's stories about the client's stories. As Corrie and Lane (2010) argue, clients typically present themselves and their concerns through the stories they tell. In presenting for coaching as an individual (with their own story) or as a collective (with a co-constructed story), the process will centre on some aspect of their self or relationships that they want to explore – a point of tension. There will be some sense of a reason for undertaking the journey involved (its purpose). They will bring concerns and difficulties, hopes, fears and expectations, and implicit or explicit theories of causation and the roles they take in causing or alleviating problems or seeking solutions (their perspectives).

These perspectives will vary culture by culture, family by family, team by team, organization by organization, community by community and individual by individual, representing a multitude of intersectional positionalities. To return to Ratele's (2019) question, what does the world look like from here, and here and here? As argued in the exploration of how to approach formulation (Chapter 2), it is necessary to start from that position, "What does the world look like from here, when here is the worldview of the client?" However, in approaching a coach, there is an implied assumption that the client believes they have something useful to add to this story to help bring about a resolution to the tension. They will come with some sense of how coaching might unfold (the process). The client and coach start with separate reflexive narratives (as we argued earlier) about the issue and how coaching might help. This represents an initial positional identification. Each party becomes an audience for these stories and co-authors in a rewriting of the scripts to create a new narrative that hopefully enables movement forward. In the coaching encounter a new relational narrative identification is co-created.

In understanding formulation as a story, Corrie and Lane (2010) explore different ways in which they can be constructed. They make the point that there is an extensive literature on how clients use stories to make sense of their lives but much less on how professional accounts are themselves stories about stories. Quoting Mishler (1986), they remind us that the impulse to narrate our lives is so strong that clients persist in their efforts to tell their story even when professional interpretations stifle their ability to do so. The importance of allowing the client's narrative to unfold is clear – space is needed for that to happen. The concept of illness narratives raised above (Burchardt, 2019) is also relevant to understanding this impulse. This increased understanding of the narration of self or personal story has appeared in both psychotherapy (Neimeyer, 2000) and coaching (Stelter, 2009). Formulation can be conceptualized as a way to assist clients to re-story their lives and to assist making sense of disparate sources of information. This is the way that diverse worldviews can be incorporated so that the formulation includes the view from here and here and here.

This requires, as Keise et al. (1993) argued, a substantial shift in our belief systems. We have to recognize that our systems of working, theoretical models and the organizations that provide services may be part of the problem, not the solution.

She argues that we must recognize that (questions have been slightly adapted here from the original text which focused just on children):

- We have to learn to listen – it is not enough to talk about partnership with clients when dealing with those who are vulnerable or marginalized; we have to see the difference between protection and rights.
- The impact of stereotyping at the individual and institutional level is an ever-present process – we have to be vigilant in monitoring ourselves as well as the contexts in which we work.
- Our theories may contribute to stereotyping; hence we have to seek ways to understand how our client sees the world.
- This requires some sense of history and recognition of the relationships between different groups in society so that a sense of the individual and structural components of "isms" is developed.
- Effective practice requires a personal awareness of the stance taken on issues – our own positionality and our openness to others.
- Our clients want to see programmes that positively impact on their lives, so we must be prepared to confront the belief systems that undermine them, and our own power in relation to them.

In the context of a person's sense of self (whatever form this takes), this becomes even more critical so that coaches can attend to the fundamental features of the stories they are trying to tell. For example, Corrie and Lane (2010) describe a way of working they term "a story motif". This works entirely from the client's frame of reference using their story as the basis for enquiry or discovery. It is not elaborated with theory from the practitioner. Within the context of a culture with which the coach is not familiar, this provides a useful way into the encounter. They also explore the idea of story structures, that is, culturally embedded prototypes that provide a way to understand the structure of the story being told. These include:

1 Where the story is set
2 The event that initiated the current concern
3 The way the client responded to this internally
4 The goal they want to achieve
5 The actions they want to take
6 The outcome achieved
7 The ending process for the intervention

The concept of positionality is also relevant here. How might ways of seeing the world, based in different categories, influence how the stories are being told. Ubuntu and Ershad illustrate alternative ways in which stories might be structured. Ubuntu prioritizes seeking to understand the structure in terms of community and belonging, and in Ershad the focus is how the client conceptualizes the right path and their intention. Thus, when we think about developing a formulation with our clients, we have to be constantly aware that the purpose sought will be influenced by culture and the positionality of the client, our self and the context for the work. Particular attention must be paid to the story they are trying to tell, how they choose to set the story and its meaning to them at that point in time. Why does it matter and why is an intervention meaningful now?

The perspectives brought to understand the concern will have an origin in those features that are privileged. These are derived from ways of seeing the world that emerge from their own sense of their position within it, their sense of our role in the encounter and our sense of how we are seeking to understand them and their needs. What perspectives are we adopting to seek that understanding informed by a sense of the role of diversity in practice?

The options for change will also have both limits and possibilities, that they constrain and enable, as we jointly devise a process to move forward. If coaching is seen as a collaborative encounter, as argued above, bringing the different stories into a shared but bigger perspective becomes a possibility. The client comes with their reflexive narrative and we ours. In working together, a new relational narrative identity is established. Client and coach can seek to understand each other and what the ideas can contribute to a desired outcome with the aim of being able to adopt a bigger, diverse and appropriate perspective. This enables the building of a new narrative to live by, which is both believable and actionable by the client (Gergen & Gergen, 2006).

Conclusion

The central theme of this chapter is that we work in diverse communities and need to draw upon approaches that reflect the world as it is. For too long the world of coaching has looked as if it is constructed by Western largely male ideologies. To address this, it is necessary to adopt a critical approach to dominant discourses. This applies to any such discourse whatever the source. Increasingly, coaching approaches have sought to incorporate diversity by adapting current theories to work in global settings. However, there is an alternative which is to build models consistent with the way the world is seen from different positionalities. This requires starting not with a set of existing assumptions that are adapted but to ask what the principles and practices might look like from here.

Questions to Consider

As a coach who is exploring how to create a more diverse approach to practice, it is important to reflect upon how your own positionality impacts both the stories you tell and those you enable being heard.

1   How do you foster storytelling that seeks to understand the client and their positionality, and which aspires to break down stereotyping and prejudice?

2 How do you demonstrate your own personal and professional values while understanding others to arrive at shared formulations?
3 How do you facilitate coaching relationships that promote inclusiveness and leverage the synergies between you and the client?
4 How might you contribute to a global network to seek to share experiences of diversity and coaching and contribute to a greater good?

Conclusion

Coaches spend a significant amount of their time and energy attempting to understand the dilemmas, concerns and requests for support with which their clients present. This is the basis for designing an effective way forward. Formulation, as the process by which coaches come to arrive at this understanding – either in the privacy of their own thoughts and reflections or in a co-created conversation with a client – has been the focus of this book.

Formulation is a unique, valuable and increasingly necessary form of sense-making, a method for finding one's way through a client's story that has historically been under-represented in both the coaching literature and on coach training programmes. Yet, it is our belief that coaches (and ultimately their clients) will benefit significantly from underpinning their work with a formulation, as it can provide a thorough and systematic way of making sense of the client's needs and guide coaching conversations into areas of exploration likely to have optimal benefit. It is this belief that has underpinned the writing of this book, and each of the preceding chapters has sought to illuminate and examine in detail one specific aspect of this complex yet highly rewarding and highly impactful task. From building an understanding of what formulation actually is, and identifying its widely espoused benefits (the focus of Chapter 1), to exploring approaches to formulation that have historically been dominant in the professional practice literature beyond coaching (the focus of Chapter 2), the intention has been to help the reader understand the origins of formulation, the benefits of its application and why it matters for coaching practice.

The book has also introduced the reader to a new contribution to the formulation literature – the 4P Framework (the focus of Chapters 3–8). Attending to each of the 4Ps – Positionality, Purpose, Perspective and Process – provides a new approach to formulation that we believe can deepen and enrich coaching conversations as well as empower the coach and client to identify relevant and potentially fruitful avenues of exploration and enquiry. We have sought to amplify and extend engagement with these four areas through both brief case vignettes and more detailed case studies as well as prompt questions to help the reader consider the implications of the chapter for their particular frames of reference and practice contexts.

As declared at the outset, our priority has been to meet the needs of those engaging in coaching practice and those who train them rather than contributing

DOI: 10.4324/9781003174585-22

to academic debate. Nonetheless, in seeking to provide an authoritative text, we have included concepts, theories and models that can take coaches beyond a simple checklist approach in order to reflect on their practice in deeper and hopefully more profound ways. We have, therefore, selected for consideration those ideas from the coaching literature and beyond that we think will be most useful for coaches without artificially simplifying the dilemmas encountered in real-world practice settings, particularly as professional practice becomes more complex.

Formulation and the Future

Formulation has a central place in the skillset of the effective coach and is, we believe, likely to become increasingly important for coaching in the years ahead. It is uncontroversial to suggest that the world is now facing unprecedented challenges in the form of multiple global socio-political events that span economic instability, international conflicts and disruptive technologies alongside climate change and the ongoing consequences of the COVID-19 pandemic. These events – sometimes termed "wicked problems" (Brown et al., 2010; Chan, 2023) because of their complex and enmeshed nature and resistance to traditional problem-solving approaches – have been noted to have significant implications for coaching practice (Kovács & Corrie, 2021).

Effective problem-solving skills for the modern world need to be couched within ways of knowing how to adapt to dynamic and volatile environments. They also require an ability to evaluate and use information that is ambiguous and sourced from settings that are equally problematic, and skill in tolerating and learning how to thrive within high levels of uncertainty and unpredictability. These coaching environments are likely to require highly honed capabilities for making decisions in the real world, enhanced resilience, cognitive agility, a more sophisticated understanding of the complexities of systems and a stronger emphasis given to self-care – both by coaches and by their clients.

Not every coaching assignment will involve the need to navigate complexity, but it seems to us reasonable to predict that complexity will feature more significantly, more of the time and in more of the dilemmas for which clients seek the services of a coach. While simple, linear models can facilitate significant positive benefits for some clients, they will not suffice for an emerging number of coaching contexts where the connections between cause and effect are impossible to directly impact or even detect. Models based on practices from the past and present, including those that have informed the development of competence frameworks, can provide no guarantees of relevance for future practice (Probert & Turnbull James, 2011).

Of course, formulation offers no artificially simplistic solutions to the dilemmas of practice, no sets of clearly articulated competences that can be methodically acquired and no checklists that can provide a sense of security against the prevailing unpredictability of the modern, globalized world. Indeed, formulation might at times raise more questions than it answers, identifying multiple potential courses of action that could be available to the coach and client in their work together. However, the aim of formulation is not to simplify practice into formulaic responses, specific protocols or prescriptions for action. Rather its aim is to enrich practice. In this sense, we would concur with the recommendation of M. Scott Peck (1998) to:

> Abandon the urge to simplify everything, to look for formulas and easy answers, and to begin to think multidimensionally, to glory in the mystery and paradoxes of life, not to be dismayed by the multitude of causes and consequences that are inherent in each experience – to appreciate the fact that life is complex (p. 14).

By writing this book we hope we have supported you in this endeavour.

Next Steps on the Journey

In the Introduction to this book we invited you to engage with a series of questions to support you in clarifying what you might need from the chapters that followed. By way of conclusion, we invite you to revisit and reconsider your original responses, to notice anything that might have changed in your thinking or practice (or that might be worthy of further thought or experimentation) and any ideas, perspectives or practices that might have aroused your interest. To support you in this endeavour, we offer you the following questions:

- Based on your reading and engagement with the material in this book, how do you now seek to understand the client, their issues and the factors which are impacting them? What, if anything, has changed in your approach?
- How might you now explore your own personal and professional values while understanding those of your client to arrive at a shared understanding? What if anything has changed and what might you wish to explore further as a result of having read this book?
- How, having read this book, might you facilitate coaching relationships that can enable an open sharing of your own and your clients' perspectives to leverage the synergies between you? Are there any areas you would explore with clients now that you might not have before?
- What else might you take away from this book to guide your future practice?

A Final Word

Whatever your reasons for engaging with us on the journey, we hope that this book might have given rise to as many questions as it has provided answers. After all, professional practice in any discipline requires the ability to operate with confidence while accepting that the status of our knowledge is always partial, that much of our evidence can be contested and that the ability to ask good questions is often preferable to seeking "correct answers" (however seductive the promise of the latter may seem). In this sense, therefore, we hope that the end of this journey with us might represent the beginning of a new one for you in thinking about the role that formulation has played and might play in your own coaching practice. To quote the poet T. S. Eliot (1942), "to make an end is to make a beginning. The end is where we start from."

References

Abbott, G. (2018). Cross-cultural coaching: A paradoxical perspective. In E. Cox, T. Bachki-rova, & D. Clutterbuck (Eds.), *The complete handbook of coaching* (pp. 378–398*)*. Sage.

Abrams, D., & Hogg, M. A. (1990). An introduction to the social identity approach. In D. Abrams & M. A Hogg (Eds.), *Social identity theory: Constructive and critical advances* (pp. 1–9). Harvester-Wheatsheaf.

Absolon, K. (2022). *Kaadossiwiin: How we come to know. Indigenous re-search methodologies* (2nd ed.). Fernwood Publishing.

The Academy of Medical Sciences. (2016). *Improving the health of the public by 2040*. https://acmedsci.ac.uk/file-download/41399-5807581429f81.pdf. Accessed 04/12/2023.

Acevedo, S. M., Aho, M., Cela, E., Chao, J. C., Garcia-Gonzales, I., MacLeod, A., Moutray, C., & Olague, C. (2015). Positionality as knowledge: From pedagogy to praxis. *Integral review: A Transdisciplinary & Transcultural Journal for New Thought, Research, & Praxis, 11*(1), 28–46.

Addison, L., & Shapiro, J. (2023). Coach for positive (Coach4+): Using the intersection of positive psychology, positive organisational psychology and executive leadership coaching to facilitate positive leadership outcomes. *Coaching: An International Journal of Theory, Research and Practice, 16*(2), 219–232. https://doi.org/10.1080/17521882.2023.2216776

Adelman, C. (1993). Kurt Lewin and the origins of action research. *Educational Action Research, 1*(1), 7–24.

Ahmadinia, H., Eriksson-Backa, K., & Nikou, S. (2022). Health-seeking behaviours of immigrants, asylum seekers and refugees in Europe: A systematic review of peer-reviewed articles. *Journal of Documentation, 78*(7), 18–41. https://doi.org/10.1108/JD-10-2020-0168

Ahmann, E., Leikin, S., Smith, K., Ellington, L., & Pille, R. (2020). Exploring health literacy and its relationship to health and wellness coaching. *International Journal of Evidence Based Coaching and Mentoring, 18*(2), 83–100. DOI: 10.24384/9qz4-w404

Ahmann, E., Smith, K., Ellington, L., & Pille, R. O. (2019). Health and wellness coaching and psychiatric care collaboration in a multimodal intervention for attention-deficit/hyperactivity disorder: A case report. *The Permanente Journal, 24*(18), Article 256. DOI: 10.7812/TPP/18.256

Alcoff, L. (1988). Cultural feminism versus post-structuralism: The identity crisis in feminist theory. *Signs: Journal of Women in Culture and Society, 13*(3), 405–436. https://dx.doi.org/10.1086/494426

Allan, P. (2007). The benefits and impacts of a coaching and mentoring programme for teaching staff in secondary school. *International Journal of Evidence Based Coaching and Mentoring, 5*(2), 12–21.

Anthony, E. L. (2017). The impact of leadership coaching on leadership behaviors. *Journal of Management Development, 36*(7), 930–939. https://doi.org/10.1108/JMD-06-2016-0092

Antonovsky, A. (1979). *Health, stress, and coping.* Jossey-Bass.

Antonovsky, A. (1987). *Unraveling the mystery of health: How people manage stress and stay well.* Jossey-Bass.

Antonovsky, A. (1996). The salutogenic model as a theory to guide health promotion. *Health Promotion International, 11*(1), 11–18. https://doi.org/10.1093/heapro/11.1.11

APA. (2024). Roads to Resilience. https://www.apa.org/topics/resilience

Armstrong, C., Wolever, R., Manning, L., et al. (2013). Group health coaching: Strengths, challenges, and next steps. *Global Advances in Health and Medicine, 2*(3), 95–102. https://doi.org/10.7453%2Fgahmj.2013.019

Arnold, T., Kleve, H., & Roth, S. (2023). Within a mesh of expectations: Dealing with dilemmas in business families using systemic tools from family coaching. *Systems Research and Behavioral Science, 40*(4), 713–722. https://doi.org/10.1002/sres.2962

Association for Coaching. (2023). *AC team coaching accreditation scheme: Competency framework.* https://cdn.ymaws.com/www.associationforcoaching.com/resource/resmgr/accreditation/teamcoachingaccreditation/ac_team_coaching_competency_.pdf. Accessed 22/05/2024.

Association for Professional Executive Coaching and Supervision (APECS). (2024). *Team coach accreditation.* https://www.apecs.org/team-coach-accreditation. Accessed 22/05/2024.

Athanasopoulou, A., & Dopson, S. (2018). A systematic review of executive coaching outcomes: Is it the journey or the destination that matters the most? *Leadership Quarterly, 29*(1), 70–88. https://doi.org/10.1016/j.leaqua.2017.11.004

Atter, N. (2009) Interim supplementary guidance for chartered psychologists seeking approval and acting as Approved Clinicians. *Forensic Update, 98*, 7.

Auda, J. (2021). *Re-envisioning Islamic Scholarship Maqasid Methodology as a new approach.* Claritas Books.

Bachkirova, T. (2015). Self-deception in coaching: An issue in principle and a challenge for supervision. *Coaching: An International Journal of Theory, Research and Practice, 8*(1), 4–19. https://psycnet.apa.org/doi/10.1080/17521882.2014.998692

Bachkirova, T. (2016). The self of the coach: Conceptualization, issues and opportunities for practitioner development. *Consulting Psychology Journal: Practice and Research, 68*(2), 143–156. https://psycnet.apa.org/doi/10.1037/cpb0000055

Bachkirova, T., Jackson, P., Gannon, J., Iordanou, I., & Myers, A. (2020). Re-conceptualising coach education from the perspectives of pragmatism and constructivism. *Philosophy of Coaching: An International Journal, 2*(2), 29–50. http://dx.doi.org/10.22316/poc/02.2.03

Bachkirova, T., & Kemp, R. (2024). AI coaching: Democratising coaching service or offering an ersatz? *Coaching: An International Journal of Theory, Research and Practice,* 1–19. DOI: 10.1080/17521882.2024.2368598

Bachkirova, T., Spence, G., & Drake, D. (2017). *The SAGE handbook of coaching.* Sage.

Baldwin, D. R., & Cherry, M. (2019). Exploring the use of internal coaches. *Consulting Psychology Journal: Practice and Research, 71*(3), 2–10.

Baptist, J., Hamon, R. R. (2022). Family systems theory. In K. Adamsons, A. L. Few-Demo, C. Proulx, & K. Roy (Eds.), *Sourcebook of family theories and methodologies* (pp. 209–226.). Springer International Publishing. http://dx.doi.org/10.1007/978-3-030-92002-9_14

Barber, H. F. (1992). Developing strategic leadership: The US army war college experience. *Journal of Management Development, 11*, 4–12. DOI: 10.1108/02621719210018208

Barden, S. (2021). *How successful leaders do business with their world: The navigational stance.* Routledge.

Baron, H., & Azizollah, H. (2019). Coaching and diversity. In S. Palmer & A. Whybrow (Eds.), *Handbook of coaching psychology: A guide for practitioners* (pp. 500–511) Routledge.

Baron, L., & Morin, L. (2009). The coach-coachee relationship in executive coaching: A field study. *Human Resource Development Quarterly*, *20*(1), 85–106. https://doi.org/10.1002/hrdq.20009

Baron, L., Morin, L., & Morin, D. (2011). Executive coaching: The effect of working alliance discrepancy on the development of coachees' self-efficacy. *Journal of Management Development*, *30*(9), 847–864. https://psycnet.apa.org/doi/10.1108/02621711111164330

Baron, R. S., & Kerr. N. L. (2003). *Group process, group decision, group action* (2nd ed.). McGraw-Hill Education.

Baucom, D. H., Fischer, M. S., Corrie, S., Worrell, M., & Boeding, S. E. (2020). *Treating relationship distress and psychopathology in couples: A cognitive-behavioural approach*. Routledge.

Baucom, D. H., Kirby, J. S., Fischer, M. S., Baucom, B. R., Hamer, R., & Bulik, C. M. (2017). Findings from a couple-based open trial for adult anorexia nervosa. *Journal of Family Psychology*, *31*(5), 584–591.

Bavelas, J. B., & Segal, L. (1982). Family systems theory: Background and implications. *Journal of Communication*, *32*, 89–107.

Bayeck, R. Y. (2022). Positionality: The interplay of space, context and identity. *International Journal of Qualitative Methods*, *21*(1).

Beck, A. T., Rush, A. J., Shaw, B. F., & Emery, G. M. (1979). *Cognitive behavioral therapy of depression*. Guildford Press.

Bell, R. (2017). *Psychosocial pathways and health outcomes: Informing action on health inequalities*. Public Health England.

Benishek, L. E., & Lazzara, E. H. (2019). Teams in a new era: Some considerations and implications. *Frontiers in Psychology*, *10*, 1006. https://doi.org/10.3389/fpsyg.2019.01006

Bentley, H., et al. (2020). *How safe are our children? An overview of data on adolescent abuse*. NSPCC.

Berger, P. L., & Luckman, T. (1967). *The social construction of reality: A treatise in the sociology of knowledge*. Anchor.

Berkowitz, B., Wadud, E. (2023). *Identifying community assets and resources*. The Community Tool Box. https://ctb.ku.edu/en/table-of-contents/assessment/assessing-community-needs-and-resources/identify-community-assets/main

Berry, P. (2020). Developing adaptive expertise in executive coaching. *International Journal of Evidence Based Coaching and Mentoring*, *S1*, 32–45. DOI: 10.24384/yxxf-fk14

Bietti, L. M., Tilston, O., & Bangerter, A. (2018). Storytelling as adaptive collective sensemaking. *Topics in Cognitive Science*, *11*(4), 710–732. https://psycnet.apa.org/doi/10.1111/tops.12358

Bignall, T., Jeraj, S., Helsby, E., & Butt, J. (2019). *Racial disparities in mental health: Literature and evidence review*. Race Equality Foundation.

Bickenbach, J., Rubinelli, S., Baffone, C., & Stucki, G. (2023). The human functioning revolution: Implications for health systems and sciences. *Frontiers in Science*, *1*, 1118512.

Blakey, M. L. (2020). Archaeology under the blinding light of race. *Current Anthropology*, *61*(S22), S183–S197.

Bleck, J., DeBate, R., Garcia, J., & Gatto, A. (2023). A pilot evaluation of a university health and wellness coaching program for college students. *Health Education Behavior*, *50*(5), 613–621. DOI: 10.1177/10901981221131267

Boal, K. B., & Schultz, P. L. (2007). Storytelling, time and evolution: The role of strategic leadership in complex adaptive systems. *The Leadership Quarterly*, *18*(4), 411–428. https://doi.org/10.1016/j.leaqua.2007.04.008

Boje, D. M. (1991). The storytelling organization: A study of story performance in an office-supply firm. *Administrative Science Quarterly*, *36*(1), 106–126.

Boje, D. M. (2018). *Organizational research: Storytelling in action*. Routledge. https://doi.org/10.4324/9781315205854

Bolam, R. (2008). Professional learning communities and teachers' professional development. In D. Johnson & R. Maclean (Eds.), *Teaching: Professionalization, development and leadership: Festschrift for Professor Eric Hoyle* (pp. 159–179). Springer Netherlands.

Bolden, R., & Gosling, J. (2006). Leadership competencies: Time to change the tune? *Leadership, 2*(2), 147–163. https://psycnet.apa.org/doi/10.1177/1742715006062932

Boniwell, I., & Smith, W. A. (2018). Positive psychology coaching for positive leadership. In S. Green & S. Palmer (Eds.), *Positive psychology coaching in practice* (pp. 159–175). Routledge.

Boulton, J. G., Allen, P. M., & Bowman, C. (2015). *Embracing complexity: Strategic perspectives for an age of turbulence.* Oxford University Press.

Bourne, A., & Whybrow, A. (2019). Using psychometrics in coaching. In S. Palmer & A. Whybrow (Eds.), *Handbook of coaching psychology: A guide for practitioners* (2nd ed.) (pp. 512–526). Routledge. https://doi.org/10.4324/9781315820217

Bowen, M. (1978). *Family therapy in clinical practice.* Jason Aronson.

Boyatzis, R. E. (2006). An overview of intentional change from a complexity perspective. *Journal of Management Development, 25,* 607–623. https://psycnet.apa.org/doi/10.1108/02621710610678445

Boyce, L. A., Jackson, R. J., & Neal, L. J. (2010). Building successful leadership coaching relationships: Examining impact of matching criteria in a leadership coaching programme. *Journal of Management Development, 29*(10), 914–931. https://psycnet.apa.org/doi/10.1108/02621711011084231

Boyd, R. L., Blackburn, K. G., & Pennebaker, J. W. (2020). The narrative arc: Revealing core narrative structures through text analysis. *Science Advances, 6*(32), eaba2196. https://dx.doi.org/10.1126/sciadv.aba2196

Brabender, V. M., Smolar, A. I., & Fallon, A. E. (2004). *Essentials of group therapy.* John Wiley & Sons.

Bradley-Cole, K., Denicolo, P., & Daniels, M. (2023). It's the way I tell them. A personal construct psychology method for analysing narratives. *Journal of Constructivist Psychology, 36*(4), 467–482. https://doi.org/10.1080/10720537.2023.2168806

British Psychological Society. (2005). *Subject benchmarks for applied psychology.* British Psychological Society.

British Psychological Society. (2011). *Good practice guidelines on the use of psychological formulation.* Division of Clinical Psychology, British Psychological Society.

Brower, T. (2021, August 22). *The power of purpose and why it matters now.* Forbes. https://www.forbes.com/sites/tracybrower/2021/08/22/the-power-of-purpose-and-why-it-matters-now/?sh=3e5e86dd163a

Brown, J. (1999). Bowen family systems theory and practice: Illustration and critique. *Australian and New Zealand Journal of Family Therapy, 20*(2), 94–103. https://psycnet.apa.org/doi/10.1002/j.1467-8438.1999.tb00363.x

Brown, S. W., & Grant, A. M. (2010). From GROW to GROUP: Theoretical issues and a practical model for group coaching in organizations. *Coaching: An International Journal of Theory, Research and Practice, 3*(1), 30–45. https://psycnet.apa.org/doi/10.1080/17521880903559697

Brown, V. A., Harris, J. A., & Russell, J. Y. (2010). *Tackling wicked problems through transdisciplinary imagination.* Earthscan.

Bruch, M. (Ed.) (2015). *Beyond diagnosis. Case formulation in cognitive behavioural therapy* (2nd ed.). Wiley-Blackwell.

Bruch, M., & Bond, F. W. (Eds.) (1998). *Beyond diagnosis: Case formulation approaches in CBT.* Wiley-Blackwell.

Bruner, J. S. (1990). *Acts of meaning.* Harvard University Press.

Buckley, A. (2007). The mental health boundary in relationship to coaching and other activities. *International Journal of Evidence Based Coaching and Mentoring, S1,* 17–23.

Burchardt, M. (2019). *Illness narratives as theory and method*. Sage.

Bushe, G. R., & Marshak, R. J. (2015). *Dialogic organization development: The theory and practice of transformational change*. Berrett-Koehler.

Butler, G. (1998). Clinical formulation. In A. S. Bellack & M. Hersen (Eds.), *Comprehensive clinical psychology* (pp. 1–24). Pergamon.

Campaign for Social Science. (2017). *The health of people. How the social sciences can improve population health*. Sage. https://doi.org/10.4135/9781473998889

Capra, F., & Luisi, P. L. (2014). *The systems view of life: A unifying vision*. Cambridge University Press. https://doi.org/10.1017/CBO9780511895555

Carkhuff, R. R., & Berenson, B. G. (1967). *Beyond counselling and therapy*. Holt, Reinhart and Winston.

Carlson, M. (2017). *CBT for psychological well-being in cancer*. Wiley-Blackwell.

Cavanagh, M. (2006). Coaching from a systemic perspective: A complex adaptive conversation. In D. R. Stober & A. M. Grants (Eds.), *Evidence based coaching handbook: Putting best practices to work for your clients* (pp. 313–354). John Wiley & Sons.

Cavanagh, M. J. (2013). The coaching engagement in the twenty-first century: New paradigms for complex times. In S. David, D. Clutterbuck, & D. Megginson (Eds.), *Beyond goals: Effective strategies for coaching and mentoring* (pp. 151–184). Ashgate.

Cavanagh, M., & Grant, A. M. (2006). Coaching psychology and the scientist practitioner model. In D. A. Lane & S. Corrie (Eds.), *The modern scientist-practitioner: A guide to practice in psychology* (pp. 146–157). Routledge.

Cavanagh, M., & Lane, D. A. (2012). Coaching psychology coming of age: The challenges we face in the messy world of complexity. *International Coaching Psychology Review, 7*(1), 75–90.

Cavanagh, M., Stern, L., & Lane, D. A. (2016). Supervision in coaching psychology: A systemic developmental psychological perspective. In D. A. Lane, M. Watts, & S. Corrie (Eds.), *Supervision in the psychological professions*. Open University Press.

Cedric, X., McGee, D. P., Nobles, W., & Luther, X. (1975). Voodoo or IQ: An introduction to African psychology. *Journal of Black Psychology, 1*(2), 9–29.

Centre for Social Justice. (2021). *Pillars of community: Why communities matter and what matters to them*. The Centre for Social Justice.

Chalmers, A. F. (2013). *What is this thing called science?* (4th ed.). University of Queensland Press.

Chan, J. K. H. (2023). The ethics of wicked problems: An exegesis. *Socio-Ecological Practice Research, 5*, 35–47. https://doi.org/10.1007/s42532-022-00137-3

Chand, A. (2008). Every child matters? A critical review of child welfare reforms in the context of minority ethnic children and families. *Child Abuse Review: Journal of the British Association for the Study and Prevention of Child Abuse and Neglect, 17*(1), 6–22.

Chapman, L. (2018). *Integrated experiential coaching: Becoming an executive coach*. Routledge.

Chapman, L. (2023). *The evidence-based practitioner coach: Understanding the integrated experiential learning process*. Routledge.

Chapman, L. S., Lesch, N., & Baun, M. P. (2007). The role of health and wellness coaching in worksite health promotion. *American Journal of Health Promotion, 21*(6), 1–12. DOI: 10.4278/0890-1171-21.6.TAHP-1

Chappell, C., Rhodes, C., Soloman, N., Tennant, M., & Yates, L. (2003). *Reconstructing the lifelong learner: Pedogogy and identity in individual, organisational and social change*. Routledge. http://dx.doi.org/10.4324/9780203464410

Charmaz, K. (2014). *Constructing grounded theory*. Sage.

Checkland, P. B. (1981). *Systems thinking, systems practice*. John Wiley Publishing.

Checkland, P. B. (1989). Soft systems methodology. *Human Systems Management, 8*(4), 273–289.

Checkland, P. (2000). Soft systems methodology: A thirty-year retrospective. *Systems Research and Behavioral Science, 17*(S1), S11–S58.

Christodoulou, J. A., Okano, K. H., Gove, A., McBride, C., Raihani, R., Strigel, C., Pérez, L. T., & Chakraborty, A. (2022). Diversity and social justice in education. In A. K. Duraiappah, N. M. van Atteveldt, G. Borst, S. Bugden, O. Ergas, T. Gilead, L. Gupta, J. Mercier, K. Pugh, N.C. Singh, & E. A. Vickers (Eds.), *Reimagining education: The international science and evidence-based education assessment.* UNESCO MGIEP.

Christoffersen, A., & Emejulu, A. (2023). "Diversity within": The problems with "intersectional" white feminism in practice. *Social Politics: International Studies in Gender, State & Society, 30*(2), 630–653. https://doi.org/10.1093/sp/jxac044

Clutterbuck, D. (2007). *Coaching the team at work.* Nicholas Brealey International.

Clutterbuck, D. (2020). *Coaching the team at work: The definitive guide to team coaching* (2nd ed.). Nicholas Brealey International.

Clutterbuck, D. (2023). *Coaching and mentoring: A journey through the models, theories, frameworks and narratives of David Clutterbuck.* Routledge. https://doi.org/10.4324/9781003323990

Clutterbuck, D., Gannon, J., Hayes, S., Iordanou, I., Lowe, K., & MacKie., D. (2019). Introduction. In D. Clutterbuck, J. Gannon, S. Hayes, I. Iordanou, K. Lowe, & D. MacKie (Eds.), *The practitioner's handbook of team coaching* (pp. 1–8). Routledge. https://doi.org/10.4324/9781351130554

Coghlan, D., & Brannick, T. (2004). *Doing action research in your own organization* (2nd ed.). Sage.

Colley, H. (2003). Engagement mentoring for "disaffected" youth: A new model of mentoring for social inclusion. *British Educational Research Journal, 29*(4), 521–542.

Collins, L., Carson, H. J., & Collins, D. (2016). Metacognition and professional judgment and decision making in coaching: Importance, application and evaluation. *International Sport Coaching Journal, 3*(3), 355–361.

Commission on Young Lives. (2022). https://thecommissiononyounglives.co.uk. Accessed 30/01/2025.

Communities Education Trust. (2021). *Report on a project at Windmill School.* Tamworth Communities Education Trust.

Cook-Greuter, S. R. (1999). *Post-autonomous ego development: A study of its nature and measurement* [Unpublished doctoral dissertation]. Harvard Graduate School of Education.

Cordingley, P., Bell, M., Thomason, S., & Firth, A. (2005). *The impact of collaborative continuing professional development (CPD) on classroom teaching and learning.* Evidence for Policy and Practice Information and Co-ordinating Centre.

Cordingley, P., & Buckler, N. (2012). Mentoring and coaching for teachers' continuing professional development. In S. J. Fletcher & C. A. Mullen (Eds.), *SAGE handbook of mentoring and coaching in education* (pp. 215–227). http://dx.doi.org/10.4135/9781446247549.n15

Corker, M., & French, S. (1999). *Disability discourse.* McGraw-Hill Education.

Corrie, S. (2009). *The art of inspired living.* Karnac Books.

Corrie, S. (2018). *The art of inspired living: Coach yourself with positive psychology.* Routledge.

Corrie, S. (2019, February 7). What do coaches need to know about mental health? Webinar for the Special Group in Coaching Psychology of the British Psychological Society.

Corrie, S. (2020). *Equipping cognitive behavioural therapists for a complex professional world: In search of a framework for training and supervision* [Unpublished doctoral thesis]. Middlesex University.

Corrie, S., & Kovács, L. (2017). Navigating client diversity: Why coaching needs formulation. *Coaching Today,* April, 6–11.

Corrie, S., & Kovács, L. (2019). The functions of formulation in coaching psychology. *The Coaching Psychologist, 15*(1), 66–75.

Corrie, S., & Kovács, L. (2021). Addressing the self-care needs of coaches through the use of formulation. *Coaching: An International Journal of Theory, Research & Practice.* DOI: 10.1080/17521882.2021.1926523

Corrie, S., Kovács, L. C., & Lane, D. A. (2021). Beyond the first session: Models of coaching, including formulation. In M. Watts, R. Bor, & I. Florance (Eds.), *The trainee coach handbook* (pp. 89–108). Sage.

Corrie, S., & Lane, D. A. (2006). Constructing stories about clients' needs: Developing skills in formulation. In R. Bor & M. Watts (Eds.), *The trainee handbook: A guide for counselling and psychotherapy trainees* (pp. 68–90). Sage.

Corrie, S., & Lane, D. A. (2010). *Constructing stories, telling tales: A guide to formulation in applied psychology.* Karnac Books. https://doi.org/10.4324/9780429473173

Corrie, S. & Lane, D. (2013). Decision-making and the coaching context. *International Coaching Psychology Review, 2*, 70–78.

Corrie, S., & Lane, D. A. (2015). *CBT supervision.* Sage.

Corrie, S., & Lane, D. A. (2021). *First steps in cognitive behaviour therapy.* Sage.

Corrie, S., & Parsons, A. (2021). The contribution of coaching to mental health care: An emerging specialism for complex times. In M. Watts & I. Florance (Eds.), *Emerging conversations in coaching* (pp. 60–77). Routledge.

Corrie, S., Townend, M. J., & Cockx, A. (2016). *Assessment and case formulation in cognitive behavioural therapy* (2nd ed.). Sage.

Cosgrove, F., & Corrie, S. (2020). Promoting well-being through the emerging specialism of health and wellness coaching. *The Coaching Psychologist, 16*(2), 35–45. https://doi.org/10.53841/bpstcp.2020.16.2.35

Cosgrove, F. L., Corrie, S., & Wolever, R. Q. (2021). An exploration of personal benefits reported by students of a health and wellness coach training programme. *Coaching: An International Journal of Theory, Research and Practice, 15*(1), 85–101.

Costa, A. C. (2024). Work teams. In M. Bal (Ed.), *Elgar encyclopaedia of organizational psychology* (pp. 692–700). Edward Elgar.

Costa, A. C., Fulmer, C. A., & Anderson, N. R. (2018). Trust in work teams: An integrative review, multilevel model, and future directions. *Journal of Organizational Behavior, 39*(2), 169–184.

Coultas, C. W., Bedwell, W. L., Burke, C. S., & Salas, E. (2011). Values-sensitive coaching: The DELTA approach to coaching culturally diverse executives. *Consulting Psychology Journal: Practice and Research, 63*, 149–161.

Council of Europe. (2022). Free to Speak Safe to Learn. https://www.coe.int/en/web/campaign-free-to-speak-safe-to-learn#:~:text=The%20Council%20of%20Europe%20project,Council%20of%20Europe's%20member%20states

Cox, E., & Bachkirova, T. (2007). Coaching with emotion: How coaches deal with difficult emotional situations. *International Coaching Psychology Review, 2*(2), 178–189.

Cox, E., Bachkirova, T., & Clutterbuck, D. (2018). *The complete handbook of coaching.* Sage.

Cranton, P. (2005). Transformative learning. In L. English (Ed.), *International encyclopedia of adult education* (pp. 630–637). Palgrave Macmillan.

Creasy, J., & Patterson, F. (2005). As cited in van Nieuwerburgh, C. (2018). Coaching in education: An overview. In C. van Nieuwerburgh (Ed.), *Coaching in education: Getting better results for students, educators, and parents* (1st ed.) (pp. 3–23). Routledge.

Crehan, K. (2016). *Gramsci's common sense: Inequality and its narratives.* Duke University Press.

Crenshaw, K. W. (1989). Demarginalising the intersection of race and sex. *University of Chicago Legal Forum, 8*, 139–168.

Crevani, L., Uhl-Bien, M., Clegg, S., & By, R. T. (2021). Changing leadership in changing times II. *Journal of Change Management, 21*(2), 133–143. https://doi.org/10.1080/14697017.2021.1917489

Cripps, B. (2017). *Psychometric testing: Critical perspectives.* Wiley.

Dagan, O., Groh, A.M., Madigan, S., & Bernard, K. (2021). A lifespan development theory of insecure attachment and internalizing symptoms: Integrating meta-analytic evidence via a testable evolutionary mis/match hypothesis. *Brain Sci., 11*, 1226. https://doi.org/10.3390/brainsci12070820

David, D., Cristea, I., & Hofmann, S. G. (2018). Why cognitive behavioral therapy is the current gold standard of psychotherapy. *Frontiers in Psychiatry, 9*(4), 1–3.

David, S., Clutterbuck, D., & Megginson, D. (2013). *Beyond goals: Effective strategies for coaching and mentoring.* Routledge. https://doi.org/10.4324/9781315569208

Davies, B., & Harré, R. (1990). Positioning: The discursive production of selves. *Journal for the Theory of Social Behaviour, 20*(1), 43–63.

Day, A., De Haan, E., Sills, C., Bertie, C., & Blass, E. (2008). Coaches' experiences of critical moments in coaching. *International Coaching Psychology Review, 3*(3), 207–218.

Day, A., Hartling, N., & Mackie, B. (2016). The psychologically healthy workplace: Fostering employee well-being and healthy businesses. In A. M. Rossi, J. A. Meurs, & P. L. Perrewé (Eds.), *Stress and quality of working life: Interpersonal and occupation-based stress* (pp. 199–217). IAP Information Age Publishing.

Day, D. V., Riggio, R. E., Tan, S. T., & Conger, J. A. (2021). Advancing the science of 21st-century leadership development: Theory, research, and practice. *The Leadership Quarterly, 32*(5), 1–10.

De Brún, A., & McAuliffe, E. (2020). Identifying the context, mechanisms and outcomes underlying collective leadership in teams: Building a realist programme theory. *BMC Health Services Research, 20*, 1–13.

DeFehr, J., (2017). Navigating psychiatric truth claims in collaborative practice: A proposal for radical critical mental health awareness. *Journal of Systemic Therapies, 36*(3), 27–38.

De Haan, E., Bertie, C., Day, A., & Sills, C. (2010). Critical moments of clients and coaches: A direct-comparison study. *International Coaching Psychology Review, 5*(2), 109–128.

De Haan, E., Culpin, V., & Curd, J. (2011). Executive coaching in practice: What determines helpfulness for clients of coaching? *Personnel Review, 40*(1), 24–44. https://doi.org/10.1108/00483481111095500

De Haan, E., Duckworth, A., Birch, D., & Jones, C. (2013). Executive coaching outcome research: The contribution of common factors such as relationship, personality match, and self-efficacy. *Consulting Psychology Journal: Practice and Research, 65*(1), 40–58.

De Haan, E., Grant, A. M., Burger, Y., & Eriksson, P.-O. (2016). A large-scale study of executive and workplace coaching: The relative contributions of relationship, personality match and self-efficacy. *Consulting Psychology Journal: Practice and Research, 68*(3), 189–207.

De Haan, E., Molyn, J., & Nilsson, V. O. (2020). New findings on the effectiveness of the coaching relationship: Time to think differently about active ingredients? *Consulting Psychology Journal: Practice and Research, 72*(3), 155–167. https://doi.org/10.1037/cpb0000175

De Haan, E., & Nilsson, V. O. (2023). What can we know about the effectiveness of coaching? A meta-analysis based only on randomized controlled trials. *Academy of Management Learning & Education, 22*(4), 1–21. https://doi.org/10.5465/amle.2022.0107

Delice, F., Rousseau, M., & Feitosa, J. (2019). Advancing teams research: What, when, and how to measure team dynamics over time. *Frontiers in Psychology, 10*, 440761. https://www.frontiersin.org/journals/psychology/articles/10.3389/fpsyg.2019.01324

Deloitte. (2019). *From employee experience to human experience: Putting meaning back into work.* https://www2.deloitte.com/us/en/insights/focus/human-capital-trends/2019/workforce-engagement-employee-experience.html

Deloitte. (2021). *Employee well-being survey: Identifying the path to success.* https://www2.deloitte.com/content/dam/Deloitte/ua/Documents/Press-release/Survey%20on%20well-being%20at%20work_EN.pdf

Deloitte. (2022). *Mental health and employers: The case for investment, pandemic and beyond.* https://www2.deloitte.com/content/dam/Deloitte/uk/Documents/consultancy/deloitte-uk-mental-health-report-2022.pdf

Deloitte. (2023). *As workforce well-being dips, leaders ask: What will it take to move the needle?* https://www2.deloitte.com/us/en/insights/topics/talent/workplace-well-being-research.html

Denham-Vaughan, S., & Gawlinski, M. (2012). Field-relational coaching for Gestalt beginners: The PAIR model. *British Gestalt Journal, 21*(1), 11–21. DOI: 10.53667/jyna2160

Denman, C. (1995). What is the point of formulation? In C. Mace (Ed.), *The art and science of assessment in psychotherapy* (pp. 167–181). Routledge.

Department of Health & Social Care. (2022). *Joining up care for people, places and populations.* https://www.gov.uk/government/publications/health-and-social-care-integration-joining-up-care-for-people-places-and-populations

Devine, M., Houssemand, C., & Meyers, R. (2013). Instructional coaching for teachers: A strategy to implement new practices in the classrooms. *Procedia-Social and Behavioral Sciences, 93*, 1126–1130.

Diamond, M. A. (2013). Psychodynamic approaches. In J. Passmore, D. Peterson, & T. Freire (Eds.), *Wiley-Blackwell handbook of the psychology of coaching & mentoring* (pp. 1–11). Wiley-Blackwell. http://dx.doi.org/10.1002/9781118326459

Dixit, R., & Sinha, V. (2023). Leveraging coaching as an instrument for training transfer: A case of learners in a Fintech Firm. *Development and Learning in Organizations, 37*(5), 1–4. https://doi.org/10.1108/DLO-07-2022-0129

Doran, G. T., Miller, A., & Cunningham, J. (1981). There's a S.M.A.R.T. way to write management's goals and objectives. *Management Review, 70*(11), 35–36.

Dossey, B. M., Luck, S., & Schaub, B. G. (2014). *Nurse coaching: Integrative approaches for health and wellbeing.* International Nurse Coach Association.

Doyle, N., & McDowall, A. (2024). *Neurodiversity coaching: A psychological approach to supporting neurodivergent talent and career potential (coaching psychology).* Routledge.

Drake, D. B. (2010). What story are you in? Four elements of a narrative approach to formulation in coaching. In S. Corrie & D. A. Lane (Eds.), *Constructing stories, telling tales: A guide to formulation in applied psychology* (pp. 239–258). Karnac Books.

Drake, D. B. (2018). *Narrative coaching: The definitive guide to bring new stories to life* (2nd ed.). CNC Press.

DuBois, D. L. (2021). *Mentoring programs for youth: A promising intervention for delinquency prevention.* https://nij.ojp.gov/topics/articles/mentoring-programs-youth-promising-intervention-delinquency-prevention. Accessed 05/01/2024.

Duncan, F., Baskin, C., McGrath, M., Coker, J. F., Lee, C., Dykxhoorn, J., Adams, E. A., Gnani, S., Lafortune, L., ... & Oliver, E. J. (2021). Community interventions for improving adult mental health: Mapping local policy and practice in England. *BMC Public Health, 21*(1), 1–14.

Dzingwa, N., & Terblanche, N. (2024). Coaching to support work-life balance of women in leadership positions. *SA Journal of Human Resource Management/SA Tydskrif vir Menslikehulpbronbestuur, 22*(0), a2509.

Ebert, C., & Hurth, V. (2022) Principles of purposeful business: Illustrative examples. *Journal of the British Academy, 10*(S5), 163–207.

Ebert, C., Hurth, V., & Prabhu, J. (2018). *The what, the why and the how of purpose. A guide for leaders.* Chartered Management Institute.

Edgerton, N., & Palmer, S. (2005). SPACE: A psychological model for use within cognitive behavioural coaching, therapy and stress management. *The Coaching Psychologist, 2*(2), 25–31.

Edmondson, A. (1999). Psychological safety and learning behavior in work teams. *Administrative Science Quarterly, 44*, 350–383.

Egan, G. (1975). *The skilled helper: A model for systematic helping and interpersonal relating.* Brooks/Cole.

Egan, T., & Hamlin, R. G. (2014). Coaching, HRD, and relational richness: Putting the pieces together. *Advances in Developing Human Resources, 16*(2), 242–257.

Eliot, T. S. (1942). *Little Gidding. Four quartets* [online]. Harcourt. http://www.davidgorman.com/4Quartets/4-gidding.htm. Accessed 08/07/2024.

Ely, R. J., & Thomas, D. A. (2001). Cultural diversity at work: The effects of diversity perspectives on work group processes and outcomes. *Administrative Science Quarterly, 46*, 229–273.

EMCC Global. (2023). EMCC Global team coaching assessment and accreditation framework (v0.8). https://emccdrive.emccglobal.org/api/file/download/knHoDVRfYcV4cs-fxxz2Gyp2Ld6cJZccOxzKsy5K1. Accessed 21/05/2024.

Engel, G. L. (1977). The need for a new medical model: A challenge for biomedicine. *Science, 196*, 129–136.

Erdös, T., De Haan, E., & Heusinkveld, S. (2021). Coaching: Client factors & contextual dynamics in the change process. *Coaching: An International Journal of Theory, Research and Practice, 14*(2), 162–183. DOI: 10.1080/17521882.2020.1791195

Eriksen, M., Collins, S., Finocchio, B., & Oakley, J. (2020). Developing students' coaching ability through peer coaching. *Journal of Management Education, 44*(1), 9–38.

Ernest, J. M., & Strichik, T. (2018). Coaching in childhood education: Using lessons learned to develop best practice for professional development in a state system. *The Excellence in Education Journal, 7*(1), 5–19.

Eronen, M. I., & Bringmann, L. F. (2021). The theory crisis in psychology: How to move forward. *Perspectives on Psychological Science, 16*(4), 779–788. https://doi.org/10.1177/1745691620970586

Farr, J., & Shepheard, M. (2018). Systemic constellations approach to coaching and coaching psychology practice. In S. Palmer & A. Whybrow (Eds.), *Handbook of coaching psychology: A guide for practitioners* (pp. 311–323). Routledge.

Fink, L., (2024). *The purpose gap.* https://thebeautifultruth.org/the-basics/what-is-the-purpose-gap/. Accessed 12/08/2024.

Fisher, J. C., Nawrath, M., Dallimer, M., Irvine, K. N., & Davies, Z. G. (2022). Connecting biodiversity and human wellbeing. In M. F. J. Aronson & C. H. Nilon (Eds), *Handbook of urban biodiversity* (pp. 141–153). Taylor & Francis.

Fleuridas, C., & Krafcik, D. (2019). Beyond four forces: The evolution of psychotherapy. *Sage Open, 9*(1), 2158244018824492.

Forrester, J. W. (1958). Industrial dynamics: A major breakthrough for decision makers. *Harvard Business Review, 36*, 37–48.

Freytag, G. (1900). *Technique of the drama: An exposition of dramatic composition and art* (E. J. MacEwan, trans., 3rd ed.). Scott, Foresman & Co. (Original work published in 1863.)

Friedman, S. (1977). The genesis of humanistic psychology. Plenary Address presented at AHP's Eighth Annual Midwest Regional Conference in Chicago, 29 April.

Frisch, M., Lee, B., Metzger, K., Robinson, J., & Rosemarin, J. (2019). *Becoming an exceptional executive coach.* HarperCollins Leadership.

Fuller, B., & Kim, H. (2022). *Systems thinking to transform schools: Identifying levers that lift educational quality.* Centre for Universal education Washington Brookings Institute.

Fyhn, B., Schei, V., & Sverdrup, T. E. (2023). Taking the emergent in team emergent states seriously: A review and preview. *Human Resource Management Review, 33*(1), 100928.

Gabriel, Y. (2000). *Storytelling in organizations: Facts, fictions, and fantasies.* Oxford University Press.

Gambrill, E. (2005). *Critical thinking in clinical practice* (2nd ed.) Wiley.

Garmezy, N., & Masten, A. S. (1986). Stress, competence, and resilience: Common frontiers for therapist and psychopathologist. *Behavior Therapy, 17*(5), 500–521.

Garvey Berger, J. (2012). *Changing on the job: Developing leaders for a complex world.* Stanford University Press.

Garvey Berger, J. (2019). *Unlocking leadership mindtraps: How to thrive in complexity.* Stanford University Press.

Gehlert, K. M., Ressler, T. H., Anderson, N. H., & Swanson, N. M. (2013). A method to improve the coach-participant match in executive coaching. *The Coaching Psychologist, 9*(2), 78–85.

Gendlin, E. T. (1996). *Focusing-oriented psychotherapy: A manual of the experiential method.* Guilford Press.

Gergen, K. (1985). The social constructionist movement in modern psychology. *American Psychologist, 40*, 266–275.

Gergen, M., & Davis, S. N. (2003). Dialogic pedagogy: Developing narrative research perspectives through conversation. In R. Josselson, A. Lieblich, & P. McAdams (Eds.), *Up close and personal. The teaching and learning of narrative research* (pp. 239–257). American Psychological Association.

Gergen, M. M., & Gergen, K. J. (2006). Narrative in action. *Narrative Inquiry, 16*(1), 112–121.

Gerson, J. (2016). *Approaching marginalized populations from an asset rather than a deficit model of education.* https://usergeneratededucation.wordpress.com/2016/05/08/approaching-marginalized-populations-from-an-asset-rather-than-a-deficit-model/

Gessnitzer, S., & Kauffeld, S. (2015). The working alliance in coaching: Why behaviour is the key to success. *The Journal of Applied Behavioural Science, 51*(2), 177–197.

Ghosh, A. (2020). Team coaches' experiences of coaching to develop conditions for shared leadership. *International Journal of Evidence Based Coaching and Mentoring, S14*, 19–31.

Giles, S. (2018, May 9). *How VUCA is reshaping the business environment.* Forbes. https://www.forbes.com/sites/sunniegiles/2018/05/09/how-vuca-is-reshaping-the-business-environment-and-what-it-means-for-innovation/?sh=78df6d0beb8d

Golawski, A., Bamford, A., & Gersch, I. (2013). *Swings and roundabouts: A self-coaching workbook for parents and those considering becoming parents.* Routledge.

Goodman, A., Joshi, H., Nasim, B., & Tyler, C. (2015). *Social and emotional skills in childhood and their long-term effects on adult life.* Institute of Education. University College London. https://discovery.ucl.ac.uk/id/eprint/10051902/1/Schoon_2015%20The%20Impact%20of%20Early%20Life%20Skills%20on%20Later%20Outcomes_%20Sept%20fin2015.pdf

Gorell, R. (2022). *Coaching self-organising teams: Helping teams flourish.* Routledge.

Gorrell, A. (2023). Creating a coaching culture to support school improvement. *Australian Educational Leader, 45*(1), 44–46.

Gosling, P. (2010). Every child does matter: Preventing school exclusion through the Common Assessment Framework. In S. Corrie & D. A. Lane (Eds.), *Constructing stories, telling tales: A guide to formulation in applied psychology* (pp. 173–198). Karnac Books.

Gould, S. J. (1981). *The mismeasure of man.* Penguin.

Gould, S. J. (1996). *The mismeasure of man* (revised). W.W. Norton.

Gov.uk. (2016). *Advisory panel to mission-led business review: Final report.* https://www.gov.uk/government/publications/advisory-panel-to-mission-led-business-review-final-report

Gov.uk. (2024). *Protected characteristics.* https://www.gov.uk/discrimination-your-rights. Accessed 20/05/2024.

Grant, A. M. (2006). An integrative goal-focused approach to executive coaching. In D. R. Stober & A. M. Grant (Eds.), *Evidence based coaching handbook: Putting best practices to work for your clients* (pp. 153–192). John Wiley & Sons.

Grant, A. M. (2011). Is it time to REGROW the GROW model? Issues related to teaching coaching session structures. *The Coaching Psychologist, 7*(2), 118–126.

Grant, A. M. (2013). Autonomy support, relationship satisfaction and goal focus in the coach–coachee relationship: Which best predicts coaching success? *Coaching: An International Journal of Theory, Research and Practice, 7*(1), 18–38.

Grant, A. M. (2016). What constitutes evidence-based coaching? A two-by-two framework for distinguishing strong from weak evidence for coaching. *International Journal of Evidence Based Coaching & Mentoring, 14*(1), 74–85.

Grant, A. M. (2017). The third "generation" of workplace coaching: Creating a culture of quality conversations. *Coaching: An International Journal of Theory, Research and Practice, 10*(1), 37–53.

Grant, A. M. (2018). Goals and coaching: An integrated evidence-based model of goal-focused coaching and coaching psychology. In S. Palmer & A. Whybrow (Eds.), *Handbook of coaching psychology: A guide for practitioners* (pp. 34–50). Routledge.

Grant, A. M., Curtayne, L., & Burton, G. (2009). Executive coaching enhances goal attainment, resilience and workplace well-being: A randomised controlled study. *The Journal of Positive Psychology, 4*(5), 396–407.

Graßmann, C., & Schermuly, C. C. (2021). Coaching with artificial intelligence: Concepts and capabilities. *Human Resource Development Review, 20*(1), 106–126.

Graßmann, C., Schölmerich, F., & Schermuly, C. C. (2020). The relationship between working alliance and client outcomes in coaching: A meta-analysis. *Human Relations, 73*(1), 35–58. http://dx.doi.org/10.1177/0018726718819725

Gray, D. E. (2009). *Doing research in the real world* (2nd ed.). Sage.

Gray, D. E., Garvey, B., & Lane, D. A. (2016). *A critical introduction to coaching and mentoring: Debates, dialogues and discourses.* Sage.

Graziano, A. M. (1971). *Behavior therapy with children.* Aldine-Atherton.

Grossman, J. B., & Tierney, J. P. (1998). Does mentoring work? An impact study of the Big Brothers Big Sisters program. *Evaluation Review, 22*(3), 403–426.

Grote, G., & Kozlowski, S. W. J. (2023). Teamwork doesn't just happen: Policy recommendations from over half a century of team research. *Behavioral Science & Policy, 9*(1), 59–76. https://doi.org/10.1177/23794607231192734

Guan, M., & Bingxue, H. (2013). Marital distress and disease progression: A systematic review. *Scientific Research, 5*(10), 1601–1606. DOI: 10.4236/health.2013.510216

Gutkin, T. B., & Curtis, M. J. (1999). School-based consultation: Theory and practice. In C. R. Reynolds & T. B. Gutkin (Eds.), *The handbook of school psychology* (3rd ed.). Wiley.

Hackshaw, K. V., Plans-Pujolras, M., Rodriguez-Saona, L. E., Moore, M. A., Jackson, E. K., Sforzo, G. A., & Buffington, C. A. (2016). A pilot study of health and wellness coaching for fibromyalgia. *BMC Musculoskelet Disord, 17*, 1–9. DOI: 10.1186/s12891-016-1316-0

Haegele, J. A., & Hodge, S. (2016). Disability discourse: Overview and critiques of the medical and social models. *Quest, 68*(2), 193–206. https://doi.org/10.1080/00336297.2016.1143849

Hagan, T., & Donnison, J. (1999). Social power: Some implications for the theory and practice of cognitive behaviour therapy. *Journal of Community & Applied Social Psychology, 9*(2), 119–135.

Hallo, L., & Nguyen, T. (2022). Holistic view of intuition and analysis in leadership decision-making and problem-solving. *Administrative Sciences, 12*(1), 1–25. https://doi.org/10.3390/admsci12010004

Hakimi, S. (2015, July 21). *Why purpose-driven companies are often more successful.* Fast Company. https://www.fastcompany.com/3048197/why-purpose-driven-companies-are-often-more-successful.

Hallam, R.S. (2013). *Individual case formulation.* Academic Press.

Hanley, R. P. (2020). *Fénelon.* Oxford University Press.

Harding, S. (1991). *Whose science? Whose knowledge? Thinking from women's lives.* Cornell University Press.

Hardingham, A. (2021). The universal eclectic model of executive coaching. In J. Passmore (Ed.), *The coaches handbook: The complete practitioner guide for professional coaches* (pp. 167–176). Routledge.

Hastings, B. J., & Schwarz, G. M. (2022). Leading change processes for success: A dynamic application of diagnostic and dialogic organization development. *The Journal of Applied Behavioral Science, 58*(1), 120–148.

Hastwell, C. (2022). *The high value of building pride in the workplace.* Great Place to Work. https://www.greatplacetowork.com/resources/blog/the-value-of-building-pride-in-the-workplace

Hauser, L. L. (2014). Shape-shifting: A behavioral team coaching model for coach education, research and practice. *Journal of Psychological Issues in Organizational Culture, 5*(2), 48–71.

Hawkins, P. (2011). *Leadership team coaching: Developing collective transformational leadership.* Kogan Page.

Hawkins, P. (2021). *Leadership team coaching: Developing collective transformational leadership* (4th ed.). Kogan Page.

Hawkins, P., & Shohet, R. (2012). *Supervision in the helping professions* (4th ed.). Open University Press.

Hawkins, P., & Smith., N. (2006). *Coaching, mentoring and organizational consultancy.* Open University Press.

Hawkins, P., & Turner, E. (2020). *Systemic coaching: Delivering value beyond the individual.* Routledge.

Hay, J. (2007). *Reflective practice and supervision for coaches.* Oxford University Press.

Hayes, W. A. (1972). As cited in Keise, C., Kelly, E., King, O., & Lane, D. A. (1993). Culture and child services. In A. Miller & D. A. Lane (Eds.), *Silent conspiracies: Scandals and successes in the care and education of vulnerable young people* (pp. 189–214). Trentham Books.

Hayes, W., & Banks, W. M. (1972). As cited in Keise, C., Kelly, E., King, O., & Lane, D. A. (1993). Culture and child services. In A. Miller & D. A. Lane (Eds.), *Silent conspiracies: Scandals and successes in the care and education of vulnerable young people* (pp. 189–214). Trentham Books.

Hays, P. A. (2019). Introduction. In G. Y. Iwamasa & P. A. Hays (Eds.), *Culturally responsive cognitive behavior therapy: Practice and supervision* (pp. 3–24). American Psychological Association.

Heider, F. (1958). *The psychology of interpersonal relations.* John Wiley & Sons. https://psycnet.apa.org/doi/10.1037/10628-000

Heifetz, R. A., & Linsky, M. (2002). *Leadership on the line: Staying alive through the dangers of leading.* Harvard Business School Press.

Heyman, R. E. (2001). Observation of couple conflicts: Clinical assessment applications, stubborn truths, and shaky foundations. *Psychological Assessment, 13*(1), 5–35.

Hindle Fisher, R., Garvey, B., & Chapman, L. (2023). Executive coaches' backgrounds – Yes, they can make a difference. *International Journal of Evidenced-Based Coaching and Mentoring, 21*(2), pp. 118–133. DOI: 10.24384/ve0b-gb52

Ho, D. Y. (1994). Face dynamics: From conceptualization to measurement. In S. Ting-Toomey (Ed.), *The challenge of facework: Cross-cultural and interpersonal issues* (pp. 269–286). SUNY Press.

Hoare, G., & Sperber, N. (2016). *An introduction to Antonio Gramsci. His life, thought and legacy.* Bloomsbury.

Hofmann, S. G., Asnaani, A., Vonk, I. J., Sawyer, A. T., & Fang, A. (2012). The efficacy of cognitive behavioral therapy: A review of meta-analyses. *Cognitive Therapy and Research, 36*(5), 427–440. DOI: 10.1007/s10608-012-9476–1

Hoggan, C. (2016). Transformative learning as a metatheory: Definition, criteria, and typology. *Adult Education Quarterly*, *66*(1), 57–75.

Hollanders, H. (2014). Integrative therapy. In W. Dryden & A. Reeves (Eds.), *The handbook of individual therapy* (pp. 519–545). Sage.

Holmes, A. G. D. (2020). Researcher positionality – A consideration of its influence and place in qualitative research – A new researcher guide. *Shanlax International Journal of Education*, *8*(4), 1–10.

Horley, J. (2012). Personal construct theory and human values. *Journal of Human Values*, *18*(2), 161–171.

Horvath, A. O., & Greenberg, L. S. (1989). Development and validation of the Working Alliance Inventory. *Journal of Counseling Psychology*, *36*(2), 223–233. https://doi.org/10.1037/0022-0167.36.2.223

Horwitz, S. K., & Horwitz, I. B. (2007). The effects of team diversity on team outcomes: A meta-analytic review of team demography. *Journal of Management*, *33*(6), 987–1015.

Huey, S. J., Park, A. L., Galán, C. A., Wang, C. X. (2023). Culturally responsive cognitive behavioral therapy for ethnically diverse populations. *Annual Review of Clinical Psychology*, *19*, 51–78. https://psycnet.apa.org/doi/10.1146/annurev-clinpsy-080921-072750

Hughes, G., Shaw, S. E., & Greenhalgh, T. (2020). Rethinking integrated care: A systematic hermeneutic review of the literature on integrated care strategies and concepts. *The Milbank Quarterly*, *98*(2), 446–492.

Humphrey, N., Lendrum, A., & Wigelsworth, M. (2010). *Social and emotional aspects of learning*. Department of Education.

Hundschell, A., Razinskas, S., Backmann, J., & Hoegl, M. (2022). The effects of diversity on creativity: A literature review and synthesis. *Applied Psychology*, *71*(4), 1598–1634.

Hurst, A. (2014). *The purpose economy*. Elevate.

Hurth, V., Ebert, C., & Prabhu, J. (2018). *Organisational purpose: The construct and its antecedents and consequences*. Working Papers 201802, Cambridge Judge Business School, University of Cambridge.

Hwang, K. K. (2012). Face and morality in Confucian society. In K. K. Hwang (Ed.), *Foundations of Chinese psychology: Confucian social relations* (pp. 265–295). Springer.

Hydén, L. C. (1997). Illness and narrative. *Sociology of Health & Illness*, *19*, 48–69.

IBM. (2010). *Capitalizing on complexity: Insights from the global CEO study*. https://www.ibm.com/downloads/cas/1VZV5X8J. Accessed 20/05/2024.

International Coach Federation. (2020). *ICF team coaching competencies: Moving beyond one-to-one coaching (v.13.11)*. https://coachingfederation.org/app/uploads/2021/10/Team-Coaching-Competencies_10.4.21.pdf. Accessed 21/05/2024.

Jackson, G. G. (1977). As cited in Keise, C., Kelly, E., King, O., & Lane, D. A. (1993). Culture and child services. In A. Miller & D. A. Lane (Eds.), *Silent conspiracies: Scandals and successes in the care and education of vulnerable young people*. Trentham Books.

Jackson, M. C. (2003). *Systems-thinking: Creative holism for managers*. Wiley.

Jackson, N., & Carter, P. (2007). *Rethinking organisational behaviour*. Prentice Hall.

Jackson, P. (2024, May 2). *Philosophies, purpose and practices* [Conference presentation]. International Conference on Coaching Supervision, Oxford Brookes University, Oxford.

Jackson, P., & Bachkirova, T. (2019). The 3 Ps of supervision and coaching: Philosophy, Purpose and Process. In E. Turner & S. Palmer (Eds.), *The heart of coaching supervision: Working with reflection and self-care* (pp. 20–40). Routledge.

Jacobson, D., & Mustafa, N. (2019). Social identity map: A reflexivity tool for practicing explicit positionality in critical qualitative research. *International Journal of Qualitative Methods*, *18*. https://doi.org/10.1177/1609406919870075

James, J., Mavin, S., & Corlett, S. (2020). A framework of modes of awareness for team coaching practice. *International Journal of Evidence Based Coaching & Mentoring*, *18*(2), 4–18.

Jamieson, M. K., Govaart, G. H., & Pownall, M. (2023). Reflexivity in quantitative research: A rationale and beginner's guide. *Social and Personality Psychology Compass*, *17*(4), Article e12735. https://psycnet.apa.org/doi/10.1111/spc3.12735

Jansen, E. (2023). *The art of effective decision-making: Insights from coaching*. Quenza. https://quenza.com/blog/knowledge-base/decision-making-coaching/#. Accessed 29/01/2024.

Jarvis, J., Lane, D. A., & Fillery-Travis, A. (2006). *The case for coaching. Making evidence-based decisions in coaching*. Chartered Institute of Personnel and Development.

Jarvis, R., Dempsey, K., Gutierrez, G., Lewis, D., Rouleau, K., & Stone, B. (2017). Peer coaching that works: The power of reflection and feedback in teacher triad teams. *McREL International*.

Jason, L. A., & Bobak, T. (2022). Using systems theory to improve intervention outcomes. *Professional Psychology: Research and Practice*, *53*(4), 415–422. https://doi.org/10.1037/pro0000467

Johnstone, L., & Boyle, M., with Cromby, J., Dillon, J., Harper, D., Kinderman, P., Longden, E., Pilgrim, D., & Read, J. (2018). *The power threat meaning framework: Towards the identification of patterns in emotional distress, unusual experiences and troubled or troubling behaviour, as an alternative to functional psychiatric diagnosis*. British Psychological Society.

Johnstone, L., & Dallos, R. (Eds.) (2006). *Formulation in psychology and psychotherapy: Making sense of people's problems*. Routledge.

Jones, K. (2018). *Every child used to matter*. Politics & Insights. https://politicsandinsights.org/2012/11/11/every-child-doesnt-matter-a-summary-of-remembering-when-every-child-mattered/

Jones, R. J., Napiersky, U., & Lyubovnikova, J. (2019). Conceptualizing the distinctiveness of team coaching. *Journal of Managerial Psychology*, *34*(2), 62–78. https://psycnet.apa.org/doi/10.1108/JMP-07-2018-0326

Jones, R. J., Woods, S. A., & Guillaume, Y. R. (2016). The effectiveness of workplace coaching: A meta-analysis of learning and performance outcomes from coaching. *Journal of Occupational and Organizational Psychology*, *89*(2), 249–277. http://dx.doi.org/10.1111/joop.12119

Jones, R. J., Woods, S. A., & Zhou, Y. (2018). Boundary conditions of workplace coaching outcomes. *Journal of Managerial Psychology*, *33*(7/8), 475–496. https://psycnet.apa.org/doi/10.1108/JMP-11-2017-0390

Jones, R. L. (1972). *Black psychology*. Harper Row.

Joo, B. K. (2005). Executive coaching: A conceptual framework from an integrative review of practice and research. *Human Resource Development Review*, *4*(4), 462–488. http://dx.doi.org/10.1177/1534484305280866

Jordan, M. (2013). *How to be a health coach: An integrative wellness approach*. Global Medicine Enterprises.

Jordan, M., & Livingstone, J. B. (2013). Coaching vs psychotherapy in health and wellness: Overlap, dissimilarities, and the potential for collaboration. *Global Advances in Health and Medicine*, *2*(4), 20–27.

Joseph, S. (2012). *What doesn't kill us: A guide to overcoming adversity and moving forward*. Basic Books.

Judge, T. A., & Piccolo, R. F. (2004). Transformational and transactional leadership: A meta-analytic test of their relative validity. *Journal of Applied Psychology*, *89*(5), 755–768. https://psycnet.apa.org/doi/10.1037/0021-9010.89.5.755

Kahn, M. S. (2011). Coaching on the axis: An integrative and systemic approach to business coaching. *International Coaching Psychology Review*, *6*(2), 194–210.

Kahn, M. S. (2014). *Coaching on the axis: Working with complexity in business and executive coaching*. Karnac Books.

Kahneman, D. (2011). *Thinking, fast and slow*. Macmillan.

Kahneman, D., & Klein, G. (2009). Conditions for intuitive expertise: A failure to disagree. *American Psychologist, 64*(6), 515–526. https://psycnet.apa.org/doi/10.1037/a0016755

Kahneman, D., Slovic, P., & Tversky, A. (Eds.) (1982). *Judgement under uncertainty: Heuristics and biases.* New York: Cambridge University Press.

Kahneman, D., & Tversky, A. (1972). Subjective probability: A judgment of representativeness. *Cognitive Psychology, 3*(3), 430–454. https://psycnet.apa.org/doi/10.1016/0010-0285(72)90016-3

Kaiser, R. B., & Overfield, D. V. (2010). Assessing flexible leadership as a mastery of opposites. *Consulting Psychology Journal: Research and Practice, 62*(2), 105–118. https://doi.org/10.1037/a0019987

Kaiser, R. B., Sherman, R. A., & Hogan, R. (2023, March 7). *It takes versatility to lead in a volatile world.* Harvard Business Review. https://hbr.org/2023/03/it-takes-versatility-to-lead-in-a-volatile-world?autocomplete=true

Kandola, R., & Fullerton, J. (1998). *Diversity in action: Managing the mosaic* (2nd ed.). CIPD.

Kegan, R. (1982). *The evolving self: Problem and process in human development.* Harvard University Press.

Kegan, R. (1994). *In over our heads: The mental demands of modern life.* Harvard University Press.

Kegan, R., & Lahey, L. L. (2009). *Immunity to change. How to overcome it and unlock the potential in yourself and your organization.* Harvard Business Press. http://dx.doi.org/10.5334/ijic.503

Keise, C., Kelly, E., King, O., & Lane, D. A. (1993). Culture and child services. In A. Miller & D. A. Lane (Eds.), *Silent conspiracies: Scandals and successes in the care and education of vulnerable young people.* Trentham Books.

Kelloway, E. K., & Barling, J. (2010). Leadership development as an intervention in occupational health psychology. *Work & Stress, 24*(3), 260–279. https://doi.org/10.1080/02678373.2010.518441

Kennel, J. (2018). Health and wellness coaching improves weight and nutrition behaviors. *American Journal of Lifestyle Medicine, 12*(6), 448–450. DOI: 10.1177/1559827618792846

Kerr, N. L., & Tindale, R. S. (2004). Group performance and decision making. *Annual Review of Psychology, 55*, 623–655. https://doi.org/10.1146/annurev.psych.55.090902.142009

Kezar, A., & Lester, J. (2010). Breaking the barriers of essentialism in leadership research: Positionality as a promising approach. *Feminist Formations, 22*(1), 163–185. http://dx.doi.org/10.1353/nwsa.0.0121

Kiecolt-Glaser, J. K., & Newton, T. L. (2001). Marriage and health: His and hers. *Psychological Bulletin, 127*(4), 472–503. https://doi.org/10.1037/0033-2909.127.4.472

Kim-Appel, D., & Appel, J. K. (2021). Bowenian Family Systems Theory: Approaches and applications. In D. Capuzzi & M. D. Stauffer (Eds.), *Foundations of couples, marriage, and family counseling* (2nd ed.) (pp. 149–172). http://dx.doi.org/10.1002/9781394266470.ch8

King, E. B., Hebl, M. R., & Beal, D. J. (2009). Conflict and cooperation in diverse workgroups. *Journal of Social Issues, 65*(2), 261–285. https://psycnet.apa.org/doi/10.1111/j.1540-4560.2009.01600.x

Kinouani, G. (2021). *Living while Black: The essential guide to overcoming racial trauma.* Random House.

Kitzinger, C. (1986). Introducing and developing Q as a feminist methodology: A study of accounts of lesbianism. In S. Wilkinson (Ed.), *Feminist social psychology: Developing theory and practice* (pp. 151–172). Open University Press.

Kleinman, A. (1988). *The illness narratives: Suffering, healing, and the human condition.* Basic Books.

Knaak, S., Mantler, E., & Szeto, A. (2017). Mental illness-related stigma in healthcare: Barriers to access and care and evidence-based solutions. *Healthcare Management Forum, 30*(2), 111–116. https://doi.org/10.1177%2F0840470416679413

Knowles, C. (2021). *Reverse mentoring: Success with OfS transformation West Midlands project.* Birmingham Newman University.

Knowles, S. (2020). *Transforming organisational culture through coaching.* Xlibris/self-published.

Korotov, K. (2016). Coaching for leadership development. In T. Bachkirova, D. Drake, & G. Spence (Eds.), *The SAGE handbook of coaching* (pp. 139–158). Sage.

Kovács, L. (2016). Enabling leaders to navigate complexity: A model for executive coaching amid ambiguity, uncertainty and change. [Doctoral dissertation]. Middlesex University repository. https://eprints.mdx.ac.uk/20827/1/LKovacsThesis.pdf

Kovács, L., & Corrie, S. (2017a). Building reflective capability to enhance coaching practice. *The Coaching Psychologist, 13*(1), 4–12.

Kovács, L. C., & Corrie, S. (2017b). Executive coaching in an era of complexity. Study 1. Does executive coaching work and if so, how? A realist evaluation. *International Coaching Psychology Review, 12*(2), 74–89.

Kovács, L. C., & Corrie, S. (2017c). Executive coaching in an era of complexity. Study 2. Applying formulation to coaching: A description of the PAIR Framework. *International Coaching Psychology Review, 12*(2), 90–100.

Kovács, L. C., & Corrie, S. (2021). Formulation as a foundation for navigating complexity in executive coaching. *Consulting Psychology Journal: Practice and Research, 73*(3), 271–288. https://doi.org/10.1037/cpb0000202

Kozlowski, S. W. J. (2018). Enhancing the effectiveness of work groups and teams: A reflection. *Perspectives on Psychological Science, 13*(2), 205–212. https://psycnet.apa.org/doi/10.1177/1745691617697078

Kozlowski, S. W., & Bell, B. S. (2020). Advancing team learning. In L. Argote & J. M. Levine (Eds.), *The Oxford handbook of group and organizational learning* (pp. 195–232). Oxford University Press.

Kozlowski, S. W., & Ilgen, D. R. (2006). Enhancing the effectiveness of work groups and teams. *Psychological Science in the Public Interest, 7*(3), 77–124. doi: 10.1111/j.1529-1006.2006.00030.x

Kozulin, A., Gindis, B., Ageyev, V. S., & Miller, S. M. (Eds.) (2003). *Vygotsky's educational theory in cultural context.* Cambridge University Press. https://psycnet.apa.org/doi/10.1017/CBO9780511840975

Kramer, A., & Kramer, K. Z. (2021). Putting the family back into work and family research. *Journal of Vocational Behavior, 126,* Article 103564.

Kreikamp, R. (2017). *The benefits of applying cultural intelligence concepts to customer satisfaction and team performance* [Unpublished doctoral dissertation]. Middlesex University.

Kreisberg, J., & Marra, R. (2017). Board certified health coaches? What integrative physicians need to know. *Integrative Medicine: A Clinician's Journal, 16*(6), 1–5. https://www.ncbi.nlm.nih.gov/pmc/articles/PMC6438087/

Kuhn, L., & Whybrow, A. (2019). Coaching at the edge of chaos: A complexity informed approach to coaching psychology. In S. Palmer & A. Whybrow (Eds.), *Handbook of coaching psychology: A guide for practitioners* (pp. 413–423). Routledge.

Kwiatkowski, R., & Winter, B. (2006). Roots, relativity and realism: The occupational psychologist as scientist-practitioner. In D. A. Lane & S. Corrie (Eds.), *The modern scientist-practitioner. A guide to practice in psychology* (pp. 158–172). Routledge.

Lai, F. Y., Tang, H-C., Lu, S-C., Lee, Y-C., & Lin, C-C. (2020). Transformational leadership and job performance: The mediating role of work engagement. *Sage Open,* 10, 1–11. DOI: 10.1177/2158244019899085

Lai, Y. L., & Palmer, S. (2019). Psychology in executive coaching: An integrated literature review. *Journal of Work-Applied Management, 11*(2), 143–164. 10.1108/JWAM-06-2019-0017.

Lai, Y. L., & Smith, H. (2021). An investigation of the three-way joint coaching alliance: A social identity theory perspective. *Applied Psychology, 70*(2), 489–517.

Lai, Y. L., & Turner, E. (2023). Ethics of multi-party contracting in coaching. In W. A. Smith, J. Passmore, E. Turner, Y. L. Lai & D. Clutterbuck (Eds.) *The ethical coaches' handbook: A guide to developing ethical maturity in practice* (pp. 215–230). Routledge.

Lane, D. A. (1973). Pathology of communication: A pitfall in community health. *Community Health, 5*(3), 157–162. http://www.jstor.org/stable/45159569

Lane, D. A. (1975). *School focussed analysis: Case formulation*. Educational Guidance Centre. ILEA.

Lane, D. A. (1978). *The impossible child*. ILEA.

Lane, D. A. (1990). *The impossible child*. Trentham Books.

Lane, D. A. (1998). Context focused analysis: An experimentally derived model for working with complex problems with children, adolescents and systems. In M. Bruch, & F. W. Bond (Eds.), *Beyond Diagnosis. Case Formulation Approaches in CBT* (pp. 103–139). Wiley.

Lane, D. A. (2002). *The emergent models in coaching*. The European Mentoring and Coaching Council.

Lane, D. A. (2013). *Game plans, game moments, game changers*. [Conference presentation]: The Rugby Football, Union, Wimbledon.

Lane, D. A., Cavanagh, M., & Smith, W. A. (2024). Case formulation: A tool for working with coaching case studies. In W. A. Smith, E. H. Pontes, D. Magadlela, & D. Clutterbuck (Eds.), *Ethical case studies for coach development and practice: A coach's companion* (pp. 18–32). Routledge. https://doi.org/10.4324/b23351

Lane, D. A., & Corrie, S. (2006). *The modern scientist-practitioner: A guide to practice in psychology*. Routledge.

Lane, D. A., & Corrie, S. (2009). Does coaching psychology need the concept of formulation? *International Coaching Psychology Review, 4*(2), 195–208.

Lane, D. A., & Corrie. S. (2011). *Making successful decisions in counselling and psychotherapy. A practical guide*. Open University Press.

Lane, D. A., & Down, M. (2010). The art of managing for the future: Leadership of turbulence. *Management Decision, 48*(4), 512–527. http://dx.doi.org/10.1108/00251741011041328

Lane, D. A., Kahn, M. S., & Chapman, L. (2018). Adult learning as an approach to coaching. In Palmer, S., & Whybrow, A. (Eds.), *Handbook of coaching psychology: A guide for practitioners* (pp. 369–380). Routledge.

Lane, D. A., Magadlela, D., Kit, I.Y.W., & Spiegel, S. (2023). Ethics and culture: Moving beyond a universal Western ethical code. In W. A. Smith, J. Passmore, E. Turner, Y. L. Lai, & D. Clutterbuck (Eds.), *The ethical coaches' handbook: A guide to developing ethical maturity in practice* (pp. 301–314). Routledge.

Lanesend Primary School. (2020) *Lanesend primary school coaching policy*. https://www.lanesendprimary.co.uk/content/S637378406959423992/Coaching%20Policy%202020.docx.pdf

Langstaff, B. (2024). *The infected blood inquiry*. https://www.infectedbloodinquiry.org.uk/reports/inquiry-report

Larson, L., & DeChurch, L. (2020). Leading teams in the digital age: Four perspectives on technology and what they mean for leading teams. *The Leadership Quarterly, 31*(1), 101377. https://doi.org/10.1016/j.leaqua.2019.101377

Laske, O. E. (1999). An integrated model of developmental coaching. *Consulting Psychology Journal: Practice and Research, 51*(3), 139–159. https://psycnet.apa.org/doi/10.1037/1061-4087.51.3.139

Lavis, P. (2016). *Our relationships with our children are critical for their healthy development*. Mental Health Foundation. https://www.mentalhealth.org.uk/explore-mental-health/blogs/why-relationships-are-so-important-children-and-young-people

Law, H. L., Ireland, S., & Hussain, Z. (2007). Conclusion, discussion and future work. In H. Law, S. Ireland, & Z. Hussain (Eds.), *The psychology of coaching, mentoring and learning* (pp. 205–224). Wiley.

Law, H. (2011). Intercultural coaching approach for Asian family business. In M. Shams & D. A. Lane, (Eds.), *Coaching in the family-owned business: A path to growth* (pp. 41–58). Karnac Books. https://doi.org/10.4324/9780429473050

Law, H. (2019). Narrative coaching – Part 1: An introduction and the first step. *The Coaching Psychologist, 15*(2), 39–42.

Law, H. (2020). Narrative coaching – Part 2: Two forms of change structures: Re-authoring and remembering. *The Coaching Psychologist, 16*(1), 59–69.

Lawlor, D., & Sher, M. (2021). *An introduction to systems psychodynamics: Consultancy, research and training* (1st ed.). Routledge.

Lawrence, P. (2019). What is systemic coaching? *Philosophy of Coaching: An International Journal, 4*(2), 35–52. http://dx.doi.org/10.22316/poc/04.2.03

Lawrence, P. (2021a). Team coaching: Systemic perspectives and their limitations. *Philosophy of Coaching: An International Journal, 6*(1), 52–82. http://dx.doi.org/10.22316/poc/06.1.04

Lawrence, P. (2021b). *Coaching systemically: Five ways of thinking about systems*. Routledge.

Leithwood, K. (2021). A review of evidence about equitable school leadership. *Educational Science, 11*, 377. https://doi.org/10.3390/educsci11080377

Lent, J. (2017). *The patterning instinct: A cultural history of humanity's search for meaning*. Prometheus Books.

Lindon, J. (2011). *Creating a culture of coaching: Upskilling the school workforce in times of change*. National College for Leadership of Schools and Children's Services.

Linley, P. A., & Joseph, S. (2005). The human capacity for growth through adversity. *American Psychologist, 60*(3), 262–264. https://doi.org/10.1037/0003-066X.60.3.262b

Lo, M-C.M. (2005). The professions: Prodigal daughters of modernity. In J. Adams, E. S. Clemens, & A. S. Orloff (Eds.), *Remaking modernity: Politics, processes and history in sociology* (pp. 381–406.). Duke University Press. http://dx.doi.org/10.1215/9780822385882

Local Government Association. (2024). *Sustainability action learning sets*. https://www.local.gov.uk/our-support/sustainability-hub/sustainability-action-learning-sets

Lofthouse, R. T., Leat, D., & Towler, C. (2010). *Coaching for teaching and learning: A practical guide for schools*. CfBT Education Trust.

Louis, D., & Fatien Diochon, P. (2018). The coaching space: A production of power relationships in organizational settings. *Organization, 25*(6), 710–731.

MacKie, D. (2023). An introduction to climate change leadership in organisations. In D. MacKie (Ed.), *The handbook of climate change leadership in organisations* (pp. 1–18). Routledge.

Madigan, S., Brumariu, L. E., Villani, V., Atkinson, L., & Lyons-Ruth, K. (2016). Representational and questionnaire measures of attachment: A meta-analysis of relations to child internalizing and externalizing problems. *Psychological Bulletin, 142*(4), 367–399. DOI: 10.1037/bul0000029

Mahrer, A. R. (2000). Philosophy of science and the foundations of psychotherapy. *American Psychologist, 55*(10), 1117–1125. https://psycnet.apa.org/doi/10.1037/0003-066X.55.10.1117

Malik, K. (2023). *Not so black and white: A history of race from white supremacy to identity politics*. Hurst.

Malkin, J. (1990). As cited in Lane, D. A. (Ed.), *The impossible child*. Trentham Books.

Malling, B., De Lasson, L., Just, E., & Steager, N. (2020). How group coaching contributes to organisational understanding among newly graduated doctors. *BMC Medical Education, 20*, 1–8. https://doi.org/10.1186/s12909-020-02102-8

Markman, H. J., Rhoades, G. K., Stanley, S. M., Ragan, E. P., & Whitton, S. W. (2010). The premarital communication roots of marital distress and divorce: The first five years of marriage. *Journal of Family Psychology, 24*(3), 289–298.

Markus, H. R., & Hamedani, M. G. (2007). Sociocultural psychology: The dynamic interdependence among self-systems and social systems. In S. Kitayama & D. Cohen (Eds.), *Handbook of cultural psychology* (pp. 3–39). The Guilford Press.

Martin, L. S., Oades, L. G., & Caputi, P. (2014). A step-wise process of intentional personality change coaching. *International Coaching Psychology Review, 9*(2), 181–195.

Masten, A. S., Lucke, C. M., Nelson, K. M., & Stallworthy, I. C. (2021). Resilience in development and psychopathology: Multisystem perspectives. *Annual Review of Clinical Psychology, 17*, 521–549. https://psycnet.apa.org/doi/10.1146/annurev-clinpsy-081219-120307

Maxton, P. J. (2021). Embracing both diagnostic and dialogic forms of organization development in order to exploit and explore. *The Journal of Applied Behavioral Science, 57*(1), 125–128.

Maxwell, C. A., Roberts, C., Oesmann, K., Muhimpundu, S., Archer, K. R., Patel, M. R., Mulubrhan, M. F., Muchira, J., … & LaNoue, M. (2022). Health and wellness for disadvantaged older adults: The AFRESH pilot study. *PEC Innovation, 1*, 100084. DOI: 10.1016/j.pecinn.2022.100084.

Mayo, A. T. (2022). Syncing up: A process model of emergent interdependence in dynamic teams. *Administrative Science Quarterly, 67*(3), 821–864. https://doi.org/10.1177/00018392221096451

McCluney, C. L., Durkee, M. I., Smith II, R. E., Robotham, K. J., & Lee, S. S. L. (2021). To be, or not to be … Black: The effects of racial codeswitching on perceived professionalism in the workplace. *Journal of Experimental Social Psychology, 97*, 104–199.

McDowall, A. (2017). The use of psychological assessments in coaching and coaching research. In T. Bachkirova, G. Spence, & D. Drake (Eds.), *The SAGE handbook of coaching* (pp. 627–643). Sage.

McFee, S. M. (2023, April 2). *Shifting from command and control*. LinkedIn. https://www.linkedin.com/pulse/shifting-from-command-and-control-autonomous-styles-sam-mcafee/

McKinsey. (2020). *Purpose: Shifting from why to how*. https://www.mckinsey.com/capabilities/people-and-organizational-performance/our-insights/purpose-shifting-from-why-to-how

McGovern, J., Lindemann, M., Vergara, M., Murphy, S., Barker, L., & Warrenfeltz, R. (2001). Maximising the impact of executive coaching behaviour change, organization outcomes and return on investment. *The Manchester Review, 6*(1).

Memon, A., Taylor, K., Mohebati, L. M. (2016). Perceived barriers to accessing mental health services among black and minority ethnic (BME) communities: A qualitative study in Southeast England. *BMJ Open*, e012337. DOI: 10.1136/bmjopen-2016-012337

Mettler, E. A., Preston, H. R., Jenkins, S. M., et al. (2014). Motivational improvements for health behavior change from wellness coaching. *American Journal of Health Behavior, 38*(1), 83–91.

Mezirow, J. (1994). Understanding transformation theory. *Adult Education Quarterly, 44*(4), 222–232. https://doi.org/10.1177/074171369404400403

Mezzina, R., Gopikumar, V., Jenkins, J., Saraceno, B., & Sashidharan, S. P. (2022). Social vulnerability and mental health inequalities in the "Syndemic": Call for action. *Frontiers in Psychiatry, 13*, 894370.

Miller, A., & Frederickson, N. (2006). Generalizable findings and idiographic problems: Struggles and successes for educational psychologists as scientist-practitioners. *The modern scientist-practitioner: A guide to practice in psychology* (pp. 103–118). Routledge.

Milner, J., Ostmeier, E., & Franke, R. (2013). Critical incidents in cross-cultural coaching: The view from German coaches. *International Journal of Evidence Based Coaching and Mentoring, 11*(2), 19–32.

Milton, M. (2014a). Sexuality: Where existential thought and counselling psychology practice come together. *Counselling Psychology Review, 29*(2), June, 15–24.

Milton, M. (2014b). *Sexuality existential perspectives*. PCCS Books.

Mishler, E. G. (1986). The analysis of interview-narratives. In T. R. Sarbin (Ed.), *Narrative psychology: The storied nature of human conduct* (pp. 233–255). Praeger Publishers/ Greenwood Publishing Group.

Misra, G., & Prakash, A. (2012). Kenneth J. Gergen and social constructionism. *Psychological Studies, 57*, 121–125. https://doi.org/10.1007/s12646-012-0151-0

Mittelmark, M. N., Bauer, G. F., Vaandrager, L., Pelikan, J. M., Sagy, S., Eriksson, M., Lindström, B., & Magistretti, C. M. (Eds.) (2021). *The handbook of salutogenesis* (2nd ed.). Springer Open.

Mohan, J. (1996). Accounts of the NHS reforms: Macro-, meso- and micro-level perspectives. *Sociology of Health and Illness, 18*, 675–698.

Molyn, J., De Haan, E., van der Veen, R., & Gray, D. E. (2022). The impact of common factors on coaching outcomes. *Coaching: An International Journal of Theory, Research and Practice, 15*(2), 214–227. https://psycnet.apa.org/doi/10.1080/17521882.2021.1958889

Murray, K. (2017). *People with purpose: How great leaders use purpose to build thriving organizations*. Kogan Page.

Nacif, A. (2021). BeWell: A group coaching model to foster the wellbeing of individuals. *International Journal of Evidence Based Coaching and Mentoring, Spec Iss 15*, 171–186.

National Board for Health and Wellness Coaching. (n.d.). Program approval. https://nbhwc. org/approved-programs. Accessed 03/04/2020.

National Fire Chiefs Council. (2024). *Action learning set guidance*. https://nfcc.org.uk/wp-content/uploads/2024/03/Action-Learning-Set-Guidance-v3-29.2.24-1.pdf

National Scientific Council on the Developing Child. (2004). Young children develop in an environment of relationships. *Working Paper No. 1*. http://www.developingchild.net

National Wellness Institute. (n.d.). *NWI's six dimensions of wellness*. https://nationalwellness.org/resources/six-dimensions-of-wellness/. Accessed 26/08/2024.

NCSL. (2013). National College of School Leadership. https://www.gov.uk/government/ organisations/national-college-for-school-leadership. Accessed 21/05/2024.

Ndaruhutse, S., Jones, C., & Riggall, A. (2022). *Why systems thinking is important for education*. Educational Development Trust.

Newlove-Delgado, T., Marcheselli, F., Williams, T., Mandalia, D., Dennes, M., McManus, S., Savic, M., Treloar, W., Croft, K., & Ford T. (2023). *Mental health of children and young people in England, 2023*. NHS England.

Nicolson, P. (1986). Developing a feminist approach to depression following childbirth. In S. Wilkinson (Ed.), *Feminist social psychology* (pp. 135–149). Open University Press.

Neimeyer, R. A. (2000). Narrative disruptions in the construction of self. In R. A. Neimeyer & J. D. Raskin (Eds.), *Constructions of disorder: Meaning-making frameworks for psychotherapy* (pp. 207–242). American Psychological Association. https://psycnet.apa.org/ doi/10.1037/10368-009

Nettleton, S. (2021). *The sociology of health and illness*. Wiley.

NHS. (2024). *Action learning sets*. https://library.hee.nhs.uk/binaries/content/assets/lks/ mobilising-knowledge/mobilising-knowledge-toolkit/als-guidance-doherty-associates.pdf

NHS England. (2023). *Working in partnership with people and communities: Statutory guidance*. https://www.england.nhs.uk/long-read/working-in-partnership-with-people-and-communities-statutory-guidance/. Accessed 14/05/2024.

NHS Race and Health Observatory. (2023). https://www.nhsrho.org/news/nhs-talking-therapies-review-identifies-barriers-in-accessing-care/. Accessed 20/05/2024.

Nielsen, K., Yarker, J., Munir, F., & Bültmann, U. (2018). IGLOO: An integrated framework for sustainable return to work in workers with common mental disorders. *Work & Stress*, *32*(4), 400–417. https://doi:10.1080/02678373.2018.1438536

Nobles, W. W. (1976). Extended self: Rethinking to so-called Negro self-concept. *Journal of Black Psychology*, *2*(2), 15–24.

NSPCC. (2024). *Keeping children safe on line*. NSPCC. https://www.nspcc.org.uk/keeping-children-safe/online-safety/inappropriate-explicit-content/. Accessed 05/01/2024.

Oberholzer, L., & Boyle, D. (2023). *Mentoring and coaching in education*. Bloomsbury.

O'Brien, J., & Cave, A. (2017). *The power of purpose: Inspire teams, engage customers, transform business*. Pearson.

O'Broin, A., & Palmer, S. (2019). The coaching relationship: A key role in coaching processes and outcomes. In S. Palmer & A. Whybrow (Eds.), *Handbook of coaching psychology* (pp. 471–486). Routledge.

Ochs, E., & Capps, L. (2009). *Living narrative: Creating lives in everyday storytelling*. Harvard University Press.

O'Connor, S. (2020). Systemically integrated approaches to coaching: An introduction. *Philosophy of Coaching: An International Journal*, *5*(2), 40–62.

O'Connor, S., & Cavanagh, M. (2013). The coaching ripple effect: The effects of developmental coaching on wellbeing across organisational networks. *Psychology of Well-Being: Theory, Research and Practice*, *3*(1), 1–23. http://dx.doi.org/10.1186/2211-1522-3-2

O'Donohue, W., Fisher, J. E., Plaid, J. J., & Curtis, S.D. (1990). Treatment decisions: Their nature and their justification. *Psychotherapy, 27*(3), 421–427.

O'Donohue, W., & Henderson, D. (1999). Epistemic and ethical duties in clinical decision-making. *Behaviour Change*, *16*(1), 10–19.

O'Donovan, B. (2014). Editorial for special issue of SPAR: The Vanguard Method in a systems thinking context. *Systemic Practice and Action Research*, *27*, 1–20. https://doi.org/10.1007/s11213-012-9247-7

O'Moore, G. (2012). PEAK: A model for use within performance coaching. *The Coaching Psychologist*, *8*(1), 39–45.

O'Neill, M. B. (2000). *Executive coaching with backbone and heart: A systems approach to engaging leaders with their challenges*. Jossey-Bass.

O'Neill, T. A., & Salas, E. (2018). Creating high performance teamwork in organizations. *Human Resource Management Review*, *28*(4), 325–331. https://psycnet.apa.org/doi/10.1016/j.hrmr.2017.09.001

Okoli, J. (2020). Improved decision-making effectiveness in crisis situations: Developing intuitive expertise at the workplace. *Development and Learning in Organisations: An International Journal*, *35*, 18–20. http://dx.doi.org/10.1108/DLO-08-2020-0169

Olthof, M., Hasselman, F., Oude Maatman, F., Bosman, A. M., & Lichtwarck-Aschoff, A. (2023). Complexity theory of psychopathology. *Journal of Psychopathology and Clinical Science*, *132*(3), 314.

Opara, V., Sealy, R., & Ryan, M. K. (2020). The workplace experiences of BAME professional women: Understanding experiences at the intersection. *Gender Work and Organization*, *27(*6), 1192–1213. https://psycnet.apa.org/doi/10.1111/gwao.12456

Orange, T., Isken, J. O., Green, A., Parachini, N., & Francois, A. (2019). Coaching for equity: Disrupt and transform practices that reveal implicit and explicit biases. *The Learning Professional*, *40*(6), 45–49.

Oshry, B. (2015). Coaching from a systems perspective. In J. Passmore (Ed.), *Leadership coaching: Working with leaders to develop elite performance* (2nd ed.) (pp. 175–196). Kogan Page.

Otter, K. (2018). Leadership coaching 2.0: Improving the marriage between leadership and coaching. *Philosophy of Coaching: An International Journal*, *2*(2), 69–82. DOI: 10.22316/poc/02.2.05

Palmer, C. A., Baucom, D. H., & McBride, C. M. (2000). A couple approach to smoking cessation. In K. B. Schmaling & T. G. Ser (Eds.), *The psychology of couples and illness* (pp. 311–336). American Psychological Association.

Palmer, S., & Whybrow, A. (2018). *Handbook of coaching psychology: A guide for practitioners*. Routledge.

Pandolfi, C. (2020). Active ingredients in executive coaching: A systematic literature review. *International Coaching Psychology Review, 15*(2), 6–30.

Parsons, T., & Smelser, N. J. (1956). *Economy and Society*. Routledge & Kegan Paul

Passmore, J. (2007). An integrative model for executive coaching. *Consulting Psychology Journal: Practice and Research, 59*(1), 68–78. https://doi.org/10.1037/1065-9293.59.1.68

Passmore, J. (2015). Leadership coaching. In J. Passmore (Ed.), *Leadership coaching: Working with leaders to develop elite performance* (pp. 5–14). Kogan Page.

Passmore, J. (2021). Developing an integrated approach to coaching. In J. Passmore (Ed.), *The coaches' handbook* (pp. 321–331). Routledge.

Passmore, J. (2024, June 13). Personal Conversation at BPS Division of Coaching Psychology Conference 2024 London.

Passmore, J., Peterson, D., & Freire, T. (2013). Psychology of coaching and mentoring. In J. Passmore, D. Peterson, & T. Freire (Eds.), *Wiley-Blackwell handbook of the psychology of coaching & mentoring* (pp. 1–11). Wiley-Blackwell. http://dx.doi.org/10.1002/9781118326459

Passmore, J., & Tee, D. (2021). Insights from qualitative coaching psychology research. In J. Passmore & D. Tee (Eds.), *Coaching researched* (pp. 141–143). Wiley. DOI: 10.1002/9781119656913

Pavlović, J. (2021). Team coaching psychology: Toward an integration of constructivist approaches. *Journal of Constructivist Psychology, 34*(4), 450–462. https://psycnet.apa.org/doi/10.1080/10720537.2019.1700856

Pearson, T. (2017). *How creativity is killed in the majority world*. New Internationalist. https://newint.org/features/web-exclusive/2017/11/15/poverty-creativity

Peters, B., & Göhlich, M. (2024). Transformative learning through group coaching. *Journal of Transformative Education, 22*(2), 157–179. https://doi.org/10.1177/15413446231178897

Peters, J., & Carr, C. (2013). *High performance team coaching*. FriesenPress.

Peterson, D. B. (2011). Executive coaching: A critical review and recommendations for advancing the practice. In S. Zedeck (Ed.), *APA handbook of industrial and organisational psychology, Vol 2. Selecting and developing members for the organisation* (pp. 527–566). American Psychological Association. https://psycnet.apa.org/doi/10.1037/12170-018

Phoenix, D. (2023). *English higher education social mobility index*. Higher Education Policy Institute.

Plaister-Ten, J. (2016). *The cross-cultural coaching kaleidoscope: A systems approach to coaching amongst different cultural influences*. Karnac Books.

Probert, J., & Turnbull James, K. (2011). Leadership development: Crisis, opportunities and the leadership concept. *Leadership, 7*(2), 137–150. https://doi.org/10.1177/1742715010394810

Quenk, N. N. (2009). *Essentials of Myers-Briggs Type Indicators Assessment*. Wiley.

Rajan, A., & Lane, D. A. (2000). *Employability: Bridging the Gap Between Rhetoric and Reality. Executive Summaries*. Centre for Research in Employment and Technology in Europe.

Ramakrishnan, V. (2011). Understanding the impact of family dynamics on the family business coaching approach. In S. Manfusa & D. A. Lane (Eds.), *Coaching in the family owned business: A path to growth* (pp. 103–124). Karnac Books.

Ramanayaka, A. R. N. D., Dickson, G., & Rayne, D. (2023). Heuristics in sport: A scoping review. *Psychology of Sport and Exercise, 71*, 102589. DOI: 10.1016/j.psychsport.2023.102589

Rapp, T., Maynard, T., Domingo, M., & Klock, E. (2021). Team emergent states: What has emerged in the literature over 20 years. *Small Group Research, 52*(1), 68–102. https://psycnet.apa.org/doi/10.1177/1046496420956715

Ratele, K. (2019). *The world looks like this from here: Thoughts on African psychology.* Wits University Press.

RCPsych (2008). *Rethinking risk to others in mental health services.* Royal College of Psychiatrists.

Reid, K. (2005). The implications of Every Child Matters and the Children Act for schools. *Pastoral Care in Education, 23*(1), 12–18. DOI: 10.1111/j.0264-3944.2005.00317.x

Reissner, S. C., & Du Toit, A. (2011). Power and the tale: Coaching as storyselling. *Journal of Management Development, 30*(3), 247–259. http://dx.doi.org/10.1108/02621711111116171

Rethorn, Z. D., Pettitt, R. W., Dykstra, E., & Pettitt, C. D. (2020). Health and wellness coaching positively impacts individuals with chronic pain and pain-related interference. *PLoS ONE, 15*(7), e0236734. https://doi.org/10.1371/journal.pone.0236734

Revans, R. W. (1982). *The origin and growth of action learning.* Chartwell-Bratt.

Riessman, C. K. (2012). Analysis of personal narratives. In J. F. Gubrium & J. A. Holstein (Eds.), *Handbook of interview research: Context and method* (pp. 695–710). Sage. https://doi.org/10.4135/9781412973588

Robbins, P. (2015). *Peer coaching to enrich professional practice, school culture and student learning.* ASCD.

Roberts, V. Z., & Brunning, H. (2018). *Psychodynamic and systems-psychodynamics coaching.* In S. Palmer & A. Whybrow (Eds.), *Handbook of coaching psychology. A guide for practitioners.* Routledge.

Robinson, T., & Yanagi, D. (2019). Coaching for consciousness: Team coaching to support system, relational, and internal awareness. In D. Clutterbuck, J. Gannon, S. Hayes, I. Iordanou, K. Lowe, & D. MacKie (Eds.), *The practitioner's handbook of team coaching* (pp. 163–179). Routledge.

Rogers, J. (2014). Resisting the charm of finding a scapegoat. https://jennyrogerscoaching.com/resisting-the-charm-of-finding-a-scapegoat/

Rollnick, S., Mason, P., & Butler, C. (1999). *Health behaviour change: A guide for practitioners.* Churchill Livingstone.

Rosinski, P. (2003). *Coaching across cultures: New tools for leveraging national, corporate and professional differences.* Nicolas Brealey International.

Ross, J. A. (1992). Teacher efficacy and the effect of coaching on student achievement. *Canadian Journal of Education/Revue canadienne de l'éducation, 17*, 51–65. http://dx.doi.org/10.2307/1495395

Ross, L. E., Doctor, F., Dimito, A., Kueli, D., & Armstrong, M. F. (2008). Can talking about oppression reduce depression? *Journal of Gay and Lesbian Social Services, 19*(1), 1–15.

Ross, L. E., & Rosser, B. R. (1996) Measurement and correlates of internalized homophobia: A factor analytic study. *Journal of Clinical Psychology, 52*, 15–21.

Roth, A. (2017). Coaching a client with a different cultural background – Does it matter? *International Journal of Evidence Based Coaching and Mentoring, Special Edition, 11*, 30–43.

Roth, A., & Fonagy, P. (2005). *What works for whom: A critical review of psychotherapy research* (2nd ed.). Guilford Publications.

Rowe, J. (2021). *Nine Rooms: Mastering the missing dimension to coaching, teaching and counselling.* John Rowe Coaching. www.ninerooms.co.uk

Ruebain, quoted in Keise, C., Kelly, E., King, O., & Lane, D. A. (1993). Culture and child services. In A. Miller & D. A. Lane (Eds.), *Silent conspiracies: Scandals and successes in the care and education of vulnerable young people* (pp. 189–199). Trentham Books.

Salas, E., Shuffler, M. L., Thayer, A. L., Bedwell, W. L., & Lazzara, E. H. (2015). Understanding and improving teamwork in organizations: A scientifically based practical guide. *Human Resource Management*, *54*(4), 599–622. https://psycnet.apa.org/doi/10.1002/hrm.21628

Salicru, S. (2020). A new model of leadership-as-practice development for consulting psychologists. *Consulting Psychology Journal: Practice and Research*, *2*(2), 79–99. https://psycnet.apa.org/doi/10.1037/cpb0000142

Sandberg, J. G., Yorgason, J. B., Miller, R. B., & Hill, E. J. (2012). Family-to-work spillover in Singapore: Marital distress, physical and mental health, and work satisfaction. *Family Relations*, *61*, 1–15. http://dx.doi.org/10.1111/j.1741-3729.2011.00682.x

Savin-Baden, M., & Major, C. H. (2013). *Qualitative research: The essential guide to theory and practice*. Routledge.

Schein, E. (2015). Dialogic organizational development: Past, present and future. In G. R. Bushe & R. J. Marshak (Eds.), *Dialogic organization development* (pp. vii–xiii). Berrett-Koehler.

Schermuly, C. C., Graßmann, C., Ackermann, S., & Wegener, R. (2022). The future of workplace coaching – An explorative Delphi study. *Coaching: An International Journal of Theory, Research and Practice*, *15*(2), 244–263. DOI: 10.1080/17521882.2021.2014542

Scott Peck, M. (1998). *Further along the road less traveled: The unending journey towards spiritual growth*. Simon & Schuster.

Seddon, J. (2003). *Freedom from command and control*. Vanguard Press.

Segal, J. (2021). *On motivation: Building better workplace cultures*. Jenny Segal.

Segers, J., & Vloeberghs, D. (2009). Do theory and techniques in executive coaching matter more than in therapy? *Industrial and Organizational Psychology: Perspectives on Science and Practice*, *2*(3), 280–283. https://psycnet.apa.org/doi/10.1111/j.1754-9434.2009.01149.x

Senge, P. (1990). *The fifth discipline. The art and practice of the learning organisation*. Random House.

Sforzo, G. A., Kaye, M. P., Harenberg, S., et al. (2019). Compendium of health and wellness coaching: 2019 addendum. *American Journal of Lifestyle Medicine*, *14*(2), 155–168. https://doi.org/10.1177/1559827619850489

Sforzo, G. A., Kaye, M. P., Todorova, I., et al. (2017). Compendium of the health and wellness coaching literature. *American Journal of Lifestyle Medicine*, *12*(6), 436–447. https://doi.org/10.1177/1559827617708562

Shafran, R. (2020). Foreword. In D. H. Bacuom, M. S. Fischer, S. Corrie, M. Worrell, & S. E. Boeding (Eds.), *Treating relationship distress and psychopathology in couples: A cognitive-behavioural approach* (pp. xiii–xv). Routledge. http://dx.doi.org/10.4324/9781315626413

Shafran, R., Clark, D. M., Fairburn, C. G., Arntz, A., Barlow, D. H., Ehlers, A., Freeston, M., Garety, P. A., Hollon, S. D., … & Wilson, G. T. (2009). Mind the gap: Improving the dissemination of CBT. *Behaviour Research and Therapy*, *47*(11), 902–909. DOI: 10.1016/j.brat.2009.07.003

Shaked, H., & Schechter, C. (2019). Systems thinking for principals of learning-focused schools. *Journal of School Administration Research and Development*, *4*(1), 18–23.

Shams, M., & Lane, D. (2011). *Coaching in the family owned business: A path to growth*. Routledge.

Shams, M., & Lane, D. (2018). Family relations: Coaching techniques for a family business. *The Coaching Psychologist*, *14*(1), 34–41.

Shaw, R. (2010). Embedding reflexivity within experiential qualitative psychology. *Qualitative Research in Psychology*, *7*(3), 233–243. https://psycnet.apa.org/doi/10.1080/14780880802699092

Shidler, L. (2009). The impact of time spent coaching for teacher efficacy on student achievement. *Early Childhood Education Journal, 36*(5), 453–460. DOI:10.1007/s10643-008-0298-4

Shoukry, H. (2017). Coaching for social change. In T. Bachkirova, D. Drake, & G. Spence (Eds.), *The SAGE handbook of coaching* (pp. 176–194). Sage.

Shoukry, H., & Cox, E. (2018). Coaching as a social process. *Management Learning, 49*(4), 413–428. https://psycnet.apa.org/doi/10.1177/1350507618762600

Sieler, A. (2020). *Coaching to the human soul: Ontological coaching and deep change, Volume I*. Newfield Institute.

Silva, C. T., & Silva, P. D. T. (2022). *Making sense of work through collaborative storytelling: Building narratives in organisational change*. Palgrave Macmillan. https://doi.org/10.1007/978-3-030-89446-7_2

Simons, T., Pelled, L. H., & Smith, K. A. (1999). Making use of difference: Diversity, debate and decisions comprehensiveness in top management teams. *Academy of Management Journal, 42*(6), 662–673.

Skakon, J., Nielsen, K., Borg, V., & Guzman, J. (2010). Are leaders' well-being, behaviours and style associated with the affective well-being of their employees? A systematic review of three decades of research. *Work & Stress, 24*(2), 107–139. https://doi.org/10.1080/02678373.2010.495262

Smail, D. (2005). *Power, interest and psychology: Elements of a social materialist understanding of distress*. PCCS Books.

Smith, W. A., Pontes, E. H., Magadlea, D., & Clutterbuck, D. (2024). *Ethical case studies for coach development and practice: A coaches' companion*. Routledge.

Spear, S., & Roper, S. (2016). Storytelling in organisations: Supporting or subverting corporate strategy? *Corporate Communications: An International Journal, 21*(4), 516–532. https://doi.org/10.1108/CCIJ-02-2016-0020

Sports Coaching UK. (2014) https://www.scottishdisabilitysport.com/wp-content/uploads/2016/07/Coaching-Disabled-People-Information-Sheet.pdf. Accessed 12/05/2024.

Spoth, J., Toman, S., Leichtman, R., & Allan, J. (2012). Gestalt approach. In J. Passmore, D. B. Peterson, & T. Freire (2012). *The Wiley-Blackwell handbook of the psychology of coaching and mentoring*. Wiley-Blackwell.

Stacey, R. D. (2007a). The challenge of human interdependence: Consequences for thinking about the day-to-day practice of management in organizations. *European Business Review, 19*(4), 292–302. http://dx.doi.org/10.1108/09555340710760125

Stacey, R. D. (2007b). *Strategic management and organizational dynamics: The challenge of complexity to ways of thinking about organizations* (5th ed.). Pearson Education (Kindle edition).

Stacey, R. D. (2010). *Complexity and organizational reality: Uncertainty and the need to rethink management after the collapse of investment capitalism* (2nd ed.). Routledge.

Stacey, R. D. (2012). *Tools and techniques of leadership and management: Meeting the challenge of complexity*. Routledge.

Stacey, R. D., & Mowles, C. (2016). *Strategic management and organisational dynamics* (7th ed.). Pearson.

Stark Taylor, S., & Blair Kennedy, A. (2018). Health and wellness coaching: Providers and practice – A commentary on Sforzo and colleagues. *American Journal of Lifestyle Medicine, 12*(6), 451–455. DOI: 10.1177/1559827618790531

Stelter, R. (2009). Coaching as a reflective space in a society of growing diversity – Towards a narrative, postmodern paradigm. *International Coaching Psychology Review, 4*(2), 209–217.

Stelter, R. (2013). *A guide to third generation coaching: Narrative-collaborative theory and practice*. Springer.

Stelter, R. (2019). *The art of dialogue in coaching*. Routledge.

Stelter, R., & Andersen, V. (2018). Coaching for health and lifestyle change: Theory and guidelines for interacting and reflecting with women about their challenges and aspirations. *International Coaching Psychology Review*, *13*(1), 61–71.

St John-Brooks, K. (2014). *Internal coaching: The inside story*. Karnac Books.

Stokes, P., Diochon, P. F., & Otter, K. (2020). "Two sides of the same coin?" Coaching and mentoring and the agentic role of context. *Annals of the New York Academy of Sciences*, *1483*(1). https://doi.org/10.1111/nyas.14316

Stout-Rostron, S. (2009). *Business coaching international: Transforming individuals and organizations*. Karnac Books.

Stout-Rostron, S. (2014). *Business coaching international: Transforming individuals and organizations* (2nd ed.). Routledge.

Stout-Rostron, S. (2019a). *Transformational coaching to lead culturally diverse teams*. Routledge.

Stout-Rostron, S. (2019b). Leadership and team coaching. In S. Stout-Rostron (Ed.), *Transformational coaching to lead culturally diverse teams* (pp. 13–29). Routledge.

Strauss, A., & Corbin, J. (1990). *Basics of qualitative research: Grounded theory procedures and techniques*. Sage.

Stucki, G., & Bickenbach, J. (2017). Functioning: The third health indicator in the health system and the key indicator for rehabilitation. *European Journal of Physical and Rehabilitation Medicine*, *53*(1), 134–138. DOI: 10.23736/S1973-9087.17.04565-8

Stucki, G., Bickenbach, J., Gutenbrunner, C., & Melvin, J. (2018). Rehabilitation health strategy of the 21st century. *Journal of Rehabilitation Medicine*, *50*(4), 309–316. DOI: 10.2340/16501977-2200.

Suite, D. H., La Bril, R., Primm, A., & Harrison-Ross, P. (2007). Beyond misdiagnosis, misunderstanding and mistrust: Relevance of the historical perspective in the medical and mental health treatment of people of color. *Journal of the National Medical Association*, *99*(8), 879–885.

Tarry, A. (2018). *Coaching with careers and AI in mind: Grounding a hopeful and resourceful self fit for a digital world*. Routledge. https://doi.org/10.4324/9780429451553

Tattum, D. P., & Lane, D. A. (1989). *Bullying in schools*. Trentham Books.

Teasdale, J. D., & Barnard, P. J. (1993). *Affect, cognition and change: Remodelling depressive thought*. Erlbaum.

Tedeschi, R. G., & Calhoun, L. G. (1995). *Trauma & transformation: Growing in the aftermath of suffering*. Sage.

Tee, D., & Passmore, J. (2022). The role of frameworks, models and approaches in coaching. In D. Tee & J. Passmore (Eds.), *Coaching practiced* (pp. 5–8). John Wiley & Sons.

Tehrani, N. (2008). Trauma support for emergency services, *Crisis Response*, *4*(3), 42–43.

Tehrani, N., & Lane, D. A. (2021). The role for coaching in psychological trauma. In M. Watts & I. Florance (Eds.), *Emerging conversations in coaching and coaching psychology* (pp. 78–94). Routledge. https://psycnet.apa.org/doi/10.4324/9781315114514-6

Terblanche, N. H. D. (2020). The coaching model derivation process: Combining grounded theory and canonical action research for developing coaching models. *Coaching: An International Journal of Theory, Research and Practice*, *13*, 45–60.

Terblanche, N. H. D. (2022). Transformative transition coaching: A framework to facilitate transformative learning during career transitions. *The International Journal of Human Resource Management*, *33*(2), 269–296.

Terblanche, N. H. D., Albertyn, R. M., & Van Coller-Peter, S. (2018). Using transformation transition coaching to support leaders during career transitions. *African Journal of Business Ethics*, *12*(1), 60–77.

Terblanche, N., Molyn, J., De Haan, E., & Nilsson, V. O. (2022). Coaching at scale: Investigating the efficacy of artificial intelligence coaching. *International Journal of Evidence Based Coaching and Mentoring*, *20*(2), 20–36.

Theberath, M., Bauer, D., Chen, W., Salinas, M., Mohabbat, A. B., Yang, J., Chon, T. Y., Bauer, B. A., & Wahner-Roedler, D. L. (2022). Effects of COVID-19 pandemic on mental health of children and adolescents: A systematic review of survey studies. *SAGE Open Medicine*. DOI: 10.1177/20503121221086712

Thompson, H. B., Bear, D. J., Dennis, D. J., Vickers, M., London, J., & Morrison, C. L. (2008). *Coaching, a global study of successful practices: Current trends and future possibilities 2008–2018*. American Management Association. https://www.opm.gov/wiki/uploads/docs/wiki/opm/training/i4cp-coaching.pdf

Thrive London. (2023). *Towards happier, healthier lives for all Londoners*. https://thriveldn.co.uk

Tindale, R., & Winget, J. (2019, March 26). Group decision-making. *Oxford research encyclopaedia of psychology*. https://oxfordre.com/psychology/view/10.1093/acrefore/9780190236557.001.0001/acrefore-9780190236557-e-262. Accessed 06/05/2024.

Tobias, L. L. (1996). Coaching executives. *Consulting Psychology Journal: Practice and Research*, *48*(2), 87–95. https://doi.org/10.1037/1061-4087.48.2.87

Toleikyte, L. (2018). *Local action on health inequalities: Understanding and reducing ethnic inequalities in health*. Public Health England.

Topping, K. (1989). Peer tutoring and paired reading: Combining two powerful techniques. *The Reading Teacher*, *42*(7), 488–494.

Topping, K. J. (2020, August 27). *Peer tutoring and cooperative learning*. Oxford Research Encyclopaedia of Education. https://oxfordre.com/education/education/view/10.1093/acrefore/9780190264093.001.0001/acrefore-9780190264093-e-1432

Tsoukas, H. (2009). A dialogical approach to the creation of new knowledge in organizations. *Organization Science*, *20*(6), 941–957. http://dx.doi.org/10.1287/orsc.1090.0435

Turner, R. A., & Goodrich, J. (2010). The case for eclecticism in executive coaching: Application to challenging assignments. *Consulting Psychology Journal: Practice and Research*, *62*(1), 39–55. https://doi.org/10.1037/a0018650

Tversky, A., & Kahneman, D. (1973). Availability: A heuristic for judging frequency and probability. *Cognitive Psychology*, *5*(2), 207–232. https://doi.org/10.1016/0010-0285(73)90033-9

Tversky, A., & Kahneman, D. (1974). Judgment under uncertainty: Heuristics and biases. *Science*, *185*(4157), 1124–1131.

Uhl-Bien, M. (2021). Complexity leadership and followership: Changed leadership in a changed world. *Journal of Change Management: Reframing Leadership and Organizational Practice, 21*(2), 144–162. https://doi.org/10.1080/14697017.2021.1917490

Uhl-Bien, M., Marion, R., & McKelvey, B. (2007). Complexity leadership theory: Shifting leadership from the industrial age to the knowledge era. *The Leadership Quarterly*, *18*(4), 298–318. https://psycnet.apa.org/doi/10.1016/j.leaqua.2007.04.002

Ullman, L. P. (1977). Foreword – Behavioral community psychology: Implications, opportunities and responsibilities. In M. T. Nietzal, *Behavioral approaches to community psychology* (pp. ix–xxviii). Pergamon.

UNESCO. (1983). *Racism, science and pseudo-science*. UNESCO.

UNESCO. (2009). *UNESCO World Report: Investing cultural diversity and intercultural dialogue*. UNESCO.

van Nieuwerburgh, C. (2012). *Coaching in education: Getting better results for students, educators and parents*. Karnac Books.

van Nieuwerburgh, C., & Allaho, R. (2017). *Coaching in Islamic culture: The principles and practice of Ershad*. Karnac Books.

van Nieuwerburgh, C., & Barr, M. (2016). Coaching in education. In T. Bachkirova, G. Spence, & D. Drake (Eds.), *The SAGE handbook of coaching* (pp. 505–520). Sage.

van Nieuwerburgh, C., Barr, M., Fouracres, A. J. S., Moin, T., Brown, C., Holden, C., Lucey, C., & Thomas, P. (2022). Experience of positive psychology coaching while working from home during the COVID-19 pandemic: An Interpretative Phenomenological Analysis. *Coaching: An International Journal of Theory, Research and Practice, 15*(2), 148–165. https://doi.org/10.1080/17521882.2021.1897637

van Nieuwerburgh, C., & Passmore, J. (2018). Creating coaching cultures for learning. In C. van Nieuwerburgh (Ed.), *Coaching in education: Getting better results for students, educators, and parents* (1st ed.) (pp. 153–172). Routledge.

Vanzella-Yang, A., Algan, Y., Beasley, E., Côté, S., Vitaro, F., Tremblay, R. E., & Park, J. (2023). The social and economic impact of the Montreal longitudinal and experimental study. *Criminal Behaviour and Mental Health, 33*(2), 116–124.

Vogler, C. (2007). *The writer's journey: Mythic structure for writers*. Michael Wiese Productions.

Von Bertalanffy, L. (1968). *General systems theory*. Penguin.

Von Schlippe, A. (2022). Family businesses in coaching: Specific dynamics. In F. Müller, H. Möller, J. Passmore, S. Greif, & W. Scholl (Eds.), *International handbook of evidence-based coaching: Theory, research and practice* (pp. 325–336). Springer. https://doi.org/10.1007/978-3-030-81938-5_27

Waley, A. (2000). *The analects*. Everyman Library.

Wang, Q., Lai, Y. L., Xu, X., & McDowall, A. (2021). The effectiveness of workplace coaching: A meta-analysis of contemporary psychologically informed coaching approaches. *Journal of Work-Applied Management, 14*(1), 77–101. http://dx.doi.org/10.1108/JWAM-04-2021-0030

Ward, R. (1990). *A descriptive bibliography of articles and books on Black and ethnic community mental health in Britain*. MIND.

Wasylyshyn, K. M. (2003). Executive coaching: An outcome study. *Consulting Psychology Journal: Practice and Research, 55*(2), 94–106. https://psycnet.apa.org/doi/10.1037/1061-4087.55.2.94

Watts, M., & Corrie, S. (2013). Growing the "I" and "We" in transformational leadership: A vision for coaching psychology. *The Coaching Psychologist, 9*(2), 86–99.

Watts, M., & Corrie, S. (2022). Growing the "I" and "We" in transformational leadership: The LEAD, LEARN & GROW Model. In D. Tee & J. Passmore (Eds.), *Coaching practiced* (pp. 139–154). Wiley.

Watts, M., & Florance, I. (Eds.) (2021). *Emerging conversations in coaching and coaching psychology*. Routledge.

Watts, M., Weinburg, J., & Lane, D. A. (2023). Coaching psychology: What it is and why it matters – An emerging conversation. In G. Davey (Ed.), *Applied psychology* (2nd ed.) (pp. 587–602). Wiley-Blackwell.

Well-Being Ambassadors. (2023). Impact Report. https://academy.worthit.org.uk/accessally_protected/wellbeing-ambassador-impact-report/

Welman, P., & Bachkirova, T. (2010). The issue of power in the coaching relationship. In S. Palmer & A. McDowall (Eds.), *The coaching relationships: Putting people first* (pp. 139–158). Routledge.

Welsh Government. (2012). *Practical approaches to behaviour management in the classroom*. Welsh Government.

West, M. A., & Lyubovnikova, J. (2012). Real teams or pseudo teams? The changing landscape needs a better map. *Industrial and Organizational Psychology, 5*(1), 25–55. https://doi.org/10.1111/j.1754-9434.2011.01397.x

Wheatley, M. J. (1999). *Leadership and the new science: Discovering order in a chaotic world* (2nd ed.). Berrett-Koehler.

Whisman, M. A. (2007). Marital distress and DSM-IV psychiatric disorders in a population-based national survey. *Journal of Abnormal Psychology, 116*(3), 638–643. DOI: 10.1037/0021-843X.116.3.638

Whisman, M. A., & Bruce, M. L. (1999). Marital dissatisfaction and incidence of major depressive episode in a community sample. *Journal of Abnormal Psychology, 108*(4), 674–678.

Whisman, M. A., & Uebelacker, L. A. (2009). Prospective associations between marital discord and depressive symptoms in middle-aged and older adults. *Psychology and Aging*, *24*(1), 184–189.

White, J. (1970). *Toward a Black psychology*. Ebony.

Whiteford, H. A., Ferrari, A. J., Degenhardt, L., Feigin, V., & Vos, T. (2015). The global burden of mental, neurological and substance use disorders: An analysis from the global burden of disease study 2010. *PloS ONE*, *10*(2), e0116820. https://doi.org/10.1371/journal.pone.0116820

Whitley, S. (2013). Group coaching as support for changing lifestyle for those diagnosed with a long-term condition. *International Journal of Evidence-Based Coaching & Mentoring*, *11*(7), 82–99.

Whitmore, J. (2010). *Coaching for performance: The principles and practice of coaching and leadership*. Hachette UK.

Whybrow, A., Turner, E., McLean, J., & Hawkins, P. (2023). *Ecological and climate-conscious coaching: A companion guide to evolving coaching practice*. Routledge.

Widdowson, L., & Barbour, P. J. (2021). *Building top-performing teams: A practical guide to team coaching to improve collaboration and drive organizational success*. Kogan Page Publishers.

Wilkinson, S. (1986). *Feminist social psychology*. Open University Press.

Winsper, C., Bhattacharya, R., Bhui, K., Currie, G., Edge, D., Ellard, D. R., Franklin, D., Gill, P. S., Gilbert, S., ... & Giacco, D. (2023). Improving mental healthcare access and experience for people from minority ethnic groups: An England-wide multisite experience-based codesign (EBCD) study. *BMJ Mental Health*, *26*(1), e300709. https://doi.org/10.1136/bmjment-2023-300709

Wolever, R. Q., Cline, T. R., Weiss, J. M., Carmack, S., Schultz, C., Arloski, M., & Lawson, K. (2024). Group health & wellness coaching: Development and validation of the required competencies. *BMC Health Services Research*, *24*(1), 392–404. https://doi.org/10.1186/s12913-024-10704-x

Wolever, R. Q., Simmons, L. A., Sforzo, G. A., Dill, D., Kaye, M., Bechard, E. M., Southard, M. E., Kennedy, M., ... & Yang, N. (2013). A systematic review of the literature on health and wellness coaching: Defining a key behavioral intervention in healthcare. *Global Advances in Health and Medicine*, *2*(4), 38–57. https://doi.org/10.7453/gahmj.2013.042

Woolfson, L., Whaling, R., Stewart, A., & Monsen, J. (2003). An integrated framework to guide educational psychology practice. *Educational Psychology in Practice*, *19*(4), 283–302.

World Health Organization. (n.d.). *Constitution*. https://www.who.int/about/governance/constitution. Accessed 08/08/2023.

Wright, N. L., Longerbeam, S. D., & Alagaraja, M. (2022). Chronic codeswitching: Shaping Black/white multiracial student sense of belonging. *Genealogy*, *6*(3), 75. https://doi.org/10.3390/genealogy6030075

Yasargil, H., & Denton, L. (2011). Family first or business first: Issues in a family business. In M. Shams, & D. A. Lane (Eds.), *Coaching in the family owned business: A path to growth* (pp. 77–90). Karnac Books.

Young, J. E., Klosko, J. S., & Weishaar, M. E. (2006). *Schema therapy: A practitioner's guide*. Guilford Press.

Yunkaporta, T. (2019). *Sand talk: How indigenous thinking can save the world*. Text Publishing.

Ziols, R., Davis, N. R., Holbrook, T., & Bridges, S. (2022). Creativity as a racializing and ableizing scientific object: Disentangling the democratic impulse from justice-oriented futures. *Review of Research in Education*, *46*(1), 345–373. http://dx.doi.org/10.3102/0091732X221089973

Zuber-Skerritt, O. (2015). Participatory action learning and action research (PALAR) for community engagement: A theoretical framework. *Educational Research for Social Change*, *4*(1), 5–25.

Index

Note: Page numbers in *italics* refer to figures and page numbers in **bold** refer to tables.

For Product Safety Concerns and Information please contact our EU
representative GPSR@taylorandfrancis.com
Taylor & Francis Verlag GmbH, Kaufingerstraße 24, 80331 München, Germany